Catholic Resistance in Elizabethan England

Early Roman Portrait of Father Robert Persons. Sketch by Charles Weld (*c.* 1857), at Stonyhurst College, from an original in Rome. Reproduced by permission of the Governors of Stonyhurst College, Lancashire.

90 0775785 2

University of Plymouth Library
Subject to status this item may be renewed
via your Voyager account
http://voyager.plymouth.ac.uk
Tel: (01752) 232323

WITHDRAWN
FROM
UNIVERSITY OF PLYMOUTH
LIBRARY SERVICES

Catholic Resistance in Elizabethan England

Robert Persons's Jesuit Polemic, 1580–1610

VICTOR HOULISTON

ASHGATE

Institutum Historicum Societatis Iesu

© Victor Houliston 2007

All rights reserved. No part of this publication may be reproduced, stored in a retrieval system or transmitted in any form or by any means, electronic, mechanical, photocopying, recording or otherwise without the prior permission of the publisher.

Victor Houliston has asserted his moral right under the Copyright, Designs and Patents Act, 1988, to be identified as the author of this work.

Published by

Ashgate Publishing Limited	Ashgate Publishing Company	Institutum Historicum
Gower House	Suite 420	Societatis Iesu
Croft Road	101 Cherry Street	Via dei Penitenzieri, 20
Aldershot	Burlington, VT 05401-4405	00193 Roma
Hampshire GU11 3HR	USA	Italy
England		

Ashgate website: http://www.ashgate.com

British Library Cataloguing in Publication Data
Houliston, Victor, 1954–
  Catholic resistance in Elizabethan England : Robert Persons's Jesuit polemic, 1580–1610.
  – (Catholic Christendom, 1300–1700)
  1. Parsons, Robert, 1546–1610 – Criticism and interpretation 2. Parsons, Robert, 1546–1610 3. Jesuits – England – Biography 4. Religious literature, English – History and criticism 5. English literature – Catholic authors – History and criticism
  I. Title
  271.5'3'092

Library of Congress Cataloging-in-Publication Data
Houliston, Victor, 1954–
  Catholic resistance in Elizabethan England : Robert Persons's Jesuit polemic, 1580–1610 / Victor Houliston.
    p. cm. – (Catholic Christendom, 1300–1700)
  Includes bibliographical references.
  ISBN-13: 978-0-7546-5840-5 (hardback : alk. paper)
  ISBN-10: 0-7546-5840-6 (hardback : alk. paper)
  1. Parsons, Robert, 1546–1610. I. Title.

BX4705.P37683H68 2007
271'.5302–dc22
2006100203

UNIVERSITY OF PLYMOUTH

9007757852

| Ashgate Publishing Ltd | Institutum Historicum Societatis Iesu |
| ISBN 978-0-7546-5840-5 | ISBN 978 88 7041 363 2 |

Printed and bound in Great Britain by Antony Rowe Ltd, Chippenham, Wiltshire.

Contents

Contents

Publishers' Note

This volume is a co-publication between Ashgate Publishing and the Jesuit Historical Institute.

As well as being part of Ashgate's *Catholic Christendom, 1300–1750* monograph series, it is the 63 volume in the Jesuit Historical Institute's series *Bibliotheca Instituti Historici Societatis Iesu.*

ASHGATE

Ashgate Publishing   *Institutum Historicum Societatis Iesu*

Series Editor's Preface

The still-usual emphasis on medieval (or Catholic) and reformation (or Protestant) religious history has meant neglect of the middle ground, both chronological and ideological. As a result, continuities between the middle ages and early modern Europe have been overlooked in favor of emphasis on radical discontinuities. Further, especially in the later period, the identification of 'reformation' with various kinds of Protestantism means that the vitality and creativity of the established church, whether in its Roman or local manifestations, has been left out of account. In the last few years, an upsurge of interest in the history of traditional (or catholic) religion makes these inadequacies in received scholarship even more glaring and in need of systematic correction. The series will attempt this by covering all varieties of religious behavior, broadly interpreted, not just (or even especially) traditional institutional and doctrinal church history. It will to the maximum degree possible be interdisciplinary, comparative and global, as well as non-confessional. The goal is to understand religion, primarily of the 'Catholic' variety, as a broadly human phenomenon, rather than as a privileged mode of access to superhuman realms, even implicitly.

The period covered, 1300–1700, embraces the moment which saw an almost complete transformation of the place of religion in the life of Europeans, whether considered as a system of beliefs, as an institution, or as a set of social and cultural practices. In 1300, vast numbers of Europeans, from the pope down, fully expected Jesus's return and the beginning of His reign on earth. By 1700, very few Europeans, of whatever level of education, would have subscribed to such chiliastic beliefs. Pierre Bayle's notorious sarcasms about signs and portents are not idiosyncratic. Likewise, in 1300 the vast majority of Europeans probably regarded the pope as their spiritual head; the institution he headed was probably the most tightly integrated and effective bureaucracy in Europe. Most Europeans were at least nominally Christian, and the pope had at least nominal knowledge of that fact. The papacy, as an institution, played a central role in high politics, and the clergy in general formed an integral part of most governments, whether central or local. By 1700, Europe was divided into a myriad of different religious allegiances, and even those areas officially subordinate to the pope were both more nominally Catholic in belief (despite colossal efforts at imposing uniformity) and also in allegiance than they had been four hundred years earlier. The pope had become only one political factor, and not one of the first rank. The clergy, for its part, had virtually disappeared from secular governments as well as losing much of its local authority. The stage was set for the Enlightenment.

Thomas F. Mayer,
Augustana College

Preface

I first became conscious of the importance of Robert Persons as a formative influence on English Catholicism when I was editing a Latin playlet from the seminary that he founded in St Omer in 1593. His name seemed to crop up everywhere I looked. Although compelling books had been written about most of the other leading Elizabethan Jesuits: Campion, Garnet, Weston and Southwell, Persons seemed to have been left out. There turned out to be good reason for this. He was not so self-evidently or unambiguously a hero as the other figures, and his career spanned so many countries, his multilingual correspondence scattered throughout Europe in so many archives, that a thorough biography would be a life's work. Not for nothing was he dubbed, unkindly, 'Polypragman Persons' – referring to the kind of meddlesome busybody Plato contrasts with the just citizen in book IV of *The Republic*.

My incipient interest in Persons led me to the Institute of Jesuit Sources in St Louis where, as I soon discovered, they were working on the lengthy manuscript of Francis Edwards's biography. There at least was a reliable guide to the correspondence and the chronology. Envisaging an old-fashioned 'Life and Works', I started at the beginning of his public writing career, which coincided with the English mission of 1580–81. It then became clear to me that there was a need for a reliable critical edition of *The Christian Directory*, so my energies were diverted into that course until my edition was published in 1998. As I worked my way systematically through the published works, I found myself drawn into several ventures of the British Academy John Foxe Project, because of Persons's rejoinder to Foxe in *A Treatise of Three Conversions*. Meanwhile, in 1998 Michael Carrafiello published his monograph, *Robert Parsons and English Catholicism, 1580–1610*. At first sight his work might seem to pre-empt my study but it has a more political focus and I challenge several of his conclusions. In attending successive meetings of the Sixteenth Century Studies Conference, I found that interest in Persons was growing. People wanted to know more about this enigmatic and powerful figure. I hope this book will do something to meet that need.

University of the Witwatersrand
May, 2006

Acknowledgements

It is a great pleasure to express my gratitude to those who have so generously given me their encouragement and assistance over the period that I have devoted to reading and thinking about Robert Persons. Through the good offices of John Gouws of Rhodes University, the late Guy Butler provided the initial impetus by passing on to me his notes towards an edition of 'Breuis dialogismus', the playlet from St Omer that launched my academic interest in the early English Jesuits. I made several visits to the Institute of Jesuit Sources in St Louis, where the director, John Padberg, SJ, gave me unfailing friendship and support. Thomas M. McCoog, SJ, archivist of the British Province of the Society of Jesus and editor of the publications of the Jesuit Historical Institute in Rome, kept me alert to material he was uncovering and processing. The seminar on 'Early Modern English Religious History' at the Institute for Historical Research at London University proved a useful stimulus, and there I was particularly fortunate to meet Michael Questier and Thomas Freeman. Several conversations with Michael Questier helped to nuance my understanding of the cross-currents in Elizabethan Catholicism. Tom Freeman invited me to participate in various activities of the British Academy John Foxe Project, and I need to pay tribute to his extraordinary care in reading and commenting on my work.

I have been privileged to be able to reside at Campion Hall, Oxford, on several occasions during the writing of this book, at the invitation initially of the then Master, Joseph Munitiz, SJ, and latterly of Gerard J. Hughes, SJ, who will be Master for only a few more months now. I am deeply grateful for their hospitality and the opportunity to share in the life of a Jesuit community. The useful conversations I have had there are too numerous to recall, but I received particular help from Graham Pugin, SJ, Michael Suarez, SJ, M. Antoni J. Üçerler, SJ and William Wizeman, SJ. T. Frank Kennedy, SJ, who was delivering the D'Arcy Lectures in 2004, gave me some fascinating information about Persons's interest in music. Other friends and colleagues whose help I would like to acknowledge are: David Attwell, Jacques Berthoud, Brian Cheadle, Timothy Clarke, Pier Paolo Frassinelli, Ann Hutchinson, Eugenie Isserow, Arlene Oseman, Alison Shell, Timothy Trengove-Jones, Merle Williams and Anthony Woodward.

No one who has spent time in Duke Humfrey's Library in Oxford can fail to enjoy the friendly support of Jeanne-Pierre Mialon, Russell Edwards and Alan Carter, to whom I am much indebted. I should also like to record my gratitude to Mgr Adrian Toffolo, former Rector of the Venerable English College in Rome, Christine Butler, archivist at Corpus Christi College, Oxford, Christine Y. Ferdinand (fellow librarian) and Sally Speir (librarian) at Magdalen College, Oxford, Wiktor Gramatowski, SJ, former archivist at the Archivum Romanum Societatis Iesu, and Dr I. Massabó Ricci, director of the State Archives in Turin, for permission to consult and quote from manuscripts in their custody.

The late Albert J. Loomie, SJ, kindly gave me permission to quote from his unpublished dissertation 'Spain and the English Catholic Exiles' (London University, 1957). The cover illustration is reproduced by permission of the Governors of Stonyhurst College, Lancashire, through the good offices of the curator, Jan Graffius.

The University of the Witwatersrand, where I teach, has been generous in granting me sabbatical leave and research funding to pursue this project. I have also received several substantial research grants from the National Research Foundation of South Africa, which I acknowledge with gratitude. I should also like to register my thanks to Tom Mayer, who accepted the work for the series 'Catholic Christendom', and to Tom Gray, the commissioning editor for Ashgate Publishing.

Material from several articles I have published over the years has been adapted in the course of preparing this book. 'The Fabrication of the Myth of Father Parsons' (*Recusant History* 22 [1994]: 141–51) and 'The Polemical *Gravitas* of Robert Persons' (*Recusant History* 22 [1995]: 291–305) inform the argument of Chapters 1 and 8 respectively. Chapter 3 includes a revised version of 'The Lord Treasurer and the Jesuit: Robert Persons's Satirical *Responsio* to the 1591 Proclamation' (*Sixteenth Century Journal* 32 [2001]: 383–401), and Chapter 4 a revision of 'The Hare and the Drum: Robert Persons's Writings on the English Succession, 1593–96' (*Renaissance Studies* 14 [2000]: 233–48). Parts of Chapter 5 are closely related to my essay 'Robert Persons's Comfortable History of England', in *Martyrs and Martyrdom in England, c. 1400–1700*, ed. Thomas S. Freeman and Thomas F. Mayer (Woodbridge, Suffolk: Boydell and Brewer, 2007). Chapter 6 is an adaptation of 'Baffling the Blatant Beast: Robert Persons's Anti-Appellant Rhetoric, 1601–2' (*Catholic Historical Review* 90 [2004]: 439–55). I am grateful to the editors of these journals for permission to use this material in this form.

List of Abbreviations

ABSI *Archivum Britannicum Societatis Iesu*
(Archives of the British Province of the Society of Jesus, London)

ARCR I A.F. Allison and D.M. Rogers, *The Contemporary Printed Literature of the English Counter-Reformation between 1558 and 1640*, vol. I: *Works in Languages other than English* (Aldershot: Scolar Press, 1989)

ARCR II A.F. Allison and D.M. Rogers, *The Contemporary Printed Literature of the English Counter-Reformation between 1558 and 1640*, vol. II: *Works in English* (Aldershot: Scolar Press, 1994)

ARSI *Archivum Romanum Societatis Iesu* (General Archives of the Society of Jesus, Rome)

CRS Publications of the Catholic Record Society (London, 1905 etc.)

CSP Domestic *Calendar of State Papers, Domestic Series 1547–1625*, ed. R. Lemon and M.A.E. Green (11 vols; London: HMSO, 1856–72)

CSP Spanish *Calendar of Letters and State Papers Relating to English Affairs Preserved Principally in the Archives of Simancas*, ed. Martin A.S. Hume (4 vols; London: HMSO, 1892–99)

For Arlene, the promise of good

CHAPTER ONE

The Legend of Father Parsons

Robert Persons, son of a Somerset yeoman, was one of the most brilliant talents in early modern England. His achievements were considerable in themselves: superior of the Jesuit English mission of 1580–81, which marked the turning-point in Catholic resistance; founder of seminaries at Valladolid, Seville and St Omer, which played such a large part in keeping English Catholicism alive; tireless leader of the English Jesuits in exile, maintaining a crucial correspondence with priests on the ground in England; author of some thirty books in English and Latin, several of which rank as masterpieces of English Reformation controversy; rector of the English College, Rome; consultant to the papacy on English and Northern European affairs. Many thought he would be created a cardinal. His stature arguably equals that of Reginald Pole or William Allen.

Although Persons is not as well known today as, say, Walter Ralegh, Francis Bacon, Edward Coke, William and Robert Cecil, Richard Hooker, William Camden or Edmund Campion, he can no longer justifiably be called a neglected figure. Perhaps the most compelling account of his career, and certainly the most lively, is that given by A.L. Rowse in his collection of lives entitled *Eminent Elizabethans*.[1] Rowse found Persons both fascinating and repellent, and, in a famous incident gleefully recalled by A.N. Wilson, reproached C.S. Lewis for ignoring Persons's claims as a writer of Elizabethan prose.[2] Like many historians, Rowse spells the name 'Parsons': the original *Dictionary of National Biography* listed him under this spelling; not surprisingly, since the entry was written by T.G. Law, a rather hostile commentator. Most of Persons's opponents during his lifetime used the 'Parsons' spelling, and they were followed in the main by both Catholic and Protestant writers of succeeding generations. The spelling 'Persons' prevails in the correspondence and in the printed works of Persons and his associates, and I have adopted it at the risk of appearing too much the advocate.

In the last two or three decades, Persons has attracted increasing attention from church historians. John Bossy has owned to admiring his realistic view of the English mission, and has burrowed into the correspondence in hopes of finding the clue to the 'Heart of Robert Persons'.[3] Persons's name is prominent in recent studies of martyrology, political theory, recusant rhetoric and Catholic

[1] A.L. Rowse, *Eminent Elizabethans* (London, 1983), pp. 41–74.
[2] A.N. Wilson, *C.S. Lewis: A Biography* (London, 1990), p. 244; cf. C.S. Lewis, *English Literature of the Sixteenth Century: Excluding Drama* (London, 1954), pp. 438–41.
[3] John Bossy, 'The Heart of Robert Persons', in Thomas M. McCoog, SJ (ed.), *The Reckoned Expense: Edmund Campion and the Early English Jesuits* (Woodbridge, Suffolk, 1996), pp. 141–58.

loyalism.[4] All the same, as a figure who was a formidable presence in English affairs in the period 1580–1610, he has not intruded on the consciousness of many non-specialists. This is a pity, because not only was his an extraordinary life in itself, but we will not understand the cross-currents of English religion, politics and literature in the late sixteenth and early seventeenth centuries without coming to terms with his career. In this study I shall chiefly be concerned with his literary output, because it has not before now received the extensive treatment it deserves. This was only one part of his very busy and multi-faceted programme, but my purpose is to show that the writing was truly integrated into his wider missionary vocation.

***

Robert Persons's life was seldom free of conflict and controversy.[5] His early life culminated in expulsion from Oxford University; his missionary activities involved him in political manoeuvres which antagonized fellow Jesuits, Catholic clerics and lay people, and the English authorities; and his writings aroused such hostility that several deliberate polemical campaigns were mounted against him.

He was born on 24 June 1546, at Nether Stowey, Somerset, to Henry and Christina Persons, the sixth of eleven children. He attended the local grammar school at Stogursey and went on to the Free School at Taunton. There he learnt his first lesson in resolution. He ran away from school, offended by the way the master treated him, only to be admonished by his mother, who took the master's side. A change of heart ensued. The parish priest of Nether Stowey, John Hayward, then took an interest in his studies, which led him to St Mary's Hall, Oxford, and finally to Balliol College.

Persons spent ten years at Oxford, from 1564 to 1574, trying to make up his mind about religion. In his day, one of the most prominent figures there was the Protestant John Rainolds, whose brilliant lectures on Aristotle's *Rhetoric* almost certainly influenced Persons's thinking about the nature of argumentation.[6] Anthony Kenny avers that he read Calvin with Thomas Hyde,

---

[4]   See Anne Dillon, *The Construction of Martyrdom in the Catholic Community, 1535–1603* (Aldershot, 2002); Peter Holmes, *Resistance and Compromise: The Political Thought of the Elizabethan Catholics* (Cambridge, 1982); Michael L. Carrafiello, *Robert Parsons and English Catholicism, 1580–1610* (Selinsgrove, 1998); Ceri Sullivan, *Dismembered Rhetoric: English Recusant Writing, 1580–1603* (Madison/Teaneck, 1995); John Coffey, *Persecution and Toleration in Protestant England 1558–1689* (Harlow, 2000); Ginevra Crosignani, 'De adeundis ecclesiis Protestantium': *Thomas Wright, Robert Parsons, S.J., e il debattito sul conformismo occasionale nell'Inghilterra dell'età moderna* (Rome, 2004); Thomas M. McCoog, SJ, *The Society of Jesus in Ireland, Scotland, and England 1541–1588: 'Our Way of Proceeding?'* (Leiden, 1996).

[5]   The standard account is by Francis Edwards, SJ, *Robert Persons: The Biography of an Elizabethan Jesuit, 1546–1610* (St Louis, 1995); see also his more general study, *The Jesuits in England: From 1580 to the Present Day* (Tunbridge Wells, 1985), pp. 17–54. See also L. Hicks, SJ (introd.), *Letters and Memorials of Father Robert Persons, S.J.: Vol. I (to 1988)*, CRS, 39 (London, 1942); Federico Eguiluz, *Robert Persons 'El Architraidor'* (Madrid, 1990); and Bernard Basset, SJ, *The English Jesuits: From Campion to Martindale* (London, 1967), pp. 55–96.

[6]   See below, Chapter 5, p. 106.

and he had an early reputation as a Calvinist.[7] But he was soon associating with Edmund Campion, who tried to help him to avoid taking the Oath of Supremacy. He did in fact take the oath, on obtaining his first degree on 31 May 1568,[8] and the inner conflict would presumably have informed his response, much later in life, to the Jacobean oath of 1606. He was so affected by the deprivation of another fellow of Balliol, Richard Garnet, in 1570 that he withdrew for a while to Somerset and London. His reputation now changed to one of 'backwardness in religion'. It is not an uncommon story: he was a lively, independent thinker who was attracted to the more defined theological positions: first Calvinism, then Catholicism. His own family was undecided: one of his brothers became a Protestant clergyman and another Catholic. His father was later converted to Rome by the missionary martyr Alexander Briant, his mother became part of the recusant underground, ending her days at White Webbs, and his niece Mary was one of the founding sisters of a convent in Brussels.[9] From such a background of family and education it is not difficult to understand Robert Persons's own blend of combativeness and sympathy: throughout his career he showed an understanding of the conflicting pressures experienced by so many of his contemporaries caught between the old religion and the new.

In November 1569 he became a fellow of Balliol College, and successively enjoyed the offices of bursar and dean, as well as lecturing in rhetoric. It was as dean that he found himself under such suspicion from the master, Adam Squire, and the majority of the foundation that he felt obliged to resign his fellowship on 13 February 1574. Given leave to stay until Easter, he provoked further hostility by trying to enforce the Lenten fast, and was (according to tradition) expelled from the college with the bells of St Mary Magdalen ringing backwards, as for a fire, in the street outside.[10] The rights and wrongs of the expulsion are still somewhat obscure. The charge was of irregularity with the accounts during his term as bursar, but the evidence is unconvincing and it seems certain that the real cause was animosity: professional rivalry, personal pique and religious tension. Persons was an able scholar and renowned tutor. There may have been some jealousy of his popularity with his pupils, and indeed it was while he was in London as the guest of the family of a pupil, James Hawley, that his colleagues intensified the pressure to have him removed. He was also, by all accounts, a strong and determined man, a stickler for discipline, and it appears that one of the fellows, Christopher Bagshaw, resented a beating. His evident leaning towards the Catholic religion must also have been a cause of estrangement.

---

[7]   Anthony Kenny, 'Reform and Reaction in Elizabethan Balliol, 1559–1588', in John Prest (ed.), *Balliol Studies* (London, 1982), pp. 17–51.

[8]   'Father Persons' Autobiography', ed. J.H. Pollen, SJ, in *Miscellanea II*, CRS, 2 (London, 1906), pp. 12–47 (p. 19).

[9]   Ibid., pp. 13, 18.

[10]   Ibid., pp. 15–22; see also Robert Persons, *A Briefe Apologie, or Defence of the Catholike Ecclesiastical Hierarchie* (Antwerp, 1601), fols 193–7, henceforth referred to as *A Defence of the Catholike Ecclesiastical Hierarchie*.

Leaving Oxford was critical in determining the direction of Persons's life. At twenty-seven he was still a relatively young man, with a fair record of achievement already, but needing to reassess his career. He retreated to London under the protection of Lord Buckhurst, and then set out, with three other young men, for Padua, a common destination for adventurous or discontented Englishmen throughout the Reformation period. What did he have in mind? En route, waiting at Louvain to travel to Frankfurt, he made the Spiritual Exercises under the direction of the Jesuit William Good, and his mind was made up then, in June 1574. From now on he would dedicate his life to the service of God. The following year he walked from near Venice to Rome, and asked to be admitted to the Society of Jesus. As a former Oxford don he progressed steadily from novice to priest and tutor at the English College.[11] He thus took his place in the English Catholic community abroad, a position that largely influenced the polemical stance of his books. There had been a significant exodus of academics from Oxford and Cambridge ever since the accession of Elizabeth in 1558, resulting in a concentration of top English scholars at Douay and Rome. Persons was among men who felt themselves to belong to a community of learning far superior to the universities they had left behind, and this contributed to the confidence of his manner.

The years from 1580 to 1585 were ones of extraordinary strain and activity for Persons as he worked tirelessly for the earliest possible reconversion of England. William Allen, leader of the Catholic exiles, arrived in Rome late in 1579 and immediately began planning for a missionary thrust. This was committed to the Jesuits: Persons was appointed leader, Edmund Campion was summoned from Prague, and the party left Rome in April 1580. The dramatic events of the Campion–Persons mission itself are very familiar: the secret meetings in London, the printing press and the defiant pamphlets, the missionary tours, the enthusiastic response, the arrest and trial of Campion, leading to his execution on 1 December 1581.[12] Persons himself took refuge in Sussex and escaped to Rouen soon after his companion was arrested in July. There he continued to occupy himself in writing and printing: not only on the questions of recusancy and persecution but also on the crucial imperative of making a resolution for Christ. This latter work, *The First Booke of the Christian Exercise, appertayning to Resolution* (commonly called *The Book of Resolution* or *The Christian Directory*),[13] was to be the cornerstone of his missionary effort. Meanwhile, he was drawn into a succession of invasion schemes involving the duke of Guise and the Catholic League in France, the

---

[11]   Henry More, SJ, *The Elizabethan Jesuits*, ed. and trans. Francis Edwards, SJ (London, 1981), pp. 47–53, 69–71.

[12]   E.E. Reynolds, *Campion and Parsons: The Jesuit Mission of 1580–1* (London, 1980); McCoog, *The Society of Jesus in Ireland, Scotland and England 1541–1588*, pp. 129–77; Richard Simpson, *Edmund Campion: A Biography*, 2nd edn (London, 1896).

[13]   I use *The Christian Directory* as the generic title for this work, which exists in three main versions: first published as *The First Booke of the Christian Exercise, appertayning to Resolution* (Rouen, 1582), revised as *A Christian Directorie Guiding Men to their Salvation* (1585) and *The Christian Directory Guiding men to eternall salvation* (1607).

prince of Parma (general of the Spanish forces in the Netherlands), Philip II of Spain, and the Pope, Gregory XIII. These entailed diplomatic missions to Lisbon, Madrid and Rome, as well as pastoral work amongst the English Catholics dispersed among Parma's armies. In the midst of all this activity he fell dangerously ill and spent the winter of 1582–83 convalescing at Bilbao and Ornate. He was also subject to alternate bouts of excitement and depression as hopes rose or were disappointed. Eventually, in a state nearing nervous collapse, he accompanied Allen back to Rome.[14]

In Rome, Persons was able to steady himself and complete his tertianship, that part of the Jesuit training that involves a time of sustained reflection before taking final vows in the society, vows that he took on 9 May 1587.[15] His understanding of his vocation developed under the influence of the Father General of the Jesuits, Claudio Acquaviva, with whom he had a significant and thoughtful correspondence.[16] Acquaviva tried to help him to be more detached from political programmes, but affairs of state still occupied his attention, especially with the build-up to the Spanish Armada. Persons and Allen busied themselves with managing the role of Catholic clergy and lay people in exile, writing in defence of the invasion and preparing a pamphlet for distribution to Catholics after the invasion. Following the failure of the Armada, he became increasingly preoccupied with the formative side of the English mission, with the seminary training and the field support of the priests. He had an agent in Antwerp, Richard Verstegan, who handled most of the printed propaganda: the printing and distribution, and even some of the writing.[17] He himself handpicked missionaries such as Garnet and Southwell and maintained an extensive correspondence with them, exercising the apostolate of letters that was so important to Ignatius and many of the early Jesuits. But his most visible activity was connected with the seminaries.

Acquaviva sent Persons to Spain in 1588–89 to negotiate with Philip II over the privileges of Jesuits in that kingdom. When he arrived there Persons took the opportunity to interest Philip in the foundation of a Jesuit seminary at Valladolid, in response to developments at Rheims: the college that had moved from Douay to Rheims was in difficulty, unable to meet the needs of the increasing numbers of students. Over the next few years Persons was instrumental in setting up another seminary at Seville, a boys' seminary at St Omer, near Calais (the origins of Stonyhurst College), and a hospice at San Lucar. These had mixed fortunes, and he had an uneasy relationship with the man appointed to direct the colleges more closely, Joseph Creswell, but Persons

---

[14] McCoog, *The Society of Jesus in Ireland, Scotland and England 1541–1588*, pp. 178–223; Bossy, 'The Heart of Robert Persons'.

[15] Thomas M. McCoog, SJ, *English and Welsh Jesuits, 1555–1650*, CRS, 74–5 (2 vols; London, 1994–95), *sub* Parsons.

[16] See 'Robert Parsons and Claudio Acquaviva: Correspondence', ed. Thomas M. McCoog, SJ, *Archivum Historicum S.I.* 68 (1999): 79–182.

[17] For Verstegan, see *Letters and Despatches of Richard Verstegan (c. 1550–1640)*, ed. Anthony G. Petti, CRS, 52 (London, 1959); and Paul Arblaster, *Antwerp & the World: Richard Verstegan and the International Culture of Catholic Reformation* (Leuven, 2004).

regarded these establishments with pride.[18] His sense of the ethos of Catholic education sustained him strongly as a controversialist, because it gave the lie to his opponents' strident denunciation of the seminary priests. The move to Spain also signalled the next stage of his writing career. He had to find ways of minimizing the damage over the Armada debacle, especially the backlash against the Jesuits and other Catholic missionary priests: his strategy was a bold one, to indict the English government, and especially Lord Burghley, before the judgment of Europe in his Latin treatise popularly known as the *Philopater*.[19] At the same time he was not prepared to give up hope of a radical change in the political dispensation in England, and so he took part in a project to promote a Catholic succession: the resulting publication, *A Conference about the Next Succession*, created a minor storm in the English court.[20]

The death of William Cardinal Allen in 1594 greatly increased Persons's sense of embattlement. He and Allen had held the centre of the Catholic enterprise for several years, but with Allen gone, English Catholicism became fissiparous, and Persons was associated with the Spanish interest. Many English Catholics felt threatened by Spain, and preferred to look to France and to some rapprochement with the English authorities. In France, the accession of the Huguenot Henry of Navarre, newly transformed into the Catholic Henri IV, shifted the balance of power away from the Catholic League with its agenda of international Catholic aggrandizement. Catholic loyalism was on the increase amongst English lay people, while fear and suspicion of the Jesuits was taking hold of some of the secular clergy: priests, that is, who did not belong to the regular orders, such as Dominicans, Franciscans or Benedictines. Dissension became chronic at places such as Wisbech Castle (where many Catholic priests were held under arrest) and the English College at Rome.[21] In 1597 Persons returned to Rome to deal with the situation at the English College. He succeeded in settling the dispute in the college, and took over as rector. His position there was a powerful one, but one that evoked envy amongst the clergy in England, and he was regarded with some disfavour by Pope Clement VIII (1597–1605). During this period he was the centre of an extremely acrimonious debate, the so-called appellant controversy, concerning the future governance of the Catholic Church in England. After initially favouring the appointment of a bishop, Persons eventually supported the establishing of an archpresbyterate. The appointment of the Archpriest, George Blackwell, was

---

[18]   Michael E. Williams, *St Alban's College Valladolid: Four Centuries of English Catholic Presence in Spain* (London, 1986), pp. 1–33.

[19]   Robert Persons, *Elizabethae Angliae Reginae haeresim Caluinianum propugnantis, saeuissimum in Catholicos sui regni edictum ... Cum responsione ad singula capita ... per D. Andream Philopatrum* (Antwerp, 1592), henceforth referred to as *Philopater*. See A.J. Loomie, SJ, 'Spain and the English Catholic Exiles, 1580–1604' (diss., London University, 1957), ch. 6.

[20]   Robert Persons [R. Doleman (pseud.)], *A Conference about the Next Succession to the Crowne of Ingland* (Antwerp, 1594 [*vere* 1595]). The book became known as *The Book of the Succession*. See L. Hicks, SJ, 'Father Robert Persons S.J. and *The Book of the Succession*', *Recusant History* 4 (1957): 104–137.

[21]   Arnold Pritchard, *Catholic Loyalism in Elizabethan England* (London, 1979), pp. 11–36, 78–81.

bitterly opposed by a group of secular priests who feared Jesuit manipulation. Much of Persons's time and energy was taken up with fielding the problems arising from a succession of appeals to Rome by the aggrieved party, and he wrote two magisterial anti-appellant tracts.[22]

The appellants' fears were allayed by the resolution of the controversy in 1602, but Persons's position was strengthened in 1605 by the accession of Pope Paul V, who was much more favourably disposed towards him than his predecessor, Clement VIII. Even so, he had become the object of fear and hatred not only of some of his fellow-Catholics but especially of the Protestant establishment in England. For almost the entire period of his rectorship at the English College, from 1597 until his death in 1610, he was engaged in an extended passage of arms with anti-Romanist English writers, chiefly about the relationship of English Catholics to the state.[23] He had to contend with accusations that Catholics posed a danger to the commonwealth, a debate that began with scare-mongering by Sir Francis Hastings in 1598[24] and modulated into questions of treason, equivocation and oaths of allegiance after the Gunpowder Plot of 1605. In 1608 he published *The Judgment of a Catholicke English-man* on King James's defence of the new oath of allegiance.[25] At the same time he was working on a longer-term project to clarify the rights of English Catholicism by writing the history of the church in England and especially the role of the papacy in forming the English nation and religion. This brought him into conflict with Foxe's *Book of Martyrs* and Coke's *Reports*, both of which tried to ground English freedom from Rome in historical precedent.[26] *A Treatise of Three Conversions of England from Paganisme to Christian Religion* and *An Answere to the Fifth Part of Reportes Lately set forth by Syr Edward Cooke* presented significant alternative versions of English history.[27]

---

[22] Robert Persons, *A Defence of the Catholike Ecclesiastical Hierarchie* (1601); and *A Manifestation of the Great Folly and bad spirit of certayne in England calling themselves secular priestes* (Antwerp, 1602). See J.H. Pollen, SJ, *The Institution of the Archpriest Blackwell: A Study of the Transition from Institutional to Paternal and Local Church Government among the English Catholics, 1595 to 1602* (London, 1916); Carrafiello, pp. 88–102; and Pritchard, pp. 120–174.

[23] Holmes, *Resistance and Compromise*, pp. 205–223.

[24] Sir Francis Hastings, *A Watchword to all religious, and true hearted English-men* (London, 1598).

[25] Robert Persons, *The Judgment of a Catholicke English-man, living in banishment for his Religion … Concerninge A late Booke set forth, and entituled; Triplici nodo, triplex cuneus, Or, An Apologie for the Oath of Allegiance* (St Omer, 1608).

[26] John Foxe, *Actes and Monuments of matters most speciall and memorable, happening in the Church, with an universall history of the same* (London, 1596), the edition with which Persons concerned himself; Sir Edward Coke, *The Fift Part of the Reports of Sr. Edward Coke Knight, the Kings Attorney Generall* (London, 1605).

[27] Robert Persons, *A Treatise of Three Conversions of England from Paganisme to Christian Religion* (2 vols; St Omer, 1603–1604), henceforth referred to as *A Treatise of Three Conversions*; and *An Answere to the Fifth Part of Reportes Lately set forth by Syr Edward Cooke Knight, the Kings Attorney generall* (St Omer, 1606), henceforth referred to as *An Answere to Coke*; see Jos. Simons (introd.), *Certamen Ecclesiae Anglicanae: A Study of an Unpublished Manuscript* (Assen, 1965).

When Persons died in 1610 he was accorded the kind of attention and honours normally associated with a cardinal. In some respects his life could be regarded as a failure: he had antagonized large sectors of English Catholicism; England was more firmly Protestant than ever, with a secure Protestant succession in prospect; foreign powers were no longer interested in restoring the faith in England. Yet he was deeply admired. He had held fast to his belief in a Catholic community, sustained by a dedicated and learned clergy, that would not compromise its loyalty to the Church of Rome. Hundreds of young men – and many women too – owed their commitment to the Catholic enterprise to his writing and leadership. The Jesuit mission was strong. And he could certainly be satisfied with his epitaph, still to be seen in the English College chapel, where he was buried alongside William Allen:

> Sacerdoti integerrimo atque doctissimo et huiusce collegii optimo moderatori qui ad animi cultum ad studium pietatis ad Angliae conversionem collegiorum domiciliis ac diversioriis per opportuna loca qua per ipsum ex integro constitutis qua collocupletatis ab ipso magnae spei convocavit magnis laboribus instituit iuventutem Hispali Vallisoleti Gadibus Ulissipone Duaci Audomari Romae quo duce et socio pater Edmundus Campianus catholicae reipublicae propugnator accerimus in Angliam primus ex societate traiecit quoque vindice et patrono veritatis hostium passim exagitata temeritas libris scriptis sermonibus literis exemplis defensa religio recreata sanctitas cum inter haec ipse nullam caperet partem concessae quietis nullum a suo capite recusaret discrimen honestissimae defensionis semper paratus semper erectus semper in mediam flammam periculosissimae concertationis irrumpens animae magnae prodigus omnino vir LXIIII explevit annos ex queis sex et triginta in Soc. Iesu per omnia virtutis exempla transegit.

> A most upright and learned priest and excellent rector of this college, who established and furnished college buildings and lodging-houses in convenient places for the cultivation of the mind, the pursuit of godliness and the conversion of England. There, at Valladolid, Seville, Douay, St Omer and Rome, he called young men together with great promise, and instructed them with all diligence. He was leader and guide when Father Edmund Campion, the keenest champion of Christendom was the first of the Society to cross over into England. As defender and patron of the truth he routed the recklessness of his adversaries. By his books, sermons, letters and example religion was vindicated and holiness restored. In the midst of all these things he enjoyed no part of the peace he sought to establish, and never refused a contest in defence of the truth. He was always prepared, always alert, always plunging magnanimously right into the flame of the most perilous conflict. He was a man who gave his all: he lived sixty-four years, thirty-six of them in the Society of Jesus.[28]

* * *

---

[28]   My transcription and translation; grateful thanks to Mgr Toffolo, former Rector of the Venerable English College, Rome, for permission to visit the college and quote from materials there; for the text, see also *ABSI* 46/12/7.

The popular image of 'Father Parsons the Jesuit' – scheming, traitorous, ruthless, over-ingenious – derives ultimately from the personal attacks made by his contemporary opponents in controversy. He was such a skilful polemicist, and he enjoyed such a notable reputation as the author of *The Christian Directory*, that the most effective way of neutralizing him was to assault his character. Protestant hostility began in response to the so-called *Philopater*, in which Persons robustly defended the seminary priests against the charges levelled against them in the wake of the Spanish Armada (see Chapter 3). Then came the infamous 'Doleman': *A Conference about the Next Succession*, published in 1595 in defiance of the Queen's ban on public discussion of the issue. This provoked such indignation in Elizabeth's court that it frightened and embarrassed the Earl of Essex, to whom the work was dedicated (see Chapter 4). Nevertheless, anti-Romanist polemic only began to target Persons systematically from 1598, when he took upon himself the role of apologist of English Catholicism under fire from Sir Francis Hastings, who warned all 'true-hearted Englishmen' against the recusants (see Chapter 5). Co-incidentally, 1598 also marked the beginning of the notorious Archpriest Controversy, in which Persons became a figure of hatred and envy to a small but significant group of secular Catholic priests, alarmed at the prospect of Jesuit domination in the English Catholic Church. Catholic sentiment against Persons had been growing steadily ever since the death in 1594 of Cardinal Allen, undisputed leader of English Catholicism and a close collaborator with Persons. Those who feared that Persons would take his place and also be created a cardinal denounced 'Doleman' to the Vatican. Abuse of 'Doleman' became a staple of the extraordinary campaign of vilification instituted by the appellants (see Chapter 6).

The 'Father Parsons' myth, as constructed in the period 1598 to 1610, consisted of three main elements: 'Father Parsons' the sophist, 'Father Parsons' the personal enemy of Queen Elizabeth, and 'Father Parsons' the bastard. Early antagonists tried to dismiss his challenge. In 1581 his pseudonym 'John Howlet' elicited scorn from John Field in a tract entitled *A Caveat for Parsons Howlet*, where he was depicted as a screech-owl.[29] The notion that England had enjoyed over two decades of religious peace until stirred up by the Jesuit mission was one that was to be used against Persons again and again in the debate about persecution. His unwelcome voice was not easily silenced, and once his polemical works, plausible and measured rather than strident, began to make an impact in the late 1590s, the best counter-strategy seemed to be

---

[29]   John Field, *A Caveat for Parsons Howlet, concerning his untimely flight and screeching in the clear daylight of the gospel, necessary for him and all the rest of that dark brood and unclean cage of papists, who with their untimely books seek the discredit of the truth, and the disquiet of this Church of England* (London, 1581). This was in response to Persons's first published book, *A Brief Discours contayning certayne reasons why Catholiques refuse to goe to Church* (London, 1580), 'dedicated by I.H. [John Howlet] to the Queenes most excellent Maiestie'. John Field, a Cambridge divinity student, edited the Protestant report of the debates in the Tower before Edmund Campion's execution; see *A Jesuit Challenge: Edmund Campion's Debates at the Tower of London in 1581*, ed. James V. Holleran (New York, 1999), p. xi n. 1, and p. 43.

to create a myth about him as a super-subtle sophister, whose every sentence would be suspect.

Persons's opponents tried to turn his virtues as a writer into signs that he could not be trusted. If he censured them for excessive warmth, they interpreted his restraint as a supercilious coolness, using wit as a cover for disrespect. His agility of mind signalled the absence of integrity, complained Matthew Sutcliffe, dean of Exeter, in 1600:

> For as *Pasquin* taketh upon him divers persons, and speaketh now like an angel, now like a devil; now like a king, and presently like a beggar; now like a Pope, and eftsoons like a poor parasite; now like a merchant, and by and by like a man of war; yea, and abhorreth not to play the part of a poet, a courtesan, or a Jebusite; so our friend *Robert Parsons* transformeth himself into all shapes, and playeth all parts, save the part of an honest man.[30]

From this point of view, the more deftly Persons managed his defence, the more he revealed his subtlety; the more reasonable his tone, the more hypocritical he was in assuming the moral high ground. Not that his opponents lacked ingenuity in exposing his secret designs. In 1608 Thomas Morton, royal chaplain and dean of Gloucester, seized on the initials 'P.R.' on the title page of Persons's *Treatise tending to Mitigation towardes Catholicke-subiectes in England*: recalling how St Augustine had characterized his adversaries, the Ps and the Rs (the Petilians and the Rogationists), as kites dressed up as doves, he demanded, 'Who could believe the Catholics' protestations that they were as harmless as doves?'[31] It was common cause among both Catholic and Protestant adversaries that Persons and his fellow-Jesuits secretly welcomed persecution for its propaganda value. The informer John Cecil claimed: 'Parsons gapes after some such windfall'.[32]

Protestants used the analogy of the Trojan horse to cast Persons in the role of Sinon, speaking peace and sweet reason with deadly intent.[33] *The First Booke*

---

[30]   Matthew Sutcliffe, *A Briefe Refutation of a certain calumnious relation of the conference passed betwixt the Lord of Plessis Marli and I. Peron, calling himselfe bishop of Evreux* (London, 1600), 'Preface to the Reader'. Pasquin was the name given to a mutilated statue in Rome, after the witty tailor near whose house it was found, because it was unclear what it represented. It was customary to paste satirical papers on the stature, which could thus speak in many contradictory voices. Sutcliffe is suggesting that Persons was elusive, impossible to pin down. 'Jebusite' was a common term of abuse for the Jesuits, after the Canaanite tribe that King David ousted from Jerusalem, just as Catholics were dispossessed in England.

[31]   Robert Persons, *A Treatise tending to Mitigation towardes Catholicke-Subiectes in England* (St Omer, 1608), henceforth referred to as *A Treatise tending to Mitigation*; Thomas Morton, *A Preamble Unto an Incounter with P.R. the Author of the deceitfull Treatise of Mitigation* (London, 1608), sigs. A1v–A2. The Petilians and Rogationists were Donatist sects denounced by Augustine.

[32]   John Cecil, Report to Lord Burghley, 23 May 1591, *CSP Domestic 1591–94*, p. 42.

[33]   For the Sinon figure, see Matthew Sutcliffe, *A Briefe Replie to a certaine odious and slanderous libel … entitled A temperate ward-word* (London, 1600), sig. A3v. It was employed by Catholics as well, e.g., William Allen, *A Treatise of Treasons against Q. Elizabeth, and the Croune of England* (Louvain, 1572), 'Preface to the English Reader', sigs. e3–i3, sometimes attributed to

of the Christian Exercise, uncontroversial as it appeared, was particularly treacherous, to the point where Edmund Bunny felt it necessary to edit out all of its half-hidden Catholic corruptions and republish it in a sanitized version (see below, Chapter 2). *A Conference about the Next Succession* affected impartiality or 'indifference'; here too both Protestants and Catholics assumed that it was merely a front to clear the way for an active, if not violent, promotion of a Spanish succession. In *A Treatise of Three Conversions* Persons sought to show how the Reformation narrative of a recovery, complete with a new martyrology, of the pure faith robbed English men and women of their true Christian inheritance; from Sutcliffe's point of view, this was no less than an attempted subversion of the entire achievement of the religious settlement in England. Ambiguously, he entitled his rebuttal, *The Subversion of Robert Parsons His confused and worthlesse worke*, in which he hoped both to subvert Persons's argument and expose it as subversive.[34] Persons, he implied, had an uncanny ability to turn settled things upside down, to turn the appearances of things inside out – in short, to expose the political and religious establishment to radical reinterpretation. He could be cast in the familiar role of the white devil, an angel with horns, tempting his readers to their ruin.

It was against Catholic polemicists such as Persons that King James I decided to found a college of writers of controversy. It was established at Chelsea in 1610 under the direction of Matthew Sutcliffe himself, with Thomas Morton appointed as one of the fellows. Ironically, Persons's educational foundations at St Omer, Valladolid and Seville, took root and flourished, while Sutcliffe's own Chelsea College failed: who, one is entitled to ask, was dealing in shadows?[35] Accusations of empty rhetoric, of the mere show of virtue and religion, shuttled back and forth between polemical adversaries, and Persons had to work hard to establish his credibility. He was constantly suspected of hidden motives: he was believed, for instance, to be consumed by personal animosity towards the Queen. The charge of treason itself was of limited propaganda value. Persons's political activities, his association with the various Armadas and his dealings with foreign powers, Spain, France and Denmark, over many years, could admittedly be invoked against his polemic.[36] Yet in the context of constant realignments of power in Europe and England's own turbulent recent history it was not enough to brand the Jesuit missionaries as rebels and traitors. Persecution could always be blamed for resistance. Persons himself wrote persuasively of men, even the Gunpowder plotters and other conspirators,

---

John Leslie; see Thomas H. Clancy, SJ, *Papist Pamphleteers: The Allen-Persons Party and the Political Thought of the Counter-Reformation in England, 1572–1615* (Chicago, 1964), p. 15.

   [34]   Matthew Sutcliffe, *The Subversion of Robert Parsons His confused and worthlesse worke, Entituled, A treatise of three Conversions of England from Paganisme to Christian Religion* (London, 1606).

   [35]   See D.E. Kennedy, 'King James I's College of Controversial Divinity at Chelsea', in D.E. Kennedy, Diana Robertson and Alexandra Walsham (eds), *Grounds of Controversy: Three Studies in Late 16th and Early 17th Century English Polemics* (Melbourne, 1989), pp. 97–126.

   [36]   This view of Persons is expressed by Coffey, p. 86.

'exasperated' by the state's inflexibility.[37] Protestant propagandists therefore took the next step, to attribute Persons's dissident writings to personal feeling rather than religious loyalty.

Towards Elizabeth, Persons tended to adopt a pastoral – almost patronizing – tone. He claimed to view her actions more in sorrow than in anger. In *A Conference about the Next Succession* he deplored her recklessness about her subjects' future. However much his opponents might also be anxious about the uncertainty of the succession, they found his attitude arrogant. In the *Philopater* he blamed the intensified persecution primarily on evil counsellors, but he called the Queen's piety into question. There was a certain irreverence, even sauciness, about his references to the Queen during her lifetime, and a presumptuous readiness to sit in judgment over her after her death, that was singularly provoking: he seemed to treat her as a mere fallible woman rather than his sovereign. Not least to be outraged by this was King James, who blustered:

> As for the English *Answerer,* my vnnatural and fugitiue Subiect; I will neither defile my pen, nor your sacred eies or eares with the describing of him, who ashames, nay abhorres not to rayle, nay, to rage and spewe forth blasphemies against the late *Queene* of famous memorie. A Subiect to raile against his naturall *Soueraigne* by birth; A man to rayle against a Lady by sexe; A holy man (in outward profession) to insult vpon the dead; nay, to take *Radamanthus* office ouer his head, and to sit downe and play the Iudge in hell; And all his quarrell is, that either her *Successour,* or any of her Seruants should speake honourably of her. Cursed be he that curseth the Anointed of God: and destroyed mought he be with the destruction of *Korah,* that hath sinned in the contradiction of *Korah.* Without mought such dogs and swine be, cast forth, I say, out of the spirituall *Ierusalem.*[38]

Persons was not above satirizing the Queen's demand for proper respect when he wanted to make an ingenious point about refusing to attend state worship. Suppose he were to discover that a civic ceremony in her honour was actually a parody? Should he participate? 'Can her majesty take it well', he asked innocently, 'or account of me, better than of a traitorous caitive, for yielding myself, to stay there, to hear them: to countenance their doings with my pretence?'[39] Why, then, should a Catholic attend a service that was a parody of praise of God?

In the characterization of Persons as a queen-baiter his Catholic opponents were all too willing to join, because it contributed to their reputation for loyalism. In 1598, when Charles Paget, perhaps Persons's most tenacious

---

[37]   *A Treatise tending to Mitigation*, Preface 'of the present division and disagreement about matters of religion in England, and of so many importunate exasperations used by divers sorts of men, to increase the same'.

[38]   James I, *An Apologie for the Oath of Allegiance: first set forth without a name, now acknowledged by James, King. Together with a premonition to all most mightie monarches* (London, 1609), p. 12.

[39]   Persons, *A Brief Discours contayning certayne reasons why Catholiques refuse to goe to Church*, fol. 55v.

Catholic enemy, was attempting to commend the anti-Jesuit party to the authorities, he attributed to Persons, for the first time, the authorship of the pamphlet commonly known as *Leicester's Commonwealth*, but innocently entitled *The Copie of a Leter, wryten by a Master of Arte of Cambridge, to his friend in London, concerning some talke past of late between two worshipful and grave men, about the present state, and some procedinges of the Erle of Leycester and his friendes in England*, originally published in 1584.[40] This prodigiously popular defamation of Elizabeth's favourite was almost certainly written in France by a group of exiled Catholic aristocrats, including Charles Arundell and Thomas Lord Paget. They were the rump of a court party outmanoeuvred by Leicester over the Anjou marriage proposals in 1580, and subsequently hounded out of the country. There is good evidence to show that Persons colluded with the authors in the publication and distribution of this work, hoping that it would undermine Elizabeth's Privy Council. But it is highly improbable that he wrote it himself.[41] Appellant writers such as William Watson and John Mush reinforced the attribution, so that the book came to be nicknamed 'Parsons' Green-coat', after the colour of the cover.[42] Protestant writers took up the cry. In 1612 Bodley's librarian, Thomas James, took it for granted that he wrote *Leicester's Commonwealth*,[43] and those responsible for republishing *Leicester's Commonwealth*, in 1641 named Persons without question.[44]

To this figure of the passionate, vindictive traitor (hidden behind the suave surface of Persons's works) could be added a picture of Persons as driven entirely by ambition and party interest. This was the thrust of the sustained attack mounted during the period 1600–1602 by the small but vociferous party of secular priests known as the appellants. From their perspective, most of Persons's activities did damage to the Catholic cause. Living in security in Catholic strongholds abroad, he could afford to demand uncompromising resistance from English Catholics, insensitive to their predicament. And so the appellants prayed to be delivered from his machinations: *a Machionationibus*

---

[40]   Edwards, *Robert Persons*, p. 227.

[41]   D.C. Peck (introd.), *Leicester's Commonwealth: 'The Copy of a Letter written by a Master of Art of Cambridge' (1584) and Related Documents* (Athens, Ohio, 1985), pp. 1–7, 23–8 agrees with L. Hicks, SJ, 'The Growth of a Myth: Father Robert Persons, S.J. and Leicester's Commonwealth', *Studies: An Irish Quarterly Review* 46 (1957): 91–105, that Persons was not the author; cf. Peter Holmes, 'The Authorship of "Leicester's Commonwealth" ', *Journal of Ecclesiastical History* 33 (1982): 424–30. It is attributed to Charles Arundell in ARCR II 31.

[42]   John Mush, *A Dialogue betwixt a Secular Priest, and a Lay Gentleman. Being an abstract of the most important matters that are in controversie betwixt the priests and the Spanish or Jesuiticall faction* (London, 1601), p. 107; William Watson, *A Decacordon of Ten Quodlibeticall Questions concerning Religion and State* (London, 1602), p. 266.

[43]   Thomas James, *The Jesuites Downefall ... Together with the Life of Father Parsons an English Jesuite* (Oxford, 1612), p. 59.

[44]   *Leicester's Commonwealth. Conceived, spoken and published with most earnest protestation of all dutiful good-will and affection towards this realm. By Robert Parsons* (London, 1641).

Parsoni, libera nos Domine.[45] Here the chief movers were Christopher Bagshaw and William Watson. Bagshaw was said to have been 'swinged' by Persons at Balliol, when the latter was Bursar, and became an implacable enemy. He was instrumental in expelling Persons from the college in 1574 and seldom missed an opportunity to crow over this disgrace. Persons was expelled for alleged mismanagement of the college accounts, and the bells of St Mary Magdalen that rang on that occasion continued to ring triumphantly in Bagshaw's pages for years to come. Bagshaw also converted to Rome but maintained a steadfastly anti-Jesuit stance, especially during the period when he was confined at Wisbech Castle: he was one of the leaders of the faction that was offended by the Jesuit William Weston's challenge to the community's religious practice. His collaborator, William Watson, acted as a kind of secretary to the appellants from 1600, writing prefaces to other men's books and compiling an anthology of insults entitled *A Decacordon of Ten Quodlibeticall Questions concerning Religion and State.* Many of Watson's satirical paragraphs were incorporated into other tracts or embellished. His stream of abuse anticipated, and contributed to, the Protestant compendium later amassed by Thomas James in *The Jesuites Downefall.*

Neither Bagshaw nor Watson, who was executed for treason in 1604, enjoyed the kind of personal reputation that could give their works much credit. Nevertheless they and their appellant partners eagerly canvassed the story of Persons's illegitimacy. This was first glanced at, in fact, by Sutcliffe in 1600, providing another example of the common cause between Protestant and Catholic detractors.[46] It was claimed that he was fathered by the local priest (hence his surname) and then foisted on a blacksmith named Cowbuck.[47] The probable basis for this slander was that he was supported by John Hayward (or Heywood), the parish priest at Nether Stowey, when he attended the Free School at Taunton. The fanciful account of Persons's bastard, Cowbuck origins prompted innumerable cheap jibes, even though two of his brothers, indignant on their mother's behalf, confirmed that he was the son of Henry and Christina Persons.[48] The frequently repeated nickname 'Cowbuck' gave the cue for many degrading suggestions. Watson sneered at Persons's leadership for displaying a narrow self-interest and beggarly manner that marked a decline from a tradition of princely prelates.[49] John Colleton, another appellant, portrayed

---

[45]   Christopher Bagshaw, *A Sparing Discoverie of our English Jesuits, and of Fa. Parsons proceedings under pretence of promoting the Catholike faith in England* (London, 1601), p. 70.

[46]   Sutcliffe, *A Briefe Replie to a certaine odious and slanderous libel lately published by a seditious Jesuite*, p. 99.

[47]   See John Mush, *Declaratio Motuum ac Turbationum quae ex controversiis inter Iesuitas ... & Sacerdotes Seminariorum in Anglia* (London, 1601), p. 58; Bagshaw, *A Sparing Discoverie of our English Jesuits*, pp. 41–2; Anthony Copley, *An Answere to a Letter of a Jesuited Gentleman, by his Cosin, Maister A.C. Concerninge the Appeale; State, Jesuits* (London, 1601), pp. 34–7.

[48]   'Father Persons' Autobiography', pp. 13–22, 36–47, and *A Defence of the Catholike Ecclesiastical Hierarchie*, fol. 197. If there were any substance to the charge, it would surely have featured in the Balliol expulsion episode.

[49]   Watson, *A Decacordon of Ten Quodlibeticall Questions concerning Religion and State*, pp. 30, 80.

him as a black-hatted merchant in Rome, peddling the crown of England to all-comers.[50]

Another social insult was to call Persons and his fellow-Jesuits 'allobrogicks' (from the Latin name of a Genevan tribe) or 'Puritans'. These terms of abuse insinuated a pharisaical, discourteous and dogmatic attitude. Unlike other religious, Jesuits did not sing in choir; this could be taken as a sign of a lowering of the tone of religious life, a falling off from the dignity of past ages. The appellants indeed represented, in an exaggerated way, that strain of feeling amongst post-Reformation Catholics that was most preoccupied with the lost glory of the institutional church. Jesuits were felt to demean themselves by meddling in politics, and Persons the bastard, it was noted, took this betrayal of the religious profession to an extreme.[51] The Protestant Thomas James added another twist: he applauded Persons for rising above his shameful origins to become an Oxford fellow and successful spiritual writer, only to sink into the mire of treason and dissent once more.[52]

The image of 'base Persons' derived some its staying power from the contrast with 'gentle Campion'. This was most memorably put by William Camden in his description of the leaders of the English mission: 'This *Parsons* was of *Somersetshire*, a valiant, fierce-natured man, and of a rough behaviour. *Campion* was a *Londoner*, of a sweet disposition, and a well-polished man'.[53] Nor was this merely a question of urbanity opposed to rusticity; Campion suffered bravely at Tyburn, but Persons fled across the Channel. According to Bagshaw he had thus re-enacted the disgrace of his flight from Balliol.[54] He had pushed away the feast-table of martyrdom for lack of a wedding-garment.[55] Cowardly, close and furtive in all his dealings, he was indifferent to the plight of his fellow-Catholics. William Watson was roused to a pitch of indignation:

> ... (cursed be the hower wherein he was borne, this *filius peccati*, *sacrilegij*, *iniquitatis*, *papuli*, *Diaboli*) how euer he durst come at Gods holy Altar, after his blasphemies, and outragious speeches, and writing against the secular Priests and Students, most falsely, irreligiously, and Pharisaically laying his owne sinnes, and the rest of the Iesuits seditious vprores, and more then heathenish impietie vpon the innocent most cruelly persecuted by them all, and by him in speciall aboue al the rest, as most cruell Iewish

---

50   John Colleton, *A Just Defence of the Slandered Priestes* (London, 1602), p. 241.

51   Mush, *A Dialogue betwixt a Secular Priest, and a Lay Gentleman*, pp. 54–5.

52   James, *The Jesuites Downefall*, pp. 57–8.

53   'Personius ille erat Somersettensis, vehemens, ferox natura, & moribus incultioribus. Campianus Londinensis, vir suauis & politissimus', William Camden, *Annales rerum Anglicanum, et Hibernicarum regnante Elizabetha, ad annum salutis MDLXXXIX* (Frankfurt, 1616), p. 319, quoted in English by Edward Gee (introd.), *The Jesuit's Memorial, for the Intended Reformation of England Under their First Popish Prince* (London, 1690), p. xii. In the same passage Camden describes Persons as 'seditioso & turbulento ingenio, audacia armatus'. On the Persons/Campion contrast, see Bossy, 'The Heart of Robert Persons', pp. 141–2.

54   Bagshaw, *A Sparing Discoverie of our English Jesuits*, p. 39.

55   Copley, *An Answere to a Letter of a Jesuited Gentleman*, p. 37. But cf. Pedro de Ribadeneira, *Bibliotheca Scriptorum Societatis Jesu* (Rome, 1676), p. 725: 'non semel tantum, sed per totam vitam quodammodo Martyr fieret, multorumque Martyrum pater': 'he was the martyr not of a moment but of a lifetime'.

harted vnnaturall ... O monster of all other ... wo woorth thee wretch: wo woorth thee and all the Iesuiticall broode: who to maintaine thy ambition, hast brought this obloquie, reproch and discredite vpon our dear countriemen and brethren, innocent, harmlesse hearts, torne out bleeding by thy massacring mercilesse crueltie.[56]

These are passionate words, but neither wild nor misdirected. Watson was trying to drive a wedge between Persons and the Jesuits on the one hand, and the bulk of the recusants on the other. The portrait of Persons as mean-spirited chimes with the slander about his birth. The appeal here is to the self-image cultivated by many loyalist Catholics: a company of the faithful clustered around the ancient nobility and gentry of the realm. Persons threatened this image because he operated so differently from Jasper Heywood, who tended to confine himself to contacts with the landed Catholic families.[57]

An important ex-Catholic associated with Heywood and the family of Thomas More was John Donne, who was indignant on behalf of the community he had himself left behind. He asserted that the Jesuit's 'continual libels, and incitatory books, have occasioned more afflictions, and drawn more of that blood, which they call Catholic, in this kingdom, than all our Acts of Parliament have done'.[58] It was alleged that his preoccupation with his own power and prestige made him callous, a motif reinforced by the frequently repeated anecdote of his expectation of the red hat. When Persons returned to Rome from Spain in 1597, rumour was rife that he would be made a cardinal. According to a (probably apocryphal) anecdote, he made the mistake of following the advice of his physicians, sending out for scarlet cloth to make a stomacher. Red was believed to have therapeutic qualities, but its association with ecclesiastical rank dominated the imaginations of the Roman merchants. A wagon appeared at the door, containing enough scarlet stuff to provide amply for a cardinal's needs. If the merchants were confused, Persons was confounded, and shuffled them out by the back door. Too late. His supposed delusions of grandeur provoked Watson to call him Nimrod, 'presum[ing] to build Babel above the welkin', and 'Corvester Parsons', the king-maker.[59]

Such attacks on Persons's character were scarcely edifying, but they arose from a crippling sense of frustration with his apparent monopoly of papal policy. In this regard Arnold Pritchard has suggested that belief in the omnipotent Jesuit was psychologically necessary for disappointed loyalist Catholics.[60] In fact, Persons encountered considerable resistance from both Popes Clement

---

[56] Watson, *A Decacordon of Ten Quodlibeticall Questions concerning Religion and State*, pp. 128–9.

[57] See Dennis Flynn, '"Out of Step": Six Supplementary Notes on Jasper Heywood', in McCoog, *The Reckoned Expense*, pp. 179–92.

[58] John Donne, *Pseudo-Martyr. Wherein out of certaine Propositions and Gradations, This Conclusion is evicted. That those which are of the Romane Religion in this Kingdome, may and ought to take the Oath of Allegeance* (London, 1610), sig. ¶1v.

[59] Bagshaw, *A Sparing Discoverie of our English Jesuits*, pp. 61–2; Watson, *A Decacordon of Ten Quodlibeticall Questions concerning Religion and State*, pp. 237, 241.

[60] Pritchard, pp. 75–91.

VIII and Paul V. The appellants nicknamed him 'Polypragman Parsons', for his indefatigable machinations, and 'Hispanized [or Hispaniolated] chameleon', for his Spanish affiliation. They called him 'emperor' and 'gubernator'. All information passing to and from the Curia on the English question seemed to bear his stamp. He was untouchable, claimed Bagshaw, with some bitterness and a great deal of sarcasm:

> And thus for this time wee leaue the Iesuits of our nation, to deale in generalities any farther with them, or with their extraordinarie illuminations or spirits of guiding soules: and doe addresse our selues to that vertuous Paragon Father *Parsons*, the vnworthie Rector of our English Seminarie at *Rome*. But before we begin with him, wee had need to entertaine you with some short Preface. For some no doubt will startle that he should be touched, what? Dare any presume to call him in question? Will you intermeddle with his actions? They are not to be sifted or canuased or discountenanced by any secular Priests whosoeuer, his holiness excepted. Beware what you doe: it is sure a note of an euill spirit: we pray God those men be found that dare take this course. He is a religious man, a Iesuit, the rarest wise man of our nation, most familiar with Princes, admired in Spaine, reuerenced in Italie, and onlie hated in England: which is a sufficient argument of his integritie.[61]

The final twist accentuates the sense of Persons as un-English. However jealous and peevish Bagshaw might be, he caught the mood of suspicion.

In a more Protestant idiom, Sutcliffe described Persons as Dagon before the Ark, one who profaned the holy places.[62] Appellants and Protestants alike, then, presented him as an alien and disturbing presence. A telling part of the Persons legend in this regard was the link with equivocation, a practice considered foreign to bluff English honesty. The abhorrence with which English Protestant writers regarded equivocation in Persons's day anticipated the horrified reaction of Victorian Englishmen to the idea of 'being economical with the truth' as expounded by some of Newman's disciples. It does not appear that Persons himself practised equivocation – in fact, he insisted that it could only be used in carefully defined circumstances – but he defended the traditional doctrine with extraordinary skill. Thomas Morton characterized him as an alchemist extracting truth from lies.[63] William Barlow suggested that the pseudonym Doleman, used for *A Conference about the Next Succession*, might be converted to *Dolus*, a byword for the kind of fraud that exploits loopholes in the law.[64] Persons was seen as the equivocator *par excellence*,

---

[61] Bagshaw, *A Sparing Discoverie of our English Jesuits*, p. 39.

[62] Matthew Sutcliffe, *A Full and Round Answer to … Robert Parsons the Noddie his foolish and rude Warne-word* (London, 1604), sig. A3.

[63] Thomas Morton, *A Full Satisfaction concerning a double Romish Iniquitie; hainous Rebellion, and more then heathenish Aequivocation* (London, 1606), p. 102, responding in part to Persons's account of Henry Garnet's trial (in which equivocation played such a major role) in *An Answere to Coke*.

[64] William Barlow, *An Answer to a Catholike English-man (so by himself entituled) who, without a Name, passed his Censure upon the Apology, made by the Right High and mightie Prince Iames … for the Oath of Allegeance* (London, 1609), p. 5.

a writer who could make treason and sedition seem virtuous. He could turn equivocation itself into a heavenly grace. In a well-known sermon on the Gunpowder Treason, Robert Tynley condemned equivocation as an unnatural practice that robs words of their meaning.[65] Conversely, the suspicion of equivocation could rob Persons's words of their effectiveness: a consummation that for his adversaries, Protestant and Catholic alike, was most devoutly to be wished.

* * *

Persons survived his controversies with Sutcliffe and Morton and the appellants, and it would probably be fair to say that he had the better of both disputes. But the legend of 'Father Parsons', Jesuit mastermind with a hidden Hispanic agenda, has persisted almost to the present day. Even so astute a popular historian as Paul Johnson describes him as 'sinister Father Parsons ... a professional international conspirator'.[66] Rather like Newman, he is regarded as capable, subtle, persuasive, yet somehow suspect, as if his writings conceal some sleight of hand. And like Newman, he attracted the scorn of Charles Kingsley. In *Westward Ho!*, Kingsley's novel about the derring-do of Ralegh and the men of Devon, the activity of Campion and Persons is assumed to be augmenting the Spanish threat. In contrast with the meek, timid, kind-hearted Campion, Persons appears as a bold, irascible bully. Able to hold his seat on a horse and his own in an argument, he is no gentleman in any sense that Kingsley will recognize.[67] On the Catholic side, the adulation of Campion has kept Persons in the shade. Gerard Manley Hopkins wrote in extravagant terms of Campion's literary gifts, comparing them with Shakespeare's.[68] Persons may not have been as polished a writer as Campion, but his writing career was by any standards much more significant. Even Catholic historians have kept their distance. A characteristic, and widely read, account of Persons's allegedly baneful contribution to the Catholic reformation in England was given by Hugh Tootel (better known as Charles Dodd) in *The Church History of England*, edited with memorable prejudice by M.A. Tierney.[69] T.G. Law, who wrote the entry for 'Parsons' in the late-nineteenth-century *Dictionary of National Biography*, cast him as the villain of the conflicts among Elizabethan Catholics, concluding: 'He was impetuous and self-willed, and moreover

---

[65]   Robert Tynley, *Two Learned Sermons. The one, of the mischievous subtiltie, and barbarous crueltie, the other of the false Doctrines, and refined Haeresies of the Romish Synagogue* (London, 1609), p. 6.

[66]   Paul Johnson, *The Offshore Islanders: A History of the English People*, rev. edn (London, 1985), p. 161.

[67]   Charles Kingsley, *Westward Ho!* (Cambridge, 1855), ch. 3.

[68]   Gerard Manley Hopkins, Letter to R.W. Dixon, 1 December 1881 (Feast Day of St Edmund Campion), in *Poems and Prose*, ed. W.H. Gardner (Harmondsworth, 1953), pp. 195–7.

[69]   Hugh Tootel [Charles Dodd (pseud.)], *The Church History of England: From the Commencement of the Sixteenth Century to the Revolution in 1688*, ed. M.A. Tierney (5 vols; London, 1839–43); Tootel's work was first published in 1737–42.

... he was subject to "inveterate prejudices", and therefore could be easily deceived'.[70]

A succession of able Jesuit historians, J.H. Pollen, Leo Hicks, Francis Edwards and Thomas McCoog, has helped to correct the legend of 'Father Parsons'.[71] Nor, to give them their due, did hostile writers such as Tierney, Law and Taunton descend to the levels of vituperation applied by Persons's contemporaries.[72] Law dismissed as 'worthless' the collection of insults masquerading as a biography published in 1612 by Bodley's librarian, Thomas James, and entitled *The Jesuites Downefall*.

In disentangling Persons the man from Persons the bogey, it is crucial to understand the nature of the legend as a rhetorical construct. In classical rhetoric, one of the most important strategies of persuasion is to establish your trustworthiness as a speaker.[73] This explains much of the personal insult that pervades religious controversy of the early modern period. Nevertheless there is an important issue behind all the mud-slinging, and that is the tension between the formative and the polemical in Persons's writing, brought into focus by the stark contrast between his most influential work, *The Christian Directory* – sweet, reasonable and even ecumenical – and his viciously sharp-tongued attacks on Protestant and appellant writers. *The Christian Directory* enjoyed remarkable success, and has been described as the most popular book of devotion in English of its day. Hostile critics could find little to cavil at in the work itself, although Protestants found some of the implied doctrine, especially on earning merit, dangerous or offensive. Intrinsically there was nothing to suggest that the author, who invited his religious opponents to join with him in amendment of life, was anything other than holy, and wholly concerned for the moral and spiritual state of his readers. Yet commentators found it hard to reconcile this irenic Persons with the political activist who promoted resistance to the state and humiliated his polemical antagonists. Rather than reconsider their judgment of him as a man, it was simpler, and often more convenient, to assume that there was something hypocritical about the writing of *The Christian Directory*. It might be a kind of Trojan horse, smuggling in Catholic doctrine to ambush the unsuspecting Protestant reader,

---

[70]   Law based his judgment on an unsympathetic reading of Persons's participation in the Archpriest Controversy. See *The Archpriest Controversy: Documents Relating to the Dissensions of the Roman Catholic Clergy, 1597–1602: from the Petyt MSS. of the Inner Temple*, ed. T.G. Law; Camden Society, 56 and 58 (2 vols; London, 1896, 1898). He also gave credence to one of Persons's most inveterate enemies, the Belgian Provincial Oliver Mannaerts.

[71]   See, for instance, J.H. Pollen, SJ, 'The Politics of English Catholics during the Reign of Queen Elizabeth. No. III. – Revival of Spiritual Life and of Political Aspirations, 1580–1582', *The Month* 99 (January–June 1902): 290–305; Hicks (introd.), *Letters and Memorials of Father Robert Persons*; Edwards, *Robert Persons*; McCoog, *The Society of Jesus in Ireland, Scotland, and England 1541–1588*.

[72]   Ethelred L. Taunton, *The History of the Jesuits in England 1580–1773* (London, 1901), esp. pp. 96–7.

[73]   Technically, this dimension of persuasion is known as *ethos*, as opposed to *logos* (formal argument) and *pathos* (appeal to emotion). See Brian Vickers, *In Defence of Rhetoric* (Oxford, 1988), pp. 19–20 and *passim*.

lured by the promise of holiness. It might be a propaganda ploy, advertising holiness of life as a Catholic commodity, to be obtained by various kinds of surrender to priestcraft. Or it might be a case of appropriating a reputation for piety simply by adapting the works of the popular Spanish Dominican writer, Luis de Granada.[74] No one could doubt his facility with words and literary structure, but how sincere was his concern for personal spiritual formation?

The argument of this study entails a reversal of the assessment made of *The Christian Directory* by Persons's hostile contemporaries. I see it as representing his core interest rather than as a self-contained project isolated from the rest of his career as a missionary and activist. Even from my brief biographical account, it is clear that his first encounter with Ignatius and the Spiritual Exercises, shortly after his expulsion from Oxford, was the most significant experience of his life, and that it informed his thinking and decisions from then on. *The Christian Directory* was his attempt to pass this transforming experience on to others. He wrote it for those who were unable, for lack of a priest, to perform the Exercises, or would be suspicious of them as an overtly Catholic instrument. But conditions in post-Reformation England were not favourable to such reading or such a resolution. There was a fight to be fought and Persons was the one to fight it. Still, he never lost sight of the goal: to promote the life-changing direction of souls that is at the heart of the Jesuit enterprise. The more closely we study his published works, the more evident are their affinities to and their correspondence with *The Christian Directory*. It was, in a sense, the book he was always writing, extending, deferring; the mission he was always rewriting.

To see Persons's polemical writing in this way is to see all his books, tracts and pamphlets as part of an apostolate of letters. It was an established Jesuit tradition to write letters of spiritual direction and comfort. Many of Ignatius' own letters are models of this kind,[75] and Persons himself conducted an extensive correspondence not only with his fellow priests but with lay men and women in need of counsel and encouragement. There is abundant evidence of the appreciation expressed by those affected by his ministry in this way. His published works were not, of course, personal letters, nor were they written primarily for Catholic readers: they were thrown into the fray in a battle of books. But the non-combatants could watch, as it were, from the sidelines. They could take comfort in the palpable hits and they could detect the pastoral concerns implicit in what Persons had written in defence of the faith and as part of a power struggle.

Persons's prose style has always had its admirers, most notably Jonathan Swift, who claimed that the only Elizabethan prose that was still readable in

---

[74]   On the adaptation of Luis de Granada, see *The Christian Directory (1582): The First Booke of the Christian Exercise, appertayning to Resolution*, ed. Victor Houliston (Leiden, 1998), pp. xxxii–xxxviii and appendix III.

[75]   See the 'Select Letters' in St Ignatius of Loyola, *Personal Writings*, ed. Joseph A. Munitiz, SJ and Philip Endean, SJ (Harmondsworth, 1996).

the eighteenth century was that of Hooker and 'Parsons the Jesuit'.[76] Casual references to its vigour and lucidity abound, in the writings of A.L. Rowse, Garrett Mattingly, Evelyn Waugh and Thomas Clancy,[77] amongst others, but there has been little sustained analysis, apart from a short essay by Joseph Crehan and a chapter of a dissertation by Edwin Broderick, both written in the 1950s.[78] The present study does not offer a literary appreciation so much as an analysis of rhetorical strategies, in an attempt to show how the pastoral vision was inflected by the historical moment.

In the most comprehensive critical overview that exists of recusant writing, Ceri Sullivan has assessed the importance of books in post-Reformation English Catholic culture, in the context of persecution and isolation. She analyses the various kinds of formation that different categories of books supported, distinguishing such books carefully from the polemical.[79] The distinction is an important one, but it is not absolute, and it would be a mistake to allow the more aggressive features of Persons's works of controversy to obscure the integrity of his vision. He is clearly one of the most significant recusant writers, at least as important as Thomas Stapleton, Edmund Campion and Robert Southwell, and it is our business to try to see his work as a whole.

Campion's *oeuvre* is small, inviting such adjectives as 'jewel-like': the play *Ambrosia*, the defence of the faith entitled *Decem rationes*, the personal apologia and challenge known as *Campion's Brag*, and the description of Ireland that found its way into Holinshed.[80] He also composed a rhetorical exercise about the moon, for the entertainment of the Queen when she visited Oxford in 1566, and an heroic poem entitled *Sancta salutiferi nascentia semina verbi*.[81] These are supremely elegant but they do not amount to a substantial body of writing with a distinctive literary presence. Campion's greatness was in his oratory, both as a preacher and a disputant. We can observe his skill in the records of the debates in the Tower before his execution.[82] There are hints there of the kind of settled conviction, the sense of belonging to the centre, that informs most of Persons's polemic. In this way it is possible to appreciate

---

[76]   *The Tatler*, no. 230; in Jonathan Swift, *Prose Works*, ed. Herbert Davis et al. (14 vols; Oxford, 1939–68), vol. 2, p. 177.

[77]   Rowse, *Eminent Elizabethans*; Garrett Mattingly, *The Defeat of the Spanish Armada* (London, 1959), p. 72; Evelyn Waugh, *Edmund Campion, Jesuit and Martyr* (1935), in *Two Lives: Edmund Campion – Ronald Knox* (London, 2001), p. 51; Clancy, *Papist Pamphleteers*.

[78]   Joseph Crehan, SJ, 'Father Persons, SJ', in Charles Davis (ed.), *English Spiritual Writers* (London, 1961), pp. 84–96; Edwin B. Broderick, 'Robert Persons *The Christian Directory*: Prolegomena to an Edition' (diss., Fordham University, 1951), pp. 96–139.

[79]   Sullivan, *Dismembered Rhetoric*, esp. p. 37.

[80]   Edmund Campion, SJ, *Rationes decem quibus fretus, certamen aduersariis obtulit in causa fidei* (Stonor Park, 1581); *A Historie of Ireland (1570)*, ed. Rudolf B. Gottfried (New York, 1940); *Ambrosia*, ed. Jos. Simons (Assen, 1969). *Campion's Brag* has been widely reproduced, e.g., in Reynolds, *Campion and Parsons*, pp. 78–81. On the drama, see Alison Shell, '"We are Made a Spectacle": Campion's Dramas', in McCoog, *The Reckoned Expense*, pp. 103–18.

[81]   See Gerald Kilroy, 'Eternal Glory: Edmund Campion's Virgilian Epic', *Times Literary Supplement* (8 March 2002): 13–15, and his study, *Edmund Campion: Memory and Transcription* (Aldershot, 2005).

[82]   See Campion, *A Jesuit Challenge*.

how close Persons and Campion were in their attitudes and understanding, much closer than the conventional 'black and white' contrast between them will allow.

Southwell has an established reputation as a minor Elizabethan poet, his religious lyrics prefiguring the greater achievement of Donne, Herbert and Crashaw. It is now becoming clearer how his verse output formed part of his missionary career, supporting the spiritual direction given in *A Short Rule of Good Life*, published posthumously in 1622. In the latter, he explains how his writing relates to Persons's:

> Before thou begin to practise these Rules, containing in them great perfection, … acquaint thy selfe with an other Booke entituled The Exercise of a Christian life, or such other-like, lest thou attempt to build a great house with slender foundation; and climing to the toppe of a high ladder; without passing by the middle steppes, as vnawares thou receiue a fall.[83]

Southwell offers practical advice on the formation of a life of disciplined devotion and service, presupposing the commitment that Persons enjoins in *The Christian Directory*. He wrote the book that Persons would have liked to write as the completion of his own work, but was continually deferring. Southwell's poems, too, are really for those who have entered on the resolved life. This difference between their books of devotion signals a larger difference in emphasis in their writing vocations. Persons remained always at the point of confrontation: each of his works confronts some difficulty or obstacle in the way of resolution. This means there is always something strained, something provisional, about his writing; it lacks Southwell's finish and Campion's grace. But it is always energetic, strategic, making things happen.

---

[83]   Robert Southwell, SJ, *A Short Rule of Good Life. To direct the devout Christian in a regular and orderly course* (St Omer, 1622), preface, pp. 13–14. On Southwell's writing career as a vocation, see Scott Pilar, SJ, *Robert Southwell, S.J. and the Mission of Literature* (Aldershot, 2003). See also Anne Sweeney, *Robert Southwell: Snow in Arcadia: Redrawing the English Lyric Landscape, 1586–1595* (Manchester, 2007).

CHAPTER TWO

The English Mission:
Writing *The Christian Directory*

The most important event in Robert Persons's life occurred in Louvain in 1574, when the Jesuit William Good guided him through the Spiritual Exercises. Twenty-eight years old, in exile from England, ousted from his fellowship at Balliol, tentatively attached to the University of Padua, he was full of energy and talent, but without prospects. Henry More, Provincial of the English Jesuits in the seventeenth century, gave the official version of what happened:

> As [Fr Good] worked through them, he roused in Persons a distaste for the mundane which eventually overcame every other feeling ... Good hoped that he would send down deep roots into goodness, and offered him sound advice to that end ... [He should] put every other thought aside save that of getting nearer to God. He should think over what he ought to do now, and come to his decision in calm and tranquillity ... He had now set his mind on a more spiritual life, and in his fresh awareness of the transitoriness of things took a new and strange delight.

His considered response to completing the Spiritual Exercises was to join the Society of Jesus. In Rome, in July 1575, after an interview with the Jesuit Father General, Everard Mercurian,

> [he] fell on his knees and made the total offering to God. He so overflowed with inner joy that then and there he made away all he possessed. With no hesitant afterthought, he adopted the Society's way of life. In it he lived henceforth in complete peace of mind.[1]

He was accepted into the novitiate on July 25, the Feast of St James, entering into a life of commitment to the service of God as it had been revealed to him.[2] A sense of mission was to consume him from now on.

To put it like this is to take More's account at face value, but there is no reason to question More's judgment. It echoes the response that Persons elicited from his fellow Jesuits. There were those who thought he was misguided in his chosen means, fanatical or driven in his pursuit of Catholic or Jesuit advantage, but no-one questioned his single-minded devotion to the mission, most memorably stated by Pedro de Ribadeneira when he wrote that Persons was the martyr not of a moment but of a lifetime.[3]

---

[1] Henry More, SJ, *The Elizabethan Jesuits*, ed. and trans. Francis Edwards, SJ (London, 1981), pp. 15, 49–53.

[2] Thomas M. McCoog, SJ, *English and Welsh Jesuits, 1555–1650*, CRS, 74–5 (2 vols; London, 1994–95), *sub* Parsons.

[3] Pedro de Ribadeneira, *Bibliotheca Scriptorum Societatis Jesu* (Rome, 1676), p. 725.

* * *

Persons's reception into the Catholic Church and the Society of Jesus was timely because he was an active proponent of the English mission from its inception.[4] William Allen, leader of the English Catholics in exile, came to Rome in 1579, resolved to launch a missionary venture. The twenty-one years since Elizabeth's accession had been a period of regrouping and consolidation: Allen founded the college at Douay to accommodate the Catholic priests and theologians, and the exiles found refuge chiefly in the Spanish Netherlands, Brittany, Spain and Italy. Catholics in England were not yet subject to heavy penalties, but they were demoralized and uncertain, lacking leadership, spiritual counsel and access to the sacraments. They were confused about church attendance and felt isolated from Rome. Allen believed that the majority of English people were still Catholic at heart, but there was a danger that their loyalty or affection would gradually dwindle until the nation lost its Catholic character and Catholicism became the religion of a persecuted minority. It was time for action.

The alliance and friendship between William Allen and Robert Persons, which began in 1579 and continued until Allen's death in 1594, was crucial in the formation of the post-Reformation English Catholic community: together they directed the activities of the mission in England and the activities of Catholics in exile: the seminaries, the involvement in the Spanish armies, and the publication of English Catholic books. Allen was 14 years older than Persons and a man of remarkable foresight. After leaving Oxford, where he had been Principal of St Mary's Hall, he joined the exiles in Louvain but spent some time in England in the early 1560s. He was among the first to recognize that church attendance posed a real problem to the survival of Catholicism. In 1568 he established the college at Douay, a move that helped to concentrate the energies of English Catholic exiles so that they could begin to work together towards a common future. Persons found himself in complete agreement with Allen: he shared these priorities and also the fundamental attitude to the English Protestant establishment.[5] They both believed that English Protestantism was a blend of political expediency and theological sectarianism, and that there were two ways to combat it: challenge the complacency and acquiescence of the lay people, and threaten or destroy the political structures underpinning the Protestant church hierarchy. It was important to strengthen the network of powerful Catholic families in order to provide encouragement and protection to the community and logistic support to the mission, but the cultivation of great houses played less part in their thinking than in that of Persons's fellow-Jesuits Jasper Heywood and William Crichton.

---

[4]   For a full account, see E.E. Reynolds, *Campion and Parsons: The Jesuit Mission of 1580–1* (London, 1980); and Richard Simpson, *Edmund Campion: A Biography*, 2nd edn (London, 1896).

[5]   See Thomas H. Clancy, SJ, *Papist Pamphleteers: The Allen-Persons Party and the Political Thought of the Counter-Reformation in England, 1572–1615* (Chicago, 1964).

Persons was still a fairly inexperienced Jesuit when he was placed in charge of the English mission early in 1580. With his academic background his course of study had been accelerated: ordained priest in July 1578, he found himself playing an advisory role in a dispute between disaffected English students at the English College, Rome, and the Welsh rector, Maurice Clynogg. When the Italian, Alfonso Agazzari, took over as rector in 1579, Persons was becoming used to associating with decision-makers in the world of English Catholic exiles. Besides William Allen, he befriended Claudio Acquaviva, who was soon to succeed Mercurian as Father General of the Jesuits.[6] Because of the way Persons assumed the leadership at this time, it is easily forgotten that he was considerably younger than Edmund Campion, who was recalled from Prague to spearhead the mission. If it is asked why Persons was chosen to be the superior, the answer may be that he was the man on the spot in Rome; he and Allen were manifestly like-minded (unlike Campion, he had been agitating for the mission), and Allen presumably felt he could trust Persons's judgment. This faith was justified, albeit in a negative way, in that it was through ignoring Persons's instructions that Campion was captured at Lyford Grange in July 1581. Much of the practical success of the mission can be attributed to Persons: the conferences, the missionary tours and the operation of printing presses.

The most vexed question about the English mission was the political agenda, subject of controversy both then and now. Several challenges have been made to the familiar image of the innocent missionaries, idealistically trusting that preaching and conversion would by themselves reverse the English Reformation, then devastated by Campion's arrest and brutal execution. This view, which is substantially that of Evelyn Waugh's influential biography of Campion, has been dismissed as a 'fairy tale' by historians more conscious of the historical pressures of 1579–81. John E. Parish has suggested that if Persons were really ignorant, as he and his party set off from Rome in April 1580, of the contemporaneous papal invasion of Ireland, he was 'one of the least informed Englishmen in Europe'.[7] Michael Carrafiello has argued that he was already committed to the violent overthrow of the Elizabethan regime, with the help of Spain and Scotland, and that this was his settled purpose (whatever the immediate project) throughout Elizabeth's reign. Carrafiello also believes that Persons was deeply influenced by the political theory of Francesco Suarez, which could arguably have predisposed him to tyrannicide or rebellion.[8] Much debate centres on the instructions given to the missionaries by Mercurian in 1580, in which they were forbidden to 'mix themselves in affairs of state'. Moreover, to protect them from accusations of treason, they

[6]   Francis Edwards, SJ, *Robert Persons: The Biography of an Elizabethan Jesuit, 1546–1610* (St Louis, 1995), pp. 14–24; Robert Persons, Letter to William Good, Rome, after 19 March 1579, in *Letters and Memorials of Father Robert Persons, S.J.: Vol. I (to 1988)*, ed. L. Hicks, SJ; CRS, 39 (London, 1942), pp. 5–28.

[7]   John E. Parish, *Robert Parsons and the English Counter-Reformation*, Rice University Studies, 52 (Houston, 1966), p. 13.

[8]   Michael L. Carrafiello, *Robert Parsons and English Catholicism, 1580–1610* (Selinsgrove, 1998), pp. 20–26, 51–4.

were authorized by the Pope, Gregory XIII, to release English Catholics from the obligation to treat the excommunicate Queen as an illegitimate monarch, 'rebus sic stantibus' (under present conditions). This was taken by the Protestant authorities to mean nothing more than that direct hostilities were suspended while the missionaries consolidated the community and the foreign powers marshalled their forces. From another point of view, the concession can be seen as the first step towards recognizing the Queen's legitimacy.[9]

Not long after their arrival in London, Campion and Persons were approached by Thomas Pounde, representing the Catholic prisoners at the Marshalsea, to draw up a declaration of their intentions in advance, to serve as evidence in case of arrest. Persons was the more persuaded: he had to urge the hesitant Campion to respond. The well-known document known as *Campion's Brag* was one result, and Persons's *'Confessio Fidei'* the other. It is telling that both Jesuits founded their apologias on their certainty of the truth of the Catholic religion, to which the questions of legality were subordinated. There was, therefore, no inherent contradiction between the fundamentally pastoral and evangelical character of the mission and the limited political objectives with which it can be associated. Thomas McCoog has noted the coincidence of the mission with the negotiations over the projected marriage between Elizabeth and the Duke of Anjou, 'Monsieur' (formerly Alençon).[10] In the event the marriage project failed, and those Catholic courtiers who hitched their wagons to that star had to go into exile. They formed the nucleus of English Catholics who remained involved in French politics and gradually became estranged from Persons and Allen. One of the purposes of the mission, to be sure, was to raise the profile of the Catholic community, to advertise its presence and to make it clear that it was not going to disintegrate. This was not so much to attract persecution as to render it futile. The question of church attendance was in fact top of the agenda. Allen and Persons wanted to halt the slide towards conformity, especially the fragmentation of Catholic confession into multiple forms of resistance. Recent research has shown just how many options there were, short of full recusancy, for Catholics to register dissent from the state church: occasional absenteeism, conspicuous inattention, crypto-Catholic worship, and partial attendance.[11] But for Persons, it was crucial that they understood that recusancy was indeed the 'gold standard'. It would keep Catholics united and would send a clear message to the authorities.

---

[9]   J.H. Pollen, SJ, 'The Politics of English Catholics during the Reign of Queen Elizabeth. No. III. – Revival of Spiritual Life and of Political Aspirations, 1580–1582', *The Month* 99 (January–June 1902): 290–305.

[10]   Thomas M. McCoog, SJ, 'The English Jesuit Mission and the French Match, 1579–1581', *Catholic Historical Review* 87 (2001): 185–213.

[11]   Alexandra Walsham, ' "Yielding to the extremity of the Time": Conformity, Orthodoxy and the Post-Reformation Catholic Community', in Peter Lake and Michael Questier (eds), *Conformity and Orthodoxy in the English Church, c. 1560–1660* (Woodbridge, Suffolk, 2000), pp. 211–36. The term 'gold standard' is from Questier's essay 'Conformity, Catholicism and the Law', in the same collection, pp. 237–61 (p. 238).

Besides the consolidation of recusancy the mission also had hopes for large-scale conversion. Even *en route* to England the party tried out its mettle by engaging Theodore Beza in dispute in Geneva. Both *Campion's Brag* and Persons's 'Confession of Faith' were written in a spirit of confidence that any moderately fair dispute would prove the superiority of the Catholic position beyond reasonable doubt. Campion wrote:

> I doubt not but you her Highness' Council being of such wisdom and discreet in cases most important, when you shall have heard these questions of religion opened faithfully, which many times by our adversaries are huddled up and confounded, will see upon what substantial grounds our Catholic Faith is builded, how feeble that side is which by sway of the time prevaileth against us.[12]

It was only to be expected that there would be a mounting influx of converts.[13]

It is best to think of the English mission neither as a purely apolitical spiritual endeavour nor as a front for papal or Spanish aggrandizement, but as a strategic intervention to strengthen the English Catholic community on all fronts. Persons's actions and writings during this period are all of a piece. He presided over the conference at St Mary Ovary (the so-called 'Southwark Synod') to discuss the basic question of recusancy. He organized the missionary tours: Persons to Gloucestershire, Herefordshire, Worcestershire and Derbyshire; Campion to Berkshire, Oxfordshire and Northamptonshire. Above all, he set great store by written propaganda. After the Southwark synod, he toured the west midlands and returned to London for the Michaelmas law term in September 1580. With the support of a printer, Stephen Brinkley, he set up a printing press in London – which migrated to various venues in the city – and settled down, chiefly at Uxenden Manor near Harrow, to write.[14]

* * *

The three kinds of books Persons wrote in 1580–82 reflect the priorities of the mission. His first book vigorously explained the insistence on recusancy: entitled *A Brief Discours contayning certayne reasons why Catholiques refuse to goe to Church*, but better known as *Reasons of Refusal*, it was printed at the Greenstreet house of Robert Brookesby in 1580 under the pseudonym John Howlet.[15] His next task was the championship of Catholic theology and

---

[12] Article viii, reprinted in Reynolds, p. 80.

[13] Thomas M. McCoog, SJ, ' "Playing the Champion": The Role of Disputation in the Jesuit Mission', in McCoog (ed.), *The Reckoned Expense: Edmund Campion and the Early English Jesuits* (Woodbridge, Suffolk, 1996), pp. 119–39.

[14] William Weston, SJ, *The Autobiography of an Elizabethan*, trans. Philip Caraman, SJ (London, 1955), p. 3 and n. 10. See also More, *The Elizabethan Jesuits*, p. 241. Details of the printing presses are given in A.F. Allison and D.M. Rogers, *The Contemporary Printed Literature of the English Counter-Reformation between 1558 and1640* (2 vols; Aldershot, 1989–94).

[15] Robert Persons [John Howlett (pseud.)], *A Brief Discours contayning certayne reasons why Catholiques refuse to goe to Church* (London, 1580), 'dedicated by I.H. [John Howlet] to the

ecclesiastical polity. *Campion's Brag* had elicited two replies, by William Charke and Meredith Hanmer, to which Persons responded in *A Brief Censure*.[16] The press had now moved to the house of Francis Browne, and in March 1581 was transferred to Stonor Park, near Henley. There Persons printed *A Discoverie of I. Nicols Minister, misreported a Jesuite, lately recanted in the Tower of London*.[17] This, as the title indicates, was a counter to a Protestant propaganda coup involving a renegade Catholic priest. The disputational dimension of the enterprise reached a climax in June 1581 with the daring printing and distribution of Campion's *Rationes decem*.[18] From Stonor Park the books were shipped up the Thames and insinuated into the university church in time for the 'Act' when degree candidates were to defend their theses:

> Great was the consternation of the university when the copies were found. There was at first a most unusual silence, and so furtively intent were many in perusing the book that never perhaps was discourse listened to with greater apathy than on this occasion. The professors and fellows, who knew not as yet what had occurred, wondered at the unusual silence. When the meeting came to a close and the whole affair was noised abroad, men's minds were swayed according as devotion or hatred moved them.[19]

Campion was arrested not long afterwards, and Persons had to wait until he had set up another press in Rouen to print his final contribution to this debate, *A Defence of the Censure*.[20] His first consideration on arrival in France, though, was the question of persecution and martyrdom, with Campion's impending fate foremost in his mind. He responded to the news of the execution of the priest Everard Hanse, on 31 July, by writing a sensational account of the antics of a Protestant, Richard Atkins, who was burned for heresy in Rome on 2 August. This book, entitled *The Copie of a Double Letter … containing the true aduises of the cause, and maner of death, of one Richard Atkins* was printed in Rheims,[21] but Persons himself printed his next work on the subject,

Queenes most excellent Maiestie'; henceforth referred to as *Reasons of Refusal*.

[16]   Robert Persons, *A Brief Censure uppon two bookes written in answere to M. Edmonde Campions offer of disputation* (London, 1581).

[17]   Robert Persons, *A Discoverie of I. Nicols Minister, misreported a Jesuite, lately recanted in the Tower of London. Wherein besides the declaration of the man, is contayned a ful answere to his recantation, with a confutation of his slaunders, and proofe of the contraries, in the Pope, Cardinals, Clergie, Studentes, and private men of Rome. There is also added a reproofe of an oration and sermon, falsely pretended by the sayd Nicols to be made in Rome, and presented to the Pope in his Consistorye. Wherto is added a late information from Rome touching the autentical copie of Nicols recantation* (Stonor Park, 1581).

[18]   Edmund Campion, SJ, *Rationes decem: quibus fretus, certamen aduersariis obtulit in causa fidei* (Stonor Park, 1581).

[19]   Quoted in Reynolds, pp. 102–103.

[20]   Robert Persons, *A Defence of the Censure, gyven upon two bookes of William Charke and Meredith Hanmer mynysters, whiche they wrote against M. Edmond Campian preest, of the Societie of Jesus, and against his offer of disputation. Taken in hand since the death of the sayd M. Campian, and broken of agayne before it could be ended, upon the causes sett downe in an epistle to N. Charke in the begyninge* (Rouen, 1582).

[21]   Robert Persons, *The copie of a double letter sent by an Englishe Gentilman from beyond the seas, to his frende in London, containing the true aduises of the cause, and maner of death, of*

De persecutione Anglicana, epistola at Rouen, with the assistance of George Flinton.[22] The two works complemented each other: one giving the English reader a continental perspective, the other giving readers in Europe a window on events in England. Throughout this period, he was also busy composing *The Christian Directory* (popularly known as *The Book of Resolution*), his persuasion to a godly life, formally entitled *The First Booke of the Christian Exercise, appertayning to Resolution.*[23]

The particular configuration of these books set a pattern for Persons's writing career: a combination of the occasional – even the opportunistic – with the deliberate promotion of Ignatian spirituality and Tridentine renewal. The question of recusancy was urgent and strategic, but not unanticipated. It was the first, important step towards Catholic restoration. Persons's book on the subject, accordingly, is measured and sequacious: it is a logically structured defence of a principle, based on nine carefully articulated 'reasons'. Alexandra Walsham has shown that refusal to be a recusant did not necessarily imply the weakness and cowardly compromise that Persons – and many others after him – assumed,[24] but his argument in *Reasons of Refusal* is impressive and convincing. The urgency of this little book (it runs to 142 octavo pages in large black letter) lies in its being a call to awake from sleep, that 'manye of oure bad Catholiques in Ingland, may see in some parte, the miserable daungerous case wherein they stande, by sleeping soe careles as they doe, in this sinne'.[25] Most Catholics were uneasy about attending Protestant worship, but they had the excuse of compulsion, and the English services were not so very different from Roman practice that they felt obliged to be scrupulous. To this Persons had two basic answers: consorting with heretics put one in extreme peril not only of damnation but of the utmost rigour of God's wrath, and the time was critical to stand up and be counted. Each Catholic's individual salvation was at stake, as well as the Catholic cause in England.

Church papism (as it is often called), the practice of going to church while remaining true in one's heart to the Catholic faith, laid one open not only to possible 'infection', or corruption, but to the deadly sins of causing scandal and abetting schism – in Persons's judgment, the two worst offences against Christ:

---

one Richard Atkins, executed by Fire, in Rome, the second of August 1581 (Rheims, 1581).

[22] Robert Persons, *De persecutione Anglicana, epistola. Qua explicantur afflictiones, aerumna, & calamitates grauissimae, cruciatus etiam & tormenta, & acerbissima martyria, quae Catholici nunc Angli, ob fidem patiuntur* (Rouen, 1581).

[23] Robert Persons, *The First Booke of the Christian Exercise, appertayning to Resolution. Wherein are layed downe the causes and reasons that should move a man to resolve hym selfe to the service of God: And all the impedimentes removed, which may lett the same* (Rouen, 1582). I use *The Christian Directory* as a generic title for the work, which exists in three main forms: *The First Booke of the Christian Exercise, appertayning to Resolution* (1582); *A Christian Directorie Guiding Men to their Salvation* (Rouen, 1585); and *The Christian Directory Guiding men to eternall salvation* (St Omer, 1607).

[24] Alexandra Walsham, *Church Papists: Catholicism, Conformity and Confessional Polemic in Early Modern England* (Woodbridge, Suffolk, 1993).

[25] *Reasons of Refusal*, fol. 20r.

> Scandale ... is a sinn more mentioned, more forwarned, more forbidden, more detested, more thretned in the Scripture, then any sinn ... except it be Idolatrie.[26]

> There is nothinge doeth soe prouocke God as the diuision of the Churche. And albeit we should doe innumerable good deedes, yet not-withstandinge we shall be punished as greuouslye as they which did rende Christe his owne fleshe and bodye, if wee disseuer in peeces the full integrytie and vnytie of the Churche.[27]

Such a solemn warning was in effect a calling to account, and anticipated the stringent morality of *The Christian Directory*, with its view of sin:

> [Of] the intollerable injurie donne unto God, in everie mortall sinne committed: whiche in deede is suche an opprobrious injurie and so dishonorable, as no meane potentate could beare the same at his subjectes handes: and much lesse God hym selfe.[28]

An array of patristic authorities, as well as Aristotelian logic, is brought to bear on the nature of conformity. From the very beginning of the mission, then, Persons was calling Catholics to a more bracing morality, from intellectual and moral laziness.

In presenting the case for recusancy, Persons made increasing use of the kind of logical pressure that would become characteristic of *The Christian Directory*. This is conspicuous in his treatment of the loss of Catholic benefits.[29] Here he gives the sacraments such value that any suffering would be worthwhile to avoid deprivation. Tellingly, the greatest care is lavished on the custom of hearing mass, rather than communicating: an emphasis reflected in the progress of the mission itself, when Catholics would flock to witness, or rather uphold in prayer, each Jesuit saying his mass:[30]

> The which action of offering of this sacred Hoste (the Sonne of God to his Father,) is of such dignitye, excellencie, and merit, not only to the Priest, but also to the standers by assisting him: as all the other good woorkes which a man can doe in his lyfe, are not to be compared with it, seeing that the verye Angels of heauen doe come downe at that tyme, to adore (after the consecration) that sacred Bodye, and to offer the same up with us, to God the father for the whole world ... If this be soe, then the hearinge of Masse, is not onelye worth the venturynge of an hundred Marckes, or sixe

---

[26] Ibid., fol. 9r.

[27] Ibid., fols 19v–20r.

[28] *The First Booke of the Christian Exercise*, part I, ch. 6, p. 52. All quotations from the 1582 version are taken from *The Christian Directory (1582): The First Booke of the Christian Exercise, appertayning to Resolution*, ed. Victor Houliston (Leiden, 1998).

[29] The eighth reason, 'Loosing the benefit of Catholique religion', *Reasons of Refusal*, fol. 44v.

[30] Robert Persons, Letter to A. Agazzari, August 1581, in *Letters and Memorials of Father Robert Persons*, pp. 78, 86. For an imaginative reconstruction, see Evelyn Waugh, *Two Lives: Edmund Campion – Ronald Knox* (London, 2001; *Edmund Campion* first published 1935), pp. 78–9.

monethes imprisonment, but also of an hundrede thousande lyues, if a
man could loose euerye one for that cause sixe tymes.[31]

Given the premises, no Catholic reader could have any excuse but to face
persecution for practising his faith. When he came to write *The Christian
Directory*, Persons had so developed this technique that he was able to corner
his readers systematically and compel them from one irresistible conclusion to
the next. In a sense, *Reasons for Refusal* not only anticipated *The Christian
Directory* but created the need for it, lest any readers escape.

Persons was concerned to put to shame those who kept making excuses for
attending church. At the end of the work, the nine 'reasons' are supplemented
with four 'conclusions' that skilfully incorporate and marshal the arguments
already used. The most striking case is the third conclusion, an exuberant
catalogue of all that is involved in going to church, raising the stakes with
each added consideration, until anyone who persisted in church papism after
reading it must feel that he had indeed put himself in the position of Pontius
Pilate, well-meaning but weak, who, as Persons laconically put it 'by this time
[i.e. having spent so much time in hell] ... hath felt, that he was deceaued'.[32]

Less conspicuous than these moral considerations, but no less urgent, was
the assault on complacency about the political effect of conformity. From
Persons's perspective it was critical that the Catholic community be seen as one
body and heard as one voice. Concealment – or, as he called it, 'dissimulation'
– put the church into hiding; going to church was a sign of the triumph of
heresy. And for some to conform while others recused themselves was to
rend the body of Christ asunder. This was of course just what the authorities
wanted: the recusancy laws were intended to be divisive. But whereas a true
Machiavellian (an identity ritually foisted on Persons) might have calculated
that it was better to maintain a hidden unity, refusing to allow the laws to
have their desired effect and leaving the resources of the Catholic community
intact, for Persons the church was not the church unless it was visible, and
visibly one. Unity consisted not only in purity of doctrine and intention but in
manifest allegiance to Rome, the sacraments and liturgy of the Roman Church.
It was not possible to separate the outward and visible signs from the inward
and spiritual grace.

Once the Queen realized that enforcing church attendance was futile, she
might see that it was also unjust. Persons's final, ninth reason is designed to
induce that recognition. He gives the example of heretics and infidels who
would not attend the Catholic Church, and then develops a series of analogies
of rulers or noblemen who would not suffer themselves to be dishonoured by
their friends or subjects giving countenance to mockery. In trying to persuade
the Queen to have the imagination to see the recusants differently, Persons
also repudiated all imputations that Rome supported the subject's right of
rebellion.[33] Recusancy was not a stalking horse for sedition. Such protestations

---

[31]   *Reasons of Refusal*, fols 45v, 47r.
[32]   Ibid., fol. 60r.
[33]   Ibid., fol. 69r.

might be regarded as disingenuous, given Persons's own political activism, but in practice he treated the question of the overthrow of the Protestant regime as a matter for other sovereign princes, not for Catholic subjects, to initiate. In *Reasons of Refusal* he explicitly denies that obedience is merely a matter of expediency, thus anticipating the charge that papal permission for Catholics to obey the Queen, despite her excommunication – *rebus sic stantibus* – was temporary: the notion that 'if the subiecte were of abilitye to resist his Prince, he might without sinne doe the same' is condemned as 'erroneous and seditious'.[34] Recusants would disobey, but they would not rebel: they would submit to the penalty for their actions.

At the very end of the book Persons explains why he has not been able to write the second and third parts, on strategies for appealing to the Queen for toleration of recusancy and for dealing with the distress if she refused. He was forced, he wrote, by illness and sudden business to leave the place where he was writing, and could not complete it before the messenger 'hast[ed] away into Englande'.[35] Persons was of course actually in England himself, and the book was printed under his direction in London, although it bears the imprint 'Doway'. This was the first of many stratagems of 'disinformation' about the production of Persons's books. These need to be treated as rhetorical devices. One should never take as literal biographical evidence anything that Persons says in his printed works about the circumstances of composition. The second and third parts were not really necessary, but it was useful to hint at their argument, sketching briefly the alternate scenarios depending on Elizabeth's response to the 'reasons of refusal': this subtly increased the pressure for relaxation of the recusancy laws. The image of the author falling ill in the midst of many cares also contributed to the *ethos* created by the conventional ending of the first part: the pious commendation of the book to God and the gentle reader.

* * *

If *Reasons of Refusal* thus claimed the moral high ground on a matter of permanent principle, *A Brief Censure uppon two bookes* (of Hanmer and Charke), *A Defence of the Censure* and *A Discoverie of I. Nicols* were more strictly occasional. They were prompted by the newly stimulated climate of disputation. *Campion's Brag*, which was meant to be kept sealed until needed, was prematurely and perhaps deliberately 'leaked' by Thomas Pounde: copies reached the Queen's Privy Council within days. Hanmer and Charke evidently felt it would do their careers no harm to be first in the lists against the Catholic champion.[36] John Nichols was a former student of the English College, Rome,

---

34   Ibid., fol. 69r.

35   Ibid., fol. 68r.

36   William Charke, *An answere to a seditious pamphlet lately cast abroade by a Jesuite, with a discoverie of that blasphemous sect* (London, 1580; rpt. 1581); Meredith Hanmer, *The great bragge and challenge of M. Champion a Jesuite, commonlye called Edmunde Campion, latelye arrived in Englande, contayninge nyne articles here severallye laide downe, directed by him to the*

who changed his mind and did the state some service by making his public recantation in the Tower. These books enter into a debate that was most dramatically mounted first by the infiltration of Campion's *Rationes decem* into St Mary the Virgin, Oxford, and then by the disputes in the Tower after Campion's arrest, in which William Charke once again debated against Campion.[37] No one would ever concede defeat in this kind of head-to-head, but Persons played his part at this time in ensuring that Catholicism remained the thinking person's option. *The Christian Directory*, on the other hand, became the book he was to continue writing, on and off, directly or indirectly, for the rest of his life.[38]

It began very modestly. In his contact with Catholic lay people Persons soon recognized a need for spiritual reading matter. Books of controversy were one thing; books that nurtured the spiritual disciplines of prayer, devotion, fasting, alms-giving and so on, were another, especially in view of the shortage of priests. Stephen Brinkley may have prompted Persons to intervene personally, for he had himself translated a work by Gaspar de Loarte with the English title *The Exercise of a Christian Life*.[39] This work provided practical guidelines for lay people, but not the motivation. Persons's *Christian Directory* was originally conceived as a prelude to Loarte, urging his readers to a fundamental inner shift of gravity, on the basis of which to institute a life of Christian exercise. Hence the title, *The First Booke of the Christian Exercise*.

It is unclear how much Persons had written before he left England in August 1581 in the aftermath of Campion's arrest. He continued with the writing in Rouen, where he took refuge with Monsignor de Monsi, a close connection of the Guise family. At some point he must have realized that to treat of 'resolution', the prerequisite or foundation of Christian exercise, involved more than enjoining the reader to 'enter into earnest consideration and meditation of our estate' (the title of part I, chapter 2). He would have to guide him or her through the whole of the first week of the Spiritual Exercises. Accordingly, he wrote powerfully about the purpose of life, accountability to God, the Day of Judgment, heaven and hell. Effectively, this entailed adapting to an Ignatian scheme a great deal of material from the popular writings of a contemporary Spanish Dominican, Luis de Granada.[40] The chapters became

---

Lordes of the Counsail, confuted & aunswered by Meredith Hanmer, M. of Art, and Student in Divinitie (London, 1581).

[37] Edmund Campion, SJ, *A Jesuit Challenge: Edmund Campion's Debates at the Tower of London in 1581*, ed. James V. Holleran (New York, 1999), pp. 72–3.

[38] For earlier studies of *The Christian Directory*, see Edwin B. Broderick, 'Robert Persons *The Christian Directory*: Prolegomena to an Edition' (diss., Fordham University, 1951); and Robert McNulty, 'Robert Parsons's *The First Booke of the Christian Exercise* (1582): An Edition and a Study' (diss., Columbia University, 1955); see also David A. Solomon, 'Examinations of Conscience: Robert Parsons' *Christian Directory* and Catholic Spirituality in Post-Reformation England' (diss., University of Connecticut, 1999).

[39] Gaspar de Loarte, *Essercitio della vita christiana* (Venice, 1561), trans. Stephen Brinkley as *The Exercise of a Christian Life* (London, 1579; rpt. Rouen, 1584).

[40] Luis de Granada, *Guia de Pecadores* (Salamanca, 1556–57; rev. edn 1567), trans. Francis Meres as *The Sinners Guide: A Worke Contayning the whole regiment of a Christian*

progressively longer as he moved on from motives to make a resolution (part I) and discussed the impediments that hinder us (part II).

The idea of merely perfecting and editing Loarte was being overtaken by a much larger design, hinging on the concept of resolution. The 'first book', as it appeared in 1582, dealt with the motives for resolution; but there was more to come. In 'The Summarie of the Christian Exercise, as it is intended', Persons projected a second book on the establishment of resolution in practice, and a third on bringing the resolved life to perfection. In the light of this reconception of the book he felt it necessary to add a preliminary explanation 'To the Christian reader towchinge two editions of this booke': the 'Christian Exercise' now existed both as a book by Loarte (translated by Brinkley) and an entirely new work by Persons.

Brinkley had been arrested in a raid on Stonor Park, so when Persons reached Rouen he had to find a new printing assistant, George Flinton. Together they produced his *De persecutione Anglicana* and *A Defence of the Censure*. These books were rapidly distributed in England through a network organized by a lay brother, Ralph Emerson.[41] On 11 April 1582 Persons wrote to Mercurian's successor as Father General, Claudio Acquaviva, to report that he had completed 'a book ... in English on resolution suited to our [present] needs'.[42] This was book I only, and one must ask why this should be particularly relevant to the situation in 1582. The answer that most readily presents itself is that resolution was just what was needed for those wavering between recusancy and church papism. Persons's correspondence over the next few years contains frequent reference to the 'resolution' shown by Catholics in the face of persecution.[43] The alignment of the deeper work of Catholic commitment with the practical decision Catholic lay people had to make about outward conformity to the state religion is significant because over the next two years Persons was heavily involved in plans for a military coup in England, even as he continued to work on *The First Booke of the Christian Exercise*, which was republished, in greatly expanded form, as *A Christian Directorie*, in 1585.[44] There is not a word in either version to give even the

---

life (London, 1598); *Libro de la Oración y Meditación* (Salamanca, 1554, rev. edn 1556), trans. Richard Hopkins as *Of Prayer, and Meditation* (Paris, 1582; Rouen, 1584); *Memorial de lo que debe hacer el cristiano* (Lisbon, 1561), trans. Richard Hopkins as *A Memoriall of a Christian Life* (Rouen, 1586). Persons was closely associated with the Hopkins translations. For a discussion of Persons's use of material from Luis, see the introduction to *The Christian Directory*, ed. Houliston, pp. xxxii–xxxviii and appendix III.

41   Robert Persons, Letter to A. Agazzari, August 1581, in *Letters and Memorials of Father Robert Persons*, pp. 77, 85.

42   'Liber quidam editus de resolutione anglice accommodatus temporibus nostris': Robert Persons, Letter to Acquaviva, 11 April 1582, *ARSI*, Fondo Gesuitico 651/640, in 'Robert Parsons and Claudio Acquaviva: Correspondence', ed. Thomas M. McCoog, SJ, *Archivum Historicum S.I.* 68 (1999): 79–182, p. 116. Translations are my own unless otherwise indicated.

43   *Letters and Memorials of Father Robert Persons*, pp. 172–3; 'Punti per la Missione d'Inghilterra', ed. and trans. J.H. Pollen, SJ, in *Miscellanea IV*, CRS, 4 (London, 1907) pp. 26–7.

44   Robert Persons, *A Christian Directorie Guiding men to their Salvation. Deuided into three Bookes. The first wherof apperteining to Resolution, is only conteined in this volume, devided into two partes, and set forth now againe with many corrections, and additions by th'Authour himself,*

slightest hint of rebellion, or even of likely increased persecution, but it seems to have been Persons's assumption that a restored Catholic monarchy would need reflective Catholic subjects, just as much as Catholics needed a godly state in which their faith could grow.

The capture and execution of Campion certainly shifted Persons's priorities from missionary to military strategy. But the fact that he continued writing *The Christian Directory* suggests that he regarded pastoral encouragement and political responsibility as complementary. The way Campion was treated as a traitor after his arrest surely convinced him that England was an intolerably hostile environment for priestly activity, so that an early overthrow of the regime was desirable. Whereas during the mission he had attended to political negotiation only intermittently, he now threw himself wholeheartedly into plans for an invasion, with the help of the Catholic League in France, and the Spanish monarchy. In April 1582 he attended a conference in Paris, involving Henry, Duke of Guise, William Beaton, Archbishop of Glasgow, William Cardinal Allen and de Tassis, the Spanish ambassador. With James VI of Scotland temporarily in the care of his Catholic cousin Esmé Stuart, Duke of Lennox, the time seemed propitious for a simultaneous invasion from Scotland and a landing site on the coast of England. Persons was sent to Portugal to sound out Philip II, who had recently managed to win the Portuguese crown. In the event, the military plan came to nothing, because Protestants wrested control of James back from Lennox by the raid of Ruthven on 23 August, but Persons and Philip formed a lasting alliance.[45]

During his return journey, Persons fell dangerously ill and spent much of the winter convalescing in Ornate and Bilbao. Allen was anxiously awaiting his arrival in Paris because another military plan was in train: hopes were pinned on the dazzling skill of Alessandro Farnese, Prince of Parma, who was proving such a devastating military commander in Belgium. Back in Paris in July 1583, Persons was asked to travel to Rome to obtain the support of Pope Gregory XIII. It is worth asking why Persons was chosen to go on both these diplomatic errands. A cynical interpretation would be that it kept him away from the detailed military planning – the dirty work, so to speak – and released him to present the 'enterprise of England', as it came to be called, in idealistic terms to the high-minded most Catholic king (as the Spanish monarch was ceremonially designated) and the Pope. In fact, Persons later showed quite an interest in military strategy, but in his writing, both public and private, he was consistent in subordinating the political to the spiritual, and this no doubt commended him to the politicians when they needed a diplomat.

---

with reprofe of the corrupt and falsified edition of the same booke lately published by M. Edm. Buny (Rouen, 1585).

[45]   John Bossy, 'The Heart of Robert Persons', in McCoog (ed.), *The Reckoned Expense*, pp. 141–58 (pp. 144–5).

Whatever Persons's persuasions to political action, they led to acute internal conflict, especially since Father General Acquaviva was trying, in his letters, to dampen his enthusiasm for these negotiations. In John Bossy's phrase, he evinced 'a zealous tepidity towards Persons' Spanish dealings'.[46] Even after the abortion of the second invasion plan, Persons was close to the power struggles in France and Belgium. He spent the first few months of 1584 in Tournai, ministering to English Catholics in the service of Parma, and he helped to promote the Guise faction by lending a hand with the scurrilous publication *Leicester's Commonwealth*. The heir to the French throne, the Duke of Anjou, died in June 1584, leaving France with the prospect of a Protestant successor, Henry of Navarre. Henri III, the present king, lacked all conviction, according to the Catholic League, and was altogether too favourable towards the English. In this context, some English Catholic aristocrats in exile, including the Lords Arundell and Paget, wrote a satire on the queen's favourite and had it translated into French as a propaganda ploy. In later years a rift was to develop between English Catholics who sought favour from France and those who inclined to Spain, but for the present Persons, who controlled much of the Catholic book trade, gave what assistance he could to the lobbying. This brought him into disfavour at the French royal court and he had to take cover in Rouen in November 1584.[47]

All this activity wore Persons out, both physically and emotionally. It can only be imagined what the loss of Campion – his admired charge and ally – meant to him. During June and July 1584, while staying in the professed house in Paris, he had a new companion, William Weston, who was soon to become superior of the mission in England. Weston was a noted scholar, and may have helped him with some material for revision.[48] After observing at first hand how complex and contradictory were the pressures acting upon the princes of state and church, Persons wrote to Mary Queen of Scots that 'uppon consyderation of ... the small successe our former labors had brought forth wee had resolved I say to leave cogitation of such matters and to follow only owr spiritual course wheruppon all dependeth thowgh in longer time'.[49] Perhaps he meant that the 'spiritual course' was the slow track and political action the fast track. The more likely interpretation is that the spiritual work was fundamental and non-negotiable, while politics was always contingent and supplementary. A few months later he begged:

---

[46]   Ibid., p. 148.

[47]   D.C. Peck (introd.), *Leicester's Commonwealth: 'The Copy of a Letter written by a Master of Art of Cambridge' (1584) and Related Documents* (Athens, Ohio, 1985), pp. 26–7.

[48]   Robert Persons, Letter to Acquaviva, 11 June 1584, in *Letters and Memorials of Father Robert Persons*, pp. 203, 205; 'Punti per la Missione d'Inghilterra', pp. 156–7.

[49]   Robert Persons, Letter to Mary Queen of Scots, 10 Oct 1584, in *Letters and Memorials of Father Robert Persons*, p. 246.

[I should like to be] allowed to make the third year of probation in order to recollect myself ... I feel myself very weakened as a result of these dealings with the world; and although I have had keener desires [to make a retreat], nevertheless, the importunity of affairs in no ways allows me to satisfy myself.[50]

It was in this mood that the revisions and expansions of *The Christian Directory* were made in 1584–85.

* * *

The Christian Directory formed the bedrock of Persons's thinking and experience throughout these vicissitudes. The revision of 1584–85 reflects a deepening of his conception of 'resolution'. In the 'Induction to the Three Bookes Followinge', prefaced to the 1582 *First Booke of the Christian Exercise*, he had made a distinction between the 'theorike' and the 'practike' parts of 'Christian divinitie ... that is, all the busines that man hath withe God in this lyfe'.[51] The second, he argued, was far more difficult than the first, and he insisted further that if we could only get the second right, God would guide us into truth about the first. If Catholics and Protestants could lay aside their differences and 'ioyne together in amendment of [their] lyues, and prayeng one for an other ... God (no doubt) [would] not suffer [them] to perish finallye for want of right faith'.[52] This was incidentally in conformity with the Jesuit belief that heresy, being usually the result of evil inclination, was better countered by moral instruction than theological dispute.[53] Here was a way of suspending theological controversy, chiefly for the sake of Catholics who might otherwise waste their energies on scrutinizing the doctrinal debate. At the same time it might induce serious-minded Protestants to embark on the way of holiness, in the course of which their eyes would be opened to the light of Catholic truth. But the more Persons thought about the motives and inducements to resolution, the more he realized that it depended on a mental revolution, an entirely new way of seeing the world. He was, in fact, dealing with the 'theorike' part: if not with the points of controversy between Catholic and Protestant, at least with the grounds of faith, the essential state of mind implied by Christian belief.

It was with this understanding that Persons revised *The First Booke of the Christian Exercise* so substantially and renamed it *A Christian Directorie Guiding Men to their Salvation*. He now conceived of the whole work of Christian exercise – motivating, beginning, perfecting resolution – as divided

---

50 'Liceat mihi ad me recolligendum, tertium novitatus annum ... facere ... Sentio enim me diuturnis his cum saeculo commerciis debilitatum valde, et licet nunquam acriora habuerim desideria; tamen negotiorum importunitas nullo modo mihi ipsi satsifacere me permittit': Robert Persons, Letter to Acquaviva, 12 Feb 1585, *ARSI*, Fondo Gesuitico 651/640, in 'Robert Parsons and Claudio Acquaviva: Correspondence', ed. McCoog, p. 161.

51 *The First Booke of the Christian Exercise*, p. 8.

52 Ibid., p. 7.

53 John W. O'Malley, SJ, *The First Jesuits* (Cambridge, Mass., 1993), pp. 70–71.

into two parts: the first 'speculatiue', on making one's resolution, and the second 'practiue', on implementing it. Where the original *First Booke of the Christian Exercise* took as its starting-point man's accountability to God, Persons now pushed the argument back to the questions of God's existence and the truth of the Christian religion: matters uncontroversial in the Catholic–Protestant confessional conflict but relevant to the spiritual state of Elizabethan England. It was not so much that people did not believe in God or Christianity; it was rather that this belief did not inform their minds in a way that issued in dedicated Christian lives. This is what Persons meant by 'a secret kinde of Atheisme': living to all intents and purposes as if God did not exist.[54] In writing two new chapters on these themes (of the existence of God and the supremacy of the Christian religion), which might seem excessively long and in some sense redundant in a Christian country where the debate was over the valid form of Christianity, Persons was aiming at a shift of consciousness from mere assent to the kind of belief that makes a difference – in this sense anticipating Newman's distinction between notional and real assent.[55] As he put it, the first book of *A Christian Directorie* was neither 'theorike' nor 'practiue' but 'speculative', containing 'matter of discourse, knowledge, speculation and consideration, to moue us to resolve'.[56]

Speculation or consideration, then, is the frame of mind Persons regards as crucial to the kind of spirituality on which a reformed Catholic England could be built. It is worth dwelling on this idea, as it took root in Persons's thinking, because its ramifications ultimately determined his writing career. He puts it strikingly in the 1582 version:

> We beleeve in grosse the mysteryes of our Christiane faythe, as that there is a hell, a heaven, a rewarde for vertue, a punyshement for vice, a judgement to come, an accompt to be made, and the lyke: but for that we chue them not well by depe consideration, nor doe not digest them well in our hartes, by the heate of meditation: they helpe us litle to good lyfe, no more than a preservative putt in a mans pockett can helpe his healthe.[57]

Consideration, then, is the mental exercise by which understanding is turned into a motive for action. It is the means of appropriating the truth, making it one's own. Persons wanted to raise the Catholic community from inertia to living faith, where Catholic truth would inform a godly nation. He would be satisfied with nothing less, and everything he was to write can be referred to this compulsion.

The kind of thinking represented by the term 'consideration' characterizes *The Christian Directory*. Persuasive, challenging, but thoroughly reasonable and reflective, the prose style is readable as few Elizabethan works are. There is none of the knotty, periodic syntax that puts a strain on comprehension

---

[54]   *The First Booke of the Christian Exercise*, part II, ch. 6, p. 310.
[55]   J.H. Newman, *An Essay in Aid of a Grammar of Assent* (1870), ed. Nicholas Lash (Notre Dame, 1979), ch. 4.
[56]   *A Christian Directorie*, fols 4v–5r.
[57]   *The First Booke of the Christian Exercise*, part I, ch. 2, p. 16.

at the expense of understanding. One example may suffice to illustrate Persons's characteristic manner in *The Christian Directory*, as he enforced the consequences of belief by giving received doctrine a heightened reality. After a physical description of the Last Judgment he draws out its implications for the reader. We are invited to imagine the feelings of those surprised without a defence on that day:

> Oh (deare brother) it is unpossible to expresse, what a great treasure a good conscience wilbe at this daye: it wilbe more worth then tenne thowsande worldes. For wealth will not helpe: the judge will not be corrupted with monye: no intercession of worldly frindes shall prevaile for us at that daye, no not of the Angels them selves: whose glorie shalbe then as the prophet saieth, *to binde kynges in fetters, and noble men in yron manacles, to execute upon them the judgment prescribed, and this shalbe glorie to all his sainctes.* Alas what will all those wyse people do then, that now lyve in delites, and can take no paine for their salvation? what shyft will they make in those extremities? whether will they turne them? whose helpe will they crave? they shall see all thinges crye vengeance about them, all thinges yelde cause of feare and terror: but nothinge to yelde them anye hope or comforte. Above them shalbe their judge offended with them for their wickednes: beneath them hell open, and the cruell fornace readie boilynge to receave them: on their right handes shalbe their sinnes accusinge them: on their left handes the devilles redye to execute Gods eternall sentence upon them: within them their conscience gnawinge: without them, their frendes bewaylinge: on everie side the world burninge. Good Lorde what will the wretched sinner doe, environed with all thes miseries? how will his harte sustaine thes anguishes? what waie will he take? to goe backe is impossible: to goe forwarde is intollerable: what then shall he doe, but (as Christ foretelleth) he shall drie up for verie feare: seeke death, and death shall flye from him: crye to the hilles to fall upon him, and they refusinge to doe hym so much pleasure, he shall stande there as a most desperate forlorne, and miserable caytife wretch, untill he receave that dreadfull and irrevocable sentence: *Goe you accursed into everlastinge fyre.* [58]

The passage is built on the rhetorical scheme known as *anthypophora*, that is, asking questions and answering them. In this case there is a progression through three separate groups of questions: the first is an indirect question: 'How great a treasure will a good conscience be at this day?' The second is a series of variations on: 'What will all those "wise" [i.e. foolish] people do then?' What shift will they make? Whither will they turn? Whose help will they crave? Finally, we focus on one wretched sinner: what will he do? Each group of questions is followed by a more or less parallel amplification of the answer, namely that without a good conscience there is no hope. The first question is answered negatively, that is to say, the treasure of a good conscience is expressed by the futility of other means of avoiding conviction: 'For wealth will not helpe: the judge will not be corrupted with monye: no intercession of worldly frindes shall prevaile for us at that daye'. From this annihilation of the familiar world where there is always the chance of evading justice, to the dreadful and pitiless surroundings on every side of those about

---

[58]   *The First Booke of the Christian Exercise*, part I, ch. 5, pp. 48–9.

to be damned, to the desperate impulses of a single trapped sinner, the sense of hopelessness increases markedly. The emphasis shifts from menacing perils all around to desperate impulses within:

> to go back ...
> to go forward ...
> dry up for very fear ...
> seek death ...
> cry to the hills ...
> stand there ... [and] receive

These are all verbs, as opposed to the prepositional phrases:

> above ... beneath ...
> on their right hands ... on their left hands ...
> within them ... without them ... on every side.

The technique employed in this passage involves the substitution of the reality of the world to come for the reassuring familiarity of the world as we know it.[59] But if the book is challenging, it succeeds also by an appeal to the past, a lost world but one that still stirs the reader. There is no explicit *apologia* for life before the Reformation, yet the prose often contains an undertow towards the forsaken ways. The underlying plot of the syntax may be called that of 'coming home'. Satirical passages, especially, recall the reader to a stable norm:

> Now then let our worldlinges goe and solace them selves with sinne as muche as they will: let them excuse and pleasantlye defend the same, sayinge, pryde is but a pointe of gentrye: glouttonie good fellowship, lecherye and wantonnes a trycke of yowth: and the lyke: they shall finde one daye that these excuses will not be receaved: but rather that these pleasant devises, wilbe turned into teares. They shall prove that God will not be jested with, but that he is the same God still, and will aske as severe accounte of them as he hathe done of other before, although it please not them now to keepe any accounte of their lyfe at all: but rather to turne all to disporte and pleasure, persuadinge them selves, that how soever God hath delt with other before, yet he will forgeeve all to them: but the holye scripture reasoneth after an other manner, which I would have everie wise Christian to consider.[60]

Concession and rebuff form the pattern here, and the rejoinder derives some of its force from the authority of Catholic tradition. God has always meant this, He has always acted thus: we who have remained faithful to Rome are the guardians of this unbroken heritage; we are not the ones who have twisted Scripture into new-fangled doctrines, nor will we countenance any ingenious self-flattering reinterpretations of the seven deadly sins.

---

[59]   For an analysis of Persons's treatment of 'dying well', which involves an acceptance of the greater reality of the afterlife, see John X. Evans, 'The Art of Rhetoric and the Art of Dying in Tudor Recusant Prose', *Recusant History* 10 (1970): 247–72, esp. pp. 256–60.

[60]   *The First Booke of the Christian Exercise*, part I, ch. 6, p. 61.

***

The mental state induced by the book, then, was one of intense awareness of truth in its application to life, and of steadfast assurance in the ancient tradition. The focus on and development of mental formation was probably the most important factor for Persons in expanding *The First Booke of the Christian Exercise* into *A Christian Directorie*, partly prompted by comments and criticism from his colleagues, partly from his own recognition that 'practical Christianity' presupposed a great deal more than he had at first anticipated. The other stimulus to revision, not unrelated, was the misappropriation of the 1582 version by the Protestants. It was never Persons's intention that his book should be used to produce better Protestants; indeed, his assumption was that a sincere resolution based on an uncontroversial understanding of basic Christian truth would inevitably lead the reader to embrace Catholicism. But the idea of accountability, on which so much of the argument of the book depends, proved to be more problematic. In this book as he wrote it, the living of a resolved life, accountable to God, involved the building up of merit, an idea which, though associated with the Catholic understanding of the perfection of repentance by charity, echoed the kind of instinctive semi-Pelagianism that most English Christians accepted unless thoroughly schooled in the Protestant doctrine of justification by faith alone.[61] From a committed Protestant point of view, therefore, the book was subversive of the entire preaching programme, even where it did not convert. It reinforced a popular, non-Protestant understanding of salvation – just what the Calvinist preachers were trying to correct – with an appeal to a more reflective or dedicated life. In some alarm, Edmund Bunny, the Calvinist chaplain to Edwin Sandys, the Archbishop of York, set out to emend the underlying theology of grace.[62] By eliminating all the corruption in the text – references to merit, feast days, Catholic devotions and practices, and the operation of fortune or chance in human affairs – he could make the book support the Protestant programme and win the man in the pew from lukewarm conformity to a hotter gospel.[63]

Bunny's change of the title, from *The First Booke of the Christian Exercise* to *A Booke of Christian exercise*, is telling. It indicates that for him 'Christian exercise' was a single process, consisting in making the resolution itself; there was

---

[61] Alan Sinfield, *Literature in Protestant England, 1560–1660* (London, 1983), pp. 151–2.

[62] *A Booke of Christian exercise, appertaining to Resolution, that is shewing how that we should resolv our selvs to becom Christians indeed: by R.P. Perused, and accompanied now with a Treatise tending to Pacification: by Edmund Bunny* (London, 1584).

[63] For Bunny's editorial interventions, see Robert McNulty, 'The Protestant Version of Robert Parsons' *The First Booke of the Christian Exercise*', *Huntington Library Quarterly* 22 (1959): 271–300; Elizabeth K. Hudson, 'The Catholic Challenge to Puritan Piety, 1580–1620', *Catholic Historical Review* 77 (1991): 1–20; Brad S. Gregory, 'The "True and Zealouse Seruice of God": Robert Parsons, Edmund Bunny, and *The First Book of the Christian Exercise*', *Journal of Ecclesiastical History* 45 (1994): 238–68; Ceri Sullivan, 'Cannibalizing Persons's *Christian Directorie, 1582*', *Notes and Queries* 239 (1994): 445–6; Victor Houliston, 'Why Robert Persons would not be Pacified: Edmund Bunny's Theft of *The Book of Resolution*', in McCoog (ed.), *The Reckoned Expense*, pp. 159–78; and *The Christian Directory*, ed. Houliston, pp. xxiii–xxvi.

no hint of second and third books about adopting the disciplines and practices thought necessary for Catholic devotion. Presumably the Protestant readers, having come to resolution, would turn to the Scriptures to help them work out their salvation, go to more sermons, take more heed and come to understand justification by faith and all it entailed. To apply the term 'exercise' to the lifelong practice of Christian religion was fundamentally alien to Protestants: it spoke too much of mechanical observations and regular obligations. In English, the word could mean the practical application of a particular virtue, 'the exercise of charity', for example, and later came to mean the performance of religious ceremonies, but it did not embrace the idea of the orderly, directed growth in and development of one's entire religious disposition.[64] It was to stress the larger conception of 'exercise' and 'resolution' that Persons renamed the work *A Christian Directorie*.

According to the evidence in *A Christian Directorie*, Persons responded to Bunny in two ways. Receiving reports of what had happened to his book, he decided to give it a more decidedly Catholic flavour without disturbing the fundamental character of the work as non-polemical. He added a chapter on 'despaire of Godes mercie' as a possible impediment to resolution. He claimed that this was in response to his readers' comments that the book failed to balance mercy and judgment, but the new material also helped to distance the work from the Puritan mentality. He also inserted a chapter of 'examples of true resolution' that linked it with recusant adversity. Finally, he added a reading scheme apportioning chapters to a two-week schedule, another feature that reinforced the Catholic sense of 'exercise' as devotional discipline. In all, *A Christian Directorie* was much less open to misappropriation.

When an actual printed copy of Bunny's *Booke of Christian exercise* came to hand, *A Christian Directorie* was already in press. Persons now turned himself into a doughty pastor warding off the wolf. The printing had reached the end of chapter 5; from that point on, Bunny's alterations were denounced in the margins. Wherever Bunny had dared to cast aspersions on the scholarship or biblical exegesis of *The First Booke of the Christian Exercise*, Persons refuted his sidenotes with a mixture of scornful satire and magisterial pity. Ironically, these responses to Bunny, which appear in sidenotes and preliminaries, spoilt the effect of *A Christian Directorie*. Typographically, the work is more impressive and complete than the 1582 version, partly because of the re-employment of Stephen Brinkley, released from the Tower in 1584, but the sidenote arguments detract from the timeless, universal, neutral quality for which Persons was striving. They link it with contemporary hostilities and give an impression of unfinished business. Persons was in a hurry to leave for Rome with Allen and embark on his tertianship, the thirty-day retreat Jesuits undertake before making their final vows.[65] It was to be another seven years before he appeared in print again.

---

[64]   See *OED*, *sub* 'exercise', especially senses 3 and 4, and the relevant citations.

[65]   See above, p. 37, n. 50.

A *Christian Directorie*, as published in 1585, was reprinted in 1598, and Persons revised it again for publication in 1607 as *The Christian Directory Guiding men to eternall salvation*, the final edition to appear in his lifetime.[66] The 1607 version retains the expansions and revisions of 1585, but drops the two long chapters on the existence of God and the truth of Christianity. The reason for this is hard to gauge. Persons had hoped that *The Christian Directory* would fulfil the need for 'some one sufficient direction for matters of life and spirit',[67] and in 1585 he presumably felt he had completed what was necessary for the first, speculative part of the work. One might have expected him to apply himself to the 'practive' part, books II and III, but although he often complained that he was being kept from this project, there is no evidence of his ever actually embarking on or making progress with the second part. In the years intervening between 1585 and 1607, his interest as a controversialist was continually being brought back to the issues that precede resolution, especially the centrality of the Catholic Church, its history, integrity and holiness. The 1622, posthumous edition of *The Christian Directory* contains further revisions to the first part.[68] Whether or not these revisions are by Persons, the fact remains that his focus was, throughout his career, on persuading men and women to make their resolution. His readers considered God's service and resolved upon it; he left their further spiritual direction to others.

The underlying reason why Persons never seemed to be satisfied with the first part of *The Christian Directory* may be that it was not really possible to limit the 'one sufficient direction' to the non-controversial. The problems of atheism and non-Christian religion were perhaps, in the end, less pressing than the practical and ecclesiastical restrictions on leading a resolved life. Dealing with these external 'impediments', to use the term from the second part of the first book, was the story of his further writing career.

***

The Christian Directory had a phenomenal impact. John Gerard, that most adventurous of the Elizabethan Jesuits, described it as 'a most useful and wonderful book which I believe has converted more souls to God than it contains pages'.[69] Bunny's version can lay claim to be the most popular work of devotion in English of its day, outstripping William Perkins's *Foundation*

---

[66] Robert Persons, *A Christian Directorie, Guiding Men to their Salvation* (Louvain, 1598); and *The Christian Directory Guiding men to eternall salvation ... consisting of two Partes, wherof the former layeth downe the motives to Resolution: and the other removeth the impediments: both of them having byn lately reviewed, corrected, and not a little altered by the Author himselfe* (St Omer, 1607).

[67] *The First Booke of the Christian Exercise*, 'To the Christian Reader', p. 5.

[68] *A Christian Directory, Guiding men to Eternall Salvation: commonly called the Resolution. The first wherof, teacheth how to make a good Resolution. The second, how to begin well. The third, how to perservere, and end happily. Written By the R. Father Robert Persons, Priest of the Society of Jesus. The Sixt. and last Edition* (St Omer, 1622).

[69] John Gerard, SJ, *The Autobiography of an Elizabethan*, trans. Philip Caraman, SJ (London, 1951), p. 2.

of Christian religion (19 editions, 1590–1638) and Arthur Dent's *Plaine man's path-way to heaven* (25 editions, 1601–1640).[70] In 1585 alone it went through 15 impressions: 32 altogether by 1640. Persons need not have worried so much about Bunny's editing, because the Protestant version was instrumental in the conversion of Benet of Canfield, the celebrated Capuchin preacher and spiritual writer who, when imprisoned at Wisbech Castle, gained a reputation as a fearsome anti-Protestant disputant.[71] However, the place of *Parsons' Resolution* (as the Bunny version was often called) in late Elizabethan culture was that of a call to repentance from a libertine or worldly life. Literary allusions tend to bear the traces of the conflict between the Puritans and the poets. Robert Greene's famous sickbed conversion from wastrel playwright was attributed to *The Christian Directory*. He wrote extravagantly of its effect on him in *The Repentance of Robert Greene*:

> Sodainly taking the booke of Resolution in my hand, I light vpon a chapter therein, which discouered vnto mee the miserable state of the reprobate, what Hell was.... After that I had with deepe consideration pondered vpon these points, such a terrour stroke into my conscience, that for very anguish of minde my teeth did beate in my head, my lookes waxed pale and wan, and fetching a great sigh, I cried vnto God, and said: If all this be true, oh what shall become of me?[72]

Not surprisingly, Gabriel Harvey, the noted Puritan man of letters, commended it.[73] Thomas Middleton treated it as a byword for a book to cure a courtesan.[74] Richard Baxter, the great seventeenth-century Puritan hymn-writer and preacher, found his vocation by reading Persons.[75] Sir John Harington responded to *A Christian Directorie* (the 1585 version) as a fearful warning against licentious authors.[76]

This was not exactly what Persons had in mind. More to his liking, many young men were called to the Catholic priesthood by reading *The Christian Directory*, according to the 'Book of Responses' at the English College Rome, the record of interviews with scholars entering the college. Thomas Poulton, who was ordained in 1613, testified:

---

[70]   Gregory, pp. 239–40.

[71]   Benet of Canfield, *The Miraculous Life, Conversion and Conversation of the Reverend Father Bennett of Canfield* (Douay, 1623).

[72]   Robert Greene, *The Life and Complete Works in Prose and Verse of Robert Greene*, ed. A.B. Grosart (15 vols; London, 1881–86), vol. 12, pp. 164–70. Many references to *The Christian Directory* are given in Robert McNulty, 'Robert Parsons's *The First Booke of the Christian Exercise* (1582)'.

[73]   Gabriel Harvey, *Pierces Supererogation* (1593), extracted in *Elizabethan Critical Essays*, ed. G. Gregory Smith (2 vols; London, 1904), vol. 2, p. 280.

[74]   Thomas Middleton, *A Mad World, My Masters*, I, ii, 47–9, in *Selected Plays of Thomas Middleton*, ed. D.L. Frost (Cambridge, 1978), pp. 14–15.

[75]   Richard Baxter, *Reliquiae Baxterianae* (London, 1696), p. 3.

[76]   Sir John Harington, preface to *Orlando Furioso* [1591], ed. R. McNulty (London, 1972), p. 558.

Patris Personii faelecis memoriae librum inscriptum de Resolutione instrumentum conversionis meae mihi porrexit: quo lecto mirabile quoddam lumen mihi affulsit; imbres lacrimarum per multos dies de oculis decurrebant, tremendum insuper Dei iuditium semper in auribus meis insonuit, adeo ut nec cibus nec somnus nec alia solita solatia mihi cordi fuerint, sed in orationibus pernoctare, fortunas in elemosinis impendere, Bedam Stapletonum aliosque de Conversione Angliae libros lectitare mundum relinquere.

As the instrument of my conversion [the divine mercy] laid before me the book of Resolution, written by Father Persons of happy memory. When I had read it, a certain marvellous light appeared to me. Tears streamed down from my eyes for several days. The tremendous judgment of God sounded continuously in my ears, so much so that I could bear no food or sleep nor anything else that used to comfort my heart, except spending the night in prayer, pouring out my wealth in alms, reading the works of Bede and Stapleton about the conversion of England, and renouncing the world.[77]

The effusiveness of this can be put down to the recent death of the author so fulsomely praised, and to the need to create an impression of fervent piety. Superficially, Pulton recalls Greene's emotional reaction; but it is worth noting that he went on to read Bede and Stapleton, seriously probing the credentials of the Catholic religion. As late as 1655 James Gogley (alias Drury) attributed his conversion to reading Persons, who was mentioned in the same breath as Thomas à Kempis.[78] Persons's rhetoric clearly had the power to attract readers to a life of self-sacrifice and dedication.

---

[77] *The Responsa Scholarum of the English College, Rome*, ed. Anthony Kenny; CRS, 54–5 (2 vols; London, 1962–63), vol. 1, p. 234 (my translation).

[78] Ibid., vol. 2, p. 556.

CHAPTER THREE

The Spanish Connection:
Satirizing Burghley

It was not long after Persons arrived in Rome on 4 November 1585 that he became involved with plans for what the Spanish called the *impresa*. His hopes for a military acceleration of 'the enterprise of England' – her restoration to the ancient faith – depressed in 1584, rose once again. He and Allen paid an unsuccessful visit to the son of Alessandro Farnese, the general of the Spanish forces in the Netherlands, but he kept up contact with Farnese himself. By June 1587, following the execution of Mary Queen of Scots, he was proposing to Philip II that a treatise, justifying the action, should be written and distributed with the invading force.[1] With Pope Sixtus V grudgingly assenting to the enterprise, Persons became more and more sanguine. He expected to be in England soon, in the wake of the Armada, and was suspected of composing the papal bulls identifying the invasion as a crusade.[2] So closely were both Allen and Persons associated with the undertaking that after its failure in August 1588 they considered withdrawing in embarrassment to Flanders.

In November 1588 Persons's link with Spain was strengthened when he was sent to Madrid to negotiate with Philip II on the position of Jesuits in Spain. Tension between the Inquisition and the Jesuits made Philip's dealings with the Society somewhat unpredictable, and the negotiations were inconclusive.[3] But Persons himself was generally able to obtain his requests from Philip. He was chiefly concerned now with the training of priests; he gained a promise of a grant for Douay on 6 February 1589, and later, in July, obtained authorization to found a seminary at Valladolid. Within the next four years he was also instrumental in founding a seminary at Seville, a hospice at San Lucar, and (at a distance) a college for boys at St Omer, Belgium.

Persons's activity in founding these seminaries is well known and well documented.[4] But we need to ask why he threw himself so energetically into this project so soon after his disappointment over the Armada. In 1592 and again in 1596 he pinned hopes on further Armadas; in 1593 he was writing *A*

[1]   Robert Persons, Memorandum, June 1587, in *Letters and Memorials of Father Robert Persons, S.J.: Vol. I (to 1988)*, ed. L. Hicks, SJ; CRS, 39 (London, 1942), pp. 303–309.

[2]   A.O. Meyer, *England and the Catholic Church under Queen Elizabeth*, trans. J.R. McKee, 2nd edn (London, 1967; New York, 1969), p. 277 and n. 2, p. 323.

[3]   Thomas M. McCoog, SJ, *The Society of Jesus in Ireland, Scotland, and England, 1541–1588: 'Our Way of Proceeding?'* (Leiden, 1996), p. 260.

[4]   L. Hicks, SJ, 'Father Persons, S.J., and the Seminaries in Spain', *The Month* 157 (1931): 193–204, 410–17, 497–506, and *The Month* 158 (1931): 26–35, 143–52, 234–44; Michael E. Williams, *St Alban's College Valladolid: Four Centuries of English Catholic Presence in Spain* (London, 1986).

Conference about the Next Succession in anticipation of the Queen's death and a possible Catholic succession.[5] He was, it is true, a nervous man of affairs, and it is tempting to see him darting from one project to another, his emotions and intentions fluctuating accordingly. Father General Acquaviva often needed to steady him. But it was not simply a matter of oscillating between the political and pastoral options. They concerned him simultaneously.

As an exile Persons evidently felt no compunction about supporting attempts by foreign princes to overthrow what he regarded as an illegitimate regime in England – illegitimate because it suppressed and persecuted the true faith. Contrary to popular belief, he did not encourage assassination attempts on the life of Queen Elizabeth, nor did he foment sedition among English Catholics abroad. But if sovereign princes were prepared to wage just war on England with a view to restoring Catholicism, he believed it was the duty of English Catholics, in the event of invasion, to support the foreign forces. He anticipated that a large proportion of the population would in fact rise up to support the invading Spaniards in 1588: a perception that entered into Spain's strategic thinking. The fact that English Catholics stood firm for the Queen during the Armada scare did something to discredit him and contributed to the divisions in English Catholicism that grew increasingly apparent in the 1590s.

During this period Allen and Persons advocated a somewhat qualified form of citizenship for English Catholics. They were to be good subjects, law-abiding and virtuous; they would refuse to go to church, but submit to the penalties attendant on civil disobedience; they would succour priests: which was against the law, but these priests would be involved purely in pastoral ministry, not in political subversion. If asked what they would do if the Pope tried to enforce Catholic religion by conquest – the notorious 'bloody question' – they were to equivocate. They would do as their conscience dictated, that is, act in the best interests of the commonwealth. They would never betray England, and an unjust regime would have to take responsibility for the actions their true patriotism would demand. Thus the doctrine of the Pope's deposing power did indeed, as the Protestant authorities contended, turn all English Catholics potentially into active opponents of the regime, 'traitors' in the monarch's eyes. Fortunately for Elizabeth, most lay people kept this article of faith as hypothetical as possible. And Persons himself assumed that priests on the mission would keep themselves completely free from military and diplomatic operations. These were strictly the business of the secular arm, which might on occasion call on the religious for assistance. Even the latter contribution became questionable as Acquaviva pressed Persons to eschew such involvement.

It is worth noting that Persons did not, during the 1580s and 1590s, publish any potentially inflammatory English accounts of persecution.[6] His

5   Robert Persons [R. Doleman (pseud.)], A *Conference about the Next Succession to the Crowne of Ingland* (Antwerp, 1594 [*vere* 1595]), henceforth referred to as A *Conference about the Next Succession.*

6   See Thomas M. McCoog, SJ, 'Construing Martyrdom in the English Catholic Community, 1582–1602', in Ethan H. Shagan (ed.), *Catholics and the 'Protestant Nation': Religious Politics*

De persecutione Anglicana epistola (1581) was followed by John Gibbons's compilation, *Concertatio Ecclesiae Catholicae in Anglia* (1583 and 1588),[7] itself incorporating a Latin version of Allen's tribute to Campion, *A Briefe Historie of the Glorious Martyrdom of xij Reverend Priests*.[8] Both Latin works were intended for a continental audience receptive to suggestions of the illegitimacy of the Elizabethan regime. Soon after his arrival in Spain, Persons also published his *Relacion de algunos martyrios* (1590),[9] which in addition to martyrological narratives included an account of the sufferings of the Bridgettine order of nuns, expelled from England in 1559. Some of the nuns returned in 1578 to live precariously in England until 1581, staying in various Catholic houses such as Lyford Grange, at the very time of Campion's arrest. Persons's support of their establishment at Rouen, and his interest in their piety, indicates the comprehensiveness of his conception of the cause in which he was engaged.[10]

* * *

Persons's chief writing objective during the period after the Armada, then, was to defend the innocence of the priestly vocation, under extremely difficult circumstances. The story of the print war of 1591–92, which climaxed in the publication of his notorious *Philopater* – entitled *Elizabethae Angliae Reginae Haeresim Caluinianum propugnantis, saeuissimum in Catholicos sui Regni edictum … Cum responsione ad singula capita … Per D. Andream Philopatrum* – bears telling again.[11] Justifiably assuming that the failure of the

---

and Identity in Early Modern England (Manchester, 2005), pp. 95–127.

[7]   Robert Persons, *De persecutione Anglicana, epistola. Qua explicantur afflictiones, aerumna, & calamitates grauissimae, cruciatus etiam & tormenta, & acerbissima martyria, quae Catholici nunc Angli, ob fidem patiuntur* (Rouen, 1581); John Gibbons, *Concertatio Ecclesiæ Catholicæ in Anglia, adversus Calvinopapistas et Puritanos, a paucis annis singulari studio quorundam hominum doctrina et sanctitate illustrium renovata* (Trier, 1583; rpt. 1588).

[8]   William Allen, *A Briefe Historie of the Glorious Martyrdom of xij Reverend Priests, executed within these twelve monethes for confession and defence of the Catholike Faith* (Rheims, 1582).

[9]   Robert Persons, *Relacion de Algunos martyrios, que de nueuo han hecho los hereges en Inglaterra, y de otras cosas tocantes a nuestra santa y Catolica religion. Traduzida de Ingles en Castellano, por el padre Roberto Personio, etc.* (Madrid, 1590).

[10]   D.M. Rogers (introd.), Diego de Yepes, *Historia Particular de la Persecucion de Inglaterra*, (London, 1971), p. viii; the *Historia* was first published in Madrid in 1599; see also 'A Preface, written by Father Robert Parsons, S.J., to the History of the Wanderings of Syon', in Dom Adam Hamilton, OSB, *The Angel of Syon: The Life and Martyrdom of Blessed Richard Reynolds, Bridgettine Monk of Syon, Martyred at Tyburn, May 4, 1535* (Edinburgh, 1905), pp. 98–113. I am grateful to Ann Hutchison for drawing my attention to this material.

[11]   Robert Persons [Andreas Philopater (pseud.)], *Elizabethae Angliae Reginae haeresim Caluinianum propugnantis, saeuissimum in Catholicos sui regni edictum, quod in alios quoque Reipub. Christianae Principes contumelias continet indignissimas:Promulgatam Londini 29. Novemb. 1591 Cum responsione ad singula capita: qua non tantum saevitia, & impietas tam iniqui edicti, sed mendacia quoque, & fraudes ac imposturae deteguntur, & confutantur. Per D. Andream Philopatrum presbyterum ac Theologum Romanum, ex Anglis olim oriundum* (Antwerp, 1592), henceforth referred to as *Philopater*. The standard accounts are by Thomas H. Clancy, SJ, *Papist*

1588 Armada did not spell the end of the Spanish threat, Lord Burghley (for Persons was surely right in assuming it was he) composed the royal proclamation 'Establishing Commissions against Seminary Priests and Jesuits',[12] in which, drawing on many arguments he had previously used in his *Execution of Justice in England*,[13] he accused the insurgent Roman Catholic clergy of acting as agents of Philip II and fomenting disloyalty to the crown. His assumptions were reinforced by disclosures made to him by a secular priest, John Cecil, recently arrived in England from Spain, where he had been working closely with Persons. John Cecil reported that he had been deputed to canvass English Catholics about support for Spain. Uncertainty about the succession to the crown also contributed to Burghley's alarmist stance; while a prohibition was in force against discussion of the succession, Catholics were actively seeking a suitable candidate. The priest Cecil claimed, for example, that he was meant to contact Ferdinand Lord Strange on behalf of Cardinal Allen.[14] The language of the proclamation was unrestrained, accusing Philip of unnaturally prolonging 'the former violence and rigor of [his] malice' into 'his declining years meetest for peace'. With the authority of the new Pope, Gregory XIV, 'hanging at his girdle',

> [he had] practiced with certain principal seditious heads, being unnatural subjects of our kingdom (but yet very base of birth), to gather together with great labors upon his charges a multitude of dissolute young men, who have, partly for lack of living, partly for crimes committed, become fugitives, rebels, and traitors, and for whom there are in Rome and Spain and other places certain receptacles made to live in and there to be instructed in school points of sedition.[15]

It would be difficult to find terms more offensive to Philip II, Gregory XIV, Persons or the seminaries at Douay, Rome and Valladolid. The King of Spain and the Pope were effectively accused of harbouring traitors, while the colleges were assumed to be propaganda factories, schooling the seminarians in abstract theories justifying deposition of monarchs, based on scholastic logic.

Pamphleteers: The Allen-Persons Party and the Political Thought of the Counter-Reformation in England, 1572–1615 (Chicago, 1964), pp. 14–43; and A.J. Loomie, SJ, 'Spain and the English Catholic Exiles, 1580–1604' (London, 1957), ch. 6. See also J.B. Code, *Queen Elizabeth and the English Catholic Historians* (Louvain, 1935), pp. 47–102; and Peter Milward, SJ, *Religious Controversies of the Elizabethan Age: A Survey of Printed Sources* (London, 1978), pp. 113–14.

[12]   *A declaration of great troubles pretended against the realme by a number of seminarie priests and Jesuits* (London, 18 Oct 1591), in *Tudor Royal Proclamations*, ed. Paul L. Hughes and James F. Larkin (3 vols; New Haven, 1964–69), vol. 3, pp. 86–95.

[13]   Sir William Cecil, *The Execution of Justice in England for maintenance of publique and Christian peace, against certeine stirrers of sedition, and adherents to the traytours and enemies of the Realme, without any persecution of them for questions of Religion, as is falsely reported and published by the fautors and fosterers of their treasons* (London, 1583).

[14]   Francis Edwards, SJ, *Robert Persons: The Biography of an Elizabethan Jesuit* (St Louis, 1995), p. 147. For details of the two letters from Persons disclosed by Cecil, see Godfrey Anstruther, *The Seminary Priests: Vol. I: Elizabethan 1558–1603* (Durham, 1968), pp. 63–8.

[15]   *Tudor Royal Proclamations*, vol. 3, pp. 87–8.

The measures to be taken to counter this threat amounted to an inquisition by which each householder was made responsible for the people under his roof.

The original text of the proclamation was dated 18 October 1591. Robert Southwell, the Jesuit missionary in hiding in England, replied almost immediately with *An Humble Supplication to her Maiestie*, the first draft dated 14 December. This work did not, however, participate publicly in the print war under discussion because it was not published until 1600, when Persons's Catholic opponents, the appellants, brought it out to contrast Southwell's moderate tone with Persons's alleged intransigence: to give it more weight they issued it under a false date, 1595, the year of Southwell's martyrdom. The work concludes with a powerful appeal for sympathy addressed directly to the Queen:

> We haue bene long enough cutt of from all Comfort, and stinted to an endles taske of sorrowes, growing in griefs as we grow in yeares, one misery ouertaking another, as if euery one were but an earnest for a harder payment. We had some small hope, that our continued patience, and quiet effusion of our bloud at your Maiesties feete, would haue kindled some sparkle of remorse towards vs: But still we see that we are not yet sunke to the depth of our misfortunes. We must yet tread the restles Maze of new aggreivances, sith we perceaue by this proclamation, that our Case is soe farr of from being pitied, that it is not so much as knowne where it can only be redressed.[16]

The first printed response came from another figure with whom Persons has often been unfavourably compared, namely Thomas Stapleton, probably the most erudite of the Elizabethan exiles. Considering that the edict was proclaimed only 15 months after Philip II secured Stapleton's appointment to the Chair of Scripture at the University of Louvain, it is hardly surprising that his contribution, dated March 1592, should be entitled *Apologia pro Rege Catholico Philippo II*.[17] Stapleton admonished Burghley to remember the fate of former evil counsellors to English princes, and to lead Elizabeth back to honourable ways that would ensure the true safety of the realm:

> Think of the Spencers, the Gavestons, the Empstons, the Dudleys and the Cromwells, who in their day enjoyed the favour of their princes no less than you in yours; and since you know that virtually no trace, no memory remains of them except in disgrace and cursing, consider what will be the case with you, who surpass them all in the impiety of your heresy, the fierceness of your cruelty, the rapacity of your avarice, the insatiability of your ambition, and the arrogance of your pride. You are not safer, or richer, or stronger than they, no more eminent in authority nor more powerful in

---

[16]   Robert Southwell, SJ, *An Humble Supplication to her Maiestie* [composed 1591, publ. 1600], ed. R.C. Bald (Cambridge, 1953), p. 45.

[17]   Marvin R. O'Connell, *Thomas Stapleton and the Counter Reformation* (New Haven, 1964), pp. 44–55. The letters patent were signed 13 July 1590. Stapleton was also indebted to Philip for the income of the deanery of Lilverenbeck in the diocese of Bois-le-duc. The date (presumably of composition) is given at the very end of the work: Thomas Stapleton [Didymus Veridicus Henfildanus (pseud.)], *Apologia pro Rege Catholico Philippo II ... Contra varias & falsas accusationes Elisabethae Angliae Reginae* (Antwerp, 1592). See ARCR I 1141.

the number of your friends, allies and clients ... But nevertheless come to your senses at last: behold the afflicted state of England, and make some concession now to the safety of your fatherland, to the peace of Christendom. Consider that you took your origin from them, that you owe everything to them, that you will entrust your posterity to them. Return to favour with my most serene king, with your own sweetest fatherland, with the noblest citizens, with the provinces you have so offended and ruined, with the Catholic Church of Christ. This is meet for your declining age, your years and your grey hairs. Then the realm of England will not regret that you were English: thus you will more truly care for yourself; thus you will best look after your posterity.[18]

'Didymus', as the work was popularly called (after the pseudonym adopted), thus made an appeal to Burghley's supposed better nature – a form of criticism disguised as friendly warning – while maintaining a fundamental diplomatic courtesy.

Unlike Southwell and Stapleton, both of whom replied directly and as it were innocently to the edict, the Jesuit Joseph Creswell initiated a pattern of artful responses. From his vantage point at the English College, Rome, he wrote a series of fictional letters, supposedly by an English traveller, about continental reactions to the edict. This compilation, in turn, he 'edited in Leipzig' as 'Ioannes Pernius' for the benefit of the Lord Treasurer as *Exemplar literarum, missarum, e Germania, ad Guilielmum Cecilium, Consilium Regium*, pointedly dated the ides of March (15 March 1592).[19] It has often been conjectured that the *Exemplar* was the result of consultation between Persons and Creswell. This is unlikely. Although Creswell was transferred to Spain later in 1592 to assist Persons in the establishment of English seminaries there, he was not made privy to the detailed contents of the major response Persons was preparing, the *Philopater*. Persons, however, planned to add substance to what Creswell had written, possibly recognizing that the *Exemplar* had been an over-hasty response.[20]

---

[18] 'Cogita Spenceros, Gauerstonos, Empstonos, Dudleos, Cromuellos, qui suis, suo tempore, Principibus non minus quam tu tuae, in deliciis fuerunt: & cum nullum fere eorum vestigium, nullam nisi cum probro & maledictione memoriam superesse intelligis, quid de te fiet considera, qui eos omnes, haeretica impietate, cruenta feritate, rapaci auaritia, insatiabili ambitione, superbo fastu longe antecedis. Non tu illis cautior, non ditior, non fortior, non authoritate eminentior, non amicorum, affinium, clientium, numero potentior ... Sed resipisce tamen aliquando; Angliae statum afflictum respice, aliquid nunc tandem patriae tuae incolumitati, aliquid Christianae reipublicae paci concedas. Quibus ortus es, quibus omnia summa debes, quibus posteros tuos crediturus es considera. Cum Serenissimo Rege meo vt voles, cum dulcissima patria tua, cum optimis ciuibus, cum tot offensis ac vastatis prouincijs, cum Ecclesia Christi Catholica, redi in gratiam. Hoc affecta aetate tua, hoc annis & canis tuis dignum est. Sic te Anglum fuisse, Regnum Anglicanum non poenitebit: sic tibi rectius consules; sic posteritati tuae optime prospicies' (*Apologia pro Rege Catholico Philippo II*, pp. 272–3). All translations are my own unless otherwise indicated.

[19] Joseph Creswell, SJ [Ioannes Pernius (pseud.)], *Exemplar literarum, missarum, e Germania, ad Guilielmum Cecilium, Consilium Regium* (Rome, 1592).

[20] A.J. Loomie, SJ, 'The Authorship of *An Advertisement written to a Secretarie of M.L. Treasurer of England* ...', *Renaissance News* 15 (1962): 201–207, citing a letter from Persons to Acquaviva, 12 August 1592 (pp. 204–205). On Creswell, see Thomas M. McCoog, SJ, *English and Welsh Jesuits, 1555–1650*, CRS, 74–5 (2 vols; London, 1994–95), *sub* Creswell. It was assumed

Meanwhile there was produced in Antwerp the first pamphlet of what appears to have been a concerted propaganda campaign. *A Declaration of the True Causes of the great troubles, presupposed to be intended against the realm of England*, dated 26 March, blamed Burghley and his fellow privy councillors for England's instability, because of their innovation in religion and destruction of the ancient nobility of the realm.[21] This sally proved a strategic success of unforeseen magnitude. Burghley instructed his agent in Antwerp, Michael Moody, to probe the authorship, and in the same letter gave an extended defence of his noble ancestry. Embarrassingly, the letter was leaked, giving his opponents a heaven-sent opportunity to lampoon his wire-drawn attempts to claim descent from the Sitsilts of Wales.[22] A more convincing *apologia* for the edict came from Francis Bacon, who undertook the defence of his patron, Burghley, by writing 'Certain Observations made upon a libel Published this Present Year, 1592'. This elegant and forcefully argued work was circulated only in manuscript, perhaps because Bacon wished to promote himself in Burghley's favour by putting his case privately to influential courtiers. Of Burghley he concluded, 'though he be not canonized for a saint in Rome, yet he is worthily celebrated as *pater patriae* in England'.[23]

* * *

There is little doubt that the author of the *Declaration* was Persons's agent in Antwerp, Richard Verstegan. Persons himself had a deep personal interest in the edict: it not only abused him by name, together with his associate William Cardinal Allen, but touched him closely in the allegations against the seminaries.[24] Against these slights on his integrity he now wrote his 'Response to the Edict' (*Responsio ad Edictum*) under the pseudonym of 'Philopater', implying that he was motivated by deep love for his country suffering under the Protestant yoke.[25] Philip II offered to subsidize the book's printing and paid

---

by many of Persons's contemporaries that Creswell had a part in the *Philopater*, e.g., Matthew Sutcliffe, *A Briefe Replie to a certaine odious and slanderous libel, lately published by a seditious Jesuite, calling himselfe N.D.* (London, 1600), pp. 201, 218.

[21] Richard Verstegan, *A Declaration of the True Causes of the great troubles, presupposed to be intended against the realm of England* (Antwerp, 1592), henceforth referred to as *Declaration*. The title purposely echoes the title of the proclamation of 18 October 1591, *A declaration of great troubles pretended against the realme by a number of seminarie priests and Jesuits*.

[22] See below, pp. 60 and 63.

[23] *The Works of Francis Bacon*, ed. James Spedding, R.L. Ellis and D.D. Heath (14 vols; London, 1857–74), vol. 8 (published as *The Letters and Life of Francis Bacon*, vol. 1), p. 201. Several MS copies survive, e.g., 'Lord Burleigh's Commonwealth' (Oxford, Corpus Christi College, MS CC 200). I am indebted to the archivist, Christina Butler, for permission to consult this MS.

[24] William Allen founded the seminary at Douay in 1568; it moved to Rheims in 1578 but came under threat during the French religious wars from the late 1580s and returned to Douay in 1594. Persons also established Jesuit houses in the Iberian peninsula, at San Lucar (1591) and Lisbon (1593).

[25] Cf. John E. Parish, *Robert Parsons and the English Counter-Reformation* (Houston, 1966), p. 42, who speculates that 'Philopater' might mean 'Pope-lover'.

for an authorized translation into English. Richard Verstegan was entrusted with both these tasks.[26]

First came the translation, transparently but nevertheless effectively disguised as a 'leak' to Burghley, by a concerned informer, of the contents of the *Philopater*. *An Advertisement written to a Secretarie of my L. Treasurers of Ingland, by an Inglishe Intelligencer as he passed through Germanie towards Italie* was ostensibly an advertisement in the Elizabethan sense of 'warning', but doubled as an advertisement, in the modern sense, of the fearful power and wit of the coming *Philopater*.[27] The preface to the *Advertisement* was dated 31 August 1592, whereas the *Philopater* was still only a quarter way through the press at the end of October.[28] Already the alarm was being sounded in England. On 8 November Mr Edward Jones sent Anthony Bacon a copy of the *Advertisement* from Hertford, calling it 'a *seditious vile book*, which he desired might be kept from any but such as were affected, and knew how to use such things'.[29] The attempt to suppress the *Advertisement* was inevitably futile: besides the printed copies that infiltrated the English market, many manuscript copies were made.[30] Furthermore, Persons was clearing the way for the *Philopater* by producing yet another short work in English, describing King Philip II's visit to the English College at Valladolid.[31] Ostensibly this was a letter, dated 20 August 1592, from a priest in the college to a refugee couple. Besides offering morale-boosting comfort to those who felt under increased pressure – such that some had had to flee from England – it was designed to show how very different were the English colleges in Spain and the Netherlands from the breeding grounds of viperous rebels as portrayed in the edict, and

---

[26] See Loomie, 'The Authorship of *An Advertisement written to a Secretarie of M.L. Treasurer of England*', and 'Philip II and the Printing of "Andreas Philopater" ', *The Library*, 5th series, 24 (1969): 143–5. A fuller translation may have been intended, according to Henry Walpole's (somewhat unreliable) 'Confession': 'it was begunne to be translated and augmented by Sr Francis Englefield who being with Fr. Parsons gave me the residue to prosecute'. See *Unpublished Documents Relating to the English Martyrs: Vol. I: 1584–1603*, ed. J.H. Pollen, SJ; CRS, 5 (London, 1908), pp. 265, 267. The various editions of the *Philopater* in 1592–93 are listed in ARCR I 885–92, including translations into French and German; the place of publication of the Prague and Cologne editions is given as 'Germany?'

[27] Richard Verstegan, *An Advertisement written to a Secretarie of my L. Treasurers of Ingland, by an Inglishe Intelligencer as he passed through Germanie towards Italie* (Antwerp, 1592), henceforth referred to as *Advertisement*.

[28] Richard Verstegan, Letter to Persons, Antwerp, 29 October 1592, in *Letters and Despatches of Richard Verstegan (c. 1550–1640)*, ed. Anthony G. Petti; CRS, 52 (London, 1959), p. 86.

[29] E. Jones, Letter to A. Bacon, 8 November 1592, London, Lambeth Palace Library, MS 648 (Bacon Papers, vol. 2) para. 172 (fol. 305), quoted in *Memoirs of the Reign of Queen Elizabeth, From the Year 1581 till her Death*, ed. Thomas Birch (2 vols; London, 1754), vol. 1, p. 90. Birch incorrectly assigns this to 1591 and identifies the book as the *Declaration*, while Spedding believes it was the *Philopater*. See *The Works of Francis Bacon*, vol. 8, p. 143. The chronology points to the *Advertisement*.

[30] E.g. London, British Library, MS Harleian 35 # 36.

[31] Robert Persons, *A Relation of the King of Spaines Receiving in Valliodolid, and in the Inglish College of the same towne, in August last past of this yere, 1592* (Antwerp, 1592).

seemed all the more persuasive in that it made only incidental mention of the controversy surrounding the edict.

The *Philopater* duly appeared at the end of 1592. It was published more or less simultaneously in Antwerp, Prague, Rome, Cologne and Lyons, according to the wishes of Philip II. Philip deliberately concealed the identity of 'Philopater' from his envoys in the cities where the work was to be published, as well as the fact that it was being printed elsewhere. This was to take the strategy of surprise to the limit, giving the impression of a spontaneous response from all over Europe. Persons reinforced it with a carefully calculated collection of Latin translations of official decrees and letters illustrating the Privy Council's determination to root out opposition, including material concerned with proceedings against the Brownists (or pseudo-Brownists) Henry Barrow and John Penry, who were hanged on 6 April 1593. The *Acta in comitiis parlamentaribus Londini* thus extended the range of the attack on Burghley by creating a fellowship in suffering with the Puritans.[32]

Another anonymous traveller's report gave further support to the *Philopater*. This was *Newes from Spayne and Holland*, ostensibly dated from Amsterdam, 1 September 1593.[33] The Spanish news complemented the earlier *Relation* from Valladolid by giving an account of the opening ceremonies of the English College at Seville, while the news from Holland described a gathering of concerned Englishmen in Amsterdam to discuss the state of affairs in England. This section rehearsed many of the arguments of Verstegan's *Declaration* in blaming Lord Burghley for England's woes, but also promised a fuller report of that part of the conference which was concerned with the claimants to the English crown on Elizabeth's decease. *Newes from Spayne and Holland* thus served as an advertisement to Persons's next project, *A Conference about the Next Succession*, marking a shift in emphasis from armed intervention to the possibility of a Catholic succession. It also offered a Catholic review of the controversy, abstracting and reiterating much of the material of Stapleton's *Apologia*, and summarizing the views of Pedro de Ribadeneira. Ribadeneira, who was writing a continuation, covering the years 1588–93, of Nicholas Sander's history of the 'English Schism', condemned the proclamation as unconstitutional, impolitic and slanderous, and gave what Persons considered to be the most objective account of the state of England.[34]

---

[32]   Robert Persons (ed.), *Acta in comitiis parlamentaribus Londini die X. Aprilis huius anni praesentis 1593. tam contra Catholicos quam Puritanos seu Caluinistas rigidos ... Collecta & in sermonem latinum traducta per Ioannem Dodritium Londini commorantem* (Antwerp, 1593).

[33]   The full title is *Newes from Spayne and Holland conteyning. An information of Inglish affayres in Spayne with a conference made theruppon in Amsterdame of Holland. Written by a gentleman trauelour borne in the low countryes, and brought up from a child in Ingland, unto a gentleman his frend and Oste in London* (Antwerp, 1593), sometimes attributed to Henry Walpole.

[34]   Nicholas Sander, *De origine ac progressu Schismatis Anglicani liber ... Editus & auctus per Edouardum Rishtonum* (Cologne: n.p., 1585; enlarged edn 1586); Pedro de Ribadeneira, SJ, *Historia ecclesiastica del scisma del reyno de Inglaterra*, part 2 (Emberes, 1594). Ribadeneira had been in England from 1558–59, hoping to found a Jesuit Mission: see McCoog, *The Society of Jesus in Ireland, Scotland, and England*, pp. 34–8.

Here the printed controversy appears to have ended. The former Jesuit, Christopher Perkins, now an agent of the state, tried unsuccessfully to interest Sir Robert Cecil in a disguised response when he sent him copies of Stapleton's *Apologia* and the *Philopater* in November 1593, commenting that they were 'full of school points and verbosity, very childishly fitted'. In view of their wide circulation in Europe, he recommended an antidote: publishing a fictional exchange of letters between Didymus (Stapleton's alias) and Philopater, 'each of them signifying what the one hath heard of the other's book'; if these were written 'in some grave manner, as might delight the wise', it would bring honour to her Majesty. Just what Perkins had in mind is unclear, but presumably he thought it would even the balance if the Protestants could show themselves capable of equally ingenious and artful forms of controversy. That this suggestion was never adopted illustrates the reluctance of the authorities to be seen to 'stoop' to polemical artifice.[35]

* * *

It is tempting, when reviewing the spate of treatises connected with the proclamation of 1591, to commend the spontaneity and depth of feeling of Southwell and Stapleton at the expense of the considered calculation of the Persons–Verstegan alliance. R.C. Bald observes that Southwell's 'tone is in striking contrast to that of the protests which came from beyond the seas'.[36] Indeed, it is possible that Persons deliberately chose to outdo Southwell, since a version of the first draft of the *Humble Supplication* appears to have been forwarded to him soon after its composition.[37] In 1603 a fellow-Catholic, antagonistic to Persons, wrote that his work was 'full of most bitter rayling, & arrogant exasperations'. In his opinion the 'foolish scoffings against great persons' were ill-judged 'vnlesse he had meant to whet a double edged sword to cut Catholicks throats'.[38] Similarly, Sir Thomas Cornwallis lamented, 'I am very sorry and so (I am sure) be all good Catholics of those lewd libels. It will but exasperate matters.'[39] A.J. Loomie depreciates the *Philopater* somewhat when he opines that it was not a suitable occasion for Persons's talents, remarking that 'the relentless examination proceeds for page after page, only

---

[35]   Christopher Perkins, Letter to Sir Robert Cecil, Harrow Hill, 26 November 1593, *Calendar of the Manuscripts of the Most Honourable the Marquess of Salisbury*, Historical Manuscripts Commission (24 vols; London, 1883–1976), vol. 4, p. 423. On the use of popular tracts for official propaganda, see Joseph Black, 'The Rhetoric of Reaction: The Martin Marprelate Tracts (1588–89), Anti-Martinism, and the Uses of Print in Early Modern England', *Sixteenth Century Journal* 28 (1997): 707–725.

[36]   R.C. Bald, Introduction to Southwell, *An Humble Supplication to her Maiestie*, p. xi.

[37]   *Letters and Despatches of Richard Verstegan*, pp. 1–38.

[38]   William Clarke, *A Replie unto a certaine Libell, latelie set foorth by Fa: Parsons ... intituled, A manifestation of the great folly and bad spirit, of certaine ... secular Priestes* (London, 1603), fol. 73v.

[39]   Quoted by Patrick McGrath, *Papists and Puritans Under Elizabeth I* (London, 1967), p. 268. McGrath observes, however, that the subsequent act against popish recusants (1593) was surprisingly moderate (pp. 269–71).

at times does his familiar wit flash out'.[40] It is quite true that the work answers the edict point for point, even providing a Latin text of each section in turn. But this does not necessarily mean that it lacks a governing idea, one that animates the whole.

An analysis of the rhetorical strategies of the *Philopater* should begin with the choice of pseudonym. During his lifetime, Persons's works were almost all published anonymously, often under assumed identities or teasing initials. *The Christian Directory* was commonly known as *Parsons' Resolution*, which is the title often to be found on the binding, although the only indication of authorship in the text itself is to be found at the end of the preface 'To the Christian Reader towchinge two editions of this booke' (signed 'Thy heartie welwiller and seruant in Christ. R.P.').[41] Edmund Bunny's 1584 version conveyed 'R.P.' to the title page.[42] Persons used the pseudonym 'Doleman' for *A Conference about the Next Succession* (1595), registering distress at the state of England without a settled succession. He then adopted the initials 'N.D.' in the 'Watchword' controversy with Hastings and Sutcliffe, provoking Sutcliffe to call him 'Parsons the Noddy'. In the Archpriest Controversy he wrote anonymously, although no-one could be in doubt about the authorship of his critique of the appellants. Later he became 'a Catholicke English-man' to comment on James's defence of the oath of allegiance, and 'P.R.' in his writings against Thomas Morton. Some of this pseudonymity, clearly, was mischievous and provocative: Persons had a certain relish in the cut-and-thrust of contest, and must have been amused by overheated reactions to his sallies, which simply indicated that his adversaries were unable to sustain the protocol of debate. But the assuming of a fictional identity – Doleman, Philopater, a Catholic Englishman – went further than this. It did not disguise the authorship, but it signalled the attitude the author wished to foreground. Just as Stapleton's 'Didymus' may have been intended to indicate that he had dual loyalty,[43] and was bound to defend his patron Philip, 'Doleman' was a patriot who would examine the claims of rival candidates for the succession with due sincerity and concern. The exiled Catholic Englishman could consider the Oath of Allegiance, which he would not be obliged to take, with objectivity. It is noteworthy how many of Persons's titles invoke a continental perspective: a pamphlet on the death of Richard Atkins, 'by an Englishe gentilman from beyond the seas, to his frende in London';[44] *A Relation of the King of Spaines*

---

[40]   Loomie, 'Spain and the English Catholic Exiles', p. 369. I am indebted to the late Fr Loomie for permission to quote from this work.

[41]   Robert Persons, *The First Booke of the Christian Exercise, appertayning to Resolution* (Rouen, 1582; revd 1585, 1607), henceforth referred to as *The Christian Directory*. All quotations from the 1582 version are taken from *The Christian Directory (1582): The First Booke of the Christian Exercise, appertayning to Resolution*, ed. Victor Houliston (Leiden, 1998).

[42]   Edmund Bunny (ed.), *A Booke of Christian exercise, appertaining to Resolution, that is shewing how that we should resolv our selvs to becom Christians indeed: by R.P. Perused, and accompanied now with a Treatise tending to Pacification: by Edmund Bunny* (London, 1584).

[43]   δίδυμος is Greek for 'twin' or 'twofold'.

[44]   Robert Persons, *The Copie of a Double Letter sent by an Englishe Gentilman from beyond the seas, to his frende in London, containing the true advises of the cause, and maner of death, of*

Receiving in Valliodolid, 'Wryten by an Inglish priest of the same College'; *Newes from Spayne and Holland*, 'Written by a gentleman trauelour borne in the low countreyes, and brought up from a child in Ingland, vnto a gentleman his frend and Oste in London', and so on.

With 'Philopater', the fictional identity takes us into the realm of satire. Not only does Persons want his readers to appreciate his love of his heritage – his fatherland, the holy father, the faith of his father's fathers – but he wants them to adopt the vantage point of someone looking at England from a distance, unrestrained in perceiving the follies and crimes of the ruling clique. Latin adds to this effect: it is not only used for a European audience, but so that English readers can have their view of Elizabeth's government filtered through that medium. It recalls the outraged humanist scepticism, the Lucianic irony, of More and Erasmus, and we shall see how Persons's satire creates a grotesquely humorous image of Burghley and his policies. It was not a technique, or even a tone, that he was to employ again: the rest of his polemical works are in English, and marked for the most part by a deliberate restraint. That is why his later attack on the appellants stands out for its harshness. In 1591–92 Persons was still experimenting with his polemical voice, and he was driven by indignation over the way the seminaries and the seminary priests were treated in the edict.

Persons and Verstegan, then, mounted a co-ordinated satirical campaign against the Queen's council. In this campaign, the *Declaration* and the *Advertisement* are subordinate to the *Philopater*. Each has its own purpose to fulfil, and each its individual character. The *Declaration*, as its full title – *A Declaration of the True Causes of the great troubles, presupposed to be intended against the realm of England* – implies, is designed as a grand gesture of indictment. Accordingly, Verstegan offers a sardonic, broadly humorous narrative of Burghley's campaign of self-aggrandizement, from the moment of Elizabeth's accession. At first the Lord Treasurer is not even named: he grows from the sycophantic serpent in Eden, insinuating his sinister suggestions into the mind of the innocent young Queen, to the all-controlling '*Dictator perpetuus*' at the head of a new riff-raff aristocracy, with a transformed clergy as his performing monkeys. Overcoming his monarch's disinclination for married priests, he ensures that the Church of England completes its attachment to the unholy trinity: uniting 'the flesh vnto the world, & the deuill'.[45] From insinuating first the figure, and then, gradually and surreptitiously, the name, of Cecil (which these pamphlets use consistently in preference to his title – Lord Burghley), Verstegan comes in his concluding pages to a climax of identification of the true cause of all England's troubles: 'It is he, that ...' is proclaimed at the beginning of each of eight successive paragraphs.[46]

The *Declaration* made a lively contribution to the English literary scene of the early 1590s. Its mock-heroic caricature of one who 'would rather choose

---

one Richard Atkins, executed by Fire, in Rome, the second of August 1581 (London, 1581).

[45]   *Declaration*, p. 11.

[46]   Ibid., pp. 66–7.

to be occupied in iniquitie, then to offend in slothe'[47] recalls the Marprelate and Harvey/Nashe tracts. Word-play abounds. There is, for example, the mockery of martial vainglory, in a passage about the English garrison at Newhaven. Although the English claimed that with two thousand men they could defend this French port against all the world, they actually sent twice that number. Why? 'Perhaps to remaine in provision against *Nouus orbis*, which peradventure might come against it also'.[48] In an entertaining account of Drake's piracies, Verstegan deliberately inverts his heroic status. Cecil, too, is dishonoured by association.[49] Cecil and Philip II are contrasted in a way that recalls Edmund Spenser's brilliant distinction between English Protestant 'Una'-nimity and papist doubleness (allegorized in 'Duessa') in *The Faerie Queene*, book I, published in 1590.[50] Now, two years later, Verstegan reverses the terms. Whereas Philip of Spain subordinates himself to the will of God: 'he attempteth nothing, nor wageth any warres, that are not iust, honorable, and allowed bothe by the lawes of God and man',[51] Cecil's foreign policy is characterized by two-facedness. The sea-piracies and the strategic interventions in support of the Dutch rebels are prosecuted without proper declaration of war. The exception is the Portuguese voyage (to assert Don Antonio's claim to the throne of Portugal against Philip's): unlike 'the double faced actions before rehearsed', this at least has been 'an ordinary expedition of war'.[52] Verstegan's use of the term 'ordinary' is devastating in its satirical force. To be 'ordinary' is to conform to accepted standards, even as a belligerent and even in the wrong cause, while Cecil's actions are beyond accepted limits. To be 'ordinary' is also to 'demean' oneself, in a certain sense, to submit to one's 'Christian neighbours',[53] rather than strut around in the self-appointed role of 'pacifier' accusing others of wrecking the 'repose of Christendom' whilst seeking, oneself, that 'vniuersall peace, which passeth all vnderstanding' – from which the only beneficiaries will be the Grand Turk and the ruling junta of England. The emptiness of such posturing is exposed by the ignoble alliance with the '*Bere-bruers*, and *Basketmakers* of *Holland*' and the futile one with the Huguenots who, though fellow-Protestants, 'are ... still French vnto the English'. The Scots too, offer a friendship that 'will ... prove Scotish in the end'.[54] In short, not even Cecil's cleverness can alter the face of such realities as the Frenchness of the French and the Scottishness of the Scots.

To the grotesque caricature of the *Declaration*, the *Advertisement* adds the whiff of the hostelry. Verstegan departs several times from his original in this

---

[47] Ibid., p. 14.
[48] Ibid., p. 15.
[49] Ibid., pp. 25–6.
[50] Edmund Spenser, *The Faerie Queene* (books I–III; London, 1590); Verstegan's familiarity with Spenser's works is evident from an explicit reference on p. 68 to *Prosopopoia. Or Mother Hubberds Tale* (London, 1591).
[51] *Declaration*, p. 36.
[52] Ibid., p. 30.
[53] Ibid., p. 39.
[54] Ibid., pp. 48–9.

summary to remind his English readers of Cecil's descent from an innkeeper. Of the Lord Treasurer's attempt to inflate the number of lions in his coat of arms to the six of his newly-claimed Sitsilt ancestry, he writes: 'a good fatt capon, or a rosted pigg seemeth a fitter cognisaunce for an Inneholders grandchild as this man affirmeth, seing that those things are more commonly to be found in Innes, and Osteries then are Lyons'.[55] No wonder, then, if such a 'malignant and wrangling worme'[56] should write calumnies of the seminarians. These young men are set apart. The surest way for a seminary priest to hoodwink the pursuivants is to imitate 'protestantical good felowes ... that is to wit, that he will eate, and drincke & tosse pottes with any man, that he will fight, and brawle, sweare, and stare, and folow queanes; cutt, and hacke, and take a purse when opportunitie is offered'.[57] Who would think that a popish priest, however superstitious or seditious, would descend to such behaviour? In these tavern terms Verstegan adapts the more cerebral logic of the *Philopater* to a popular audience, bringing the controversy to street level and countering any suggestion that the Catholic cause is alien or remote.

* * *

The skilfulness with which Verstegan tailors his own prose to his English audience, presenting Persons's arguments obliquely and even gingerly, lends conviction to his characterization of the style of the *Philopater*:

> I do assure you it is the moste sharpe, bitter, and odious thing that euer I thinck was written by the papistes, though the writer pretende great modestie, and doeth not in deede vse open rayling tearmes, but by a close, fluente, and cutting stile, and by discussing ... of many, and curious perticularities, and by pretending to proue all he saith, by our owne bookes, lawes, cronicles, and recordes, he filleth his reader with infinite desire to reade al through out.[58]

These remarks are designed to arouse curiosity, and so should be treated with some caution. But it is noticeable that Verstegan here alludes to the very features that modern commentators such as Loomie and Bald treat as signal weaknesses, and turns them into recommendations: the craftiness of the abuse and the methodical detail of the response. The polemical strategy has evidently been thought through.

---

[55]   *Advertisement*, p. 40.

[56]   Ibid., p. 43.

[57]   Ibid., p. 44. These passages are inserted into the equivalent material from the *Philopater*, pp. 140 and 151. Significantly, the 'good felowes' paragraph, which has no equivalent in the *Philopater*, is at least as long as Verstegan's version of Persons's extended assessment of the state of the universities of Oxford and Cambridge.

[58]   *Advertisement*, p. 7. Cf. Persons's assessment of his own rhetoric: 'this man gueth him many wayes such rough hewing and vttereth so many particulers of the present state of Ingland, and vseth so often your owne lawes stories, and cronicles to proue it, as it maketh all sortes of straungers wonderfully desirous to reade it' (*Newes from Spayne and Holland*, fol. 14v).

The *Philopater*'s satirical assault on Cecil is energized by the view that the Lord Treasurer is fighting a futile campaign, with makeshift weapons, against Providence.[59] Persons consistently contrasts Cecil's impudent and puny stratagems with the steady, unstoppable force of English Catholic resistance, the solid achievements of the most Catholic king of Spain, and the secure judgment of Catholic Europe. Cecil is an actor, a comedian, a rhetorician. Verstegan alludes to this characterization in his *Advertisement* when he writes:

> Yf a foole ... vpon a stage shoulde auouch such stuffe in a comedy, he would be hissed out, and not permitted, whereas this man telleth it both as an accuser, a witnes, and a Iudge in a most bloudy tragedy, in the sighte, and hearing of the whole worlde.[60]

These histrionics, as Verstegan implies, have both a tragic and a comic dimension, which the tone of Persons's satire has to accommodate. Since the edict in Persons's opinion is both ridiculous and destructive, it enacts a complex *hamartia*, an error of judgment that elicits derision on the one hand and pity on the other. Derision, because the edict was self-defeating: its natural effect would be to strengthen Catholic resolve. England's enemies, therefore, deride her folly:

> They can't help but rejoice publicly and even burst out laughing when they notice how the wickedest of men, by God's most just sentence, cut their throats with their own swords and cast themselves headlong down the road to manifest ruin.[61]

In this light, the writings of Persons and his allies in protest would seem redundant, if not actually impolitic; but the recusants also pity the realm and pray for God's mercy on Elizabeth. Persons himself assumes a third stance: the prophet's role, warning those who will listen, and calling down God's justice upon those who will not.

The work begins by dissociating the edict from the Queen. Persons provides satirical portraits of the five privy councillors – Bacon, Hatton, Leicester, Walsingham and Cecil – responsible for the religious policy now revealed in its sternest aspect. The characterization of Elizabeth's government concludes with the well-known description of Ralegh and his 'schoole of Atheisme'. In Persons's language 'atheism' primarily means indifference to God rather than

---

[59]   Persons's Protestant adversary Matthew Sutcliffe called it 'satyricall' in his *Briefe Replie to a certaine odious and slanderous libel*, p. 218, but was not paying a compliment to its literary style.

[60]   *Advertisement*, p. 49.

[61]   'Laetari palam & cachinnos etiam sustollere coguntur, quod iustissimo Dei iudicio, iniquissimos homines suis se gladijs iugulare, & in manifestam se perniciem praecipites agere animaduertant' (*Philopater*, p. 137, para. 199). References to the *Philopater* give the page number of the Antwerp edition, followed by the paragraph number.

philosophical disbelief,[62] but here he conflates the two: the Privy Council, with its opportunism, cynicism and blatant injustice, is atheist in the former sense, but it is associated with the blasphemies of Ralegh and his circle, who were said to teach their scholars to spell God backwards. Ernest A. Strathmann has justly cautioned against taking the Ralegh material literally, since it is an 'ironic burlesque of the Proclamation'; the point here is not what it tells us about Ralegh but how it contributes to the Cecil theme.[63] Persons uses the satirical technique of putting an extreme case, in order to destabilize his readers' view of authority. Suppose Ralegh were to become a privy councillor and proclaim, on the Queen's behalf, a ban on belief in God, who would accept it? Yet, if Burghley's policies are rightly viewed, that is effectively what they do: embody atheism. The outcome is to efface royal authority, to rob it of its divine authentication. There are several variations on this theme: Persons presents Leicester as the representative of atheistic impertinence: his scandalous matrimonial affairs and his murky death identify him as the atheistic subject *par excellence*, one who in consequence becomes impudent towards the Queen.[64] Conversely, an atheistic royal edict carries no weight because it stands contrary to the laws of all Christian princes, of all previous English monarchs, even of her own father Henry VIII.[65]

One can observe this line of thought moving in the direction of *A Conference about the Next Succession*, which asserts the people's right to remove a monarch who has failed to defend the faith.[66] For the present, however, Persons stops short of arraigning Elizabeth as a tyrant; instead, he places the smallest possible distance – but still a distance – between her and the tyrannical actions of her government. There is a shift of tone whenever he turns to address her directly, as if to warn her that ultimately she will be held responsible. These are, he cautions (with a dramatically sudden, accusatory intrusion of the possessive *'tua'*), *your* judges, *your* gallows. The logic by which the edict turns papists into traitors is uncivilized and anti-Christian: 'They are papists; *consequently*, whatever they say, they are traitors' (my emphasis: a series of parallel *ergo* constructions follows). This 'barbarous, heretical and ultra-Turkish inference made by your judges (Elizabeth), your prosecutors, magistrates, agents and executioners' is a non-sequitur worthy of the Turks and heathens but enacted by five different sets of her officers. The seminarians, who might have been ornaments to her realm, now hear God's call to return 'to your crosses, your prisons, your racks, your gibbets'.[67] In both cases the careful juxtaposing of

---

[62]   See *The First Booke of the Christian Exercise*, part II, ch. 6: 'a secret kinde of Atheisme, or denieing of God: that is, of denieing him in life and behaviour' (p. 310).

[63]   Ernest A. Strathmann, 'Ralegh and the Catholic Polemicists', *Huntington Library Quarterly* 4 (1945): 337–58, attributes the *Advertisement* to Sir Francis Englefield, Henry Walpole and Joseph Creswell (see above, n. 20). For Cecil's 'atheism' see *Philopater*, p. 135, para. 197.

[64]   *Philopater*, p. 17, para. 14.

[65]   Ibid., pp. 37–8, para. 45.

[66]   Thomas Preston, *Apologia Cardinalis Bellarmini pro iure principum* (London, 1611), pp. 98–100, denounces *Philopater* for just this doctrine.

[67]   'Papistae sunt: *ergo* quicquid dicant, proditores sunt ... haec Barbara, haeretica, & plusquam Turcica, tuorum (Elizabetha) Iudicum, Quaestorum, Procuratorum, actorum, &

the vocative 'Elizabetha' with some form of the possessive 'tua' is designed to appeal to her honour, assigning ultimate responsibility without directly attributing blame.

In dealing, next, with the edict's calumnies against Philip, Persons indicts Cecil for turning Elizabeth into a kind of monster. In a characteristic court-room manoeuvre, he counters the edict's 'story' with an opposite and alternative narrative, whose coherence and plausibility are designed to make one wonder how the other version could ever seriously have been entertained. After weighing up the international records of Elizabeth and Philip at some length and with a deliberate show of fairness, he asks:

> Since (I say) these things are most certain, and clearly evident to anyone with the eyes to see, what ultimately can be the purpose of this rhetoric of Cecil's that goes to the very limit of falsehood? Why are so many fantastic fabrications piled senselessly on top of each other? Unless, perhaps, he proposes to make himself a laughing-stock and his royal mistress a rock of offence to the whole world?[68]

His interpretation of Philip's career resonates with Stapleton's *Apologia* and with the more sober parts of Creswell's *Exemplar*, and is closer to the truth than popular historiography, with its myth of the Elizabethan golden age, would suggest.[69] But Persons is more interested in the mendacity of the teller than in the falsity of the tale. Cecil's over-heated rhetoric, he argues, arises from envy of Philip's power. Without it, he has to resort to fabricating a grotesque mimic world, filled with strange creatures of fantasy. Queen Elizabeth herself is made into Behemoth 'the purpose of whose creation was that he should fear nothing'.[70] Taken out of the ordinary course of human life, she has become freakishly fearless and shameless.

The inner core of emptiness in Cecil's case, that which makes it a 'vaine Bubles shadow' (to steal a phrase from Donne),[71] is exposed in the matter of genealogy. Trying to lend credibility to the charge of treason, Cecil has imputed low and even base birth to Allen and Persons, so that nothing honourable could be expected from them. Persons trumps this with the publication of Cecil's humiliating 'Sitsilt' correspondence. Ultimately this has no bearing on

---

carnificum consequentia:'; 'ad tuas cruces, tuos carceres, tuos eculeos, tua patibula, Elizabetha' (*Philopater*, p. 57, para. 74).

[68] 'Si haec (inquam) certissima sint, & omnium sensibus patentissima, quorsum ista Cecilij mendacissima tandem rhetorica … qua tot figmenta sine causa conglomerantur, nisi forte vt se omnibus ridendum, & Dominae suae causam vniuerso mundo detestandam proponat?' (ibid., p. 101, para. 143).

[69] McCoog, *The Society of Jesus in Ireland, Scotland, and England*, pp. 75–7 and 82–3. McCoog is himself concerned to correct the glowing martyrological style of Catholic historiography (pp. 6–9). Code, *Queen Elizabeth and the English Catholic Historians*, p. 77 n. 1, argues that Catholic historians, despite the unreliability of their sources, were more or less correct about the rights and wrongs of the war with Philip II.

[70] 'Behemoth … qui factus est vt nullum timeret' (*Philopater*, p. 104, para. 149, alluding to Job 40).

[71] 'Loves Alchymie', in *The Poems of John Donne*, ed. Herbert J.C. Grierson (2 vols; Oxford, 1912), vol. 1, p. 39.

the question of treason, as Persons admits, 'since virtue is the mother, nurse and guardian of all true nobility';[72] but that is his point: even Cecil's irrelevancies are without foundation.

The substantial 'other' that Persons puts forward in place of this bubble-world is the history of the seminaries, which he can acclaim with great authority and confidence. Not one seminarian, he notes, has ever been accused of a crime other than the traditional priestly practices that have now been turned into treasonable offences.[73] Nor, despite torture, threats and promises, has any gone over to the Lord Treasurer's opinion ('vestram sententiam') which he does not even dignify with the name of religion.[74] When they seek to convert others, there is no dressing up ('fucum') of the truth: 'We put the bare truth on display'.[75] In contrast, he then outlines the dire state of the English universities, with a show of emotion at the loss of their ancient splendour. Apart from the degeneration of morals and the profanation of religion, he points to the abandonment of scholasticism as the reason why the products of Oxford and Cambridge are no match for the exiled seminarians.[76] The superficiality of contemporary scholarship, indeed, is of a piece with Cecil's threadbare rhetoric. In casting sound principles aside the university men are like foolish boys who reject a golden urn in favour of a brightly ornamented potsherd, or obtuse fishermen who miss the pearls enclosed in the plainer shells.[77] Persons's way of dealing with Cecil's extravagant language is to seize on key terms and re-interpret them. For example, there is the proclamation's description of the origin of the seminaries: 'to *gather together* ... a multitude of dissolute young men' (my emphasis). Persons retorts that he *gathered together* the scattered flock by command of the king of heaven, 'king of kings, and shepherd of all', alluding to John 11:52, where it is recalled how it was prophesied that the Messiah would 'gather into one the children of God who are scattered abroad'.[78] In this way Persons turns Cecil's language inside out, as it were, so as to recreate the reality it has suppressed.

Up to this point the dominant satirical mode has been comical, exposing Cecil's monstrous inventions, which are superseded by, or even transformed into, the workings of Providence. But as Persons approaches the question of martyrdom and the 'bloody questions', his tone becomes more sober. Still, the theme of Cecil the rhetorician is sustained. Tyranny consists in a freedom with

---

[72] 'Cum virtus mater sit, & nutrix, & conseruatrix omnis verae nobilitatis' (*Philopater*, p. 142, para. 207).

[73] Ibid., p. 147, para. 215.

[74] Ibid., p. 149, para. 218. On patterns of conversion in this period, see Michael Questier, *Conversion, Politics and Religion in England, 1580–1625* (Cambridge, 1996).

[75] 'Veritatem nudam ostentamus' (*Philopater*, p. 150, para. 220).

[76] Ibid., p. 161, para. 236.

[77] Ibid., pp. 160–61, para. 236. On developments in Oxford after the emigration of Roman Catholic dons in the 1560s and 1570s, see Penry Williams, 'Elizabethan Oxford: State, Church and University', in T.H. Aston et al. (eds), *The History of the University of Oxford* (8 vols; Oxford, 1984–2000), vol. 3 (ed. James McConica), pp. 397–440. Leicester and Burghley were the chancellors of Oxford and Cambridge respectively.

[78] 'Regisque regum, ac pastoris vniuersalis' (*Philopater*, p. 150, para. 220).

words, when legal terms such as 'treason' are given such a liberal interpretation that innocent priests are put to death for lese-majesty. In Persons's view, this is a quibbling with words, a damnable form of nominalism, and an unmatched 'licence for injustice and instability'.[79] This argument about language gives an intriguing slant on the question whether Catholic priests were executed for treason or religion under Elizabeth. To support his assumption that Cecil's terminology is irresponsible, Persons cites Stow's independent record of Catholic martyrdoms. Here he makes good what Verstegan had warned about his method of using the Protestants' own writers as evidence.[80] A detailed account of the trial of Campion and his associates, again, emphasizes how serious are the consequences of Cecil's rhetorical 'confectio',[81] even if from another point of view it is a trifling fallacy, 'nugax fallacia'.[82]

In keeping with this indignant mood, the Queen's predicament now appears more pitiful than before. Cecil has accused Persons of being Philip's confessor, a notion dismissed as ludicrously improbable, the product of a feeble attempt to make fun of the appellation 'most Catholic king'. It is no more than an 'ignorant use of words to misappropriate things': these words are usurpers, just as others are tyrants.[83] What Cecil has meant in jest now becomes Persons's heartfelt aspiration: if only he could have been Elizabeth's confessor, he might have saved her from the spiritual peril of her approaching hour of death, when she will be 'without any of this sacrament's benefit, without any examination of conscience, without remorse or remedy' as she 'piles one sin upon another, offence upon offence'.[84] What consolation will Cecil be able to give her in that day, he asks, what fanciful mitigation of her plight ('quid leuaminis deceptae')?[85] Earlier, he has underlined the pathos of her situation by once again shifting the perspective radically. 'Put the case' that the Queen were under the kind of pressure now being applied to recusants. Suppose she were a Protestant in a Catholic kingdom, feeling obliged to hold out against invitations to conform. What a genuine relief it would be for her to return to

---

[79] 'Iniustitiae & inquietatis licentiam' (ibid., pp. 187–8, para. 275–6). The question of martyrs and pseudo-martyrs was bitterly contested; see Clancy, *Papist Pamphleteers*, pp. 131–42. The 'bloody question' was an authorized form of interrogation designed to convict recusants of treason by asking the accused which side he would support in the event of an invasion by a Catholic power authorized by the pope to restore the faith. See Philip Hughes, *Rome and the Counter-Reformation in England* (London, 1942), pp. 261–2, and Patrick McGrath, 'The Bloody Questions Reconsidered', *Recusant History* 20 (1991): 305–319.

[80] *Philopater*, pp. 184–6, para. 267. A revised edition of Stow appeared in 1592 as *The Annales of England, faithfully collected out of the most autenticall Authors, Records, and other Monuments of Antiquitie* (London, 1592).

[81] *Philopater*, p. 199, para. 292.

[82] Ibid., p. 187, para. 275.

[83] 'Ironica verborum vsurpatio' (ibid., p. 201, para. 294): 'ignorant' is the most likely sense of 'ironica'.

[84] 'Sine vllo sacramenti huius beneficio, sine vllo conscientiae scrupulo, remorsu, aut remedio, peccata peccatis, & delicta delictis accumulans' (ibid., pp. 206, para. 304).

[85] Ibid., p. 207, para. 304.

the Catholic faith of her ancestors![86] In this way the impression is given that Elizabeth is an unwilling partner in a Protestant government that is out of sympathy with the nation as a whole.

Persons is now in a position to denounce the Protestant 'religion of the word'. In a paradoxical elaboration of the theme of hypocrisy, he suggests that Catholic devotional practices are a more reliable vesture of piety than the verbal protestations of the reformed religion. While the edict frequently invokes God's name in a 'praetensa deuotio' (affectation of piety), Elizabeth and her court eschew the outward signs of devotion, treating that 'garment of ours' as 'a kind of false semblance of holiness':[87] not for Elizabeth the genuflexion, the beating of the breast or the moving of the lips in prayer.[88] In this, Persons asserts, the Protestant regime of England goes one further than the Arian persecutors of the early church, who at least veiled themselves in Catholic devotion. Unlike the emperor Constantius (a wolf in sheep's clothing), Elizabeth sheds her wool and pursues her 'lupina opera' (wolfish deeds) quite unashamedly.[89]

The *Philopater* concludes with stirring words of encouragement to the recusants. The theme of Providence persists: the Protestant regime will not prevail against them, because its structure is so shaky:

> For [our] struggle (to say nothing of anything else) is not against bronze or marble enemies, but some or other servile and imbecilic opponent, decrepit and moth-eaten; although his hatred and envy may be immense, his strength nevertheless is limited, his life short, and his end doubtful.[90]

With Providence goes the practice of sound words. Persons's reassurance, 'non … contra hostes aeneos', alludes to a familiar literary motif, derived from Horace's 'I have built a monument more enduring than bronze' and most memorably developed in English by Shakespeare's 'Not marble, nor the guilded monument / Of Princes shall out-liue this powrefull rime'.[91] Where the poets contrast the durability of their verse with the transience of marble and bronze, Persons dismisses Cecil's words and rhetoric as well as his more material

---

[86]   Ibid., pp. 196–7, para. 288. Here Persons may be responding to the ostentatiously even-handed arguments made by Edmund Bunny, in his *Treatise tending to Pacification* (1584), appended to his adaptation, *A Booke of Christian exercise, appertaining to Resolution*, to show that Catholics have more to gain than lose in converting to the state religion.

[87]   'Vestimentum nostrum … falsa quadam sanctitatis specie'.

[88]   *Philopater*, pp. 215–16, para. 311. But when it suits his argument, Persons makes much of Cecil's show of devotion in the time of Queen Mary (ibid., p. 25, para. 28).

[89]   'Nec vlla ouis indumenta … prae se ferat: nor does she display any of the sheep's clothing' (ibid., p. 220, para. 319).

[90]   Non enim (vt caetera omnia taceam) contra hostes aeneos aut marmoreos certamen illis est, sed contra vnum vel alterum vetulum & imbecillum, decrepitum, & exesum; quorum odium & inuidia licet immensa sit, vires tamen limitatae, vita breuis, & exitus incertus' (ibid., p. 249, para. 361).

[91]   'Exegi monumentum aere perennius', Horace, *Odes* III, xxx; William Shakespeare, *Shakespeares sonnets Never before imprinted* (London, 1609), Sonnet 55. Although the *Sonnets* were probably composed after 1592, they testify to the currency of the idea. *Aeneus* (bronze, brazen) is derived from *aes*.

efforts as Lord Treasurer. To those intimidated by the edict's measures, or perhaps lured away from the faith by the prospect of riches and other vanities, he cites the oration of Nazianzus against Julian the Apostate: they will see 'how unstable, hoary and contemptible all those things are, that commonly appear great and formidable to the carnal eye'.[92] Once the comedy is over, the actors' masks are put aside.

* * *

It will be apparent from my reading of the *Philopater* that the work was animated by Persons's experience with the English seminaries in Spain, not only because they were misrepresented in the proclamation but because they were a foil to Cecil as Persons saw him. His other writings about the seminaries bear this out. *A Relation of the King of Spaines Receiving at Valliodolid* charges the edict with defiance against Providence. The introductory section is built on a skilful contrast between the edict as the work of a man (Cecil) and the seminary at Valladolid as the work of God. Persons claims that the edict was itself a response to news of the erection of the seminary and detects a consummate irony in the circumstances following. So far from deterring prospective students, the proclamation had publicized the seminary, 'so as that which my Lord Treasorer's wilynes in Ingland did inuent, to terrifie and diuerte men from coming hither, that doth Gods goodnes, & powerfull hand in heauen (far ouerreaching my Lords simple pollicies) turne to an incitation for men to repaire this waie'.[93]

So concerned was Persons to show that the college was not part of a master-strategy of Spanish intrigue, but a work of Providence, that he downplayed his own hand in its foundation. According to the edict, Philip II had 'practiced with certain principal seditious heads [Persons and Allen] to gather together with great labors upon his charges a multitude of dissolute young men ... to be instructed in school points of sedition'. In the *Relation* Persons noted how several chance events coincided to bring the college into being. Various groups of English priests and students, some from the struggling college at Rheims and some from England, met 'by chaunce' in Valladolid in late 1588 and early 1589; 'by good chance, or rather by Gods particular prouidence', Persons was in the Spanish court when they made their appeal to the King. At that moment, and not before, he realized that God wanted him to found a seminary. He strongly denied that anyone 'began this Seminarie vppon any precedent deliberation, nor thought of any such matter at the beginning thereof, but onelie God himself, in such speciall and particular manner began the same', reinforcing the point at the very end of the work:

---

[92]   'Quam incerta, cana & contemptibilia sunt haec omnia, quae magna ac tremenda carnis oculi videri solent' (*Philopater*, p. 252, para. 361).

[93]   *A Relation of the King of Spaines Receiving in Valliodolid*, pp. 6, 13. Further references to Cecil and the proclamation are on pp. 23, 59, 60.

oftentymes I haie [sic] heard F. Persons saie that, in all the cogitations, speeches or conferences betwene the Cardinall and him ... for the beginning helping or furthering of this cause, it neuer came in talke or deliberation or in any mans mynde to begin Seminarie or college in Spaine.[94]

This emphasis made for a compelling story. But by the time (almost 30 years later) when John Blackfan was writing the annals of the college, the narrative had taken on a different shape. He credited Persons with a rapid and decisive response to the post-Armada difficulties at Rheims: 'But in the midst of this fear and trepidation Father Persons wrote to them from Rome suggesting that they send some students abroad, especially to Spain. Plucked out of this fear of destruction they would be able to see how happily they could establish a settled dwelling-place and fixed abode in that region.'[95] Blackfan went on to assert that it was as a result of this advice that the first students set off from Rheims. Michael Williams argues in favour of Persons's contemporary version, and Edwin Henson, Blackfan's editor, points out – against Blackfan's later version – that this author was concerned to give the Society of Jesus, and Persons in particular, all the credit for the foundation.[96] Indeed, in 1620 it was no longer necessary to avoid any hint of a grand design. Nevertheless, there is sufficient plausibility in Blackfan's account to suggest that in 1592–93 Persons was so preoccupied with his theme of Providence that he found the details of his story shifting naturally into that pattern.

Persons's following report on the seminaries, *Newes from Spayne and Holland*, develops a further antithesis between the seminaries in Spain and England's religious policy. Here he plays with the notion of 'consequentia': each ill-judged act of persecution leads to a new foundation in a divinely ordered series, until the influx of priests into England reaches alarming proportions: 'and in the mean space her Maiestie waxeth old, the realme groweth to more dissention and confusion in religion, the Puritans become very hoat and heady, the people wearyed and amazed'. 'Whith thes manner of procedings', Cecil is asked, 'what then shalbe the end at lenght of this course think you?'[97] In addition to that 'consequentia', there is the dangerous slide 'from papists to Lutherans, from Lutherans to Swinglians, from Swinglians to Caluinists, from Caluinists to puritans, and now last of al from puritans agayne of a mylder

---

[94] Ibid., pp. 6–7, 9–11, 59–60. The latter declaration ('oftentymes ...') was inserted into the first (before 'but onelie God himself') in a Spanish version printed in 1592, *Relacion de un Sacerdote Ingles ... de la venida de su Magestad ... al colegio de los Yngleses* (Madrid, 1592). See Edwin Henson (introd.), *Registers of the English College at Valladolid, 1589–1862*, CRS, 30 (London, 1930), p. x.

[95] 'In hoc autem timore et trepidatione scripsit eis Roma Pr Personius ut emitterent aliquos in exteras nationes et maxime in Hispaniam qui erepti huic quam timebant vastationi despicerent qua fœliciter in ora possent sedem et domicilium collocare' (John Blackfan, 'The Revised Annals of the English College, Valladolid', in *Registers of the English College at Valladolid*, appendix III, p. 263).

[96] Williams, *St Alban's College Valladolid*, pp. 4–8; Henson (introd.), *Registers of the English College at Valladolid*, p. viii. For Persons's diplomatic mission to Spain, see Edwards, *Robert Persons*, pp. 129–34, and Hicks, 'Father Persons, S.J., and the Seminaries in Spain'.

[97] *Newes from Spayne and Holland* (fols 28v–30r [vere 29r]).

sort, vnto heddy Brownists'.[98] If we collate these with the 'consequently' (*ergo*) passage in *Philopater*,[99] Persons appears to be suggesting that poetic justice is in operation: tyrannical imputation of guilt by non-sequitur leads inexorably to ruin.

* * *

Persons offers, in the *Philopater* and its supporting pamphlets, a consistent interpretation of Burghley's practices both in the edict itself and in his religious policy generally. In contrast with the English Catholics whose dependence on Providence is evident in their solid learning, their loyalty to the faith of their ancestors and the church Fathers, and the sobriety and self-sacrifice of their lives, Burghley appears as the great dissimulator, a political opportunist driven by passionate personal ambition. He is the '[filius] huius Saeculi', the child of this generation who seems wiser than the sons of light.[100] The Lord Treasurer's rhetoric consists entirely of makeshift stratagems, futile in trying to cheat the operation of Providence. For Persons, English policy is like a stage-play, Marlovian in its theme of the over-reacher over-reached.

The *Philopater* was one of the most trenchant attacks on the religious policy of William Cecil. In the heated post-Armada atmosphere, the pseudonym Andreas Philopater rapidly became a by-word for seditious papist propaganda. Despite its contemporary reputation, and despite growing recognition of Persons's political and literary impact, the work remains obscure today, to the extent that Carrafiello, in his 'political biography' of Persons, is able to dismiss it at second hand in a single sentence.[101] Ironically, the Latin employed by Persons to appeal to all of Europe has helped to relegate it to the footnotes. A case in point is Curtis Breight's monograph on the politics of Marlowe's plays. His thesis is that the career of Piers Gaveston in Marlowe's *Edward II* (published 1594) was a coded version of, or at least an allusion to, the contemporary Roman Catholic discourse in which Gaveston's name is occasionally invoked in categorizing Cecil (Lord Burghley) as an 'evil counsellor'. This is a plausible if speculative attempt to gauge the impact of religious controversy on contemporary drama. Tellingly, however, Breight's examples from the Catholic pamphlets are restricted to Verstegan's two short English pieces, the *Declaration* and the *Advertisement*, to the neglect of the weightier *Philopater*.[102] The omission would be defensible, on the grounds that Marlowe's audience would be more likely to be familiar with the English pamphlets, were it not that it blurs the differences, both in style and content,

---

[98] Ibid., fol. 32r.

[99] See above, p. 62.

[100] *Newes from Spayne and Holland*, fol. 34r, alluding to Luke 16:8.

[101] Michael L. Carrafiello, *Robert Parsons and English Catholicism, 1580–1610* (Selinsgrove, 1998), p. 75.

[102] Curtis C. Breight, *Surveillance, Militarism and Drama in the Elizabethan Era* (London, 1996), pp. 111–26. Breight overlooks the fact that the Gaveston/Cecil identification is not a hallmark of the *Philopater*, but appears more frequently in French political controversy at this time.

between what we might call the cheeky English galleys and the fully rigged Latin man-of-war. Still, Breight alerts us to the fact that the lively exchanges connected with the Armada and its aftermath were at the forefront of Londoners' minds. Religious controversy had street appeal.

In some respects the *Philopater* was an attempt at damage-control after the failure of the Spanish Armada. Satire is intrinsically unfair, and the assault on the Elizabethan regime was one way of securing a propaganda advantage that might ease the pressure on recusants and clergy by weakening the government's resolve. But it was also the first of a series of political writings that developed an ideal of the English Catholic state. It was not a coincidence that *Newes from Spayne and Holland* gave notice both of the growth of the seminaries and the possibility of a Catholic succession. As Catholic piety and learning increased, so the inadequacy of the current political establishment became more manifest. In the *Philopater* Persons insisted on the emptiness of English religious forms, the dangerous attachment to a merely external structure of social cohesion, a world where people were kept in order by keeping them from the truth. In his *saeva indignatio* against Cecil's government he was beginning to sense that something more serious was happening to England than the temporary ascendancy of heresy. Now, as he recognized the urgency of the need for the institution of a Catholic prince – whether by invasion or by succession – he was also having to think more carefully about the role of the Catholic laity.

The *Philopater* argues specifically that the recusants and their clergy were occupied in spiritual formation and virtuous living; they were not responsible for political action. But the larger political critique creates an alarming awareness how corruption was affecting the nation, such that it was going to take more than local prayer and foreign pikestaffs to put it right. As Persons started to think about the succession, he saw the Catholic community as potential political participants, fully understanding the relationship between royal power and Catholic faith as the informing and renewing force in the body politic. In the development of this conception of resistance politics, the *Philopater* was thus a significant first step.

CHAPTER FOUR

The Myth of England's Catholic Destiny: Persons's Political Vision

It was not only the failure of the Spanish Armada that led Persons to turn his attention to the succession as the source of hope for Catholic restoration. It had a great deal to do with his ambivalence towards James VI of Scotland, heir to Mary Queen of Scots and always the front-runner to succeed Elizabeth. He was later to claim that he had been firmly committed to James's interest, either indirectly through his mother or, after her death, in his own person, until 1592–3.[1] This is hard to reconcile with the way Persons and Allen dealt with Philip II's claim at the time of the Armada in 1588. At that time they recommended that Philip remain silent about his own prospects of acceding to the throne of England until after the successful completion of the invasion.[2] This looks like a scheme of concealment to maximize internal support for the invasion, although Persons may in fact have been prevaricating with Philip, whose motivation for the Armada needed constant spurring. Persons and Allen may well have been pinning their hopes on a post-Armada scenario where the English Catholic Church would be able to play off Philip and James in order to direct the reconstruction of the nation as a Catholic state.

Whatever Persons had in mind at the time of the Armada, the fact is that by 1593 James was not a candidate he could whole-heartedly endorse. Even William Crichton, the Scottish Jesuit with powerful connections among the Catholic Scottish earls and great expectations of being able to influence the king, had virtually given up hope of James's conversion and was backing the earls against him.[3] In this light, Persons's decision to get involved in a project to set out, as objectively as possible, the strengths of the claims of the various candidates, for the information of the English public, was to some extent determined by the need to exert pressure on James to consider how important the Catholic 'vote' was going to be in tipping the balance in his favour.

---

[1]   Robert Persons, Letters to James I, Rome, 18 August 1602, *ABSI*, Anglia III, 20, and 18 October 1603, *ABSI*, Anglia III, 36, transcribed in Thomas M. McCoog, SJ, 'Harmony Disrupted: Robert Parsons, S.J., William Crichton, S.J. and the Question of Queen Elizabeth's Successor, 1581–1603', *Archivum Historicum S.I.* 73 (2004): 149–220 (pp. 208–215), see esp. p. 211.

[2]   'Memorandum drawn up by Dr William Allen and F. Robert Persons concerning the succession to the English crown and the expedition against England', Rome, after 24 March 1587, *Letters and Memorials of Father Robert Persons, S.J.: Vol. I (to 1988)*, ed. L. Hicks, SJ; CRS, 39 (London, 1942), pp. 295–303.

[3]   Francisco de Borja Medina, SJ, 'Intrigues of a Scottish Jesuit at the Spanish Court: Unpublished Letters of William Crichton to Claudio Acquaviva, 1590–1592', in Thomas M. McCoog, SJ (ed.), *The Reckoned Expense: Edmund Campion and the Early English Jesuits* (Woodbridge, Suffolk, 1996), pp. 215–45; McCoog, 'Harmony Disrupted', pp. 156–8.

Persons's authorship of the notorious outcome of this project, *A Conference about the Next Succession to the Crowne of Ingland*, which was published in 1595 under the name of R. Doleman,[4] has been the source of contention from the very start.[5] He was himself very cagey about the extent of his role, claiming that it was chiefly the work of Allen and Sir Francis Englefield and that the pseudonym used, Doleman ('*vir dolorum*'), indicated that the work was a generic expression of Catholic disappointment with James. But these disclaimers were written under circumstances where it was crucial for Persons to counteract attempts to isolate him from the main body of English Catholics, both in England and abroad. In diplomacy with James, he needed to make it clear that he was an important representative of Catholic opinion, and in negotiations with Acquaviva and the papacy he was the target of a succession of pressure groups trying to challenge his leadership in English Catholic affairs. It was thus in his interest that *A Conference about the Next Succession* be seen as a cooperative venture, a working document produced by a group of Catholic scholars and churchmen concerned about the succession and governed by no particular party feeling.[6] The ascertainable facts appear to be these: in the short pamphlet entitled *Newes from Spayne and Holland*, published in 1593, Persons advertised a forthcoming, fuller record of a supposed debate on the succession.[7] Sir Francis Englefield, an adviser to the Spanish court on English Catholic affairs, had been occupying himself for some years in detailed genealogical researches connected with the succession, and had set out a book on the pretenders to the crown and 'who are likely to prevail', according

---

[4]   Robert Persons [R. Doleman (pseud.)], *A Conference about the Next Succession to the Crowne of Ingland, divided into two partes. Whereof the first conteyneth the discourse of a civill Lawyer, how and in what manner propinquity of blood is to be preferred. And the second the speech of a Temporall Lawyer, about the particuler titles of all such as do or may pretende within Ingland or without, to the next succession. Where unto is also added a new and perfect arbor or genealogie of the discents of all the kinges and princes of Ingland, from the conquest unto this day, whereby each mans pretence is made more plaine. Directed to the right honorable the earle of Essex of her Maiesties privy councell, & of the noble order of the Garter* (Antwerp, 1594 [*vere* 1595]), henceforth referred to as *A Conference about the Next Succession*. Doleman was, unluckily, also the name of a seminary priest, Alban Dolman, whom Persons was accused of defaming; see Ann M. Hutchison, 'The Life and Good End of Sister Marie', *Bridgettiana* 13 (2002): 33–89, p. 79, n. 114. This was a mere coincidence; the name was intended to signal the doleful prospect of England without an heir, especially with the disappointment over James.

[5]   Much of the documentary evidence discussed here is set out by L. Hicks, SJ, in 'Father Robert Persons S.J. and *The Book of the Succession*', *Recusant History* 4 (1957): 104–137.

[6]   Robert Persons, Letter to Acquaviva, Madrid, 4 and 16 June 1594, *ABSI*, Persons Letters, 46/12/3, fols 265–68 (Spanish), 271–74 (English translation). See also Persons, *A Briefe Apologie, or Defence of the Catholike Ecclesiastical Hierarchie* (Antwerp, 1601), fol. 187v, henceforth referred to as *A Defence of the Catholike Ecclesiastical Hierarchie*; and *A Manifestation of the Great Folly and bad spirit of certayne in England calling themselves secular priestes* (Antwerp, 1602), fol. 63r, henceforth referred to as *A Manifestation of the Great Folly*.

[7]   See above, Chapter 3, p. 55. The full title is *Newes from Spayne and Holland conteyning. An information of Inglish affayres in Spayne with a conference made theruppon in Amsterdame of Holland* (Antwerp, 1593), sometimes attributed to Henry Walpole. The news from Spain concerned the founding of the seminary at Seville; from Holland, the succession debate supposedly held in Amsterdam.

to a confession deposed by Thomas Wright in 1595.[8] It seems that William Allen, too, had intended to write a book on the succession but instead sent his papers to Persons.[9] One of Persons's most vociferous enemies, William Gifford, somewhat confusingly asserted both that the book was composed by Persons and that the original English manuscript was in the hand of Richard Verstegan, supplemented by material in Persons's hand.[10]

This evidence led Leo Hicks to the conclusion that Persons was 'not the sole author, but ... he had some part in the production of the work'.[11] Indeed, Hicks's view was that Persons's was not even the major part. I would argue, on the contrary, that although Allen and Englefield, and possibly others, provided material for the book, Persons compiled and wrote the final version. To begin with Gifford's account of the manuscript (which he obtained briefly in Antwerp by bribing the printers): one must regard it as no more trustworthy than his biased summary of the contents (as represented to the authorities in Rome). Verstegan was Persons's agent in Antwerp, and took responsibility for the printing of his works, so that it is quite possible that there was a fair copy in his hand. But since his name is not mentioned in any of the other correspondence about the authorship, we can be fairly safe in discounting his part in it. Englefield's researches were presumably incorporated into *A Conference about the Next Succession*, but nothing extant of his writing suggests that he was capable of developing the kind of overarching argument that makes the book what it is. On balance, we can be fairly confident that Persons was responsible both for the rhetorical disposition and the theoretical underpinning of the book. It is most likely that he assembled the material and wrote the treatise during the latter part of 1593, following the publication of *Newes from Spayne and Holland*. By March of the next year he reported that a Latin translation was already in progress.[12]

During the period of composition the Fifth General Congregation of the Society of Jesus took place in Rome, while Persons remained in Madrid to monitor the situation at court during the absence of the most prominent Spanish Jesuits.[13] There followed a considerable delay before the book was

---

[8] See A.J. Loomie, SJ, *The Spanish Elizabethans* (New York, 1962), pp. 14–51, esp. pp. 43–7. For the Wright confession, see *CSP Domestic 1595–97*, p. 156.

[9] 'The opinion and judgement of C.A. [Cardinal Allen] before his death, concerning the late printed Booke of Succession of England and certayne poyntes therunto apperteyning', signed B.S. (probably Roger Baines, Allen's secretary), cited by Hicks in 'Father Robert Persons S.J. and *The Book of the Succession*', p. 128.

[10] W. Gifford, Letter to T. Throgmorton, 5/15 June 1595, *CSP Domestic 1595–97*, p. 55; and *Calendar of the Manuscripts of the Most Honourable the Marquess of Salisbury*, Historical Manuscripts Commission (24 vols; London, 1883–1976), vol. 6, p. 512; Hicks, 'Father Robert Persons S.J. and *The Book of the Succession*', pp. 107, 126–7.

[11] Hicks, 'Father Robert Persons S.J. and *The Book of the Succession*', p. 126.

[12] Robert Persons, Letter to Acquaviva, Madrid, 10 March 1594, *ABSI*, Persons Letters 46/12/3, fol. 226.

[13] Francis Edwards, SJ, *Robert Persons: The Biography of an Elizabethan Jesuit, 1546–1610* (St Louis, 1995), pp. 158–9; Robert Persons, Letter to Acquaviva, Valladolid, 2 Nov 1593, *ABSI*, Persons Letters 46/12/3, fol. 202.

actually published in Antwerp in mid-1595, chiefly because of confusion in Rome over its contents and purpose. Father General Acquaviva, prompted by Crichton, was very uncertain about the wisdom of publishing the work, and expressed disquiet over Jesuit involvement. Discussion of the succession was strictly banned in England, and any benefits of airing the question from abroad had to be weighed against political and diplomatic repercussions.[14] There was an anxious exchange of letters between him and Persons in March 1594; the presses were stopped in Antwerp, and Persons sought both Allen and Acquaviva's approval of the manuscript.[15] Eventually Acquaviva was persuaded, but only after discreet circulation of the Latin and Spanish versions. The situation was indeed very delicate.

* * *

Bearing in mind Persons's perspective on the political situation in the mid-1590s, we can detect some immediate political strategies and also a more comprehensive intellectual design in *A Conference about the Next Succession*. Baldly summarized, the treatise argues, in part I, that 'proximity of blood' is not the only, nor even necessarily the most important, consideration in settling the succession. Part II sets out the genealogical evidence and concludes that no candidate has a clear-cut advantage. The claim of James VI of Scotland is admitted to be the most compelling on first sight, but strong counter-arguments are advanced which reduce him to the same level as other candidates. Much of the argument hinges on the Lancaster–York dispute, with the author favouring Lancaster and, tellingly, discounting the claim of Henry VII and his descendants (including, of course, the king of Scots) to belong to that house.

The whole argument of Persons's arbitration among the pretenders rests on the vindication of Henry Bolingbroke's rebellion against Richard II. To begin with, John of Gaunt, as the eldest surviving son, should have succeeded Edward III, rather than his nephew Richard. Moreover, his duchess Blanch, as heiress to the duchy of Lancaster, passed on to her son, Henry Bolingbroke, the royal lineage she inherited from Edward I's younger brother Edmund Crookback. Bolingbroke also had the right to depose Richard by reason of the latter's evil government and the general choice of the people. Wearing the crown both by hereditary right and reason of state, he combined the principles

[14]   The statutes forbidding discussion are 13 Eliz. c. 1 (1571) and 23 Eliz. c. 2 (1581), in *Select Statutes and Other Constitutional Documents Illustrative of the Reigns of Elizabeth and James I*, ed. G.W. Prothero; 4th edn (Oxford, 1946), pp. 59–60, 78–9. On the prosecution of Peter Wentworth, for raising the question in Parliament, see *Proceedings in the Parliaments of Elizabeth I*, ed. T.E. Hartley (3 vols; Leicester, 1981–95), vol. 3, pp. 42, 44, 68–9. On Acquaviva, see Hicks, 'Father Robert Persons S.J. and *The Book of the Succession*', p. 126, and Edwards, *Robert Persons*, pp. 171–3.

[15]   Robert Persons, Letter to Acquaviva, Madrid, 10 March 1594, *ARSI*, Hisp. 136, fols 245r–246v; Claudio Acquaviva, Letter to Persons, Rome, 30 March 1594, *ARSI*, Tolet. 5/II, fol. 333v; Persons, Letter to Acquaviva, Madrid, 4 and 16 June 1594, *ARSI*, Hisp. 136, fols 362r–363v; Acquaviva, Letter to Persons, Rome, 1 August 1594, *ARSI*, Cast. 6, fol. 183r; Acquaviva, Letter to Crichton, Rome, 2 March 1596, *ARSI*, Fl. Belg. 1/II, fol. 595.

of kingship that are carefully spelt out in the first part of *A Conference about the Next Succession*. But since Henry IV's line died out with Henry VI and his son Edward Prince of Wales, it was difficult to determine his true heir. Ultimately there were only two candidates: James VI of Scotland, and Isabel Clara Eugenia, the Infanta of Spain. James was descended from Henry VII and his wife Elizabeth and thus could claim, like the Tudors, to combine the white and red rose: Elizabeth being the daughter of the Yorkist King Edward IV, and Henry Tudor being descended from John of Gaunt's third wife Catherine Swynford. But since neither John of Gaunt nor Catherine Swynford was of the house of Lancaster by blood, the true Lancastrian line could be said to run through Blanch's eldest daughter Philippa (Bolingbroke's sister), who married the King of Portugal. Her nearest descendant, via King Emmanuel of Portugal, the Emperor Charles V and then Philip II of Spain, was the Infanta Isabella. As it happened, the Infanta was also descended from Arthur Duke of Brittany, the rightful heir to the throne, murdered by King John.

It will be noticed that Persons not only favoured the house of Lancaster above York, he sought to demolish the Tudor myth of the incorporation of the white and red rose. Instead of upholding Henry Tudor's right to the throne, and using him as the point of departure for settling the succession, he took the genealogical argument back into the uncertainties of the Wars of the Roses. It meant, in effect, that whoever succeeded Elizabeth would be the equivalent of Henry Bolingbroke, one whose claim by birth would be at best confused and uncertain, yet whose right to rule would be vindicated by a combination of other critical factors.

It has often been assumed, despite Persons's protestations, that *A Conference about the Next Succession* is at the very least a covert promotion of the candidature of Isabella, the Infanta of Spain, in opposition to that of James Stuart. Certainly it creates the circumstances, and provides the materials, on the basis of which a strong case could be made and a campaign launched, but it stops short of endorsing hers as the strongest claim. In the course of time Persons was to support the Infanta's candidature actively and deliberately, but there is no evidence that he had already decided to do so in 1593 when the book was written.[16] He was, however, very wary of James's intentions, explaining in 1596 that there was no substantial proof of the king's serious interest in Catholicism and that if he took the Catholics' part it would be a matter of prudence rather than conviction.[17] Throughout the 1590s Persons was careful not to burn his bridges with any candidate, because personal allegiance to a prince was less important than the 'cause'.

His stated concern was to alert his Catholic readers, in the absence of officially sanctioned information or public debate, to the simple facts of

---

[16] See L. Hicks, SJ, 'Sir Robert Cecil, Father Persons, and the Succession, 1600–1601', *Archivum Historicum S.I.* 24 (1955): 95–139.

[17] Robert Persons, Letter to Crichton, Seville, 10 May 1596, *ABSI*, Coll P, fol. 316 (copy in *ABSI*, Persons Letters 46/12/3, fols 456–66).

the succession issue, as he saw them (based on Englefield's researches).[18] He hoped that the Catholics would form a united party behind one candidate and strove to make it clear that no Catholic could in conscience support a non-Catholic candidate. In this regard he warned against wishful thinking about toleration. As things stood, all these considerations did tend to point towards the Infanta, the only definitely Catholic pretender, but hopes were still alive for the conversion of James, while the religious convictions of Ferdinand Stanley, fifth earl of Derby, were matter for speculation. In the event, Stanley died in the interval between composition and publication.[19]

A Conference about the Next Succession, then, was intended to be a first step towards a Catholic policy on the succession, rather than a crafty manoeuvre on the part of a scheming Jesuit. Its immediate publishing context, however, appears to have been somewhat mischievous. The edition printed in Antwerp sported a dedication to Robert Devereux, Earl of Essex. It is just possible, if Persons or Verstegan (supervising the printing) believed that Essex might be willing to favour the recusants, that this was a genuine overture. If so, it was singularly inept. Essex was gravely embarrassed at court.[20] Although the storm soon passed, the Queen's favourite could hardly be expected to welcome being implicated in a treatise on a subject she had explicitly and passionately banned from discussion. It is, therefore, far more likely that the dedication was intended to discredit Essex with James, who at this stage looked to Essex rather than the Cecils for support.[21] Such a stratagem would be consonant with the book's unambiguous thrust, not to exclude James from consideration, but to dislocate him from any position of advantage.

***

This account of the book's political strategy may appear unduly naive. Persons, after all, was seldom free of involvement in some or other short-term plan for the 'liberation' of England, despite his well-known disclaimer in 1584: 'Doctor Allen and I … had resolved I say to leave cogitation of soch matters and to follow only owr spirituall cowrse wheruppon all dependeth thowgh in longer time'.[22] This raises the question of the relationship between his polemical writings and his political activism, one of the most vexed and

---

[18]   Robert Persons, Letter to Crichton, Madrid, 2 Nov 1596, *ABSI*, Coll P, fol. 318 (copy in *ABSI*, Persons Letters 46/12/3, fols 514–520).

[19]   A.J. Loomie, SJ, 'The Armadas and the Catholics of England', *Catholic Historical Review* 59 (1973): 385–403; Edwards, *Robert Persons*, p. 146. Attempts to link the Stanleys' title with Catholic hopes – and thereby ruin them – have usually been attributed to Cecil's intrigues. On 29 November 1593 Richard Hesketh was executed for approaching the fifth earl, who immediately gave him up. On Hesketh, see *Letters and Despatches of Richard Verstegan*, ed. Anthony G. Petti; CRS, 52 (London, 1959), p. 200 n. 8 and pp. 203–204.

[20]   Rowland Whyte, Letter to Sir Robert Sidney, London, 5–12 Nov 1595, *Report on the Manuscripts of Lord de L'Isle and Dudley Preserved at Penshurst Place*, Historical Manuscripts Commission (6 vols; London, 1925–66), vol. 2, pp. 182–4.

[21]   Hicks, 'Sir Robert Cecil, Father Persons, and the Succession, 1600–1601', pp. 107–112.

[22]   *Letters and Memorials of Father Robert Persons*, p. 246.

intriguing questions about Robert Persons.[23] To put it simply: the works of controversy present a reasonable face, firm but conciliatory, while the political actions range from passive resistance to violent invasion. It may be helpful to observe that his published works adhere in some measure to the principle whereby priests engaged on the English mission scrupulously refrained from political involvement while they were on English soil. In their training, political issues were avoided.[24] Persons does not eschew political topics, but he ensures that every sentence projected into the public domain can be defended against a charge of treason. This is a rhetorical decorum maintained throughout his literary career, whatever shifts one might detect between 'resistance and compromise'.[25] The pressure of such decorum can be felt particularly in *A Conference about the Next Succession*, where, if my interpretation of the evidence about authorship is correct, he conscientiously undertook the writing, or 'writing up', as representative of the English Catholics as a whole, not his own party or interest. It would explain his indignation over accusations of being the sole author or prime mover.

The most striking feature of *A Conference about the Next Succession*, as part of Persons's literary output, is the contrast in style with the *Philopater*.[26] The satirical style has been abandoned in favour of the studied impartiality of the historian. One should be careful of interpreting this as a neutral or artless manner: the impersonal, representative voice, the predominance of historical fact and the restrained, provisional argumentation are all deliberate rhetorical strategies. Time replaces language as the distancing device: where the *Philopater* invites the reader to view English affairs from a wide European perspective and with humanist irony, *A Conference about the Next Succession* scrutinizes the current succession predicament in relation to centuries of dynastic confusion and religious stability. It makes England's Protestant religious settlement look as eccentric historically as it does geographically. Historiography, rather than Latinity, thus becomes the symbol of hope for English Catholicism. Even so, some geographical distance was helpful. Persons set his fictional discussion of the succession in Amsterdam, offering a slightly detached view of English affairs as the supposedly well-informed, objective and disinterested observers considered the likely outcome of the succession, with Elizabeth ageing and court politics unstable.

---

[23] See Thomas M. McCoog, SJ, *The Society of Jesus in Ireland, Scotland, and England 1541–1588: 'Our Way of Proceeding?'* (Leiden, 1996), p. 266.

[24] William Allen, *A True, Sincere and Modest Defence of English Catholiques* (Rouen, 1584), p. 64.

[25] Peter Holmes, *Resistance and Compromise: The Political Thought of the Elizabethan Catholics* (Cambridge, 1982).

[26] Robert Persons [Andreas Philopater (pseud.)], *Elizabethae Angliae Reginae haeresim Caluinianum propugnantis, saeuissimum in Catholicos sui regni edictum ... Cum responsione ad singula capita* (Antwerp, 1592), henceforth referred to as *Philopater*.

The critical effect aimed at in *A Conference about the Next Succession* is to inculcate 'consideration', a habit of mind commended especially in *The Christian Directory*.[27] In 1582 Persons described it as:

> The keye whiche openeth the doore to the closet of our harte, where all our bookes of accompte doe lye. It is the lookinge glasse, or rather the very eye of our soule, wherby shee seethe her selfe, and lookethe into all her whole estate, her riches, her debtes, her duetyes, her negligences, her good gyftes, her defectes, her safftie, her daunger, her way she walkethe in, her pase shee holdeth, and, finallye, the place and ende which shee drawethe unto. And without this consideration, shee runnethe on blindlye into a thousande brakes and bryers, stumbling at every steppe into some one inconvenience or other, and continualie in perill of some great and deadlie mischiefe.[28]

The whole of the rest of the work guides the reader through a process of consideration of the state of his or her soul in Ignatian fashion. I would argue that this is apposite, *mutatis mutandis*, to the design of *A Conference about the Next Succession*. To begin near the end of the latter book, the Infanta's title is indirectly recommended to the reader's 'consideration' thus:

> Which [that this lady the infanta of Spaine, is of the true and ancient blood royal of Ingland] being graunted, they inferr, that seing matters are so doubtful at this day, about the next lawful succession, and that diuers of the pretendores are excluded, some for bastardie, some other for religion, some for vnaptnes to gouerne, and some for other causes, & seing the common wealth hath such authoritie to dispose in this affaire, as before the Ciuil lawyer hath declared, why may there not *consideration* be had among other pretenders, of this noble princesse also (saie these men) especially seing she is vnmarried and may therby commodate many matters, and salue many breaches, & satisfie many hopes, and giue contentment to many desires, as the world knoweth.[29]

The treatise can be said to promote, not simply one candidature, but a certain frame of mind or mental disposition in the reader. Persons himself claimed that the book was a warning of the dangers of *ignorance* in this matter;[30] equally, he might have warned against *inconsideration*, repeating the terms of a chapter title from his earlier work: 'Howe necessarie it is to enter into earnest consideration and meditation of our estate'.[31]

Consideration that leads to a state of being resolved in the service of God has much in common with the consideration Persons invokes for the settlement

---

[27]   *The First Booke of the Christian Exercise, appertayning to Resolution* (Rouen, 1582; revd 1585, 1607), henceforth referred to as *The Christian Directory*. All quotations from the 1582 version are taken from *The Christian Directory (1582): The First Booke of the Christian Exercise, appertayning to Resolution*, ed. Victor Houliston (Leiden, 1998).

[28]   *The Christian Directory*, part I, ch. 2, pp. 17–18.

[29]   *A Conference about the Next Succession*, part II, pp. 157–8; emphasis added.

[30]   Robert Persons, Letter to Crichton, Madrid, 2 Nov 1596; *A Manifestation of the Great Folly*, fol. 64r.

[31]   *The Christian Directory*, part I, ch. 2.

of the succession. Both involve 'indifference'. In his correspondence Persons consistently protested that he was indifferent who should succeed, so long as he or she were Roman Catholic,[32] and in *A Conference about the Next Succession* he imputed such an attitude to all his co-religionists: 'it is thought, that these other of the Roman religion do remayne very *indifferent*, to follow any one that shalbe set vp for their religion, and is lykest to restore and mayntayne the same, be he strainger or domestical'.[33] Similarly, *The Christian Directory* calls on his Protestant readers to peruse the work indifferently: 'Wherfore (gentle reader) if thow be of an other religion than I am, I beseche the most hartelye, that layenge a side all hatred, malice and wrathfull contention, let us joyne together in amendment of our lyves'.[34] In context, the phrase 'amendment of our lyves' means careful attention to the deliberately non-partisan or *indifferent* directives of the work. Just as *The Christian Directory* urged a devotional withdrawal from controversy, so *A Conference about the Next Succession* invited the Catholic community to consider its political well-being without passion or partisanship.

Francis Edwards quotes one of Persons's declarations of indifference with the comment: 'He was lukewarm towards the principle of legitimism'.[35] Yet indifference has no association with lukewarmness in this context. In the religious controversy of the sixteenth century it normally meant something much more positive: a bracketing of 'things indifferent' in order to promote agreement on essentials. Annabel Patterson, in her treatment of Holinshed's *Chronicles*, extends the meaning of the word to the realm of the history of the monarchy, the very subject with which *A Conference about the Next Succession* engages. She argues that indifference is central to the entire Holinshed project: what appears to be shapeless or incoherent in the *Chronicles* derives from a deliberate attempt to allow the reader to confront the past indifferently in all its multivocal diversity and self-contradiction.[36] In an obvious sense this applies to part II of *A Conference about the Next Succession* where each claim is allowed to speak for itself. One could argue that it also applies in a more subtle sense to part I, where the reader is prompted to take greater responsibility for his or her political future. 'Indifference' here means an unwillingness to allow matters of state to be mystified and so prejudged, and an insistence that they be brought to the bar of dispassionate right reason.

The argument of part I is incremental and very carefully constructed. It is easy to misunderstand it. But we have to make a conscious effort to be 'indifferent'. There are arguments for removing a corrupt monarch, by force if

---

[32]   E.g. Robert Persons, Letter to Crichton, Seville, 10 May 1596, *ABSI*, Coll P fol. 316; *A Defence of the Catholike Ecclesiastical Hierarchie*, fols 187v–188r.

[33]   *A Conference about the Next Succession*, part II, p. 247; emphasis added.

[34]   *The Christian Directory* , 'To the Christian Reader', p. 7.

[35]   Edwards, *Robert Persons*, p. 244, quoting Robert Persons, Letter to William Douglas, Earl of Angus, Rome, 24 Jan 1600, *ABSI*, Coll P fols 414–18, transcribed in McCoog, 'Harmony Disrupted', pp. 202–208.

[36]   Annabel Patterson, *Reading Holinshed's Chronicles* (Chicago, 1994), preface and *passim* (see index, *sub* 'indifference').

necessary (ch. 4). Much is made of the blessings God has poured upon those rulers who in times past replaced the tyrannical or the incompetent (ch. 3). Such arguments could be taken to mean that the author was in favour of the assassination of Queen Elizabeth or invasion by the Spaniards, and presumably were so taken, to judge by some of the epithets used of the book by Persons's political opponents, who described it as vile and dangerous. Persons did in fact lend his support to the Spanish Armadas, and John Bossy has argued that he may have been implicated in the assassination proposal by George Gifford in 1583.[37] But this was not the point of the argument. Rebellion was justified because the monarchy was a creation of the commonwealth and accountable to it.[38] If so, the members of the commonwealth had a grave responsibility to consider carefully before consenting to the accession of the next monarch at such a doubtful juncture, giving due weight to the ends for which a commonwealth exists. That end, the true worship of God, is accordingly the subject of the final chapter of part I.

The purpose of part I of *A Conference about the Next Succession*, as I have suggested, is to bring politics out of the realm of the ineffable and into the domain of reason, to create subjects who make considered choices. The particular target is the *Apologia Catholica* (1584) by Pierre de Belloy, heavily attacked again and again in *A Conference about the Next Succession*.[39] Belloy's was the most extreme formulation of the absolutist version of the divine right of hereditary monarchs. He supported the claim of Henry of Navarre to the French throne despite his Huguenot affiliation. For Persons, this doctrine turns birthright into a kind of magic whereby God alone determines the destiny of a nation: 'to say that god only doth thes things & leaueth nothing to mans iudgement therin is agaynst al reason vse and experience of the world'.[40] King James took Belloy's doctrine even further and insisted that royal policy was between the king and his God, for only the king was privy to God's secret counsels of state policy.[41] Persons, on the other hand, seeks to habituate his readers to their responsibility to judge between tyrants and good kings; to

---

[37]   John Bossy, 'The Heart of Robert Persons', in McCoog (ed.), *The Reckoned Expense*, pp. 141–58, esp. pp. 149–50; cf. Edwards, *Robert Persons*, pp. 84–6.

[38]   *A Conference about the Next Succession*, part I, p. 73.

[39]   Pierre de Belloy, *Apologia catholica ad famosos et seditiosos libellos Coniuratorum* (Paris, 1584), translated as *A Catholicke Apologie against the Libels, Declarations, Advices, and Consultations made, written and published by those of the League, perturbers of the quiet estate of the Realme of France* (London, 1590). The work was published under the name Edmond de L'Allouette, probably a pseudonym. Persons refers to the Latin title regularly in *A Conference about the Next Succession*. On the influence of French political theory on English writers of this period, see Lisa Ferraro Parmelee, *Good newes from Fraunce: French Anti-League Propaganda in Late Elizabethan England* (Rochester, 1996), esp. chs 1, 4 and 5, referring to *A Conference about the Next Succession*.

[40]   *A Conference about the Next Succession*, part I, pp. 123–4. See also part I, pp. 2, 35–6, 64–9.

[41]   James I, *Basilikon doron, Or His Maiesties instructions to his dearest sonne, Henrie the prince* (London, 1603).

distinguish, for instance, between the rightful deposition of Richard II and the unlawful wresting of power from Henry VI.[42]

The ambivalent treatment of royal birthright can be illustrated by contrasting Persons's treatment of the career of Henry V with that of Shakespeare. In *King Henry V*, the young warrior-king seeks to atone for the sin of his father's rebellion by building chantries for Richard's soul, and prays on the eve of Agincourt that God will not visit on him his father's fault, by demoralizing his men in battle.[43] Whatever the justification for Bolingbroke's *coup* – and Shakespeare in *King Richard II* deliberately leaves the rebels' motives and procedures equivocal – there is an irreducible sense of sacrilege attached to the displacing (and subsequent assassination) of the Lord's anointed. Where Shakespeare exploits the imaginative appeal of the divine right of kings (extravagantly urged in the *Apologia catholica*), without fully endorsing it, Persons will admit no frisson of transgression when he narrates the 'putting back' of an unworthy king:

> In this man's place by free election was chosen for king the noble knight Henry Duke of Lancaster, who proved afterwards so notable a king, as the world knoweth, and was father to King Henry the Fifth, surnamed commonly the Alexander of England.[44]

These exploits simply confirm Henry V's title; they do not atone for sin or symbolize divine grace to a tainted house. Persons resists the attempts of the propagandists of divine right to invest kingship with an occult mystery. He reclaims the question of majesty from the secret counsels of God for the domain of human action and choice, declaring, 'God will not always bind himself to work miracles, or to use extraordinary means in bringing those things to pass, which he hath left in the hands of men and of commonwealths to effectuate by ordinary way of wisdom and justice.'[45] His intention was to dislodge the habit of mind that was being inculcated by such official propaganda as the now infamous 'Homilie against disobedience and wilfull rebellion' (1571).[46] Abrogation of political choice was always a temptation to Catholics, with their respect for authority; as witness their general acquiescence in Elizabethan religious and foreign policy.

Against this creeping tendency to overvalue obedience, Persons offered his own version of the divine right of kings. So far from depreciating royal authority, he declared that 'as nothing vnder God is more honorable, amiable, profitable or soueraine, than a good Prince: so nothing is more pestelent or

---

[42]   *A Conference about the Next Succession*, part II, pp. 95–6.

[43]   William Shakespeare, *King Henry V*, IV, i, 264–279. The play was first performed in 1599; *King Richard II* was first performed in 1595; see Andrew Gurr (introd.), *King Richard II* (Cambridge, 1984), p. 1; and *King Henry V*, rev. edn (Cambridge, 2005), p. 1.

[44]   *A Conference about the Next Succession*, part I, pp. 59–60.

[45]   Ibid., part II, p. 68.

[46]   'An Homilie against disobedience and wilfull rebellion', in *Certaine Sermons or Homilies appointed to be read in Churches*, 2 parts (London: J. Bill, 1623), extracted in Andrew Gurr (ed.), *King Richard II* (Cambridge, 1984), pp. 215–20.

bringeth so general destruction and desolation as an euel Prince'.[47] To expose tyranny was to affirm the holiness of the office. The glory of a prince, therefore, lay not in immunity from popular censure but in the grace conferred by (or through) the consent of the commonwealth. Just as a marriage turns into a sacrament when the consent of the bride is given in church, so divine authority accrues to a king when his subjects have given free consent to his sovereignty in a religious coronation. Persons writes that the 'contract betwene the king and his common wealth, at his first admission, is as certayne and firme … as any contract or mariage in the world can be, when it is solemnized by wordes *de praesenti* (as our law speaketh) betwene parties espoused before by wordes *de futuro*'.[48] That is, right of birth is like a pre-contract of marriage, while the coronation oath, with the people's consent, seals the contract *de praesenti*, God conferring his blessing.[49] Thus a king is made not by birth, nor by God nor by the people, but by all three consenting. The lengthy description Persons gives, right in the middle of part I (ch. 5), of the ceremonial attached to the coronation oath creates a vivid and compelling image of monarchy as it should be: when the archbishop and bishops participate in full splendour and approval, as they do at the coronation of the French king,[50] monarchy has reached its zenith. As for England – *Ichabod*.

The ceremony itself is crucial to Persons's political thinking. Where divine-right theorists such as Belloy concentrated the supernatural operation in kingship on the mystery of birth, Persons diffused grace amongst a range of contributory elements. Providence works by coincidence of human circumstances, and this interaction is dramatized in the coronation ritual. This is not a mere outward manifestation of an antecedent reality, an absolute and inalienable right to rule based on succession by birth. Coronation, in Persons's view, effects a real change in the status of the monarch, 'for as much as not nature, but the election and choice of the people, had made their first Princes from the beginning of the world'.[51] Coronation is a 'form of agreement and convention between the commonwealth and their Christian head or king … reduced to a more sacred and religious kind of unity and concord',[52] where 'agreement' means, first, a coming to one mind, and only then, and arising from this unity, a contract.

The beneficent combination of succession and election in the making of a king, as Persons sees it, is enhanced by a telling medicinal metaphor. As sole determinant of a king's right, each has its disadvantages, but these can be cancelled out by reference to the other: 'so as election by succession, and succession by election is salved, and the one made a preservative and treacle to the other: and this is the wisdom and high policy left by God and nature to

---

[47]   *A Conference about the Next Succession*, part I, p. 38; see also p. 78.

[48]   Ibid., part I, pp. 119–20.

[49]   For a full discussion of this distinction, as it was applied historically, see Christopher Brooke, *The Medieval Idea of Marriage* (Oxford, 1989), ch. 6, 'Marriage in Law and Practice'.

[50]   *A Conference about the Next Succession*, part I, pp. 101–113.

[51]   Ibid., part I, p. 82.

[52]   Ibid., part I, p. 84.

every commonwealth'.[53] Here Persons draws on an understanding of health as an equilibrium of potentially conflicting elements in the body. Contemporary treatises make a careful distinction between 'meat' and 'physic': treacle is not to be taken as nourishment but as an antidote to poison. It is often a case of one poison driving out another. Thus Thomas Moffet, at one time physician to Sir Philip Sidney, comments on a treacle made from the flesh of a hernshaw fed entirely with adders: 'Wherefore howsoever we use such birds for physic, yet let us not feed upon them as meats, lest we take poison instead of nourishment.'[54] If, then, election and succession are to be seen as treacles to each other, Persons attributes the political well-being of the commonwealth to a balance of potentially dangerous principles. Divine favour, the seal of such wholeness, is not to be presumed; an appeal is made to the collective judgment of 'every man that is of reason and judgement, and void of passion' to discern God's favour, to recognize his anointed.

It would be a mistake, therefore, to focus exclusively on the subversive or rebellious dimension of *A Conference about the Next Succession*. In this work Persons is much more concerned to redefine or reinvent monarchy than to license the toppling of the Elizabethan regime. An indication of how the book has been misread is the tendency to align it with the 'monarchomachs': Buchanan, Hotman and du Plessis Mornay, as Persons's contemporary opponents did.[55] It is more probable that he was influenced by his fellow-Jesuits, Francisco Suarez and Juan de Mariana, especially in view of his meeting with Suarez in 1593:

> Fr Francis Suarez passed by here last week and, seeing what great facilities there are for printing his books, he spoke to me about it ... We for our part [have] regard both to the merits of the work itself as well as to the person of one who deserves so well of all men, and especially of the English nation.[56]

It is likely enough that Suarez and Persons discussed the issues of political theory to be found in part I of *A Conference about the Next Succession*. Even here one needs to be cautious. Michael Carrafiello attempts to position Persons's political theory very precisely 'somewhat to the left of Suarez, but

---

[53] Ibid., part I, p. 131.

[54] Thomas Moffet, *Healths Improvement: or, Rules Comprizing and Discovering The Nature, Method, and Manner of Preparing all sorts of Food Used in this Nation* (composed 1596; published London, 1655), p. 93.

[55] Henry Constable, *A Discoverye of a Counterfecte Conference helde at a counterfecte place, by counterfecte travellers, for thadvancement of a counterfecte tytle, and invented, printed, and published by one (PERSON) that dare not avowe his name* (Cologne [*vere* Paris], 1600), p. 57; William Watson, *A Decacordon of Ten Quodlibeticall Questions concerning Religion and State* (London, 1602), p. 228; William Clarke, *A Replie unto a certaine Libell, latelie set foorth by Fa: Parsons* (London, 1603), fol. 76r. George Buchanan, *De iure regni apud Scotos, dialogus* (Edinburgh, 1579); Francois Hotman, *Francogallia* (1573); Junius Brutus (pseud.), *Vindiciae contra Tyrannos: siue, De principis in populum, populique in principem, legitima potestate* (Basle, 1579), usually attributed to Philippe de Mornay.

[56] Robert Persons, Letter to Acquaviva, Valladolid, 2 November 1593, *ARSI*, Hisp. 136, f. 207 (copy in *ABSI*, Persons Letters 46/12/3, fol. 205).

also somewhat to the right of Goodman, Knox, Buchanan and Mariana ... closest to Hotman and Mornay's resistance theory'. In a detailed analysis of the precise differences between the views of Persons and Suarez on the legitimacy of rebellion against tyrants he attributes to both writers more definitive positions than the rhetorical disposition of either's writings will allow. It is by no means certain that Persons was so familiar, in detail, with Suarez's theory that he consciously intended to revise it in *A Conference about the Next Succession.* Much of that thinking is embodied in Suarez's *De legibus ac deo legislatore,* which was not published until 1612.[57] He taught in Rome from 1580–85 and thereafter in Salamanca, and Persons may have attended some of his lectures before he left Rome in April 1580, but we cannot assume extended exposure to Suarez's ideas. Thus it seems best merely to observe some significant affinities between them.[58]

Suarez is concerned to define the relationship between human and divine elements in constituting royal *potestas*: the right of a king derives immediately from men, a necessary consequence of living in a community, but mediately from God.[59] What one might call the marital model of royal authority, which we have seen in Persons, emerges in Suarez when he 'puts the case' of a false application of such a model:

> Moreover, one might adduce as an argument the fact that, as I remarked above, if we assume that men have willed to gather together into one political community, it is not in their power to set up obstacles to this jurisdiction; and this is an indication that the jurisdiction does not flow proximately from their wills as from a true efficient cause. Thus, in regard to matrimony, we rightly infer that the husband is the head of the wife by grant of the Author of nature Himself, and not by the will of the wife; for though they may contract the marriage by their own will, nevertheless, if they do contract it, they cannot prevent the establishment of this superiority.[60]

On the contrary, he argues, it is God's special will for the human race that laws should be made 'proximately' by man (as the immediate cause) while actually

---

[57]   Francisco Suarez, *Tractatus de legibus ac deo legislatore* (Coimbria, 1612).

[58]   Michael L. Carrafiello, *Robert Parsons and English Catholicism, 1580–1610* (Selinsgrove, 1998), p. 16 n. 26 and pp. 51–5; cf. J.H.M. Salmon, 'Catholic Resistance Theory, Ultramontanism, and the Royalist Response, 1580–1620', in J.H. Burns and Mark Goldie (eds), *The Cambridge History of Political Thought, 1450–1700* (Cambridge, 1991), pp. 219–53, who notes that Suarez's scholastic form of presentation creates many ambiguities and apparent contradictions.

[59]   'Hanc potestatem esse immediate ab hominibus, & mediate a Deo': Francisco Suarez, *De legibus* III iv 8, in *Selections from Three Works of Francisco Suarez, S.J.*, trans. G.L. Williams et al. (2 vols; Oxford, 1944), vol. 1, p. 209, col. a (Latin) and vol. 2, p. 389 (English). I am indebted to Michael J. Suarez, SJ, for drawing my attention to the link between Persons and Suarez.

[60]   'Et potest suaderi, quia, vt antea dicebam, supposita voluntate hominum conueniendi in vna politica communitate, non est in potestate eorum impedire hunc iurisdictionem; ergo signum est proxime non prouenire ex eorum voluntatibus, quasi ex propria causa efficienti. Sicut in matrimonio recte colligimus, virum esse caput mulieris ex dono ipsius auctoris naturae, & non ex voluntate vxoris, quia licet ipsi voluntate sua matrimonium contrahant, tamen si matrimonium contrahant hanc superioritatem impedire non possunt' (*De legibus* III iii 2, in *Selections from Three Works of Francisco Suarez, S.J.*, vol. 1, p. 204, col. a and vol. 2, p. 378).

deriving from eternal law.[61] Thus, while Suarez insists that 'human positive laws', including the institution of the monarchy, are contingent rather than absolute, he makes this the very basis for asserting that such laws are the most significant legal manifestation of divine grace working through his people.

It is noteworthy that the custodians of the will of the people are not, in the narrative sketched by *A Conference about the Next Succession*, their representatives in parliament but the presiding archbishop and bishops at the time of the coronation oath. Persons does not in fact concern himself with the possible constitutional mechanisms by which popular consent might be withdrawn. Nevertheless, his book was found useful during the constitutional conflicts of the seventeenth century. During the Civil War, Parliamentarians appropriated it to justify the forcible removal of Charles I,[62] and later, even more ironically, Algernon Sidney was accused of drawing on it in his bid to exclude the Roman Catholic James, Duke of York, from the succession.[63] Jonathan Swift, an admirer of Persons's prose style, possessed a copy of Sidney's reprint, in which he entered marginalia such as: 'The latter part of this chapter [part I, ch. 9] savours much of the Jesuit, and is calculated to raise an inevitable War at the death of Qu. Eliz.'[64]

Persons's contribution to the development of parliamentary democracy was somewhat fortuitous, therefore. Some commentators have emphasized its opportunism. A.L. Rowse memorably if extravagantly pronounced that Persons 'argued Philip's claims, as a descendant of the house of Lancaster, on behalf of his daughter, the Infanta: any clever fool, it seems, can find arguments for anything he wants'. Attempting a similar rhetorical flourish, Michael L. Carrafiello has averred that Persons provided 'ample ideological ammunition to set off the actual big bang that Fawkes and company planned for king and Parliament in November 1605'. Nevertheless, *A Conference*

---

[61]   *De legibus* I iii 17–20, in *Selections from Three Works of Francisco Suarez, S.J.*, vol. 1, pp. 19–20 and vol. 2, pp. 47–50.

[62]   For a review of seventeenth-century reprints, under various guises, see J.B. Williams [*vere* J.G. Muddiman], 'Puritan Piracies of Father Persons' "Conference" ', *The Month* 117 (1911): 270–78. The best known was in *Severall Speeches Delivered at a Conference concerning the Power of Parliament, to proceed against their King for Misgovernment* (London, 1648), an adaptation by Henry Walker. There was also an abridgement entitled *A Treatise Concerning the Broken Succession of the Crown of England. Inculcated, about the later end of the Reign of Queen Elizabeth. Not impertinent for the better Compleating of the General Information intended* (London, 1655).

[63]   The reprint of Robert Persons, *A Conference About the Next Succession to the Crown of England* (London, 1681), occasioned a response by Edward Pelling, *The Apostate Protestant. A Letter to a Friend, occasioned by the late Reprinting of a Jesuites Book. About Succession to the Crown of England* (London, 1682). See also William Assheton, *The Royal Apology: or, An Answer to the Rebels Plea: wherein, the most noted anti-monarchical tenents, first, published by Doleman the Jesuite, to promote a bill of exclusion against King James. Secondly, practised by Bradshaw and the regicides in the actual murder of King Charles the 1st. Thirdly, republished by Sidney and the associators to depose and murder his present Majesty, are distinctly consider'd. With a parallel between Doleman, Bradshaw, Sidney and other of the true-Protestant party* (London, 1684).

[64]   Jonathan Swift, *Prose Works*, ed. Herbert Davis et al. (14 vols; Oxford, 1939–68), vol. 5, pp. 241–3 (marginalia); cf. vol. 2, p. 177 for his opinion of Persons as a stylist.

about the Next Succession has taken a modest but noteworthy place in the history of resistance theory. Peter Holmes has boldly applauded it as arguably the most significant work of political theory by an Englishman between More and Hobbes;[65] although this claim has not subsequently been reasserted, the book has become a convenient reference point for cultural historians and Shakespearian scholars wishing to debunk the supposedly Tillyardian myth of an Elizabethan consensus against rebellion.[66]

My analysis of *A Conference about the Next Succession* suggests that its real interest lies in the promotion of a historically informed Catholic political conscience. As political theory, it came at a significant moment in the debate over church–state relations, and particularly in the debate over the definition of the Jesuit vocation. Persons lays himself open to the charge that his notion of the popular will is chimerical (in that he treats a ceremonial form as a substantive choice) and consequently that he places the real power in the hands of the presiding clergy. *A Conference about the Next Succession*, in other words, could be seen as merely a disguised *apologia* for the papal power of deposition and for the role of the clergy, and especially the Jesuits, in controlling state policy. Such a scenario would be deeply ironic in view of the fact that the Fifth General Congregation of the Society of Jesus, which was meeting at the very time of the composition of this treatise, was to issue a stern prohibition against Jesuits meddling in affairs of state.[67]

Persons, who was very close to Acquaviva, the Father General of the Jesuits, throughout this period, protested that the politicization of religion by the English government had made it impossible for him and his colleagues to avoid encroaching on political territory: the 'interests of Catholic religion in England', he wrote, 'are so bound up and intermingled with those of state that one cannot deal with the former without treating the latter'.[68] There is in Persons's political theory, accordingly, an alignment of the orders of grace and nature. The 'acts of the commonwealth' by which evil kings are deposed re-enact the 'particular ordinations of God Himself' in Old Testament days.[69] Conversely, if a king acts by arbitrary power, irrespective of justice, he defies the law of God:

---

[65]   A.L. Rowse, *The England of Elizabeth* (London, 1950), p. 462; see also his *Eminent Elizabethans* (London, 1983), pp. 41–74, esp. pp. 61–5; Carrafiello, p. 117; Holmes, *Resistance and Compromise*, pp. 146–57. For analysis of the thinking of Persons and his colleagues on the succession, see Thomas H. Clancy, SJ, *Papist Pamphleteers: The Allen-Persons Party and the Political Thought of the Counter-Reformation in England, 1572–1615* (Chicago, 1964), pp. 44–78, and Arnold Pritchard, *Catholic Loyalism in Elizabethan England* (London, 1979), pp. 11–36.

[66]   A conspicuous early example is Wilbur Sanders, *The Dramatist and the Received Idea: Studies in the Plays of Marlowe and Shakespeare* (London, 1968), ch. 8.

[67]   *For Matters of Greater Moment: The First Thirty Jesuit General Congregations*, ed. John W. Padberg, SJ et al., (St Louis, 1994), p. 200 (decree 47).

[68]   Robert Persons, Letter to Acquaviva, Marchena, 12 May 1594, *ARSI*, Hisp. 136, fol. 318; see Edwards, *Robert Persons*, p. 171; and McCoog, *The Society of Jesus in Ireland, Scotland and England 1541–1588*, pp. 279–80.

[69]   *A Conference about the Next Succession*, part I, p. 39.

But if they be bound to no justice at all, but must be borne and obeyed, be they never so wicked, then is this end and butt of the commonwealth, and of all royal authority, utterly frustrate: then may we set up public murderers, ravishers, thieves and spoilers to devour us instead of kings and governors to defend us, for such indeed are kings that follow no law but passion and sensuality, and do commit injustice by their public authority.[70]

Without the consonance of political legitimacy and the needs of the commonwealth, monarchy becomes a monstrosity, offending against God and nature. True kingship is ordained by God through the people for whom he cares, but primarily through the presiding archbishop at the coronation ceremony: just as the priest has authority to consecrate the elements of the Eucharist, the archbishop is authorized to bestow divine grace upon a concord of human wills.

* * *

In August 1596 the Scottish Jesuit William Crichton registered his dismay over the publication of *A Conference about the Next Succession* by protesting to Persons, the presumed author: 'There is a French proverb: you don't catch a hare by a drum. Ministers are now beating it in the pulpits both of England and Scotland.'[71] He implied that the book, so far from increasing the likelihood of a Catholic restoration, had aggravated the fears of a Catholic rebellion. The English Protestant clergy were using it to rekindle rumours of foreign invasion plans and plots to secure a succession that would overthrow the existing ecclesiastical order. Recusants would be viewed with even greater suspicion of disaffection and treason; persecution would surely be intensified. In short, the book had done the Roman Catholic cause a disservice. In response, Persons claimed that such alarms were based on hearsay or, at best, a misreading of the book, that persecution had if anything diminished since its publication in mid-1595, and that its fair and objective investigation into the question had done credit to English Catholics. The book had been written, he asserted, to combat ignorance and unpreparedness. The book was a drum: a drum to frighten off the wolf, protecting English Catholics from having a heretic foisted on them; it would also alert the Pope and Catholic princes to the facts of the situation, enabling them to make informed decisions.[72] Once the book was published, it became subject to the shifts in the political situation and was interpreted accordingly: the author of an anonymous, widely circulated manuscript argued that *A Conference about the Next Succession* had actually improved

---

[70]   Ibid., part I, pp. 66–7.

[71]   William Crichton, Letter to Persons, n.p., 20 August 1596, English translation in *ABSI*, Persons Letters 46/12/3, fol. 470.

[72]   Robert Persons, Letter to Crichton, Madrid, 2 Nov 1596, *ABSI*, Coll P 318 (copy in *ABSI*, Persons Letters 46/12/3, fols 514–20).

James's chances by showing the strength of his claim.[73] But during the year following publication, support grew, at least among the exiles in Spain, for the candidature of Isabella, the Infanta of Spain, leading to a petition to Philip II in September 1596 urging him to declare openly in her favour.[74] In the same month, with manoeuvres over the succession beginning to gain momentum, and with his sojourn in Spain about to come to an end,[75] Persons set himself to write *A Memorial for the Reformation of England* for the consideration of the Infanta, and any other likely Catholic candidate.[76]

A Conference about the Next Succession had created an expectation of a royal master or mistress wooing Catholic England. As a work of historiography it constructed a myth of popular investment in the crown, borrowing from the past a form of wedding scenario for the 1590s. The Infanta of Spain never really declared her interest, but just as Persons appealed to his countrymen to consider indifferently who they would want to succeed Elizabeth, so he invited the Infanta to consider, with equal indifference, what kind of commonwealth England might become. This was not to be *her* England so much as England under a generic Catholic Prince. Persons was almost ready to be Pole to her Queen Mary.

Persons had given considerable thought to the policies of restoration pursued under Mary Tudor, and the fruit of this thought is evident in his advocacy of patience and caution. In 1553, when she succeeded Edward VI, the nation could truly be said to be predominantly Catholic. The embattled Protestant minority, recognizing that there had not been time to break the hold of the old religion on the people, was desperate enough to support Lady Jane Grey's claim to the succession – a very different case from the interest in the Infanta at the end of Elizabeth's reign. By the 1590s, the people had become accustomed to Protestant ways. There could be no simple reversion to the *status quo* as if all that had happened over the past 40 years were a mere aberration. Persons would, in his further history-writing, endeavour to present the English Reformation as exactly that,[77] but he was realistic enough to know that the Catholic Prince would be dealing with a radically divided population, a large proportion of which would be sceptical about Catholic religious claims.

For a clearer picture of how he envisaged the church might operate in a reformed Catholic commonwealth, we need to turn to *A Memorial for the Reformation of England*, which in this matter may be treated as a gloss on *A Conference about the Next Succession*. Although it was not published in Persons's day, but was edited by a Protestant scare-monger a century later, it

---

[73]   'An Apologie and Defence of the King of Scotland', in *Documents Illustrating Catholic Policy in the Reign of James VI*, ed. T.G. Law; Publications of the Scottish History Society, 15 (Edinburgh, 1893).

[74]   *CSP Spanish 1587–1603*, pp. 636–7.

[75]   Persons was summoned to Rome to help with the dispute in the English College.

[76]   *The Jesuit's Memorial, for the Intended Reformation of England Under their First Popish Prince*, ed. Edward Gee (London, 1690), henceforth referred to as *A Memorial for the Reformation of England*.

[77]   See below, Chapter 5.

was known to many contemporaries.[78] At the conclusion of part I of the earlier work Persons asserts that the chief end of political life and power is the spiritual welfare of all the people. The *Memorial,* accordingly, presents a picture of the commonwealth in which the entire nation is as it were saturated with agencies for spiritual upliftment: 'Veins and Arteries spread throughout Man's Body to give Blood and Spirit to the fleshy parts that lye about them'.[79] The essential function of the monarchy is to protect and promote these agencies. Chief of them is the delicately named 'Council of Reformation' which would oversee the process of national debate on religious controversy during a limited initial period of religious toleration; in addition, almost every major issue of royal policy, such as the distribution and settlement of church lands and revenues, would be referred to it (part I, chs 7–9). Edward Gee, the Protestant divine who printed *A Memorial* for the first time in 1690, put every reference to the Council (which Persons admitted was just another name for the Inquisition) into 'scare Gothic', as a fearful warning against ever admitting a papist prince. Indeed, Persons's various proposals for centralized control and review have a strongly totalitarian flavour. All local concentrations of independent power, episcopal, aristocratic and judicial (he ignores municipal authorities for the most part) are regarded with some suspicion and placed under royal surveillance.[80]

The history of revolutions and restorations does not inspire confidence in national councils of reform. One is tempted to dismiss the Council of Reformation as a mere instrument to ensure political obedience. Still, the purpose of the kinds of surveillance Persons proposes is to direct all the energies of the realm towards 'the end for which they were created': that all should have justice in court, that God should be honoured in every church and the people edified, that the lands and livelihood of the poor should be free of encroachment from the rich, that recreation should be just that and not licence, and that the young should all enjoy education and employment. In some respects Persons is progressive: protesting vigorously against rack-renting,[81] against the denial of counsel in English trials,[82] against the death penalty for minor offences,[83] and against beating in schools.[84] In his enthusiasm for custom, tradition and conformity, on the other hand, he can be seen as more conservative.[85] His

---

[78] Persons included extracts from the work in *A Manifestation of the Great Folly,* ch. 5, noting that his Catholic opponents 'fondly terme it … the high *counsel of Reformation*' (fol. 55v).

[79] *A Memorial for the Reformation of England,* p. 186.

[80] Ibid., pp. 121–3, 223–4, 240.

[81] Ibid., pp. 233–6.

[82] Ibid., pp. 248–50.

[83] Ibid., pp. 212–13.

[84] Ibid., p. 160.

[85] For modern evaluations of Persons's proposals, see Thomas H. Clancy, SJ, 'Notes on Persons's "Memorial for the Reformation of England" (1596)', *Recusant History* 5 (1959): 17–34; and John J. Scarisbrick, 'Robert Persons' Plans for the "True" Reformation of England', in Neil McKendrick (ed.), *Historical Perspectives: Studies in English Thought and Society in Honour of J.H. Plumb* (London, 1974), pp. 19–42. Holmes, *Resistance and Compromise,* pp. 161–5, treats the *Memorial* as marking a shift away from resistance towards compromise. Carrafiello,

picture of an industrious, equitable England free of corruption and the abuse of power has much imaginative appeal, sufficient perhaps to awaken his fellow-Catholics to the desirability of reaching consensus on the succession. Thus it is not surprising that in 1602, defending the *Memorial* against imputations of Jesuit power-seeking, he should employ the same terms, 'indifference' and 'consideration', associated with the raising of consciousness in *A Conference about the Next Succession:* 'he proposeth with all indifferency such matters as he hath obserued and noted to be thought and considered of at that tyme'.[86] The most dubious aspect is the degree of coercion and the extent to which the whole scheme cloaks an interest in clerical domination.

Concerning these suspicions of a hidden clerical agenda, it may be helpful to examine Persons's proposals for educational reform, especially in the universities. He has a claim to be treated as a significant figure in the history of education: not only was he responsible for the foundation of seminaries at Valladolid, Seville and St Omer, two of which continue to flourish to the present day; he had sufficient insight into student psychology to settle, as no-one else could, the disturbances at the English College, Rome, and he was reputed to be an exceptionally able scholar and tutor at Balliol College in his earlier years. He even showed an intelligent interest in the musical life of the students, and its attendant dangers.[87] Accordingly, he devotes a large portion of the *Memorial for the Reformation of England* to educational institutions,[88] and there are many incidental references scattered throughout the work. He is concerned with thoroughness from top to bottom: from ensuring that doctorates are awarded deservedly, to smoothing the path for the sharp-witted sons of the poor.[89] Perhaps the most telling proposal deals with the division of labour in the universities between the colleges and schools. In his judgment the colleges are unlikely to have men of sufficient learning to be entrusted with lectures: these should be centralized in the schools (such as the Divinity School), while the colleges would handle 'repetition' and other exercises. Lectureships should be both desirable and competitive. Every topic, for example, would be treated simultaneously in two different venues by rival lecturers competing for listeners. Remuneration would be concentrated in the most prestigious lectureships so as to attract men to the lower-paid posts in hopes of moving up.[90]

---

pp. 56–87, analyses it as a well-informed, pragmatic scheme aimed at eliminating the state of clerical and legal corruption caused by the 'prince's arrogation of ecclesiastical power'.

[86]   *A Manifestation of the Great Folly*, fol. 56r.

[87]   T. Frank Kennedy, SJ, 'Jesuits and Music: Reconsidering the Early Years', *Studi Musicali* 17 (1988): 71–100, translates a letter written by Persons to Paul Hoffaeus, the Assistant General for the German provinces on 6 June 1587: 'When the young students are sitting every feast day as canons in the church which is quite small, various ladies come to sit very close, almost in front; other youths and foreign gentlemen come to gaze around very indecently, whereby, I know in particular that some students have received great detriment, and one can only fear for the others' (p. 91). My thanks to Fr Kennedy for drawing my attention to this material.

[88]   *A Memorial for the Reformation of England*, pp. 148–84.

[89]   Ibid., pp. 162–3, 260–61.

[90]   Ibid., pp. 153–5.

In all this one can recognize Persons's assumption that quality can be assured only by centralization. Considered as a whole, the success of the *Memorial*'s proposals for reform depends on the availability of a large corps of visitors, dedicated royal officials who would review the activities of judges, schoolmasters, parish priests and the like. That Persons shows little anxiety about such a group attests to his confidence in the effectiveness of humanist education: the result of his experience with the seminaries in Spain and his knowledge of the Rheims–Douay college. Observing the commitment, self-sacrifice and sheer ability of the young men at Valladolid and Seville, he perhaps overestimated the possibilities of creating an exemplary class of public servants.

Two further optimistic assumptions underlie the *Memorial*. One is that the Catholic hierarchy represented by the Council of Reformation might be disinterested and united. The other is that conformity in religion could be achieved by a patient and objective public examination of the evidence, with both Protestants and Catholics given leisurely opportunity to put their case.[91] In view of the amount of hostility Persons had to endure personally, not least from his fellow-Catholics, these might seem peculiarly and even incomprehensibly naive. Yet it should be remembered that in 1596 Persons had not yet encountered at first hand the squabble at the English College in Rome, that the notorious 'archpriest controversy' still lay in the future, and that the divisions between the Scottish Catholic exiles and the English Jesuits had not yet become marked.[92] Cardinal Allen, symbol of English Catholic unity, was not yet two years dead. As for the settlement of religious disputes, Persons's career as a controversialist helps to explain, if it does not justify, the confidence he shows here. He was not a theologian *per se*: his polemical works deal with such matters as the morality of attending Protestant church services, accusations of treason against seminary priests and Jesuits, definitions of true and false martyrdom, the appropriate form of governance for English Catholicism, the taking of oaths of allegiance and the practice of equivocation. Seldom are strictly theological points at issue. Instead, he deals with the political and ethical predicaments arising out of adopting certain theological positions; that is (to use Persons's terms) of accepting the truth of the Catholic faith. At no time after his conversion in 1574 did Persons show the slightest doubt of that truth. Moreover, the remarkable success of *The Christian Directory* in drawing men and women into lives of devoted Catholic service must have

---

[91]   Cf. the disputations between Mornay and Perron before the King of France in 1600 (narrated by Persons in an annexure to *A Treatise of Three Conversions of England from Paganisme to Christian Religion* [3 vols; St Omer, 1603–1604], vol. 2) and between Laud and Fisher before James I in 1622. Peter Milward, SJ, *Religious Controversies of the Elizabethan Age: A Survey of Printed Sources* (London, 1978), pp. 139–40, suggests that Persons's war of books with Matthew Sutcliffe (1600–1604) was roughly analogous.

[92]   J.H. Pollen, SJ, 'The Accession of King James I', *The Month* 101 (1903): 572–85, esp. p. 575. Persons himself noted the irony of his disappointed trust in English priests in *A Manifestation of the Great Folly*, fol. 58v.

encouraged him to believe that most people will act reasonably when a few incontrovertible propositions are pointed out to them.

The rhetoric of these works on the succession, then, is founded on an educational mission. As a Jesuit, Persons wholeheartedly endorsed the company's ideal of the apostolate.[93] In a well-known letter from this period he expressed his desire to spend the rest of his life moving from village to English village ministering to the needs of the flock:

> [When I am called to political negotiations] and then turn back to contemplate this my present way of life, so free from care and full of consolation, more profitable too for myself and haply for others also – when I set this, I say, before my eyes and certain other things which for many years back it has been in my mind to do, viz. to travel through the towns and villages of England expounding the precepts of the Christian doctrine, if England should be converted in my lifetime – I feel myself to be so averse to that other kind of life.[94]

This was not entirely a personal vision: he envisaged thousands of others enthusiastically embracing the same calling. In company with Edmund Campion on the English mission of 1580–81 he had briefly experienced such a ministry. The events and legislation of the intervening decade and more had convinced him that it could not be repeated under a Protestant regime. If by writing *A Conference about the Next Succession* he could awaken his fellow-Catholics to their responsibilities for the succession, and if by writing *A Memorial for the Intended Reformation of England* he could inspire the Infanta or another Catholic candidate with the prospect of social and religious transformation in England, he could at least be satisfied that he had done all in his power to give his vision a chance of fulfilment.

---

[93]   For the term 'company' (from the Italian *compagnia*, the equivalent of the Latin *societas*), see John W. O'Malley, SJ, *The First Jesuits* (Cambridge, Mass., 1993), pp. 33–4, see also pp. 200–242.

[94]   Robert Persons, Letter to Englefield, Seville, 10 May 1595, English translation by Leo Hicks, SJ, in *ABSI*, Persons Letters 46/12/3, fol. 327; cf. Francis Edwards's translation in Henry More, SJ, *The Elizabethan Jesuits* (London, 1981), pp. 291–2, which takes Persons's project to be the precondition of England's redemption – 'This must be done if England is to be redeemed in my time' – rather than the happy consequence of a Catholic succession: 'if England should be converted in my life time' (as Hicks puts it).

CHAPTER FIVE

Reclaiming the Past:
Combating Foxe and Coke

A Memorial for the Reformation of England was the work of an exile in Spain, still hopeful of restoration.[1] Even before Persons left Spain late in 1596 to attend to the problems at the English College in Rome, he was turning his mind to an ambitious project that would make history benefit English Catholicism even under continued persecution. This he was to entitle the *Certamen Ecclesiae Anglicanae*,[2] a title that bears witness to the struggle or contestation of the church in England: that is, the conflict between church and state. If Protestants thought of the history of the church as a history of the English people trying to cast off the Roman yoke, Persons insisted that English secular rulers were culpable for stifling the flow of grace from Rome on which the spiritual health of the nation depended. The *Certamen*, which occupied him from 1597 to 1604 or even later, never got beyond the stage of compilation of divers materials, but it stood behind two major polemical works: namely, *A Treatise of Three Conversions of England*, which was directed at the Foxe tradition of representing Catholicism as an oppressive burden on the English spirit,[3] and *An Answere to the Fifth Part of Cokes Reportes*, which refuted the claim that autonomy from Rome was implicit in the common law.[4] Published at a critical period around the beginning of James's reign when the question of toleration was open, both works tended to claim for the Catholic community the right

---

[1]   Robert Persons, *The Jesuit's Memorial, for the Intended Reformation of England Under their First Popish Prince*, ed. Edward Gee (London, 1690), henceforth referred to as *A Memorial for the Reformation of England*.

[2]   See Jos. Simons (ed.), *Robert Persons, S.J.: Certamen Ecclesiae Anglicanae: A Study of an Unpublished Manuscript* (Assen, 1965).

[3]   Robert Persons, *A Treatise of Three Conversions of England from Paganisme to Christian Religion. The First under the Apostles, in the first age after Christ: The Second under Pope Eleutherius and K. Lucius, in the second age. The Third, under Pope Gregory the Great, and K. Ethelbert in the sixth age; with divers other matters thereunto apperteyning. Divided Into three partes, as appeareth in the next page. The former two whereof are handled in this booke, and dedicated to the Catholikes of England. With a new addition to the said Catholikes, upon the news of the late Q. death and succession of his Maiestie of Scotland, to the crowne of England. By N.D. author of the Ward-word* (3 vols; St Omer, 1603–1604), henceforth referred to as *A Treatise of Three Conversions*.

[4]   Robert Persons, *An Answere to the Fifth Part of Reportes Lately set forth by Syr Edward Cooke Knight, the Kinges Attorney generall. Concerning The ancient & moderne Municipall Lawes of England, which do appertayne to Spirituall Power and Iurisdiction. By occasion wherof, & of the principall Question set down in the sequent page, there is laid forth an evident, plaine & perspicuous Demonstration of the continuance of Catholicke Religion in England, from our first Kings christened, unto these dayes. By a Catholicke Devyne* (St Omer, 1606), henceforth referred to as *An Answere to Coke*.

to be regarded as the authentic historical embodiment of the Christian faith in England.

A number of factors coincided at the very end of the sixteenth century to focus attention on the Englishness of Catholicism. The possibility that the Catholic candidate for the succession would be a foreigner was one. Another was the allegation that the Pope, to whom Catholics in some sense owed their ultimate allegiance, was a foreign prince. More subtly, and therefore more insidiously, there was the Reformation myth about the purity of the English church. Although Puritans and Protestants (to use the contemporary appellations) might differ on the extent to which the Church of England had been cleansed of popish corruptions, they were agreed that the Reformation was restoring Christianity to the English people by freeing them from practices, doctrines and legal restrictions imposed from without. The historical researches of Foxe and Coke, as they were disseminated in the period 1596–1605, played a major role in the consolidation of this climate of opinion. Within the Catholic community, therefore, the imperative to prove one's loyalty intensified, leading to tensions within both the laity and the clergy which in turn were exploited and complicated by government overtures and the appellant campaign against the Jesuits.

***

The republication of Foxe's *Actes and Monuments* in 1596 was a goad to Persons's labours on the *Certamen Ecclesiae Anglicanae* as an alternative ecclesiastical history of England.[5] He had already begun to gather materials, concentrating on the period beginning with the reign of Henry VIII. It was, thus, designed to expand the work of Nicholas Sander, the manuscript of whose *De origine ac progressu schismatis Anglicani* Persons had annotated in 1586.[6] In the course of time the *Certamen* grew to five thousand pages of manuscript. As it stands, it is a compendium rather than an original work, containing several relevant histories (by other authors) in their entirety. It would be reasonable to assume that Persons meant to work this material up into a unified ecclesiastical history, given that he was particularly adept at creating impressive and highly readable works out of material he culled from others. Such were *The Christian Directory*,[7] adapted from Luis de Granada, and, if my view of the authorship is

---

[5]   John Foxe, *Actes and Monuments of matters most speciall and memorable, happening in the Church, with an universall history of the same* (London, 1596), sig. ¶4v. Persons's copy is preserved at the Venerable English College, Rome, Pressmark P.VIII.9 (new listing 331.26). Grateful thanks to the former Rector, Mgr Adrian Toffolo, for permission to view this copy and quote Persons's annotations.

[6]   For a summary of the debate on Persons's role in the publication of the two editions of *De origine*, see Thomas F. Mayer, 'A Sticking-Plaster Saint? Autobiography and Hagiography in the Making of Reginald Pole', in Thomas Mayer and D.R. Woolf (eds), *The Rhetorics of Life-Writing in Early Modern Europe: Forms of Biography from Cassandra Fedele to Louis XIV* (Ann Arbor, 1995), pp. 205–222, esp. p. 212.

[7]   Robert Persons, *The First Booke of the Christian Exercise, appertayning to Resolution* (Rouen, 1582; revd 1585, 1607), henceforth referred to as *The Christian Directory*.

correct, *A Conference about the Next Succession*, incorporating the researches of Sir Francis Englefield.[8] Besides the manuscript of the *Certamen* itself, there remain in Rome other working documents, such as a draft history of the reign of Henry VIII. Persons called on his extensive network of correspondents to send in any relevant material they might have to hand.[9]

Persons's annotated copy of the 1596 *Actes and Monuments* is still to be seen at the Venerable English College in Rome, along with the manuscript *Certamen*, as testimony to the incomplete project. One reason why it was never finished is that the issues became entangled in a more urgent controversy arising from the republication of Foxe. In 1598 Sir Francis Hastings, whom Persons dubbed the 'Foxe-cub', drew heavily on the *Actes and Monuments* to warn his fellow-Englishmen against the Catholic threat, in his *Watchword to all religious, and true hearted English-men*.[10] Hastings, a Puritan whose brother (Sir Henry Hastings, third Earl of Huntingdon) was an outside candidate for the royal succession, drew out the implications of Foxe's depiction of the Church of Rome as an anti-Christian political force bent on the destruction of the English commonwealth. Under the initials N.D., Persons vigorously defended the record of English Catholics in *A Temperate Ward-word, to the turbulent and seditious Wach-word of Sir Francis Hastinges knight*,[11] arguing that English Roman Catholics were true-hearted Englishmen *par excellence*. Hastings went on the defensive with *An Apologie or Defence of the Watch-word*,[12] supported by Matthew Sutcliffe, Dean of Exeter, who in an attempt at one-upmanship adopted the initials 'O.E.'. Sutcliffe's *Briefe Replie to a certaine odious and slanderous libel* and *New Challenge made to N.D.* prompted Persons to write an extensive *Warn-word to Sir Francis Hastings Wast-word*.[13]

In the *Warn-word*, Persons claimed he had provided 'sufficient proof' for 'any indifferent, prudent, and discreete man, to yeeld his assent thervnto, and

[8]   Robert Persons [R. Doleman (pseud.)], *A Conference about the Next Succession to the Crowne of Ingland* (Antwerp, 1594 [*vere* 1595]), henceforth referred to as *A Conference about the Next Succession*.

[9]   For a full description of the sources and development of the *Certamen*, see Jos. Simons's introduction to his selection, *Certamen Ecclesiae Anglicanae: A Study of an Unpublished Manuscript*. Henry Garnet sent materials to Persons in 1600: see Philip Caraman, SJ, *Henry Garnet 1555–1606 and the Gunpowder Plot* (London, 1964). Letters connected with the project include Richard Hall to Robert Persons, 20 May 1600 (*ABSI*, Persons Letters 46/12/5, fols 1085–6).

[10]   Sir Francis Hastings, *A Watchword to all religious, and true hearted English-men* (London, 1598).

[11]   Robert Persons, *A Temperate Ward-word, to the turbulent and seditious Wach-word of Sir Francis Hastinges knight* (Antwerp, 1599).

[12]   Sir Francis Hastings, *An Apologie or Defence of the Watch-word* (London, 1600).

[13]   Matthew Sutcliffe, *A Briefe Replie to a certaine odious and slanderous libel, lately published by a seditious Jesuite, calling himselfe N.D.* and *A New Challenge made to N.D.* (London, 1600; bound together); Robert Persons, *The Warn-word to Sir Francis Hastinges Wast-word; Conteyning the issue of three former Treatises, the Watch-word, the Ward-word and the Wast-word (intituled by Sir Francis, an Apologie or Defence of his Watchword) ... Wherunto is adioyned a breif reiection of an insolent, and vaunting minister masked with the letters O.E.* (2 vols; Antwerp, 1602).

to rest fully satisfied of the truth'.[14] Catholics did not assent to some alien and disturbing religious system that made them irrational and untrustworthy. But the Foxian image of Roman tyranny and cruelty that lay behind Hastings and Sutcliffe was so influential that it was a question whether the *Warn-word*, or any other Catholic book, would be read with indifference, prudence or discretion. To counter that image, Persons introduced into the debate the three volumes of *A Treatise of Three Conversions of England from Paganisme to Christian Religion* in which he endeavoured to demonstrate the debt owed by the English Church to the Roman see. He was thus able to shift the ground from the heated dispute over the post-Reformation practice of both Catholic and Reformed traditions – the burning of heretics, the question of recusant loyalty, the spiritual corruption and political ambition of the papacy – to an earlier period: to search there for the roots of the truly English Church.

The first two parts of his treatise, comprised in volume 1, contained the analysis of the part played by Rome in the 'conversions' of England in the time of Joseph of Arimathea (first century), Pope Eleutherius (third century) and Augustine of Canterbury (sixth century). This was designed to refute Foxe's notion of an invisible antecedent to the Reformed Church of England: that is, a foreshadowing of the church of the Reformation, hidden in the history of the 'church apparent'. In the following two volumes, Persons offered an 'examen' of the calendar of Protestant saints prefixed to Foxe's work in 1563, commemorating the Protestant and proto-Protestant martyrs in place of the traditional saints' days.[15] Although this brought back attention to more recent history, the purpose was to dismantle Foxe's martyrological narrative and thereby honour and reinstate the Catholic heritage. Persons also took the opportunity to append two bulky additional treatises, apologies for Roman doctrine. Volume 2 contained a revised version of his account of the public disputation in 1600 between the Bishop of Evreux and the Huguenot champion, Philippe du Plessis Mornay, while volume 3 added a conspectus of the heresy trials of Foxe's martyrs, addressing issues such as transubstantiation. These annexures complemented *A Treatise of Three Conversions* and the 'examen' by defining and clarifying the faith for which the 'true' saints and martyrs died from earliest times, and which the pseudo-martyrs rejected. To the rival sets of martyrs, then, was added a contestation of ideas.

The close connection of *A Treatise of Three Conversions* with the *Watchword* controversy is shown by the fact that Matthew Sutcliffe busied himself with attacking Persons on both fronts. In 1604 he produced *A Ful and Round Answer to N.D. alias Robert Parsons the Noddie his foolish and rude Warne-word*, and two years later attempted *The Subversion of Robert Parsons His confused and worthlesse worke, Entituled, A treatise of three Conversions of England from Paganisme to Christian Religion*. In the same year, 1606, he

---

[14]   *A Treatise of Three Conversions*, vol. 1: sig. ***4r.
[15]   This calendar is missing from the Bodleian Library copy of the 1596 *Actes and Monuments* (Pressmark S.3.19.Th) but is included in Persons's working copy at the Venerable English College in Rome.

elaborated *A Threefold Answer unto the third part of a certaine Triobolar Treatise of Three supposed Conversions of England to the moderne Romish Religion published by Rob. Parsons under the continued Maske of N.D.*[16] The feebly satirical titles do at least recognize the core of Persons's argument, that the contemporary, post-Tridentine Catholic Church was at one with the faith thrice given to England in past ages, but the works themselves show little sign of ability to cope with *A Treatise of Three Conversions* in anything but a piece-meal way. Sutcliffe appears to have been thrown off guard somewhat by the fact that he had expected the 'examen' to be merely a collection of slanders against the Reformers.[17] Persons did not respond, possibly judging that Sutcliffe had added nothing new to the debate. By 1606 there was more urgent controversial business to attend to.

* * *

Much modern critical reaction to *A Treatise of Three Conversions* has been concerned with its destructive qualities. Persons claimed to find 120 lies in three leaves of the *Acts and Monuments*, and called Foxe the 'father of lies'.[18] J.F. Mozley takes exception to Persons's dismissal of 'unlearned' Protestant men and women.[19] Glyn Parry, though grudgingly admiring Persons's ability to reduce his opponent's arguments to rubble, deplores the blunt instruments used in this propaganda warfare.[20] Thomas Freeman, again, notes Persons's skill in detecting discrepancies between Foxe's text and his supposed sources.[21]

Anne Dillon maintains that Persons's martyrology, a counterblast to Foxe, was primarily targeted at Catholic loyalists, and particularly the appellants. Those who sought some form of accommodation with the Protestant regime, especially those who used anti-Jesuit action as a bargaining chip, could be seen as betraying the glorious inheritance of the Saxon martyrs and missionaries, and were undermining the Jesuits' work of building up a model Catholic Reformation Church. Dillon's analysis reflects the current characterization of Persons as pursuing a vision of the English Catholic Church that would make it a bright shining example of Catholic Reformation piety to the whole world. To what extent this was a divisive and exclusive element in the troubled

---

[16]   Matthew Suttcliffe, *A Ful and Round Answer to N.d. alias Robert Parsons the Noddie his foolish and rude Warne-word* (London, 1604); *The Subversion of Robert Parsons His confused and worthlesse worke, Entituled, A treatise of three Conversions of England from Paganisme to Christian Religion* (London, 1606); *A Threefold Answer unto the third part of a certaine Triobolar Treatise of Three supposed Conversions of England to the moderne Romish Religion published by Rob. Parsons under the continued Maske of N.D.* (London, 1606).

[17]   *A Threefold Answer*, sig. A2r.

[18]   *A Treatise of Three Conversions*, vol. 3, p. 412.

[19]   J.F. Mozley, *John Foxe and his Book* (London, 1940), pp. 176–80. Another, brief critique of *A Treatise of Three Conversions* is to be found in Richard Helgerson, *Forms of Nationhood: The Elizabethan Writing of England* (Chicago, 1992), pp. 265–6.

[20]   Glyn Parry, 'John Foxe, "Father of Lyes", and the Papists', in David Loades (ed.), *John Foxe and the English Reformation* (Aldershot, 1997), pp. 295–305.

[21]   Thomas S. Freeman, 'John Bale's Book of Martyrs? The Account of King John in *Acts and Monuments*', *Reformation* 3 (1998): 175–223, esp. pp. 206–207.

Catholic community at the turn of the sixteenth century it is hard to determine; I would argue that *A Treatise of Three Conversions* was written in a more generous spirit.[22]

At a time of potential conciliation or at least of easing of persecution, it can be the best strategy to hold the line most tenaciously. This appears to have been Persons's thinking. Ceri Sullivan offers a further suggestion why a critique of Foxe may have seemed timely. The point at issue between Persons and Foxe, she argues, is not historical accuracy but doctrinal integrity. In her opinion there were elements in the *Actes and Monuments* that were particularly damaging to Catholics in the run-up to the succession: not so much the record of Marian persecution as the trashing of Catholic doctrine. Persons's intention, she argues, was to edit these elements out of Foxe, showing that the Protestant martyrs were ineffectual witnesses to the fantasy that Catholic doctrine was no longer tenable.[23] There is some plausibility to this argument. In James's eyes – assuming that he was most likely to succeed – imputed heresy was more likely to put Catholics beyond the pale than a history of persecution restricted chiefly to the reign of Mary Tudor. His own mother had been put to death, with dubious legality, in the Protestant cause, and had some claim to martyrdom herself. James could overlook the violence of the earlier Reformation period, especially since he saw himself as the bringer of peace. But his deep interest in theology meant he was likely to heed Foxe's exposé of Catholic superstition. This could well account for Persons's preoccupation with the pseudo-martyrs' lack of learning, but there is little evidence that in composing *A Treatise of Three Conversions* he had James specifically in mind. The address to James calls for toleration, it is true, but it is toleration for a church that lays claim to the full glory of Christ's visible, known church, of which doctrinal credibility is only one part.

Ceri Sullivan is critical of Persons's rhetorical strategies in *A Treatise of Three Conversions*. She castigates him for trying to provoke what she calls a brawl in heaven by invoking Catholic saints to take revenge on Foxe and his pseudo-martyrs for the injuries done to them. This breaks decorum, she feels, and lowers the tone of the debate. But indignation on behalf of the displaced saints was not unique to Persons. Harpsfield, for example, heatedly described the new martyrs dispossessing the old and pushing violently and ambitiously into their places.[24] If Persons stands out for Sullivan as a crude and blustering spokesman for the old religion, this reflects what John Bossy has called the

---

[22]   Anne Dillon, *The Construction of Martyrdom in the English Catholic Community, 1535–1603* (Aldershot, 2002), pp. 323–69; cf. Alexandra Walsham, '"Yielding to the Extremity of the Time": Conformity, Orthodoxy and the Post-Reformation Catholic Community', in Peter Lake and Michael Questier (eds), *Conformity and Orthodoxy in the English Church, c. 1560–1660* (Woodbridge, Suffolk, 2000), pp. 211–36, esp. p. 233.

[23]   Ceri Sullivan, *Dismembered Rhetoric: English Recusant Writing, 1580 to 1603* (Madison/Teaneck, 1995), esp. pp. 114–15; and '"Oppressed by the Force of Truth": Robert Persons Edits John Foxe', in David Loades (ed.), *John Foxe: An Historical Perspective* (Aldershot, 1999), pp. 154–66.

[24]   'Qui ... antiquis Christi martyribus e possessione sua & sede deturbatis, in eorum locum tam violenter & ambitiose intruduntur': Nicholas Harpsfield, *Dialogi Sex contra Summi*

'classic twin portrait' of Campion and Persons, 'painted in contrasting white and black'.[25] Persons is represented as the blunt Somersetshire yeoman lacking the social graces of the dashing Oxford scholar and favourite of the Queen, the elegant rhetorician who died a heroic martyr's death at Tyburn. Persons was the one who got away: he carried on a tough and realistic struggle, and he was not always scrupulous about the means he used. Still, his voluminous correspondence reveals a man of remarkable tact and diplomacy. He won the favour of Philip of Spain and the Duke of Guise, and seemed always able to defuse personal hostility. This was shown especially in his handling of disputes at the English College in Rome. Young Catholic aristocrats such as George Gilbert idolized him. His opinion was so highly regarded in Rome that, according to report, the Cardinal Nephew, Pietro Aldobrandino, sent his coach daily to the gate of the English College, to take him to the Vatican.[26]

* * *

Persons's critique of Foxe is most revealing in that it helps to clarify his own intentions in writing the history of the English Church. Instead of recognizing the *Actes and Monuments* as a celebration of the revolt against Romish power and corruption, a work that generates its own expectations and rules of progression, he appears to assume that it should read like a history or a chronicle, and that the mock-calendar of saints should serve a devotional purpose.[27] It is little wonder that Foxe's work falls short of these requirements. It does not offer a coherent thematic account of the Reformation, nor does it provide systematic annual coverage of the church in England down the ages. The mock-calendar, whether Foxe himself intended it to be part of his work or

---

Pontificatus, monasticae vitae, sanctorum, sacrarum imaginum oppugnatores, et pseudomartyres (Antwerp, 1566), p. 820, see also pp. 861–2.

[25] John Bossy, 'The Heart of Robert Persons', in Thomas M. McCoog, SJ (ed.), *The Reckoned Expense: Edmund Campion and the Early English Jesuits* (Woodbridge, Suffolk, 1996), pp. 141–58 (p. 141).

[26] Henry Tichbourne, Letter to Thomas Derbyshire, 2 February 1597, *CSP Domestic Elizabeth 1595–97*, pp. 356–8, item 28. Ronald Corthell, 'Robert Persons and the Writer's Mission', in Arthur F. Marotti (ed.), *Catholicism and Anti-Catholicism in Early-Modern English Texts* (London, 1999), pp. 35–62, argues that Persons's 'authority was obtained through the arts of courtship and argumentation' (p. 35).

[27] On generic questions in the *Actes and Monuments*, see John N. King, 'Fiction and Fact in Foxe's *Book of Martyrs*', in David Loades (ed.), *John Foxe and the English Reformation* (Aldershot: Scolar Press, 1997) , pp. 12–35; Thomas S. Freeman, ' "Great searching out of bookes and autors": John Foxe as an Ecclesiastical Historian' (diss., Rutgers University, 1995), pp. 44–58; Patrick Collinson, 'Truth and Legend: The Veracity of John Foxe's Book of Martyrs' (1985), rpt. in *Elizabethan Essays* (London, 1994), pp. 151–78; D.R. Woolf, 'Erudition and the Idea of History in Renaissance England', *Renaissance Quarterly* 40 (1987): 11–48; 'The Rhetoric of Martyrdom: Generic Contradiction and Narrative Strategy in John Foxe's *Acts and Monuments*', in Thomas Mayer and D.R. Woolf (eds), *The Rhetorics of Life-Writing in Early Modern Europe* (Ann Arbor, 1995), pp. 243–82.

not, is iconoclastic, designed to affirm an entirely new conception of sainthood and its place in the church.[28]

A *Treatise of Three Conversions*, bulky as it is, does not aspire to the status of a full-length ecclesiastical history of England. That place was reserved for the projected *Certamen Ecclesiae Anglicanae*. Next to the *Actes and Monuments*, *A Treatise of Three Conversions* seems cheekily compact. It is essentially a polemical work rather than a history. Despite the title, there is no sequential account of the three conversions; the pleasure Persons gives is not 'the free walke of a story-writer', as Foxe promised,[29] but the enjoyment of witty exposé and the comfort of knowing what is to be gained from reviewing England's spiritual inheritance from Rome. This is evident from the structure of the three volumes. The *Treatise* is divided into three unequal parts: the first two, which take up the first volume only, identify the Church militant as the visible Church of Rome (part I) and not the mythical invisible Church as traced by Foxe (part II). The Church triumphant is purportedly the subject of the third part,[30] the 'examen' of Foxe's mock-calendar of saints and martyrs, which occupies volumes 2 and 3. Foxe's martyrs are excluded from the heavenly company, which consists solely of the Roman saints. The treatise is designed, then, to reassure and comfort the English Catholic faithful, united not only with the true visible Church of the ages, but also with the blessed Church of eternity. Their roots are in the historical Church, and their destiny in the Church of the world to come. Here was a reaffirmation of the traditional formula of the Church militant and triumphant, at a time when the recusants were being intimidated by a Protestant Church of England that claimed to be emerging at last triumphant from invisibility during the dark ages. They were further discouraged by the appearance of hostile and unlikely martyrs who had eclipsed the old familiar saints.

The first volume repairs the breach with Rome, repudiating the notion that true Christianity can exist in England apart from the Holy See. The breach refers primarily to Foxe's denial of the crucial first links, rather than to Henry VIII's secession; Persons treats Henry as fundamentally a Catholic king. Following John Bale, Foxe argued that the Protestant Church of England was descended from the original British Church, because the Roman Church in England had been established only with the conversion of the Saxons by St Augustine.[31] Persons preferred to call the Saxons 'English', and was concerned to attribute the conversion of the Britons, under King Lucius, to the intervention of Pope Eleutherius. The Protestant view was that Lucius' church was independent of

---

[28]   For a fuller discussion of Persons's critique of the *Actes and Monuments*, see Victor Houliston, 'Robert Persons's Comfortable History of England', in Thomas S. Freeman and Thomas F. Mayer (eds), *Martyrs and Martyrdom in England, c. 1400–1700* (Woodbridge, Suffolk, 2007), pp. 180–202.

[29]   *Actes and Monuments* (1596), fol. 645v, cited in *A Treatise of Three Conversions*, vol. 2, p. 79.

[30]   *A Treatise of Three Conversions*, vol. 2, p. 29.

[31]   See Dillon, pp. 329–37, and (on Henry) pp. 338–9.

the papacy, on the grounds that Pope Eleutherius only got involved after being approached by the Britons. Eleutherius notes:

> Ye require of vs the Roman lawes and the emperors to be sent ouer vnto yow, which yow may practise and put in vre within your realme. The Roman lawes and the emperors we may euer reproove: but the law of God we may not. Yow haue receyued of late through Gods mercy in the realme of Britany the law of Christ, &c.[32]

Persons here cites Foxe's translation, which gives precedence to the sovereign work of God in the conversion of the English; the Pope's role is to offer Roman expertise to help to set up a legal infrastructure. If so, Canterbury would seem to have a right to secede and restore the *status quo ante*. Characteristically, Persons turns Foxe's argument upside down. The letter certainly proves that when Pope Eleutherius wrote the letter, Lucius was already a Christian. But it does not prove that he was not converted by Rome. The Pope's letter must be a *second* intervention: he now provides laws for the church he has brought to birth.[33]

It is a moot point. Tellingly, Persons relies on the internal evidence of the letter rather than material from other ecclesiastical historians such as Bede, Geoffrey of Monmouth or Polydore Vergil, as Thomas Stapleton does, when he deals with the same issue.[34] Persons in effect keeps his reader involved with the text itself, thus giving the spiritual obligation to Rome a greater dramatic force. Accordingly, he satirizes the grudging way Foxe concedes some part of the British conversion to the Pope:

> So denieth he the matter, and consider, I pray you, what he attributeth to *Eleutherius* in this conuersion: *Peraduenture* (saith he) *he might help somthing to K. Lucius his conuersion*. And is not this a great matter, especially being qualified (as it is) with the restriction *Peraduenture?* Yf a man should say of Esop's fables, *that peraduenture some of them, in some points might be true:* were it not as much as *Iohn Fox* doth attribute to all this consent of authors for the conuersion vnder *Pope Eleutherius?* ... Yow may mark the diminutiues vsed by Fox to lessen the benefitt, to witt, *Peraduenture, might somthing, &c.* And thereby consider what a holy stomake he hath to Rome.[35]

By contrast with what he sees as mean-minded, grudging ingratitude, Persons aims to make the recusant faithful alive to their glorious inheritance. 'This treatise', he writes in his opening dedicatory epistle, 'doth chiefly and principally belong to yow that are Catholiques, at this day, most woorthy children of so renowned parents, most honorable ofspring of so excellent ancestors, most glorious posterity of so famous antiquity.'[36] Whether they

---

[32] *A Treatise of Three Conversions*, vol. 1, p. 90.
[33] Ibid., vol. 1, p. 93.
[34] Thomas Stapleton, *A Counterblast to M. Hornes Vayne Blast against M. Fekenham ... touching, the Othe of Supremacy* (Louvain, 1567), pp. 395–401.
[35] *A Treatise of Three Conversions*, vol. 1, pp. 87–8.
[36] *A Treatise of Three Conversions*, vol. 1, sig. ¶3v.

thought of their Christian ancestry as British or Saxon, they could hold their heads high. Although Persons's Catholic readers would have to wait for the *Certamen Ecclesiae Anglicanae* for the true monument of their church, *A Treatise of Three Conversions* would comfort his flock, under attack in the present controversy, with a foretaste of the lessons of the *Certamen*.

There is, then, a pastoral purpose underlying the martyrology of *A Treatise of Three Conversions*, polemical as it is. Persons contrasts the self-ordained way Foxe compiled his martyrology with the due process of the primitive Church: 'so ... as to haue speciall care to gather their names, write their actions, note the dayes and places of their sufferings, appoint speciall notaries to attend thervnto, and others to ouersee the same, as deacons and subdeacons ordayned and appointed to that purpose by bishops, as appeareth throughout all antiquitie'.[37] He reviews:

> 1600. yeares, wherin this ship of the Cath. Church hath passed thorow no fewer stormes then there are yeares and ouercome them all [as an excellent shipp well tackled and skilfullie guided, breaketh thorow the waues without hurt at all]; wheras many hundred sects and sectaries in the meane space haue byn broken in peeces, perished and consumed.[38]

This alludes, no doubt, to the nautical metaphor familiar from Foxe's preliminary 'Protestation ... to the true and faithfull congregation of Christes vniuersall Church ... dispersed through the realme of England', with its appeal for unity: 'because God hath so placed vs Englishmen here in one commonwealth, also in one Church, as in one shippe together: let vs not mangle or deuide the shippe'.[39] Further on, Persons repudiates Foxe's offer 'to lay hands on the great illustrious and visible Church of these first 300 yeares'.[40] This reinforces a view of the primitive church as a desirable mansion, so that the search for the authentic church in England is effectively a property dispute.[41] These reassuring figures, the vessel and the edifice, portray the Roman Church as a trustworthy organization, where each Christian has an appointed place.

Persons thus invites his readers, whether they are wavering recusants or thoughtful discreet potential converts, to come home, like the prodigal son. Since the Roman Catholic Church in England has represented Christianity on the island from the earliest times, the recusants are 'at home' while the Protestants are wandering in the wilderness, in exile in the far country:

> Wherfore to avoyd this dangerous and damnable pitt of subuersion and ouerthrow in Christian beleefe, (wherof a man may stand in danger, by so great variety, and contrariety of pretended saincts, as heere yow haue seene represented, in the two former calendars), yf yow would aske my opinion

---

[37]   Ibid., vol. 2, p. 32.

[38]   Ibid., vol. 1, p. 232.

[39]   John Foxe, *Actes and Monuments* (1596), sig. ¶4v.

[40]   *A Treatise of Three Conversions*, vol. 1, p. 323.

[41]   Ibid., vol. 1, sig. **7r. This image is ultimately derived from St Augustine's sermon *contra Donatista*; see Peter Robert Lamont Brown, *Augustine of Hippo: A Biography* (London, 1967), p. 221.

how yt might be done, and how a man might reduce his mynd after so great a tempest of contrary wynds in this behalfe, to a calme and quiett state of deuotion againe, and to the enioying of some sweet peace and tranquillity of conscience, as our forefathers did, and as we were accustomed also to do before we fell into these contentions, my counsell in this case should be, to thinke seriously of the example of the rash and inconsiderate yong man [the prodigal son] ... not much vnlike to him, who by persuasion of heretiks, or sectaryes, and by their continuall clamors, iests, and scoffs against the Popes calendar and saincts therof hath suffered himselfe to be drawne from the reuerent respect and deuotion, which he had vnto them before, and to thinke of new saincts, and so by little and little, to be drawen on, and to be lead by Iohn Fox into this wyld hogge-field of his husked saincts, wherof yow shall feele the lothsome sauour, and behould their foule behauiour afterward ... Wherfore to end this direction, I would wish the discreet Christian reader to be deluded no longer with these new fancyes, but to returne rather to the stepps of his forefathers in this behalfe, and to resolue to follow the same for the time to come, and to double his deuotion towards the honour of Christs frends in heauen, for the maledictions, slaunders, and calumniations which he hath heard vttered against them by new fangled heretiks.[42]

The term 'wyld hogge-field of ... husked saincts' is more than abusive; it implies how Foxe has missed the point of martyrology: the stories of martyrs are not intended to arouse indignation or stir up combat so much as to strengthen the faithful in an orderly structure of virtuous life. It is as if Foxe's writings have stirred up the passions – of enmity, false pity and hatred, antagonisms on both sides – thus drawing even the most sober-thinking English Christian away from home, from a restful state of devotion and good works, to a far country where ultimately there is no nutrition for the soul.

Foxe's pseudo-martyrs, then, are characterized by human, fleshly passions, as in the case of Savonarola, who, 'being of a hoate & cholericke nature' indulged it rather than subdued it, 'and preached so vehemently against them, that were his aduersaryes, as also scandalously, & with ouer much bitternes'.[43] In such a context, constancy is really a passionate stubbornness. Roman martyrs tried to imitate Christ, who went as a lamb to the slaughter; consequently, they appear unmoved by their sufferings. Foxe's heroes are flesh and blood people who fight and argue and protest. They are subject to the human weakness of playing to the gallery, with their cheeky rejoinders. Robert Smith, for example, was called the Controller, 'for commonly he controlled all that was spoken by others'. Here he challenges Bishop Edmund Bonner:

Bonner:	By my troth, *Maister Speaker*, you shall preach at the stake.
Smith:	Well sworne, my Lord, yow keep a good watch.
Bonner:	Well, *Maister Controller*, I am no Sainct.
Smith:	No, my Lord, nor yet good Bishopp.[44]

---

[42] 'A direction and instruction for vse of the two calendars', *A Treatise of Three Conversions*, vol. 2, pp. 2–3, 20–21.

[43] *A Treatise of Three Conversions*, vol. 2, pp. 454–5.

[44] Cited in *A Treatise of Three Conversions*, vol. 3, pp. 114, 116.

Foxe praises his martyrs for their combative qualities, whereas Persons commends the saints and martyrs for their constructive works of piety. His pattern of Christian exercise is based on freedom from controversy; it entails a constant struggle against the world and the flesh. In *A Treatise of Three Conversions*, as in *The Christian Directory*, he emphasizes right practice rather than right belief:

> But the principall cause and reason [for writing *The Christian Directory*] was, to the ende our countrye men might have some one sufficient direction for matters of life and spirit, among so manye bookes of controversies as have ben writen, and are in writing dailye. The whiche bookes, albeit in thes our troublesome and quarrelous times be necessarie for defence of our faith, againste so manye seditious innovations, as are now attempted: yet helpe they litle oftentymes to good lyfe, but rather do fill the heades of men with a spirite of contradiction and contention, that for the most parte hindereth devotion, which devotion is nothinge els, but a quiet and peaceble state of the sowle, endewed with a joyful promptnes to the diligent execution of all thinges that appartayne to the honour of God.[45]

This is an ideal of sanctity – the resolved life – quite antithetical to what Persons deprecates in Foxe. He admires the Fathers for invoking the help of the saints in the struggle and for venerating those very saints primarily for their 'heroicall actions'.[46] He chastises Foxe for failing to mention 'one eminent act' in the lives of his martyrs, 'ether of chasteninge their bodyes, mortifyinge their appetits, contemning the world and pleasures therof'.

The attitude to asceticism in *A Treatise of Three Conversions* is complex. In response to a perceived under-valuation of self-denial in Foxe, Persons re-affirms the virtues of mortification and virginity. Here, for example, he contrasts St Polycarp and John Hooper:

> *Polycarpe* was a great faster and louer of penance: this man, of good cheere and liberty. *Polycarpe* was a great prayser and obseruer of chastity; this man had his Burgundian sister to keep him dayly company ... [Hooper confessed] also plainly by his speach afterward, that himselfe had not the gift to lyue chast, no not in those old dayes of his, nor when he was in prison & tribulation, and shortly after like to be burned. Such was the perfection euen of these most principall Foxian Saints and Martyrs.[47]

The Protestant martyr gives appetite free reign. Again, Persons celebrates virginity by analogy:

> What difference is there betweene our Church, and them in purity of proceeding? Surely no lesse, then betweene a most honest house or exact monastery of Religious women, that admitt none to their cohabitation, but

---

[45] *The First Booke of the Christian Exercise*, 'To the Christian Reader', p. 5. Quotations from the 1582 version are taken from *The Christian Directory (1582): The First Booke of the Christian Exercise, appertayning to Resolution*, ed. Victor Houliston (Leiden, 1998).

[46] *A Treatise of Three Conversions*, vol. 2, pp. 8, 11.

[47] Ibid., vol. 2, pp. 318, 321.

pure and vnspotted Virgins: and a stewes or brodell house, that imbraceth all broken, stayned, or corrupt people, without difference whatsoeuer.[48]

The primary point is of doctrinal uniformity as opposed to the motley collection of 'Foxian' saints. Persons denounces the married clergy as 'men giuen to ther sensualityes both of women, and other like their commodityes, after the fashion of other ordinary men'. Yet this does not amount to a recommendation of an ascetically monkish life, but of a vigorous life of active service, for he goes on to demand, in any true martyr, a 'supernaturall concurrence of God with their actions'.[49]

Persons is not here concerned with miracles, which are seldom mentioned in the work. The formation of the Catholic Christian takes precedence, in *A Treatise of Three Conversions*, over extraordinary or sensational sanctity. Although they might incur the wrath of secular or heretical authorities, the saints in the Roman calendar do not seek martyrdom or even, necessarily, to confront evil structures. Persons himself was sensitive about having taken flight at the time of Campion's arrest and execution, and it is hard to believe that he did not have this in mind when he pointed out how the ancient martyrs, too, often preferred flight: 'much more godly and wisely wrote *Saint Athanasius* to the contrary, in the next age after, in a booke of his owne flight and exile vnder Arrians, shewing by diuerse proofes both of scripture and of practize in the apostles themselues, that it is lawfull to flie in tyme of persecution'.[50] Here too one recognizes the advocacy – surprising, perhaps, in so vigorous and combative a Jesuit as Persons – of quietness, the ideal of a church spacious enough for all. There may be a struggle to establish this, a struggle in which there will be heroes, but the final purpose is to establish a space where piety may be practised in peace. Thus, after the examen of the calendar, Persons describes 'the Catholike man' at length.[51] Very little of the work actually deals with the true saints and martyrs; it uses the *Actes and Monuments* as a foil for the life all Catholics are called to lead.

***

The constructive dimension of *A Treatise of Three Conversions* comes even more clearly into focus when we consider it in relation to the development of *The Christian Directory*. Persons had republished the 1585 version, *A Christian Directorie*, in 1598,[52] and was to revise the work again for publication in 1607.[53] In the process, he seemed to find it difficult to make up his mind about the two long chapters he added near the beginning of *A Christian Directorie*: 'That there is a God' (ch. 2) and 'Confirmations of Christian religion' (ch. 4).

---

[48] Ibid., vol. 2, p. 359.
[49] Ibid., vol. 2, p. 84.
[50] Ibid., vol. 2, p. 40.
[51] Ibid., vol. 3, pp. 461–64 [*vere* 474].
[52] *A Christian Directorie Guiding men to their Salvation* (Rouen, 1585; rpt. Louvain, 1598).
[53] *The Christian Directory Guiding men to eternall salvation* (St Omer, 1607).

At the beginning of *A Treatise of Three Conversions*, he discussed the form of argument used in these two chapters. The first was based on pure reason, he wrote, and the second on 'suppositional demonstration'. The latter form characterized *A Treatise of Three Conversions*.[54] With this connection in mind, we can appreciate that the later work is a natural extension of the argument of *A Christian Directorie*, as revised in 1585. The man or woman in pursuit of resolution needs first to be convinced, by pure reason, that God exists, and then (by arguments more probable than inescapable) that Christianity is the true religion, and finally (by the same kind of probable arguments) that Roman Catholicism is the authentic form of English Christianity. But if *A Treatise of Three Conversions* was a ramification of the earlier work, it also suggested that this line of argument was superfluous to the purposes of *The Christian Directory*. Instead of allowing the motives for resolution to proliferate, Persons could reduce this part of the work and begin to think of parts II and III, on making the resolution and bringing it to perfection. This may help to explain why Persons decided to cut the two chapters in question from the 1607 version.

The notion of 'suppositional demonstration' provides a key to the manner of *A Treatise of Three Conversions*. Persons may have derived this logical category from the lectures of John Rainolds delivered at Oxford during Persons's career there.[55] What is proved beyond dispute by reason alone, Persons argues, precludes a 'free assent of faith',[56] so what he will offer is a combination of revelation, 'credible proofs' and reason, all of it depending on the pure affection of the reader. Here he seems to be influenced by the Aristotelian insistence that rhetorical discourse concerns itself with credible rather than absolute proof, an insistence brilliantly elaborated by John Rainolds. With this kind of evidence, purely individual judgment is inadequate: as Persons puts it, 'neyther he nor we, as particular men, ought to iudge of these things: but the Catholike Church, which by her bishops and pastors do examine the proofes weight and moment of euery one of these things that fall out'.[57] Foxe (he claims) operates on quite the opposite principle, as for example in his treatment of Wyclif and his followers: 'The Parlament saith, that they preached heresies and notorious errors: but Iohn Foxe saith, it was true Christian doctrine.'[58] Persons wishes to move his treatise out of the combat zone of mere assertion and counter-assertion, preferring a more leisurely mode where the receptive reader is open to 'suppositional demonstration' guaranteed by the consensual wisdom of the Church.

Persons's confidence in a stable Roman ideal informs the style of *A Treatise of Three Conversions*. Buoyed up by the conviction of such a legacy, he promises

---

[54] *A Treatise of Three Conversions*, vol. 1, sigs. ***7v–8v.

[55] Lawrence D. Green (introd.), *John Rainolds's Oxford Lectures on Aristotle's 'Rhetoric'* (Newark, 1986), esp. pp. 64–76.

[56] *A Treatise of Three Conversions*, vol. 1, sig. ***8r.

[57] Ibid., vol. 1, p. 430.

[58] Ibid., vol. 1, p. 498.

much matter of 'gratefull variety both of tymes, men, and affaires',[59] drawing freely on the full range of historical matter to provide an unforced diversity, 'not indeed so much … to delight, as to moove and profit thee'.[60] He uses the analogy of London cloth-sellers to contrast his exposition of English church history with Foxe's. One displays his whole cloth freely at midday, while the other foxily offers glimpses of his fragmentary wares in dark corners.[61]

In comparison with the *Actes and Monuments*, and with his own *Certamen*, Persons's *Treatise of Three Conversions* is of modest proportions. It is, nevertheless, his most substantial printed work. In the context of his commitment to the English mission it represents his supreme effort to encourage and unify a recusant community that had not only suffered long persecution but considerable internal tension since the death of William Cardinal Allen in 1594. They were divided over the succession, over the question of loyalism and over the archpriest. When Persons began the *Treatise* in 1602 – the preface to the first volume is dated Christmas Eve, 1602 – the long wait for the Queen's demise was almost over; by the time he completed it in 1604, James's succession was assured, with dubious hope of relief for Catholics. Never had the English Catholic community been in greater need of comfort.

Just how influential the *Treatise* was, it is hard to assess. Anne Dillon judges that it came too late and was too implicated in Persons's polemical agenda about toleration and conformity to counter the anti-Romanist propaganda effectively. The debate about persecution was overtaken by the Gunpowder Plot and its aftermath, and Persons's own interest in English history got diverted into a contestation with Coke over ecclesiastical jurisdiction and the common law. But Persons's opponents did take notice. Matthew Sutcliffe wrote two outraged volumes in response. One reader took the time to check Persons's tally of saints in the two calendars and inscribed his findings in a copy of the *Actes and Monuments*.[62] John Strype, the ecclesiastical historian, indignantly challenged what Persons had to say about Cranmer; ultimately, he was moved to write a biography himself.[63] Edward Gibbon owned a copy, which suggests that by the eighteenth century it had achieved some measure of notoriety.[64]

* * *

A Treatise of Three Conversions projected onto the Catholic community at the very beginning of James's reign, the identity of the true visible church in

---

[59]   Ibid., vol. 1, sig. **8v.

[60]   D.R. Woolf argues that Foxe imposes 'figure[s] of sameness' on the diversity of his narrative, in 'The Rhetoric of Martyrdom: Generic Contradiction and Narrative Strategy in John Foxe's *Acts and Monuments*', pp. 258ff.

[61]   *A Treatise of Three Conversions*, vol. 1, pp. 629–30.

[62]   See Victor Houliston, 'The Martyr Tallies: Robert Persons and his Anonymous Respondent', in David Loades (ed.), *John Foxe at Home and Abroad* (Aldershot, 2004), pp. 47–50.

[63]   John Strype, *Memorials of the Most Reverend Father in God, Thomas Cranmer* (London, 1694), 'Epistle Dedicatory', sig. B1v. I am indebted to Thomas S. Freeman for the latter reference.

[64]   Geoffrey Keynes, *The Library of Edward Gibbon* (London, 1980), p. 214.

England, inheriting the holiness and fortitude of the early Saxon plantation. What Persons's next work did was to add a legal confirmation of the doctrinal and moral character of the recusant flock. In this respect it was not irrelevant that *A Treatise of Three Conversions* and *An Answere to the Fifth Parte of Cokes Reportes* were written in the context of the appointment of the archpriest. Institutional establishment was not the Jesuits' first concern – they tended to be much more interested in spiritual formation – yet Persons was beginning to see a new, purified but ultimately unchanged Catholic Church emerging from the Elizabethan persecution, and it was a church to which he ascribed not only purity of life and integrity of doctrine, but an inalienable right to be fully Roman.

Much Reformation historiography was concerned with pedigree and continuity. Protestants tried to trace their roots to Noah, or the primitive church or the British, pre-Saxon church, uncovering the 'true gospel church' that had all but disappeared in the days of the whore of Babylon. The Reformers' alternative was the apocalyptic woman clothed in the sun who had gone into the wilderness, only to re-emerge, manifest in the pre-Reformation sects – Wycliffites, Albigensians, Hussites, Lollards – and finally in the Protestant Reformation.[65] Catholics gloried in the visible known church. But there is also a sense in which Catholic historiography could appropriate the Protestant plot. With James established on the throne of England, the Protestant Church of England was entrenched. The true Catholic Church had gone underground and become a remnant. Robert Persons thus had a story to tell of the gradual suppression of true, Roman Catholicism in England. The story does not start with the Henrician suppression but with the whittling away of papal jurisdiction during the Middle Ages.

The story may best be understood by considering Persons's critique of what to him was a fraudulent shadow story told by Coke in *The Fift Part of the Reports*.[66] Coke wrote of a wedge of gold that lay in obscurity. The only way you could identify the true, hidden church was to use the 'touch-stone, the scripture'. In effect this meant, commented Persons, that the individual, interpreting Scripture for himself, made himself the 'touch-maister and Iudge' over the church, instead of allowing himself to be directed by mother church.[67] The golden age of the primitive church had been turned, by Coke's analysis, into the leaden age of medieval superstition. In Persons's view, this was a perverse new form of alchemy: 'And how then could come in this transfusion, and transmutation of gold into lead, which you dreame of?' If we reverse the terms of this analogy, for Persons the visible known church of the Catholic

---

[65]   Rev. 12:1. The motif is developed by Edmund Spenser in *The Faerie Queene* (London, 1590), book I, canto iii.

[66]   Sir Edward Coke, *The Fift Part of the Reports of Sr. Edward Coke Knight, the Kings Attorney Generall: Of divers Resolutions and Iudgments given upon great deliberation, in matters of great importance & consequence by the reverend Iudges and Sages of the Law: together with the reasons and causes of the Resolutions and Iudgements* (London, 1605).

[67]   *An Answere to Coke*, 'The Epistle Dedicatory to Syr Edward Cooke Knight', paragraphs 20, 24, 32, 33.

Middle Ages was all of gold, refined and purified by the Holy See of St Peter. The Reformers wanted to hide the gold, both by rewriting the history of the church and by suppressing the papal connection.

Persons's response to Coke consisted of writing English history as a progression of baleful measures to diminish papal influence in the realm. What for Coke was a blessed narrative of increasing freedom from papal ecclesiastical jurisdiction, inherent in the common law and becoming more and more clearly apparent, was for Persons an accumulation of *de facto* restrictions on a jurisdiction that remained valid *de iure*. Henry VIII was proclaimed head of the English Church by statute, by a violent, self-authorized interruption of tradition, not by some happy efflorescence of the common law.

Persons's agenda, then, was to reverse Coke's story. By interpreting all measures to restrict papal power as occasional, limited and targeted at specific local and temporary inconveniences, and not as bold assertions of an intrinsic English liberty from Rome (precedents of the Henrician secession), he could once more uncover the radiance of the English Catholic Church. *De facto* – that is, superficially – the Christian commonwealth of England seemed increasingly autonomous; but *de iure* the Roman connection was as strong as ever, even after it had been denied by statute.[68] By rights, England as a faith community still belonged to Rome. For Persons there was also a golden age. In the centuries immediately following the conversion of the Anglo-Saxons, the warmth of devotion was such that there was an intimate bond with Rome. Persons wrote of 'the acknowledgement and exercise of the Popes authority in those dayes, as also the deuoute and prompt obedience of our Christian Kings and Prelates therevnto, in that holy time of our first primitiue Church'.[69] Although this was weakened and obscured in the course of time by self-serving monarchs, it was still alive as an inspiration to the recusants.

The Reformation, then, could be viewed as merely completing a dishonest process of denying the link with Rome. As such denials were usually opportunistic, the Reformation always appears, in Persons's writing, fatally compromised by considerations of personal advantage. That is why he develops a critique of Protestant polemic as wilfully deceitful. It is not just that Protestant apologists get their facts wrong, misinterpret them or commit logical flaws in argument. Nor is it a question only of misrepresenting Catholic practice or dogma – although Persons counters both these aspects of Protestant writing. It is that these writers falsify the evidence under circumstances that make the conclusion inescapable that they must have known what they were doing. Persons's exposure of this comes to a climax in his two books against Thomas Morton arising out of the trial of Garnet and continuing the debate with Hastings and Sutcliffe over the treasonableness of recusancy. But it is against Coke that he makes the most strategic argument. He has a very ironical view of Coke's much-vaunted impartiality:

---

[68]   Ibid., pp. 63–4.
[69]   Ibid., p. 135.

There followeth the same title to knitt vp the page, this pleasing sentence of *Cicero* in his Tusculane questions. *Quid enim laboro, nisi vt veritas in omni questione explicetur, verum dicentibus facile cedem?* What doe I endeuour, but that the truth should be laied open in euery question, with resolution to yeld to them that shall speake the truth. This sentence (I say) giueth mee great comforte, yf *M. Attorney* will doe as he insinuateth, and follow the indifference of his Author alleaged, who in the matters he handled (which were of philosophye) is knowne to haue byn so equall, as he was not well resolued, what part to take. Yet doe I not exact, so much equality in this our controuersie of diuinitie (presuming my aduersary to be preoccupated with the preiudice of one parte) but shall rest well satisfied with his desire, to haue the truth examined in euery point; and much more with his readines, to yeeld vnto her, whersoeuer she shall be founde.[70]

Coke, after all, was attorney-general. He was engaged in a very important project, reinterpreting English legal history in such a way as to shape the future of legislation. If Persons could effectively expose the fraud that Coke was perpetrating, misleading king and parliament, he could strike a major blow for recusancy, that is, upholding papal jurisdiction as so embedded in the English legal tradition that no-one could reasonably deny the right to refuse to attend divine worship not sanctioned by the Pope.

An Answere to Coke was thus a vital plank in the platform of a form of resistance that assumes a moral right to toleration. There was no need to bargain or negotiate. Because papal ecclesiastical jurisdiction had been illegally denied, by mere force of the king's will, those who continued to uphold it stood in a position of distinct legal advantage. In *A Conference about the Next Succession* Persons assumed a relationship between church and state that demanded, as the priority of government, royal care for the state of the Catholic Church in England as the priority of rule. Even if the monarch did not accept this brief, recusants were informed that to settle for anything less was a betrayal. Under a hostile regime, this was their due, an obligation firmly underscored by history. In *An Answere to Coke* Persons carefully defined what he meant by the illegitimacy of the penalties faced by Catholics. It is here that the point is made that recusancy does not imply rejection of the monarch's basic right to rule. Referring to Elizabeth, Persons says that if Catholics believed her to be an unlawful monarch, this would release them from the obligation to be recusants. A lawful monarch should not command subjects to attend heretical worship. It is therefore incumbent on Catholics, as faithful subjects, to signify the unlawfulness of the laws enforcing church attendance. If the queen were unlawful, obeying her commands on matters of religion would signify nothing, because there is no implied religious contract between her and her subjects: church attendance would simply mean bowing to *force majeure*.[71]

Besides reinforcing the Catholic conscience, *An Answere to Coke* fleshed out Persons's understanding of the institutional church, especially in its legal dimension. In Calvin's *Institutes of the Christian Religion* scholastic confidence

---

[70]   Ibid., pp. 1–2.
[71]   Ibid., p. 372.

in reason is combined with Protestant confidence in the authority of Scripture to place the practice of Christian religion on a (to him) unassailable foundation.[72] These institutes are, so to speak, foundational. For Persons, the historically authenticated church provides the foundational institutes. The life of religion originates with the faith community to whom Jesus entrusted his Spirit and his teachings. Persons frequently uses terms like 'wellspring' and 'source' to register his sense of origins, and explains

> The origen of spirituall power comming not by this way of the people, nor being giuen to them at all, but immediatly by Christ our Sauiour to his Apostles, and their Successours, Bishops and Prelates, by lawfull Ordination and Succession of Priesthood, and imposition of hands to the end of the world; no temporall Tutors, or Administrators could rightly get into this authority, except they were first made Priests.[73]

To have those teachings – or some of them – without the sanction of holy church was to have the form of religion without the power thereof. Even Scripture, outside the church, lost its power to give life.[74] Hence the fatal consequences of breaking with Rome. More than this – and this is why the history of the English monarchy is so important – there is a contract between king and people to sustain the church and support it in its role of giving spiritual life to the people. Persons's historiography seeks to interrogate how kings and queens variously failed in this task: tyrannical or unjust rule, for instance, affected the conditions necessary for leading a fully devoted life (for anyone other than a confessor or martyr, that is). Illegitimacy of title – considered in *A Conference about the Next Succession* – rendered the original contract itself invalid and thus deprived the church of lawful support. *A Treatise of Three Conversions* implied that Foxe's elevation of pseudo-martyrs blackened the name of kings and queens whose legitimate power and authority had strengthened the church and supported the truth. Kings who chipped away at the pope's ecclesiastical supremacy, as celebrated by Coke, weakened or even strangled the lifeline to Rome. 'I am the vine; ye are the branches. Abide in me', Christ said, signifying the unity of the church, abiding in the viceregency of the pope. It is thus by hard work on the historical evidence of the compact between Catholic religion and the body politic that Persons emerges with a powerful idea of 'the true ancient birth-right, and best inheritance of English subiects indeed ... their right to Catholique religion'. Referring to his own historical researches, he declared that 'for seeking out and cleering the euidence of this right, [we] ought to be diligent, and to spare no labour, paine, or industrie'.[75] Here he was deliberately challenging Coke, who celebrated the Englishman's birthright

---

[72] Jean Calvin, *Institutes of the Christian Religion*, ed. J.T. McNeill; trans. F.L. Battles; The Library of the Christian Classics, 20–21 (2 vols; London, 1961), first published as *Christianae religionis institutio* (Basle, 1536) and finally revised in 1559.

[73] *An Answere to Coke*, p. 358.

[74] Ibid., p. 8.

[75] Ibid., pp. 16–17.

as the liberties of the common law. Persons denied that papal claims robbed Englishmen of their birthright.

There is, then, in Persons's enquiry in *An Answere to Coke* a combination of historical diligence and logical simplicity. This can be illustrated in his view of Elizabeth's legal position *vis-à-vis* the church. The idea of her exercising ecclesiastical supremacy is so absurd, even to serious Protestants, that there is no need to negotiate with the practical reality. The absurdity, comical as it is, is enforced both logically and historically. A woman cannot rule in the church, but no monarch has that right in any case. Persons's theory and practice have a very simple logical base, assuming that Rome's ecclesiastical supremacy represents natural law.[76] This presupposition derives from divine ordinance, not historical accident – but it is manifest in the historical instances that Persons analyses. It was essential, in this regard, for Persons to demonstrate that his examples outnumbered Coke's. In particular he paid attention to Anglo-Saxon precedents.[77] Thus for Persons there is a fusion of history and logic: natural law and the definition of the true universal church are demonstrable both logically and historically. Thus his simplicity, such as it is, is the simplicity of a clear, thorough programme, and one that has historical reach and purchase.

For a man so deeply involved in practical politics and affairs – some would simply call it 'intrigue' – Persons may seem to us singularly naive. He had an unshakeable faith in the role of the papacy, not because he was unaware of human fallibility, but because he was only too conscious of it and believed that the only remedy lay in the structures of the Catholic Church, guaranteed by the guidance of the Holy Spirit and by the accumulated weight of history and learning. The fact that he was a Jesuit definitely helped: the organization operated on a purely logical understanding of the purpose of human life before God and the means of achieving that end. The ideal is simple, and it has only an incidental connection with immediate political advantage, in the sense of advantage for the Jesuits themselves. There is a paradox here: the power and influence of the Jesuits derived from their capacity to put Christians in touch with the reality of their faith; yet the Jesuits were always being accused of serving their own interest – which was to promote this work most effectively and with the fewest hindrances.

Here we touch on the secret of Persons's historical imagination. He had an Ignatian model of the church in society; he sees England as the place where such a church could materialize – not by *creatio ex nihilo* but by distilling the truth of English history. From this point of view we could say that he has a teleological interpretation of history, and that *A Memorial for the Reformation of England* is the goal to which all tends. This furnishes another reason why, in *An Answere to Coke*, he is anxious to separate the two jurisdictions. By separating the sword of St Peter and the sword of Constantine he allows for their cooperation, rather than conflict between them. He has no desire for

---

[76]   Arnold Pritchard, *Catholic Loyalism in Elizabethan England* (London, 1979), pp. 60–61.

[77]   Donna B. Hamilton, 'Catholic Use of Anglo-Saxon Precedents, 1565–1625', *Recusant History* 26 (2003): 537–55, esp. p. 547.

Rome to have temporal jurisdiction in England, any more than he wants the English king to have ecclesiastical supremacy: 'It is ... a manifest fallacie', he pronounces, 'to saie, *he hath spirituall iurisdiction ouer me*, and *therfore also temporal*; which followeth not, and much lesse the contrarie; *he hath temporall Authoritie ouer any* ergo *spiritual also*'.[78] The division does not imply an equality, much less a rivalry. When a king abuses the exercise of temporal jurisdiction, he can be called to account, not because the pope has temporal power but because the spiritual welfare of the people is at stake. With the hope of a Catholic monarch gone, the separation restores one dimension of the hoped-for compact between church and state. If Persons is successful in establishing that the combination of the two powers – temporal and spiritual – is the work of statute, then he can force the two powers apart again (from the point of view of legitimacy) and so infer the design of a complementing of the two powers from the course of English history.[79] Later, in the debate over the oath of allegiance, he was to claim that James's apologists had effectively ceded this point.

There is another connection between the *Memorial* and *An Answere to Coke*, apart from seeing them as end and means. Both have a strongly satirical dimension. Michael Carrafiello rightly points out that the *Memorial* exposes the results of the 'arrogation of ecclesiastical power' by the monarchy.[80] These are the abuses that have to be reformed. As utopian discourse the *Memorial* thus extends the satirical programme of the *Philopater*, while *An Answere to Coke* offers an historical portrait of political vice and virtue in the monarchy's legal relations with the church. History and satire reinforce each other. The more Rome can do for England, the more she flourishes; leave everything to royal appointment and the nation suffers. We have, then, in the period 1590–1606, a nexus of history, satire and political theory in Persons's writing, all of it concerned with the position of the Roman Church in the commonwealth. It must be the Roman Church, whatever the nationality of the commonwealth. This is not to deny national character; indeed, Persons's deepest yearning, as it manifests itself in his correspondence and the tone of crucial passages in his printed works, is to bring to birth an English Church that will show the world what England can do for Christ, if only England will allow Rome to be the midwife.

***

England became a Protestant realm, permanently as it turned out, in 1558, when Persons was only 12, a Taunton schoolboy. He must have been aware of the national change of religion, but since he (and some of his family) only

---

[78] *An Answere to Coke*, p. 40.

[79] The royal proclamation of 5 November 1602 explicitly denied any such division of jurisdictions. See Pritchard, pp. 128–9; and *Tudor Royal Proclamations* (3 vols; New Haven, 1964–69), vol. 3, p. 254.

[80] Michael L. Carrafiello, *Robert Parsons and English Catholicism, 1580–1610* (Selinsgrove, 1998), p. 87.

adopted a strongly Roman Catholic identity years later, he presumably had little personal memory of Catholic life under Mary. From the time of his conversion in 1574 he spent most of his life in exile in Catholic countries abroad. Even as he was receiving detailed reports of developments by way of Verstegan's *Advices from England* from 1576 onwards,[81] he was experiencing at first hand the cooperation and conflicts of ecclesiastical, secular and military leaders in France, Belgium, Spain and Italy. He was engaged in high-level scheming and planning, and was even asked by Pope Paul V to draw up a prospectus for the reconversion of Northern Europe. His close ties with Possevino and Aldebrandino made him politically well-informed and astute. He was also familiar with the political theory of Francesco Suarez and Robert Bellarmine.

Persons was thus in a particularly advantageous position to envisage what Catholic England might be. In large part this was predicated on an interpretation of what Catholic England had been, or at least had aspired to in the past. There was in his view of English history a certain level of anachronism, as he projected onto the past a theory of kingship that had been developed by contemporary continental Jesuits, but this anachronism existed in dialogue with Protestant polemicists such as Foxe, Sutcliffe and Coke who with equal if not greater anachronism imaged English history as proto-Protestant.[82] Like them, he had a strong interest in the future, believing that a true Catholic restoration – or reformation – in England would bring to fruition all that was noblest in her past. Even though he continued writing history after the accession of James VI and I, when the disappointing manifestation of the new king's intentions had made it clear that England was not to have a Catholic monarch for the foreseeable future, his sense of what England's history implied about her true identity as a nation supported a strongly resistant ideology, unwilling to be incorporated into a Protestant state, however lenient it was prepared to be.

Persons's political theory was not of itself original or innovative, although it gained nuance by application to history and by confrontation with the emergent absolutist discourse emanating from France. He understood there to be an unwritten contract between prince and people that the monarch was obliged to uphold the doctrine of the true Church, to complement her in the struggle against vice and crime, and to patronize her in her work of sanctification. Happy the nation whose king put the spiritual state of his subjects above all other considerations. Though the blood of the martyrs was the seed of the Church, a much more cooperative relationship between Church and state was assumed to be the norm. Indeed, the veneration of true martyrs was part of the conversation by which the Church in its piety kept up the pressure on kings to perform their function as defenders of the faith.

Just what this theory – which was substantially that of Suarez – meant for the deposition of heretical monarchs was a matter of debate, and Persons's

---

[81]   A.C.F. Beales, *Education Under Penalty: English Catholic Education from the Reformation to the Fall of James II* (London, 1963), p. 68.

[82]   F.J. Levy, *Tudor Historical Thought* (San Marino, Calif., 1967), p. x.

words and actions were somewhat contradictory and erratic. It is in this area that he was – and is – most vulnerable to criticism, and much of his black reputation stems from his political activism. But what concerns us here is his use of history to intervene in the late Elizabethan and early Jacobean debate over the fashioning of the commonwealth. Persons's histories are cast in rhetorical form, lively and combative, and in each case the form is significant. The dialogue of *A Conference about the Next Succession* embodies the principle of 'indifference' by which the Catholic ideal of monarchy overshadows individual claims. By cleaning up the calendar, *A Treatise of Three Conversions* anticipates the redemption of time a new order would bring. And Coke's falsifications, as Persons sees them, epitomize the corruption of the English Church by temporal considerations.

If Persons's rhetoric adds a dimension to history, it is the commendation of an Ignatian perspective on public responsibility. He is never content merely to establish historical truth or falsehood: he is concerned to vivify the Catholic spirit he sees at work in historical events. Given that it is the Christian's business to be resolved in the service of God, every faculty subordinated to the greater glory of God, the question is: how is political power best applied to enable men and women to practise the vocation of their baptism? We find in all three works an urgent probing of the past to find the hand of God cooperating with those who do not let expediency stand in the way of the life enjoined in *The Christian Directory*. Effectively, this means giving the Church support in the work of spiritual nurturing. We could say, then, that Persons's historiography is primarily clerical in bias, except that the Church is always seen as a means to an end. There is some emphasis on the honour of the clerical estate, and we are constantly reminded that the temporal exists for the sake of the spiritual, so that respect is demanded for Rome's pre-eminence, but the final end is to release the energies that encourage the practice of virtue.

Although Persons as historian is unquestionably a polemicist, it is important to recognize that he writes deliberately in a humanist rhetorical tradition that prizes dialogue, encomium and logical coherence rather than atomistic refutation. He finds room for an ample and measured praise of those who have used secular power to promote the kingdom of God. The genres of his historical works associate them with the practice of 'counsel to princes', and he had real hopes of influencing royal policy. He was not merely concerned to demonstrate that Rome was the true Church; he was determined to prove what made a true king. He dedicated *A Conference about the Next Succession* to Essex, embarrassing the Earl, whose sympathies were unreliable, but advertising an association with an idealistic rather than an expedient style of courtesy.[83] *A Treatise of Three Conversions* was dedicated first to Elizabeth and then to James, not only appealing for recognition but also commending

---

[83] In the 1590s these were the terms associated with Essex and Burghley respectively. Persons denounced Burghley in *Elizabethae Angliae Reginae haeresim Caluinianum propugnantis, saeuissimum in Catholicos sui regni edictum ... Cum responsione ad singula capita* (Antwerp, 1592; see above, Chapter 3) and dedicated his next major book, *A Conference about the Next Succession*, to Essex.

a self-knowledge that would confess a fuller conception of kingship. In *An Answere to Coke* Persons invokes an ideal of integrity by which both attorney-general and King would submit to truth above all. The argument is not limited to ecclesiastical convenience.

The reach of Persons's rhetoric is such that his history makes myth. He counters the Protestant myth with its providentialist reading of history. The Tudors brought England civil peace and religious reform. Exploiting the romances of chivalry, writers such as Sidney and Spenser connected English Protestantism with King Arthur: the British Church, truer to primitive tradition than the later Saxon Church, had re-emerged under Henry VIII. Autonomy from Rome could actually be detected from the earliest days, and the antecedents of modern English liberty could be tracked, in Coke's *Reports*, through the intervening centuries. Persons, instead, constructed a myth of England as glorious and prosperous only when kings fulfilled their obligations as defenders of the faith, when the Church militant, publicly and recognizably directed by the Holy See, was visibly aligned with the Church triumphant: Kings paid tribute to the Pope on earth and the saints in heaven. No pseudo-martyrs inhibited the economy of grace by which the spiritual health of the present was derived from the sacrifices of the past – an economy that was properly managed by the universal Church in its authority and discernment. Nor were the channels of grace impaired, when England was at her best, by expedient suspensions of papal jurisdiction.

Recusancy thrived on this myth. Persons set great store by continuity with an heroic past. In doing so his vision of the English mission chimed with that of Edmund Campion, who wrote, in the most frequently quoted passage of recusant prose:

> And touching our Societie, be it known to you that we have made a league – all the Jesuits in the world, whose succession and multitude must overreach all the practices of England – cheerfully to carry the cross you shall lay on us, and never to despair your recovery, while we have a man left to enjoy your Tyburn, or to be racked with your torments, or consumed with your prisons. The expense is reckoned, the enterprise is begun; it is of God, it cannot be withstood. So the faith was planted, so it must be restored.[84]

The mission would replicate the earlier conversions. Persons's appeal to history thus cuts both ways; he recreates English Church history – and the political and legal adjuncts to it – in the mould of the militancy of the Catholic Reformation; and he takes inspiration for the present struggle from the primitive British and Saxon Church. The restoration Campion anticipates is implicit in the history Persons writes, because all past departures from the ideal are marked as predictors of what needs to change. England's Catholic destiny is inscribed in her fallen past.

---

[84]   *Campion's Brag*, article viii, reprinted in E.E. Reynolds, *Campion and Parsons: The Jesuit Mission of 1580–1* (London, 1980), p. 80.

CHAPTER SIX

A Jesuit Apologia: Appellant Abuse

During the same period when Persons was writing a past for the English Catholic community, he was involved in the controversy with his fellow Catholic clergy that has done much to shape his reputation down to the present day: the archpriest controversy. Persons's situation at the turn of the sixteenth century needs to be understood if we are to appreciate the rhetorical strategies and preoccupations that inform his two anti-appellant treatises, *A Briefe Apologie, or Defence of the Catholike Ecclesiastical Hierarchie in England* and *A Manifestation of the Great Folly and bad spirit of certayne secular priestes*,[1] two works that contain some of his best and most sustained, passionate writing yet do not readily attract the modern reader's sympathy.[2] In 1597, soon after his return from Spain, Persons settled for the time being the strife in the English College, Rome. In so doing he showed masterly negotiating skills, extraordinary patience and strength of character, and he was duly appointed Rector of the college, a position he was to hold for the rest of his life.[3] This meant that he was effectively in command of the entire English Catholic educational project: he had founded seminaries in Valladolid and Seville, and was on cordial terms with the President of the college at Douay, Dr Richard Barret. When Barret died in May 1599, he was replaced by Dr Thomas Worthington, three of whose nephews had been at the Valladolid college.[4] Persons was also the Prefect of the Jesuit mission to England, in

---

[1]   *A Briefe Apologie, or Defence of the Catholike Ecclesiastical Hierarchie, & subordination in England, erected these later yeares by our holy Father Pope Clement the eyght; and impugned by certayne libels printed and published of late … under the name of Priests of the Seminaries* (Antwerp, 1601), henceforth referred to as *A Defence of the Catholike Ecclesiastical Hierarchie*; and *A Manifestation of the Great Folly and bad spirit of certayne in England calling themselves secular priestes Who set forth dayly most infamous and contumelious libels against worthy men of their owne religion, and divers of them their lawful Superiors, of which libels sundry are heer examined and refuted. By priests lyving in obedience* (Antwerp, 1602), henceforth referred to as *A Manifestation of the Great Folly*.

[2]   The style of the former is singled out for praise by Vernon Blackburn in *English Prose: Selections*, ed. Henry Craik (5 vols; London, 1893–96), vol. 1, *Fourteenth to Sixteenth Century*, pp. 385–90.

[3]   Anthony Kenny, 'The Inglorious Revolution, 1594–1597', *Venerabile* 16 (1956): 240–58, and *Venerabile* 17 (1957): 7–25, 77–94, 136–55; Francis Edwards, SJ, *Robert Persons: The Biography of an Elizabethan Jesuit, 1546–1610* (St Louis, 1995), pp. 198–215.

[4]   Godfrey Anstruther, *The Seminary Priests: Vol. I: Elizabethan 1558–1603* (Durham, 1968), pp. 387–8; see A.C.F. Beales, *Education under Penalty* (London, 1963), pp. 59–60; *Registers of the English College at Valladolid*, ed. Edwin Henson; CRS, 30 (London, 1930), p. 10 n. Persons met Worthington in 1579 when the latter came to Rome in company with William Allen; see Persons's 'A Storie of Domesticall Difficulties', ed. J.H. Pollen, SJ, in *Miscellanea II*, CRS, 2 (London, 1906), p. 137.

constant communication with the superior on the ground, Henry Garnet.[5]

This was a powerful position within an otherwise weak and embattled English Catholic community. But the eruption of the appellant controversy in 1598 threatened to undo all that Persons had been working towards. The political climate was changeable, with the deaths of Burghley (4 August) and Philip of Spain (13 September), uncertainty about the effects of the Peace of Vervins (2 May) – which established the title of Henri IV of France and held a rapidly diminishing prospect of relief for the recusants – and the marriage, on 15 November, of the preferred Catholic candidate for the English succession, Isabella Clara Eugenia, Infanta of Spain, to Archduke Albert of Austria. If diplomatic pressure could be put on France to be more sympathetic to the recusants, things looked hopeful. In England, meanwhile, a fresh propaganda war was brewing with the appearance of *A Watch-word to all religious, and true-hearted Englishmen*, by Sir Francis Hastings, who characterized Catholics as dangerous dissidents. Hastings was capitalizing on the republication, in 1596, of Foxe's *Actes and Monuments*.[6] It was a delicate moment. As far as Persons was concerned, the important thing was for Catholics to stand firm and uncompromising; it was much more likely that the state would negotiate with them thus than if they began to seek accommodation through making concessions about the state's legitimacy.[7]

***

By the end of the sixteenth century it was becoming apparent that the English Catholic community was in need of clear direction. After the death of Cardinal Allen on 16 October 1594, relations between the Jesuits and the secular clergy were diversified; priests who had trusted Persons because they trusted Allen became much more wary. Disaffection with the Jesuits, among both clergy and laity, developed in several related contexts. Loyalists, especially among the laity, were reluctant to embrace the full recusant position, and the clergy connected with loyalist lay patrons became increasingly alienated from the exiles.[8] The uncertainty of the succession meant that the Catholic community was being pulled in various directions. *A Conference about the Next Succession* was designed to deter premature commitment to one candidate or another, but every new development, rumour or manoeuvre contributed to the division into

---

[5]   See Thomas M. McCoog, SJ, 'The Establishment of the English Province of the Society of Jesus', *Recusant History* 17 (1984): 121–39.

[6]   Sir Francis Hastings, *A Watchword to all religious, and true hearted English-men* (London, 1598; composed before September 1597); John Foxe, *Actes and Monuments of matters most speciall and memorable, happening in the Church, with an universall history of the same* (London, 1596). See above, Chapter 5.

[7]   *A Manifestation of the Great Folly*, fol. 79r.

[8]   Jesuits were accused of exercising undue control over their lay patrons, while seculars thought of themselves as more sympathetic; for an analysis of divisions among priests in Yorkshire, see Hugh Aveling, *Northern Catholics: The Catholic Recusants of the North Riding of Yorkshire 1558–1790* (London, 1966), pp. 163–9; on lay patronage and political allegiance, see John Bossy, *The English Catholic Community 1570–1850* (London, 1975), pp. 37–9.

separate camps, backing the Scottish or the Spanish candidature, James VI of Scotland or the Infanta Isabella.[9] Thus William Crichton seriously considered returning to Scotland in hopes of a reconciliation with James, at much the same time as Catholic refugees were petitioning Philip III to declare full support for the Infanta.[10]

Also related to politics was the long-running tension in Belgium, where a significant number of exiled Catholic noblemen and gentry was concentrated. Many of these had left England at the time of the failure of the French marriage scheme of 1580, and so regarded themselves as having a stake in English Catholic diplomacy. They were much affected by the struggle for power in France, gradually detaching themselves from the interest of the Catholic League and forming an alliance with the French court. In the process, conflict arose between the English Jesuit William Holt, a close associate of Persons's, and the Belgian Provincial, Oliver Mannaerts, who became fierce in his criticism of both Persons and Holt. In 1597 Crichton named several Catholic gentlemen who wanted to see Holt removed.[11] Ultimately Acquaviva sided with the English Jesuits, but replaced Holt with William Baldwin in 1598. Crichton no doubt echoed the sentiments of many when he protested against Persons's inflexibility: 'It is not expedient', he wrote, 'to be so severe and rigorous with erring opponents.'[12] Mannaerts seems to have made no secret of his dislike of Persons, and played a part in the growth of a strong anti-Persons faction. Persons's modern apologists such as Leo Hicks and Francis Edwards have perhaps exaggerated both the power and maliciousness of this faction, but it undoubtedly existed as a thorn in his flesh.[13]

Disaffection with the Jesuits came to a head at Wisbech Castle and the English College in Rome. Fr William Weston, Garnet's predecessor as Jesuit superior, had entered the community of jailed Catholic clerics at Wisbech Castle in 1588; in December 1594 he withdrew to his room in disgust over the lax behaviour of some of his fellow inmates, and the community was split. The conflict at Wisbech epitomized the conflict between the Jesuits – who had a very clear idea of what their religion demanded – and those among the secular

---

[9]   Robert Persons [R. Doleman (pseud.)], *A Conference about the Next Succession to the Crowne of Ingland, divided into two partes* (Antwerp, 1594 [*vere* 1595]). See above, Chapter 4.

[10]   On the Crichton plan, see Thomas M. McCoog, SJ, 'Harmony Disrupted: Robert Parsons, S.J., William Crichton, S.J. and the Question of Queen Elizabeth's Successor, 1581–1603', *Archivum Historicum S.I.* 73 (2004): 149–220; on the petition, see *CSP Spanish, 1587–1603*, pp. 633–4, cited by A.J. Loomie, SJ, 'Philip III and the Stuart Succession in England', *Revue belge de Philologie et d'Histoire* 43 (1965): 492–514, p. 497 n. 2 , rpt. in *Spain and the Early Stuarts, 1585–1655* (Aldershot, 1996). Crichton was believed to have written an 'Apologie and Defence of the King of Scotland' that offended Archduke Albert, Philip II's son-in-law. See *Documents Illustrating Catholic Policy in the Reign of James VI*, ed. T.G. Law; Publications of the Scottish History Society, 15 (Edinburgh, 1893).

[11]   William Crichton, Letter to Acquaviva, n.p., n.d., *ARSI*, Angl. 42, fols 46r–47v; McCoog, 'Harmony Disrupted', pp. 171–3.

[12]   William Crichton, Letter to Duras, Chambéry, 24 May 1602, *ARSI*, Angl. 42, fols 158r–159r; McCoog, 'Harmony Disrupted', pp. 182–3.

[13]   On the Mannaerts–Holt–Persons conflict, see Edwards, *Robert Persons*, pp. 160, 198–9, 216–20; and McCoog, 'Harmony Disrupted', pp. 174–80.

priests who resented the Jesuits' status and were wary of their commitment to a resolutely unaccommodating stance towards the Elizabethan religious and political dispensation.[14] Weston himself was a friend of Persons and may have assisted in the revision of *The Christian Directory*.[15] At the English College, Rome, divisions followed analogous lines. Many students, echoing the common cry that the Jesuits were no better than Puritans, resented the discipline at the college, which they felt to be humiliating to free-born Englishmen of gentle blood. Their resistance, in turn, was interpreted as 'mock[ing] at everything that bears on spirituality and virtue'.[16] In close quarters at Wisbech and the English College, disagreements took on larger proportions and were invested with deep spiritual significance.

Under these circumstances, it seemed intolerable to someone like Persons that the clergy should be free of central authority. In general the Jesuits were less interested in questions of ecclesiastical government than secular priests. But where the lay people faced dilemmas of citizenship and faith, and the clergy were unevenly dispersed and connected with a diversity of gentry families, there was a real danger of fragmentation. Moreover, Persons had a vision for a reformed Catholicism that could not be left simply to individual conversion and spiritual formation. The energies of resurgent Catholicism would have to be coordinated. This was a Jesuit programme, but it could not be accomplished by Jesuits alone: for one thing, there were too few of them; for another, they liked to work in an unfettered way, free of organizational responsibilities.

The appointment of an archpriest was, in the end, Persons's idea, even if he was not alone responsible. At first he would have preferred a bishop, but when it became clear that Pope Clement VIII would not agree, Persons approved of the alternative, an archpriest. To understand why this arrangement met with such spirited opposition among some of the secular clergy, we need to recognize how important bishops were in the thinking of the seculars. Bishops represented normality; as long as the Pope refrained from appointing Catholic bishops to episcopacies held by Protestants, England was being treated as a mission field, where the Jesuits would have far too much freedom of action. An archpriest, on the other hand, would have authority only over the seculars, while the Jesuits remained virtually autonomous. They would be free to operate as an elite group, pushing forward with the persuasion of strategic lay people to a new and subversive spirituality that might prove a threat to the interests of the secular priests, and the archpriest would ensure that the seculars would

---

[14]   For a full account of the 'Wisbech Stirs', see Arnold Pritchard, *Catholic Loyalism in Elizabethan England* (London, 1979), pp. 78–101; and *The Wisbech Stirs (1595–98)*, ed. P. Renold; CRS, 51 (London, 1958). Persons's analysis of what happened at Wisbech is in *A Defence of the Catholike Ecclesiastical Hierarchie*, ch. 6, fols 62v–83v.

[15]   Robert Persons, 'Punti per la Missione d'Inghilterra', ed. and trans. J.H. Pollen, SJ, in *Miscellanea IV*, CRS, 4 (London, 1907), pp. 156–7. *The Christian Directory* is the generic title for *The First Booke of the Christian Directory, appertayning to Resolution* (Rouen, 1582; revd 1585, 1607).

[16]   Robert Persons, Letter to Clement VIII, Rome, 28 September 1597, *ABSI*, Coll P, fol. 358; Edwards, *Robert Persons*, p. 211.

not be a hindrance. What for Persons seemed a reasonable means to keep English Catholicism together and allow it to grow towards perfection, seemed to others the harbinger of dissolution of the existing power structures, tenuous as they already were. The appellants were motivated by conservatism, a desire (in alliance with loyalist lay people) to keep a low profile and a resistance to new, higher standards of churchmanship. It was no accident that the appellant party drew strength especially from the faction at Wisbech Castle that rebelled against the stricter regimen introduced by William Weston: of the appellant writers, Christophet Bagshaw and Thomas Bluet were prisoners at Wisbech, while John Mush was a frequent visitor.[17]

The story of the archpriest controversy can be told in bald outline. In March 1598 the Cardinal Protector of England, Cajetan, proposed that the persecuted Church of Rome in England should be placed under the authority of an archpriest. George Blackwell was appointed, and the Jesuit superior Henry Garnet reported that there was general acceptance among the clergy. Perhaps. A relatively small but determined group of secular priests – just how representative they were of a wider feeling it is hard to establish – protested against the imposition, as they saw it, of an unwanted and unfamiliar form of church government.[18] Fundamentally, they were disaffected with the Jesuits, whom they believed to be behind the move and would stand to gain from it.

On the grounds that the appointment of the archpriest lacked explicit papal authority, the party of secular priests sent two of their number, William Bishop and Robert Charnock, to Rome in October 1598, to appeal to Pope Clement VIII. Hence the term 'appellants' used to describe the party, whose prominent members included Christopher Bagshaw, John Mush, Thomas Bluet, John Colleton, Anthony Copley and William Watson. Over the following four years, move and countermove ensued: appeals to the pope, papal confirmation of Blackwell's appointment, accusations of schism (later withdrawn), attempts to block the appeals, dissuade the appellants, lock them up in the English College, and so forth, until on 11 October 1602 a papal brief gave a final ruling, favouring the archpriest but removing the Jesuits from any governing role. Both sides in the conflict resorted to print to vilify the other. In his bibliography of Elizabethan religious controversies, Peter Milward lists 27 separate titles under the heading 'The Appellant Controversy'.[19]

* * *

It is difficult, at this distance, to judge between Persons and the recusants. Both sides stooped low. The Jesuits' methods and priorities have come under scrutiny in recent years in terms that make the appellants' suspicions quite

---

[17]   See the entries for Bagshaw and Mush in Anstruther.
[18]   Even for the appeal of 17 November 1600, only 33 priests subscribed, out of some 400 secular priests in England and Wales. See Edwards, *Robert Persons*, p. 262.
[19]   Peter Milward, SJ, *Religious Controversies of the Elizabethan Age* (London, 1978), pp. 116–24.

understandable.[20] But there can be no question that, in Persons's eyes at least, the appellant campaign was a direct and even, to some extent, a deliberate hindrance to the growth of that exemplary Catholic community that could be the pride of the counter-Reformation. It was this potential loss that so disturbed him and moved him to write so fervently against the appellants. Of this vision neither the appellants nor the English authorities who sponsored their writings had any clear idea. The appellants saw the Jesuits as meddling in traditional pastoral relationships, while the Bishop of London, Richard Bancroft, welcomed any opportunity to confuse and divide the Catholic community.

The refusal, by the appellant party, to accept the appointment of the archpriest, and their attempt to gain leverage against the Jesuits by making overtures to the English government (or, alternatively, to gain tolerance from the government by asking the Pope to withdraw the Jesuits), created a dangerous public division in English Catholicism that aroused Persons's deepest indignation. He found it hard, distanced as he was, to sympathize with the growing sentiment of Catholic loyalism, and he seems not to have perceived that his impatience with dissent in the ecclesiastical realm sat uneasily with his legitimizing of political dissent in *A Conference about the Next Succession*.[21] But what provoked him most was the portrayal of Jesuits in general, and himself in particular, as self-promoting power-seekers prepared to sacrifice their co-religionists for their own advantage. He was regularly accused of pursuing policies – Spanish invasion plans, intervention in the succession, insistence on recusancy – for which his fellow countrymen had to pay while he lived in security in Rome. But he had a vision for English Catholicism, and a deeply held conviction of the right way to go about realizing that vision. Working closely with such men as Edmund Campion, William Allen, William Weston, Robert Southwell, Henry Garnet and, among foreigners, Alfonso Agazzari (twice rector of the English College, Rome, 1579–86 and for a year in the 1590s) and Claudio Acquaviva (the Jesuit General), he knew what learning and devotion could do for the Catholic apostolate, in building up the faithful.

---

[20]   The best account of the controversy is given by Pritchard, pp. 120–74; Persons's involvement is detailed in Edwards, *Robert Persons*, pp. 235–94. See also *The Archpriest Controversy: Documents Relating to the Dissensions of the Roman Catholic Clergy, 1597–1602: from the Petyt MSS of the Inner Temple*, ed. T.G. Law; Camden Society, n.s. 56 and 58 (London, 1896–98); John Bossy, *The English Catholic Community*, pp. 35–48; and A.O. Meyer, *England and the Catholic Church under Queen Elizabeth*, trans. J.R. McKee; 2nd edn (London, 1967; New York, 1969).

[21]   See above, Chapter 4. Loyalism is treated sympathetically by Alexandra Walsham, *Church Papists: Catholicism, Conformity and Confessional Polemic in Early Modern England* (Woodbridge, Suffolk, 1993); and Alison Shell, *Catholicism, Controversy and the English Literary Imagination, 1558–1660* (Cambridge, 1999), pp. 107–168. For an analysis of appellant political thinking, see Michael L. Carrafiello, *Robert Parsons and English Catholicism, 1580–1610* (Selinsgrove, 1998), pp. 88–102; Peter Holmes, *Resistance and Compromise: The Political Thought of the Elizabethan Catholics* (Cambridge, 1982), pp. 186–204; and Lisa Ferraro Parmelee, *Good newes from Fraunce: French Anti-League Propaganda in Late Elizabethan England* (Rochester, 1996), ch. 7. Catholic loyalism developed both as a result of a conflict of allegiance, especially among lay people, and disillusionment with foreign, especially Spanish, intervention.

This was a group of men it would be hard to equal for spiritual stature at the time. His own best work had been to persuade English Christians, through his phenomenally successful *Christian Directory*, to make an unwavering commitment to the service of God, issuing from deliberate consideration (see above, Chapter 2). This was the English mission as he saw it: the bright, and bright-eyed, young men who came to the seminaries were witnesses to the work of grace. But he was not so naïve as to imagine that this could be brought to fruition without more favourable political conditions. In this regard, too, he had an unshakeable conviction: regimes existed to promote the spiritual welfare of their subjects, and he saw it as part of his brief not only to use his influence to secure, if possible, the most suitable successor to Elizabeth, but to instruct English Catholics to be politically responsible too.

Convinced as Persons was that the Jesuits had the secret to English Catholic renewal, he saw the appellant critique as slander that threatened to extinguish the light of virtue. His two attacks on the appellants are therefore a sustained treatment of the theme of slander, under extremely delicate circumstances. He needed to denounce slander and isolate his enemy without descending to the level of his opponents. The way he went about this was to develop a rhetorical protocol that would distinguish him clearly from his opponents: a form of rhetoric one might call 'exuberant apology', in contradistinction to the false copiousness, as he saw it, of his opponents. He too, wrote at length, but he wrote (he believed) to a purpose, his eloquence aroused by indignation.

The number of hostile pamphlets was daunting. The first wave followed the failure of the first appeal, censured by a papal brief in April 1599, rather heavy-handedly interpreted by Blackwell. Throughout 1600 and 1601 the appellant party grew in strength and indignation, and the second appeal, dominated by the informer John Cecil,[22] elicited more sympathy in Rome, with much lobbying for French support. Meanwhile the English Protestant authorities, and in particular Richard Bancroft, Bishop of London, were doing everything to encourage the state of disunity and strife among the Catholics by sponsoring the publication of anti-Jesuit tracts. The London printers Thomas Creede, Richard Field and Felix Kingston were prominent in this battle of books.[23] The anti-appellant campaign was launched by a work commonly known as *An Epistle of Pious Grief*, which may have been written by Persons's assistant in Rome, Nicholas Smith, SJ, and contained material from a speech by Persons himself.[24] In the next response, *A Defence of the Catholike Ecclesiastical Hierarchie*, Persons took issue with a Latin work by John Mush, *Declaratio*

---

22   See above, Chapter 3, p. 49.

23   Gladys Jenkins, 'The Archpriest Controversy and the Printers, 1601–1603', *The Library*, 5th series, 2 (1948): 180–86.

24   S.N. (pseud.), *The Copie of a Letter written to a very worshipful Catholike Gentleman in England, of greif conceaved about some scandalous dissention, and bookes set forth, tending to the disgracing one of another, by such as labour in the same cause. By S.N. that dearely loveth them all* (Antwerp, 1601). P.J. Holmes, '*An Epistle of Pious Grief*: An Anti-Appellant Tract by Robert Persons', *Recusant History* 15 (1981): 328–3', argues that Persons was the author. See ARCR II 565.5.

Motuum ac Turbationum, and an English one compiled (possibly) by William Bishop, *The Copies of certaine discourses*.[25] As he was going to press, two further works appeared, again one in Latin and one in English: *The Hope of Peace*, by John Bennet, and *Relatio Compendiosa Turbarum*, by Christopher Bagshaw. These Persons attended to in *An Appendix to the Apologie*, published separately, early in 1602.[26]

A Manifestation of the Great Folly started off in 1602 as a reply to a further work by Bagshaw, *A True relation of the faction begun at Wisbich*, and one by Thomas Bluet, *Important Considerations, which ought to move all true and sound Catholikes who are not wholly Jesuited ... to acknowledge ... that the proceedings of her Maiesty ... have bene both mild and mercifull*.[27] Although, as the titles indicate, these were not directly concerned with the archpriest issue itself, they amplified the portrayal of the Jesuits as trying to dominate English Catholicism in their own narrow interest. In the course of composing *A Manifestation of the Great Folly* Persons found that he had four more books to contend with:

- *A Sparing Discoverie of our English Jesuits, and of Fa. Parsons proceedings vnder pretence of promoting the Catholike faith in England*, by Christopher Bagshaw (London, 1601)
- *A Dialogue betwixt a Secular Priest, and a Lay Gentleman ... of the most important matters that are in controversie betwixt the priests and the Spanish or Jesuiticall faction*, by John Mush (London, 1601)
- *An Answere to a Letter of a Jesuited Gentleman ... Concerninge the Appeale*, by Anthony Copley (London, 1601)
- *A Decacordon of Ten Quodlibeticall Questions concerning Religion and State*, by William Watson (London, 1602).

Watson's was the most extravagant of them all. In addition, he contributed fiery prefaces to Bluet's *Important Considerations*, Bagshaw's *Sparing Discoverie* and Mush's *Dialogue*. In reviewing his own earlier writings, Persons also

---

[25]   John Mush, *Declaratio Motuum ac Turbationum quae ex controversiis inter Iesuitas ... & Sacerdotes Seminariorum in Anglia* (London, 1601); William Bishop, *The Copies of certaine discourses, which were extorted from divers ... to purge themselves of the most greevous crimes of schisme, sedition, rebellion, faction, and such like, most uniustly laid against them for not subscribing to the late authoritie at the first sending thereof into England* (London, 1601).

[26]   John Bennet, *The Hope of Peace. By laying open such doubts and manifest untruthes as are divulged by the Arch-priest in his Letter or Answere to the Bookes which were published by the Priestes* (London, 1601); Christopher Bagshaw, *Relatio Compendiosa Turbarum quas Iesuitae Angli ... Sacerdotibus Seminariorum populoque Catholico concivere* (London, 1601); Robert Persons, *An Appendix to the Apologie, lately set forth, for the defence of the Hierarchie, & subordination of the English Catholike Church, impugned by certaine discontented priestes. Wherin two other bookes or libels of the impugners ... are examined, and considered* (Antwerp, 1602), henceforth referred to as *An Appendix to the Apologie*.

[27]   Christopher Bagshaw, *A True relation of the faction begun at Wisbich, by Fa. Edmons, alias Weston, a Jesuite* (London, 1601); Thomas Bluet, *Important Considerations, which ought to move all true and sound Catholikes who are not wholly Jesuited ... to acknowledge ... that the proceedings of her Maiesty ... have bene both mild and mercifull* (London, 1601).

had cause to defend himself against attacks on his political works: Henry Constable's *Discoverye of a Counterfecte Conference* and Robert Fisher's 'Memorial against the Jesuits', a manuscript document dating from 1597.[28]

In the dispute with the appellants, Persons's authorship of *A Conference about the Next Succession* became a bone of contention. Many of the secular priests had loyalist affinities, and resented this work as an embarrassment to English Catholicism. Appellant outrage focused on the pseudonym 'Doleman', which came to epitomize for them the Jesuit's misappropriation and attempted monopolization of the Catholic cause. It is unlikely that Persons, in choosing the pseudonym, had in mind the Marian priest, Alban Dolman, but that is what the appellant writers claimed. Their sense of the contrast between this revered priest and the infamous 'Doleman' is a measure of the division that had grown since the English mission. In those earlier days, Alban Dolman's interests had been closely aligned with Persons's, for it seems that it was he that came to succour Mary Champney on her deathbed. Champney was a Bridgettine nun who returned from exile in 1578 and died in April 1580, just before the arrival of Campion and Persons. Two of her sister nuns were at Lyford Grange the following year when Campion was arrested. The Bridgettine house at Mechlin, Flanders, had been provided in 1572 or 1573 by Sir Francis Englefield, later to become a close associate of Persons's. Persons continued to show an interest in the embattled Bridgettines, but by 1598 the appellants were ready to paint his portrait as a narrow activist far removed from the kind of piety he, Dolman and Mary Champney all shared.[29]

***

In the hurly-burly of the appeals from 1598 to 1603 it is difficult to disentangle Persons the negotiator from Persons the writer. As negotiator he fought hard, even if he was not utterly intransigent over the appellant intervention. Fundamentally he held that the anti-Jesuit faction had put themselves in the wrong by appealing to Rome, he believed that their dissent (or, as he put it, insubordination) put the Catholic community at a political disadvantage, and so he advocated firm measures against them. In so doing he was holding on to his own position of power in determining papal policy regarding English affairs and resisting any attempt to reduce Jesuit influence on the archpriest. Even so, he was conciliatory at a personal level: for example, when he released Bishop and Charnock from their detention in the English College in 1599 he did his best to show, by acts of kindness, that there was nothing personal in his opposition.[30] He was also willing to enter into serious and frank negotiations

---

[28] Henry Constable, *A Discoverye of a Counterfecte Conference held at a counterfecte place, by counterfecte travellers, for thadvancement of a counterfecte tytle* (Cologne [*vere* Paris], 1600). For Robert Fisher's 'Memorial against the Jesuits', see Edwards, *Robert Persons*, p. 217.

[29] Ann M. Hutchison, 'Mary Champney a Bridgettine Nun under the Rule of Queen Elizabeth I', *Bridgettiana*, 13 (2002): 3–32; and 'The Life and Good End of Sister Marie', *Bridgettiana*, 13 (2002): 33–89, esp. p. 79 n. 144.

[30] *A Defence of the Catholike Ecclesiastical Hierarchie*, pp. 121–3.

with the French court, circumventing the pro-appellant ambassador to Rome, Philippe de Béthune, and winning the grudging respect of Henri IV's secretary of state, the seigneur de Villeroy.[31]

All this is in keeping with a vigorous, uncompromising but flexible attitude towards the English authorities. Politics, after all, is the art of the possible. But as a writer he had a simpler brief. It should be noted that his two anti-appellant tracts belong to that period of the dispute between the failure of the first, rather poorly conceived appeal of 1598–99 and the development of French-sponsored appellant negotiations in 1602, much better organized and focused. This was a period in which the state of public opinion in England counted most strongly, as the appellant party gathered its strength. What Persons was not prepared to countenance, and felt he had to silence at all costs, was the anti-Jesuit propaganda that was pouring off the London presses. This may in part account for the fact that *A Defence of the Catholike Ecclesiastical Hierarchie* was put out after the papal brief of 17 August 1601, forbidding further publication in the print war. The archpriest Blackwell held back the issuing of the brief until Persons's book was out; in effect, he connived in Persons's urgent need to put down his critics and affirm the Jesuit cause.[32]

The story Persons tells in *A Defence of the Catholike Ecclesiastical Hierarchie* is that of a concerted opposition to the Jesuits, an unbroken line of emulators, calumniators and dissidents beginning with the endemic conflicts in the English College in Rome (from 1579 onwards), extending to the abuse of William Holt in Brussels and William Weston at Wisbech Castle, more trouble in Rome (1596), and finally the archpriest controversy. That these were connected no-one would wish to deny, but Persons glosses over other possible factors in the discontents among the English Catholics. In turn, his foregrounding of a single thread of anti-Jesuit factionalism exaggerates the role of the Jesuits in contemporary English Catholic history. Such simplification enables him to represent his opponents as monothematic and repetitive, while his own belief in the Jesuit apostolate is so deeply held that even though that, too, is a single theme, it is capable of infinite extension.

The implicit contrast, then, is between the appellant printing extravaganza and the rich vein of Catholic truth. Where Bagshaw claims to be 'compendious', Persons satirizes the sheer bulk of his work, its manufacture of words utterly disproportionate to the matter: everything the appellants write is 'longer than standeth with the credit of the relators'.[33] What they seek is not just freedom from the archpriest's authority but licence to write what they wish, unrestricted by considerations of justice and truth, 'hauing litle care ... what they say or wryte, so they say much and vtter vgly things'.[34] With exquisite

---

[31]   See John Bossy, 'Henry IV, the Appellants and the Jesuits', *Recusant History* 8 (1965): 80–122, esp. pp. 91–4.

[32]   Edwards, *Robert Persons*, pp. 263–4, gives the details of the brief and Blackwell's response, without noting the connection with the publication of *A Defence of the Catholike Ecclesiastical Hierarchie*.

[33]   *An Appendix to the Apologie*, fol. 21r.

[34]   *A Manifestation of the Great Folly*, fol. 40v (*vere* 39v).

mimicry Persons mocks the way they batter their way past all the evidence to false allegations:

> The matter is, that *wheras* in tyme of the tumultuous proceedings of these men and their fellowes both in Rome, Flanders, and England, many things were spoken, done, & wrytten against the fathers of the Society by their vngrateful schollers of our nation, without all ground of truth, but only through passion, leuity, anger, and incitation of others, as appeareth not only by the examination of the things themselues, but by the confessions also of the partyes that did accuse, when they were out of passion, and by the sentence of all iudges appointed in these causes (all of which we haue shewed largely & particularly in the 3. 4. 5. And 6. Chapters of our Apologie) yet these men *knowing* in their consciences, and in the sight of all the world this to be true, and that those calmuniations obiected (or the most part of them) were meerly false & deuised vpon the causes aforesaid, and denyed afterward by those that obiected them, do *notwithstanding* set them downe now againe as points iustified or iustifiable, and haue put them also in print for the further infamation of Iesuits.[35]

The periodic sentence first multiplies, quite laboriously and painfully, all the unfavourable signs that should give the appellants pause, then lets slip the agent ('yet these men'), holds them up again with further considerations ('knowing ...'), and only then releases their action: '[these men] do notwithstanding set them downe now againe ... for the further infamation of Iesuits'.

Such rhetorical kicking against the pricks represents a radical division between words and things, a style that depends on 'amplifications ... exaggerations ... in words alone, scoffes and iests'.[36] Persons turns to the theme of isolation to suggest that his adversaries are reduced to endless repetition from a depleted store, fixated with volume at any expense.[37] By cutting themselves off from the appointed hierarchy, by deliberately refusing to recognize the pope's clear and unambiguous will, they effectively exclude themselves from serious debate. They become estranged from the intellectual centre, just as their new allies, the English Protestants (such as the Bishop of London) are sure to wither and perish in schismatic isolation. It is wholly characteristic of Persons's habits of mind that he should thus apply his ecclesiastical formula – *sine Roma nihil* – to polemical decorum. At various strategic moments he simply abandons the attempt to find sense in appellant arguments: 'all these poynts we say our men must accommodate themselues, for we cannot ty them to geather with any conuenience of reason, wit, religion or piety'.[38]

Besides false copiousness, Persons detects a pseudo-restraint, especially in Bagshaw's unaptly named *Sparing Discoverie of our English Jesuits*: 'the word *sparing discouery* in their title, might haue byn spared and left out, seing they spare neyther modesty shame or conscience'.[39] There is, for instance, the

---

[35] Ibid., fol. 5r, emphases added.

[36] Ibid., fol. 2r.

[37] See esp. *A Manifestation of the Great Folly*, ch. 3, 'There folly and presumptious spirit in making to them selues such aduersaries, as they do' (fols 29r–40r [*vere* 39r]).

[38] Ibid., fol. 27v.

[39] Ibid., fol. 81r.

'multitude of … parentheses' by which the style of William Watson, author of the prefatory epistle, is marked. To illustrate this, Persons quotes at length from a previous retractation by Watson. The parentheses appear to be more than a mannerism: they create a curious, even eccentric, effect of hedging about everything there is to say, suggesting an enigmatic Iago-like combination of shiftiness and affected bluntness. Here, for example, he confesses to having attended a Protestant service:

> After that I had byn two dayes in *Durance* I (hearing that I should be vrged to go to the heretical Church) wickedly determined (after a great though short conflict had with my self) to preuent their euil attempt by pernicious pollicy, in requesting conference with some learned protestant, which being graunted, I did (though faynedly yet altogeather vnlawfully) so farre condescend by a litle and a litle vnto him, that lastly I went to their heretical seruice, with this intent (and truly with none other at that tyme God he knoweth) thinking thereby to haue escaped their hands, adding herunto a blynd supposition, that in such an obscure place, I should not giue scandal to any Catholike by that wicked act, because (those being compelled oftentymes that wil not come voluntarily) it should not be knowne (til I had escaped) whether I came without or with my owne accord.[40]

With such a man, and with such a rhetoric, you cannot know where you stand. Here too we have, in effect, a multiplication of words without matter.

One of Watson's shifty confessions, wittily seized on by Persons, takes us to the heart of the matter. Watson had buckled under pressure in prison and had betrayed some of his fellow Catholics, so he accused himself of the crime *percussio clerici*, striking a cleric. This, says Persons, is an ignorant and utterly inappropriate identification of his former legal offence; but, fortuitously, it describes exactly – if taken figuratively – the current offence of writing vituperously against the Jesuits. Now indeed he is lashing out with his tongue against holy men:

> Let him consider in how farre worse case he standeth *now*, then he did *then* hauing scandalized so much the more Catholiks in *this* fall, then in *that*, by how much *this* is more publike, and preiudicial to the common cause, hurtful and iniurious to infinite particular persons belyed and slaundered by him, and that *this* is voluntary conspiring with the comon enemy wheras *that* was vpon feare and fraylty, *this* is of meere malice, enuy, pryde, and other like motyues the other vpon infirmity: so as there is much more cause for him to accuse himself of *Percussio Clerici* then before.[41]

It is worth dwelling on this riposte because it encapsulates Persons's method of turning his opponents' language inside out. Watson's literal error – he was not guilty of *percussio clerici* in the precise legal sense – turns out to be a perfect figure of his true offence: striking at the heart of the clergy. Unintentionally he produces a metaphor by which he stands condemned. From Persons's point of

---

[40]   Ibid., fol. 84v.
[41]   Ibid., fols 85v–86r; emphases added.

view, to slander the Jesuits in prose is to assault the clergy. Out of Watson's own extravagant language the truth has sprung, like an epiphany.

In *A Defence of the Catholike Ecclesiastical Hierarchie*, and even more so in *A Manifestation of the Great Folly*, Persons is not content merely to correct calumny. He wants to make manifest how crucial the Society of Jesus is to the spiritual health of the nation. This is no time for false modesty or defensiveness. And so he reinvents the appellant writings as slanders which, properly understood, figure forth the glorious truth about the Jesuits. He argues that accusations literally levelled against the Jesuits bring all Catholics, and all Catholic practice, figuratively into disrepute. When Bagshaw accuses the Jesuits of exploiting confession, he retorts: 'But now heare another impiety exercised by a sleight and figurative speech suggested to them (no doubt) by heretics to bring in contempt, suspition and auersion, the holy sacrament of Confession and holsom vse therof.' The term 'sleight and figurative speech' refers to the ambiguity surrounding 'confession' in the passage he quotes from Bagshaw:

> Our Iesuits are most rigorous in their taking of mens confessions, wherby they know as wel the seruants as by their maisters & mistresses their seueral confessions, all the secrets in those familyes: the wyues against her husband, the husbands against his wife, and the seruants of them both, &c.[42]

Here the legal and sacramental uses of the word are collapsed; deliberately, in Persons's view, to make it appear that under cover of religious confession Jesuits exact information they can use to their advantage. 'Surely this is more like some ribalds speech then of a priest or Catholike', he complains, implying that 'confession' has become a kind of dirty joke. The *OED* suggests that the legal meaning of the term developed later than the religious, so it could be said that the sacrament of confession is the literal meaning, and the confession of misdemeanour is figurative, so that Bagshaw is indeed being 'figurative', whether or not we judge him to have used sleight of hand.[43] By pointing this out, Persons invites his readers to separate the sacramental from the legal once more, and in so doing to affirm the true practice even more strongly. Conversely, Bagshaw's debasement of Jesuit confession brings down all Catholics and all Catholicism, because, as Persons believes, the Jesuits hold the key to the mystery; they are metonymically inseparable from the faith's centre.

If this implication is bold, Persons's self-praise is even more daring. He softens it, marginally, by writing of himself anonymously in the third person. Yet no one could read this assertion without recognizing how completely Persons had made himself the touchstone for discerning the truth about the Jesuits:

---

[42]   *A Manifestation of the Great Folly*, fol. 88v.
[43]   See *OED*, *sub* 'confession', I.1.b. *Law* and 2.a. 'As a religious act'. The adjective 'sleight' is defined as 'artful' or 'deceptive'.

And truly in this our English Cath. Cause & reduction of our countrey
it seemeth that God hath suffered him [Persons] to be *insignum, cui
contradicetur,* as a marke or signe set vp for all sorts of bad people, atheists,
heretikes, apostataes, seditious, contentious, tumultuous, disastred, and
dissolute to inueigh against, and this is to the immitation of his maister and
Sauiour Christ, who was, and is, and shalbe to the worlds end a signe of
contradiction in the highest degree to all wicked whatsoeuer.[44]

To be a 'sign of contradiction' is to stand as a target for the verbal barrage
of the adversary and, by redirecting it, to turn it into the opposite. It is to
confront a self-generated and self-generating rhetoric with a reality that for the
first time cannot be evaded. It is to fuse words with things once again so that
the evil-speaker, the slanderer, finds himself praising virtue against his own
will. Persons's critique of appellant rhetoric thus turns false copiousness into
apologetic exuberance, uncovering, by signs of contradiction, true metaphors
and metonymies of praise.

  A Defence of the Catholike Ecclesiastical Hierarchie and *A Manifestation
of the Great Folly* represent Persons's most sustained personal *apologia*. He
devotes chapter 12 of *A Defence of the Catholike Ecclesiastical Hierarchie* to
giving the 'full story' of his life and chapter 5 of *A Manifestation of the Great
Folly* to a defence of his most controversial writings. There are also several
extended sections in other chapters of *A Manifestation of the Great Folly* in
which the obsession of the appellants with attacking Persons personally is taken
as a sign of their 'bad spirit'.[45] At one level one could read his self-vindication
as evidence of Persons's extreme touchiness, as A.L. Rowse has done.[46] It is
noteworthy, however, just how much he is in control of this material. A good
illustration may be found in the refutation of *A Sparing Discoverie of our
English Jesuits*.[47] This work was written by Persons's arch-rival, Christopher
Bagshaw, whose personal animosity to the Jesuit stretched back to a humiliating
thrashing at Balliol in 1573.[48] In July 1602 the mysterious 'Anthony Rivers'
wrote to Persons naming Bagshaw as the author, but it seems likely that *A
Manifestation of the Great Folly* had already been written.[49] Had Persons
known the identity of his opponent he might perhaps have lost control; as
it is, his chief target is William Watson, who wrote the preface to *A Sparing
Discoverie*. For most of the chapter he adopts a tone of satirical detachment
or studiously understated censure. It is only at the end, with the ground well

---

[44]   *A Manifestation of the Great Folly*, fol. 89r.
[45]   Ibid., chs 3, 4, 7 and 8.
[46]   A.L. Rowse, *The England of Elizabeth* (London, 1950), pp. 463–4, likens Persons to Swift
(who admired his style) as a 'conjured spirit'.
[47]   *A Manifestation of the Great Folly*, ch. 7.
[48]   Edwards, *Robert Persons*, pp. 5–10.
[49]   Milward, *Religious Controversies of the Elizabethan Age*, p. 119. There has been much
speculation as to the identity of 'Anthony Rivers', who had an extensive correspondence with
Persons at this time; he was once assumed to be a Jesuit but was probably William Sterrell,
secretary to the Earl of Worcester. See Patrick Martin and John Finnis, 'The Identity of "Anthony
Rivers" ', *Recusant History* 26 (2002): 39–74; and *Records of the English Province of the Society
of Jesus*, ed. Henry Foley, SJ (7 vols in 8; London, 1877–83), vol. 1, pp. 5–62.

prepared, that he deliberately cuts short his patient exposé of falsehood and spurns his enemy with contempt:

> And heere now the very multitude of these outragious libels with the immensity of hatred, hellish spirit, & poysoned entrals discouered therin, do force vs against our former purpose to cut of and stay all further passage and proceeding in this horrible puddle of lyes, slaunderous inuectiues & diuelish detraction, for that the very looking them ouer, doth weary the hart of any true Christian, and consequently wheras before we had determined with our selues to giue yow some tastes or examples out of them all, yet now finding the multitude to be without end, and the quality so base, vile, and malitious as the venome of any lost or loose tongue armed with audacity, and defended with impudency, stirred vp with enuy and enraged with fury, and bounded no way by any limits of conscience, piety or feare of God can vomit or cast out to defame their brethren: finding this (we say) we haue thought good to cease heere without further styrring the lothsome ragges of so filthie a donghil.[50]

Read cursorily and out of context, this might appear to be just another bout of mud-slinging, the staple of so much religious controversy. Within the structure of *A Manifestation of the Great Folly* it is an act of controlled aggression, devastating in its impact.

As rhetorical compositions, both *A Defence of the Catholike Ecclesiastical Hierarchie* and *A Manifestation of the Great Folly* are carefully designed to rebuild the impaired image of Catholic Christendom, epitomized in the Jesuit apostolate, as reasonable, firmly grounded in the truth, all-embracing and magnanimous. True Catholic priests, like Persons, are in a constant state of readiness to succour the faithful or find the answers to conflict.[51] Truly edifying Catholic discourse is timely rather than time-serving, instructive to the conscience, well-adapted to the 'indifferent reader' and artistically sophisticated.[52] Above all, it keeps decent proportion between copiousness of language and fertility of argument. Persons takes pains to give several practical demonstrations of his own conformity to these rhetorical ideals, notably in his vindication of Sir William Stanley's capitulation to the Spaniards at Daventry in 1587. As an English captain, Stanley had been put in command of this town on behalf of the Dutch Protestant rebels, but felt bound by conscience to hand it over to Spanish control. After devoting two pages to expounding the relevant 'Catholike doctrine and diuinity', Persons summarizes the case for Stanley:

> And this may suffice for Catholike men and all other also that are of good conscience and louers of iustice for the cleering of *S. William Stanleys* fact concerning lawfulnes & obligation of conscince. There remayneth to say a word or two concerning his honour as a souldiar and subiect of her Ma. Wherin albeit his cheef defence and iustification be indeed the forsaid obligation of equity, right and conscience towards almighty God which

---

50   *A Manifestation of the Great Folly*, fol. 94.
51   *A Defence of the Catholike Ecclesiastical Hierarchie*, ch. 10.
52   *A Manifestation of the Great Folly*, ch. 5.

is to be preferred before all other obligation to temporal princes, yet the points before specified or insinuated by vs, are sufficient also, though this so strict diuine obligation had not byn, to excuse him from the opprobrious & contumelious calumniations of *treachery and faith-breaking* wherwith these seditious people so iniuriously do charge hym.[53]

The passage is not sparing with its terms of abuse, but it is weighted towards the two lines of argument: one of which (duty to almighty God) has already been fully set out. The other (duty to Elizabeth and the soldier's code of conduct) has been 'specified and insinuated' and is given further elaboration in the paragraph following. The precision with which Persons handles the case is noteworthy.

The most intriguing instance of rhetorical self-awareness appears in his discussion of the internal strife in the English College, Rome, in 1596–97. His pretext for reopening this issue is that the appellants, Bluet and Bagshaw, are back in Rome, still harping on the same anti-Jesuit grievances that were supposedly settled back then, showing that they have not grown up since their student days. This gives him a good opportunity to reiterate what Cardinal Sega, the visitor, said in 1597, and incidentally to commend 'the pure and elegant stile also of that learned man besids his wisdome, piety & experience'.[54] Good letters are always on the side of the Jesuits. But Persons handles this in a curious way. When he quotes exemplary passages from Sega they are in fact no more than elegantly courteous. The meat of Sega's judgment, his praise of the Jesuits, is given in Persons's own words: he assumes the mantle of the eloquent humanist.

The positive achievement of these two works, then, lies in refracting argument, or refutation, into praise. This could be seen as the counterpart – mirror image in reverse – of allowing argument to disintegrate into slander, but it is more than a rhetorical trick of self-congratulation; it requires witty engagement with the adversary, adroit integration of specific points of contention into a moral theme, and strategic placement of individual, highly wrought eulogies. Such, for instance, is the tribute to Father William Holt, who died in Barcelona in May 1599.[55] To use technical rhetorical terms, Persons shifts from the judicial to the demonstrative form, so as to undo the work of slander and make virtue manifest.[56] Yet it is also a deliberate alignment of Rome with the central humanist tradition as Persons emulates such exponents of literary apology as

---

[53]   *A Manifestation of the Great Folly*, fol. 52v. Cf. William Allen, *The Copie of a Letter written by M. Doctor Allen: concerning the yeelding up, of the citie of Daventrie* (Antwerp, 1587). For a discussion of the debate over the morality of Stanley's action – the kind of dubious act the Jesuits were accused of condoning – see Thomas M. McCoog, SJ, *The Society of Jesus in Ireland, Scotland, and England, 1541–1588: 'Our Way of Proceeding?'* (Leiden, 1996), pp. 230–33, although Persons's contribution lies outside the period covered.

[54]   *A Manifestation of the Great Folly*, fol. 72v.

[55]   *A Defence of the Catholike Ecclesiastical Hierarchie*, ch. 7. Holt was a close associate of Persons.

[56]   Judicial rhetoric is concerned with establishing the true facts of the case; demonstrative (or epideictic) rhetoric elaborates praise and blame. For a full exposition, see Brian Vickers, *In Defence of Rhetoric* (Oxford, 1988), pp. 53–62.

Erasmus, More and Sidney: at one point he even invokes Plato and Cicero, to defend his use of imaginary (or, as his opponents called it, 'counterfeit') dialogue in *A Conference about the Next Succession*.[57] As I have tried to show, he is quite self-conscious and deliberate in structuring and composing these two works as a studied stylistic antithesis to the opposing pamphlets: organized thematically rather than countering arguments point for point; keeping decorum in the measure of praise and blame rather than reheating the same gobbets interminably; varying understatement with rounded affirmation rather than trying to sustain a constant pitch of strident indignation.

That *A Defence of the Catholike Ecclesiastical Hierarchie* and *A Manifestation of the Great Folly* belong to a superior order of rhetoric to the outpourings of Bagshaw, Mush, Bluet and Watson does not imply that they held the field. Ultimately the Jesuits' influence in the English Catholic community was eroded by the archpriests themselves, notably Blackwell's successor George Birkhead from 1606 to 1615. Persons might have felt some wry amusement over the fate of the Blatant Beast of slander at the end of book VI of Edmund Spenser's Protestant epic, *The Faerie Queene*, published in 1596:

> Thus was this Monster by the maystring might
> Of doughty *Calidore*, supprest and tamed,
> That neuer more he mote endammadge wight
> With his vile tongue, which many had defamed,
> And many causelesse caused to be blamed:
> So did he eeke long after this remaine,
> Vntill that, whether wicked fate so framed,
> Or fault of men, he broke his yron chaine,
> And got into the world at liberty againe.[58]

The mouth of slander is only temporarily stopped; the Blatant Beast escapes. Persons's reputation down the centuries suggests that Spenser knew the world as it is. Nor should we assume that Persons's inventiveness and verbal ingenuity necessarily confer a moral advantage. What I have endeavoured to show is that it would be a mistake, in discussing recusant literature, to make a sharp division between polemical works (aimed at the demolition of opponents) and works of spiritual formation.[59] The two tracts we have been discussing formed part of a long and bitter feud involving both a print war and various kinds of diplomatic manoeuvrings. They were written in response to a pressing political crisis, in the build-up to the second appeal. Yet Persons did not lose

---

[57] *A Manifestation of the Great Folly*, fol. 65r; cf. Henry Constable, *A Discoverye of a Counterfecte Conference*. Desiderius Erasmus, *Moriae encomium, sive Stultitiae laus* (Paris, 1511), known as *The Praise of Folly*; Sir Thomas More, *Libellus vere aureus nec minus salutaris quam festivus de optimo reipublicae statu deque noua insula Utopia* (Louvain, 1516); and Sir Philip Sidney, *Defence of Poesie* (London, 1595) are all based on the formal rhetorical 'praise' or *apologia*.

[58] Edmund Spenser, *The Faerie Queene* (London, 1596), book VI, canto xii, stanza 38.

[59] Cf. Ceri Sullivan, *Dismembered Rhetoric: English Recusant Writing, 1580 to 1603* (Madison/Teaneck, 1995), ch. 1.

sight of his fundamental missionary purpose, to edify and support the Catholic community in England. It is a measure of his skill that he could bridge the gap between securing an advantage and enlightening the faithful.

CHAPTER SEVEN

Making England Safe for Catholicism: Liberty of Conscience under James

The accession of James I was a disappointment to Persons, if not all English Catholics. There had been hopes that Elizabeth would be succeeded by a Catholic monarch, that James himself would convert, or that he would extend more or less full toleration to Catholics. As a ruler with a very high opinion of his own wisdom and fairness, James had himself encouraged such hopes, for in the run-up to the succession he had tried to conciliate everyone, not merely through ambition but because he seems genuinely to have believed that he could be all things to all men. He was optimistic that there would be a place for moderate Catholics in his commonwealth. He had enjoyed the friendship and support of prominent Catholics, especially Esmé Stuart, his cousin and early companion; he was conscious that the majority of English Catholics had supported his candidature for the succession, whatever their reservations, because he was the son of Mary Queen of Scots, and he found the Presbyterian party among the Protestants a real thorn in the flesh. So he was well-disposed, and not only to those who had openly declared themselves in his favour. As he travelled south to take up his kingship, Catholic petitions for liberty of conscience were confidently pressed upon him. But all they got was a temporary suspension of penalties, some moderation of persecution and a general air of benevolence.[1]

On 18 October 1603 Persons greeted the new king with a personal letter explaining his own involvement in the succession struggle and expressing his hopes that James would not make the same mistake as Elizabeth in persecuting the Catholics and in the process ruining her soul.[2] At the same time he comforted his fellow-Catholics, in a hastily rewritten preface to the final volume of *A Treatise of Three Conversions*, with the continued hope of his conversion:

> It seemeth impossible vnto mee, that such a witt, and so godly affected a mynd, as God hath bestowed vpon his Maiestie, can long be deteyned with the vanity & inanity of sects & heresies, where no grownd, no head, no

---

[1] The best general discussion of James's religious policy is by Kenneth Fincham and Peter Lake, 'The Ecclesiastical Policy of King James I', *Journal of British Studies* 24 (1985): 169–207.

[2] Robert Persons, Letter to King James I of England, Rome, 18 October 1603, *ABSI*, Anglia III, 36, transcribed by Thomas M. McCoog, SJ, 'Harmony Disrupted: Robert Parsons, S.J., William Crichton, S.J. and the Question of Queen Elizabeth's Successor, 1581–1603', *Archivum Historicum S.I.* 73 (2004): 149–220 (pp. 210–15).

certaine principle, no sure rule or method to try the truth, no one reason at all can be found, why a man should rather be of one sect, than another.[3]

But this may have expressed his confidence in the argument of his book rather than any real continued expectation that James would convert.

It seems at the very least that with the accession of James Persons abandoned further hope of securing the conditions for the wholesale reconversion of England through diplomatic or military pressure. The dream he had delineated in *A Memorial for the Reformation of England* was not to come to fruition,[4] and he would have to accept the prospect of Catholics and Protestants living together in one country in amity. But for him there was no question of concordance, no trimming down of Catholicism to measure up to royal expectations. Although he was willing to accept that not all Protestants were heretics, but merely believers in heresy, he wholeheartedly endorsed the conclusion of the convert Humphrey Leech that to remain a Protestant, having seen the truth of Catholic religion, was to be damned. Leech expressed alarm at the King's confidence that there was sufficient common ground in the early general councils to save him from the charge of heresy:

> For wheras I had with the greatest deliberation that I could possibly imagine, grounded vpon my owne peculiar experience of many yeares trauayle in the sacred volumes of Orthodox Antiquity, made before a firme irreuocable resolution to abandon the Protestant Religion vpon inuincible arguments of great solidity, and notorious discouery of execrable blasphemy, palpable and detestable heresie, against God his Christ, his Church, his Saints: building my foundation vpon the mayne rocke of Ancient Primitiue Church, Canonicall Scripture, truly sensed by them, Creedes and Councells, digested, collected, established by them; I now descried that your Maiesty intended to ground the cleane contrary Plea vpon the same heades for vindication of the Protestant Religion from the guilty crime of heresie.[5]

Here was no room for religious consensus. Persons could try to allay anxieties about the papal threat, but he wanted toleration for the Catholic faith in its entirety. The king, on the other hand, was willing to tolerate, and even favour, Catholics, but not Catholicism.[6] The last project of Persons's writing career

---

[3]   Robert Persons, *A Treatise of Three Conversions of England from Paganisme to Christian Religion*, 3 vols (St Omer, 1603–14), vol. 3, sig. *4r, henceforth referred to as *A Treatise of Three Conversions of England*.

[4]   Robert Persons, *The Jesuit's Memorial, for the Intended Reformation of England Under their First Popish Prince*, ed. Edward Gee (London, 1690), henceforth referred to as *A Memorial for the Reformation of England*.

[5]   Humphrey Leech, *Dutifull and Respective Considerations upon foure severall heads of Proofe and Triall in matters of Religion. Proposed by ... Iames King ... for clearing his Royall Person from the Imputation of Heresy* (St Omer, 1609), sig. *4v–**1r. Persons appears to have had a hand in the writing and publication of this work: see Peter Milward, SJ, *Religious Controversies of the Jacobean Age: A Survey of Printed Sources* (London, 1978), p. 111 and ARCR II 495.

[6]   James Brodrick, SJ, *The Life and Work of Blessed Robert Francis Cardinal Bellarmine, S.J. 1542–1621* (2 vols; London, 1928), vol. 2, p. 169.

was to defend the integrity of Catholicism and commend it as tolerable by a Protestant monarch.

***

During the period of the Archpriest Controversy, Persons unquestionably lost ground as a leader of English Catholics. Jesuit domination of the seminaries was accepted, but not without resentment. At Douay, Thomas Worthington's decision to send students out to classes with the Jesuits, instead of being taught in the house, met with strong opposition.[7] Blackfan's *Annals* of the Valladolid College record the conflict over rivalry between the Jesuit and Benedictine interests there between 1599 and 1603; there was considerable dissatisfaction over Joseph Creswell's handling of these affairs.[8] Worthington and Creswell were both close associates of Persons's. Even in the English College in Rome, where Persons was Rector, discontent was endemic. On the political front things were not going his way. The Infanta Isabella, the chief hope for a Catholic succession in England, had married the Archduke Albert and together they took charge of the Spanish Netherlands. After Philip III succeeded to the Spanish throne in September 1598 she viewed his support for her candidature for the English succession with suspicion. Her intuition that this would affect her position in the Low Countries was confirmed in 1601 when Philip made enquiries about the reversion of the Netherlands to the Spanish crown if the Infanta did not have an heir. Under these circumstances it is not surprising that her husband, the Archduke, showed no enthusiasm for the English succession.[9]

Persons's hopes for a Catholic prince were fading. If the Infanta was uninterested, James's attitude was ambiguous. In 1602 Persons sent word to Scotland, via the king's agent, Sir James Lindsay, that he was willing to support James to the death if only he would change his religion.[10] Meanwhile Crichton was busy again, with the financial backing of Pope Clement VIII, with a plan to return to Scotland and negotiate with James about the treatment of Catholics: Acquaviva was hesitant and by the time his permission came through in February 1603, it was too late. The queen died on 24 March 1603. Persons accepted James's accession but was disappointed that he had not been tied down to any terms of toleration. He felt that a Spanish army in readiness in Belgium, and a holding back of support from English Catholics, would have concentrated James's mind and forced him to make some definite commitments.

[7]   A.C.F. Beales, *Education Under Penalty* (London, 1963), p. 138.

[8]   Ibid, p. 125; Michael E. Williams, *St Alban's College Valladolid: Four Centuries of English Catholic Presence in Spain* (London, 1986), pp. 22–7.

[9]   See Albert J. Loomie, SJ, 'Philip III and the Stuart Succession in England', *Revue belge de Philologie et d'Histoire* 43 (1965): 492–514.

[10]   Robert Persons, Letter to King James VI of Scotland, 18 August 1602, *ABSI*, Anglia III, 20; transcribed by McCoog, 'Harmony Disrupted', pp. 208–210.

He still hoped that peace negotiations with Spain and the Netherlands would bring some relief.[11]

When Persons wrote to James in October, therefore, he could not be very optimistic either about his own reception or the prospects for the Catholic community. However cautious his political allegiances and negotiations had been, he was represented by many as a fanatical Hispanophile whose *Conference about the Next Succession* had been targeted at James's succession hopes.[12] Nevertheless he was bold with James and made it clear that as far as he was concerned Catholics would drive a hard bargain. Addressing himself to James for the first time as his king, he managed the required abasement with extraordinary nerve:

> In this great fortune, and prosperous entrance of your Majesties raiyne, when all the world doth applaud, and mightie Princes also do everywhence congratulate, I poore worme of the earth should do the same and joyne my weeke, and ingrate voyce with so stronge and pleasant soundes of others; neyther could I well be heard in so great a mutltitude nor should I offer any thing els unto your Majestie then wherwith these dayes you have byn cloyd, as I doubt not, but that your Majesties great wisdome doth easely consider of what nature and condition these acclamations are, though never so just, and due to your present fortune, yet in truth but wyndes, that follow the weather, and oftentymes are more fresh, and pleasant to the outward sense, then profitable to the inward health, if without measure, or caution they be lett in, or imbraced by us.[13]

Yes, he is a 'poore worme of the earth', but only in comparison with the 'mightie Princes'. Yes, congratulations and acclamations are rightly due, and Persons himself 'should' join in. But the king knows that all such ceremony is but empty wind. Fair-weather friends are not to be trusted. So Persons will get to grips with the issues, man to man. After clearing his own name, he earnestly warns James against persecuting the Catholics and alienating their affections, citing the miserable fate of Elizabeth, the folly of depending on the favour of the anti-Catholic faction at court, and the benefits of securing Catholic affection when trying to deal with tension between Protestants and Puritans.

It is unlikely that James was convinced by any of this. He had the option of playing off one Catholic group against another. For instance, loyalist Catholics were planning a *Petition Apologeticall* to try to secure toleration by promising to restrict the number of priests in England.[14] The Gunpowder Plot put Persons at a further disadvantage. According to the English ambassador, Sir Charles Cornwallis, writing to the Earl of Salisbury from Valladolid in 1606, Persons

---

[11]   Robert Persons, Letter to 'Antony Rivers', 6 July 1603, in *Miscellanea II*, ed. J.H. Pollen, SJ; CRS, 2 (London, 1902), pp. 212–18.

[12]   Robert Persons [R. Doleman (pseud.)], *A Conference about the Next Succession to the Crowne of Ingland* (Antwerp, 1594 [*vere* 1595]), henceforth referred to as *A Conference about the Next Succession*. See above, Chapter 4.

[13]   Robert Persons, Letter to King James I, Rome, 18 October 1603, *ABSI*, Anglia III, 36; transcribed by McCoog, 'Harmony Disrupted', pp. 210–15 (p. 210).

[14]   John Bossy, *The English Catholic Community, 1570–1850* (London, 1975), pp. 38–9.

was trying hard to appear loyal to the king, but onlookers remained sceptical: '*Parsons hath so far waded into shuffling with Practices and Turbulencie, as too late it is now to withdrawe his Foot with any hope to gaine Opinion of a quiet Disposition.*' [15] Some suspected him of complicity in the Gunpowder Treason itself, but, as Edward Coffin argued, if there had been any evidence of this, 'all pulpits, all bookes had proclaimed it, all Princes Courts, yea all cornes [sic] of Christendome had been cloyed with Embassages, pamphlets, Inuectiues, and clamors against him'.[16] Despite this atmosphere of suspicion, and the disappointments of the accession and the Gunpowder Plot, Persons was prepared to enter vigorously into the debate over toleration.

* * *

To understand what James had in mind in his dealings with Catholics it is helpful to invoke his ecumenical vision for Europe,[17] because one can see his European blueprint as an analogy for his religious policy for England. Several times in the early years of his reign James made an appeal, either to the Pope or his fellow princes, for a general council of the church, in which the Pope was to play a leading but not a dominant or supreme role. Europe's Christian princes would sponsor, support and to some extent monitor the proceedings; rather like literary patrons, they might expect the council to be accountable to them in some way. Since the Pope, *primus inter pares*, would have to accept the rulings of the general council, it was to be hoped that the result would be a re-unified church, founded on the Roman Catholic communion but mildly reformed. Not unpredictably, James's efforts were futile. The Vatican politely but firmly pointed out that the Roman Church was in full accord with all the previous general councils, most recently the Council of Trent – to which Protestants had been invited – and there was little point holding another one that would simply endorse Roman belief and practice. James might as well convert straight away.[18] Notwithstanding this failure, the evidence suggests that James's domestic religious policy owed much to this kind of thinking. Under royal guidance and patronage Catholics would be brought into the ecumenical fold, shedding their corruptions, still affording the Pope his due as spiritual leader without supreme authority. Hence his optimism that Catholics could practise their faith in peace if they simply renounced the corrupt doctrine of the papal deposing power by swearing an oath of allegiance. To use a term

---

[15]   Ralph Winwood, *Memorials of Affairs of State in the Reigns of Q. Elizabeth and K. James I, Collected (chiefly) from the Original Papers of ... Sir Ralph Winwood*, ed. Edmund Sawyer (3 vols; London, 1725), vol. 2, p. 226.

[16]   Edward Coffin, 'A Preface to the Reader', in Robert Persons, *A Discussion of the Answere of M. William Barlow, D. of Divinity, to the Booke intituled: The Iudgment of a Catholicke Englishman ... concerning The Apology of the new Oath of Allegiance* (St Omer, 1612), sig. k1r.

[17]   See W.B. Patterson, *King James VI and I and the Reunion of Christendom* (Cambridge, 1997).

[18]   Ibid., ch. 2.

now fashionable, one could describe James's policy as one of 'concordance',[19] seeking common ground among the religious traditions and purging the excesses of Presbyterianism and Romanism (that is, a clinging to the full panoply of papal pretensions).

These attitudes are evident in James's reaction to the Gunpowder Treason. He immediately made it clear that he would resist any attempt to blame Catholics in general for the conspiracy; in fact, his immediate target, apart from the conspirators themselves, was the Puritan faction among the Protestants, because the events simply confirmed his fear of religious extremism.[20] In 'A Proclamation denouncing Thomas Percy and other his adherents to be Traitors', published on the very day of the Treason, he declared: 'wee are by good experience so well perswaded of the Loyaltie of divers of our Subjects (though not professing true Religion) that they doe as much abhorre this detestable conspiracie as our Selfe'. At first he blamed only the conspirators, attributing their crime to ignorance: 'so utterly corrupted with the Superstition of the Romish Religion, as seduced by the blindnesse thereof, and being otherwise of lewde life, insolent disposition, and for the most part of desperate estate', but later he extended his displeasure to Jesuit priestcraft, while continuing to protest his conciliatory attitude:

> It is so manifest to the world by all our proceedings hitherto towards those Subjects of ours, which doe professe the Romish Religion, how slowe Wee have been to extend the severitie of our Lawes (in matter of life) even against the Romish Priests themselves, who seditiously incite and warrant the ignorant Papists to forsake their naturall love and loyaltie.[21]

The chief measure taken against non-complicit Catholics was the drafting of a new Oath of Allegiance requiring them to renounce adherence to the doctrine that the Pope had authority to depose heretical or tyrannical princes. James intervened to alter the wording so that it implicitly acknowledged the papal right to excommunicate him, as long as this did not compromise his subjects' allegiance.[22] He appears to have genuinely believed that he was thus making a friendly invitation to English Catholics to become part of a national consensus of Christian orthodoxy. 'Was there euer a more Gratious part in a King ... towards Subiects of a contrary Religion', he asked, 'then by making them to

---

[19]   See J.C. Laursen and C.J. Nederman (introd.), *Beyond the Persecuting Society: Religious Toleration Before the Enlightenment* (Philadelphia, 1998), p. 6, citing Mario Turchetti, 'Religious Concord and Political Tolerance in Sixteenth- and Seventeenth-Century France', *Sixteenth Century Journal* 22 (1991): 15–25.

[20]   See Lori Anne Ferrell, *Government by Polemics: James I, the King's Preachers, and the Rhetorics of Conformity 1603–1625* (Stanford, 1998), pp. 1–24.

[21]   'A Proclamation for the apprehension and discoverie of John Gerrard, Henry Garnet, and Oswald Tesmond, 15 Jan 1606'. For this series of proclamations, see *Stuart Royal Proclamations, Vol. 1: Royal Proclamations of King James I, 1603–1625*, ed. James F. Larkin and Paul L. Hughes (Oxford, 1973), pp. 125, 124, 131.

[22]   The Oath condemns the doctrine 'That Princes which bee excommunicated or depriued by the Pope, may be deposed or murthered by their subjects, or any other whatsoeuer', 3 Jac. I, c. 5, in *A Collection of Sundry Statutes*, ed. F. Pulton (London, 1940), p. 1304.

take this Oath, to publish their honest fidelitie in Temporall things to their Soueraigne, and thereby to wipe off that imputation and great slander which was laid vpon the whole professors of that Religion, by the furious enterprise of these Powder-men?'[23] These irenic inclinations need to be qualified, however. Even before the Gunpowder Treason, James had tightened up the recusancy laws:

> But now to make all even, and that the *Papists should not take heart upon the depressing of the Puritans*, (or that in deed they did so, *and flattered themselves with a vaine Hope of Tolleration*, or that it was cunningly imposed upon them by the contrary part,) upon *Sunday* last the King made a long and vehement Apology for himself in the Councill Chamber, that he never had any such Intention, *that if he thought his Sons would condescend to any such Course, he could wish the Kingdom translated to his Daughter*: That the Mittigation of their Payments, was in Consideration *that not any of them had lift up his Hand against his coming in*, and so he gave them a Year of Probation to conform themselves, which seeing it had not wrought that Effect, he had fortified all the Laws that were against them, and made them stronger, (saving for Blood, from which he had a naturall Aversion,) and *commanded they should be put in Execution to the uttermost*; and that this his Intention should be made known publickly.[24]

It has been claimed that this signalled that he 'never intended to pursue a public programme of toleration':[25] In fact, it shows the King a little embarrassed, protesting too much, but clearly wary of showing too much favour to Catholics. A similar sense of constraint was in evidence after the events of late 1605, as if there were some difference between King and Parliament over the appropriate treatment of Catholics, so that the Oath of Allegiance, which could be presented as conciliatory, formed part of a group of severe measures.[26]

If opinions differ on the motives behind the Oath of Allegiance, certainly the effects were contradictory. Some Protestant politicians were disquieted by the thought that the oath could be taken by Catholics without abandoning their fundamental allegiance to Rome. They need not have been anxious: the Oath had an extremely damaging and divisive effect on English Catholicism. Since the lines of division did not follow those already established by the appellant

---

[23] James I, *Triplici nodo, triplex cuneus: or, An Apologie for the Oath of Allegiance, Against the two Breves of Pope Paulus Quintus, and the late Letter of Cardinal Bellarmine to G. Blackwel the Arch-priest* (London, 1607 [*vere* 1608]), p. 77; see Anthony Milton, *Catholic and Reformed: The Roman and Protestant Churches in English Protestant Thought, 1600–1640* (Cambridge, 1995), pp. 255–63; M.C. Questier, 'Loyalty, Religion, and State Power in Early Modern England: English Romanism and the Jacobean Oath of Allegiance', *The Historical Journal* 40 (1997): 311–29.

[24] John Chamberlain, Letter to Ralph Winwood, 26 February 1604, in Winwood, *Memorials of Affairs of State in the Reigns of Q. Elizabeth and K. James I*, vol. 2, p. 49.

[25] Diana Robertson, 'Bishop Lancelot Andrewes and his Gunpowder Treason Sermons, 1606–1618', in D.E. Kennedy, Diana Robertson and Alexandra Walsham (eds), *Grounds of Controversy: Three Studies in Late 16th and Early 17th Century English Polemics* (Melbourne, 1989), pp. 49–96 (p. 51).

[26] Brodrick, vol. 2, p. 192, claims that this is why Robert Bellarmine was not taken in by the ambiguity of the Oath.

crisis, we must infer that many Catholics experienced an excruciating dilemma, and this may indeed have been the intention of those, including Bancroft, who devised the Oath.[27] Thus James need not have been so surprised and indignant when his invitation was rebuffed. The Archpriest, George Blackwell, at first called a conference to discuss the Oath, and then referred the matter to Rome for guidance. Two papal breves and a letter from Robert Bellarmine unequivocally proscribed the Oath, and this remained the official position even though Blackwell himself, under pressure from Bancroft, submitted on 24 June 1607, pleading the distress that the Catholic community would experience if the Oath were refused.[28] James responded anonymously to the three offending documents in a work entitled *Triplici nodo, triplex cuneus: or, An Apologie for the Oath of Allegiance*, published by the King's printer, Robert Barker, on 14 February 1608 (given as 1607 on the title page). The characteristically pedantic title alluded to a three-fold wedge (his book) against a threefold knot (the breves and the letter). He provoked Bellarmine into a Latin response under the name of one of his secretaries, Matthaeus Torti, some time between March and September 1608, while Persons replied in English, also under an assumed identity, in *The Judgment of a Catholicke Englishman*.[29] The broad hints Persons made about the authorship forced James into the open:[30] he republished the *Triplici nodo* (somewhat revised) under his own name, addressed a lengthy accompanying *Premonition* to his fellow princes in the hope of solidarity, withdrew the revised version from the press to make a few trivial corrections, and finally issued it on 8 April 1609 only to have it politely ignored by most of the princely presentees.[31] Eventually he had to settle for delegating the controversy to Bishops Lancelot Andrewes (to reply

---

[27]   Milton, pp. 257–8; Questier, 'Loyalty, Religion, and State Power in Early Modern England'. Bossy, *The English Catholic Community*, p. 41, points out that appellant clergy refused to take the oath.

[28]   Blackwell's submission followed the first breve (September 1606), before he had received the second breve (August 1607) and the letter from Bellarmine (September 1607). Bellarmine's letter, Blackwell's response and his further exposition of his position are to be found in *A Large Examination taken at Lambeth, according to his Maiesties direction, point by point, of M. George Blakwell* (London, 1607).

[29]   Robert Bellarmine, SJ, *Responsio Matthaei Torti Presbyteri et Theologi Papiensis, ad Librum inscriptum, Triplici Nodo Triplex Cuneus* (Cologne, 1608); Robert Persons, *The Judgment of a Catholicke English-man, living in banishment for his Religion: Written to his private friend in England. Concerninge A late Booke set forth, and entituled: Triplici nodo, triplex cuneus, Or, An Apologie for the Oath of Allegiance. Against two Breves of Pope Paulus V. to the Catholickes of England; & a Letter of Cardinall Bellarmine to M. George Blackwell Arch-priest. Wherin, the said Oath is shewed to be unlawfull to the Catholicke Conscience: for so much, as it conteyneth sundry clauses repugnant to his Religion* (St Omer, 1608), henceforth referred to as *The Judgment of a Catholicke English-man*.

[30]   On James's anonymity, see Marcy L. North, 'Anonymity's Subject: James I and the Debate over the Oath of Allegiance', *New Literary History* 33 (2002): 215–32.

[31]   'A Proclamation for the calling in of such of the Bookes of his Maiesties Apologie of the Oath of Allegiance, as were of an erronious impression, 7 April 1609', in *Stuart Royal Proclamations*, vol. 1, pp. 211–12 and n. 2; James I, *An Apologie for the Oath of Allegiance: first set forth without a name, now acknowledged by James, King. Together with a premonition to all most mightie monarches* (London, 1609), pp. 5–6.

to Bellarmine in Latin) and William Barlow (to deal with Persons).[32] By all accounts Persons tried to ignore Barlow, but eventually spent four months writing *A Discussion of the Answere of M. William Barlow, D. of Divinity, to the Booke intituled: The Iudgment of a Catholicke Englishman ... concerning The Apology of the new Oath of Allegiance,* which was incomplete at his death and finally published in 1612.[33]

James was constrained by consideration of several interest groups of which the English Catholics were but one. It is risky, therefore, to be categorical about his agenda when dealing with a particular action, publication or political measure. Moreover, his overtures were compromised throughout by his obsession with his prerogative, so that any sign of derogation from his princely authority and immunity from criticism caused an almost comical over-reaction. Any promotion of a political theory, however modestly defined, that gave independent authority in the realm to anyone or anything but himself made him recoil in horror.[34] Seeking to flatter him, William Barlow went so far as to suggest that even the Almighty had to tread warily when dealing with princes.[35] Certainly Robert Persons had to treat James's policy with vigilant suspicion.

***

The critical aspect of the new Oath of Allegiance, as drawn up and placed before Parliament in May 1606, was the denunciation of the papal deposing power. This was a doctrine that was in some dispute in Catholic circles, but the dilemma facing English Catholics was that by taking the oath they were accepting the judgment of a Protestant layman on a Catholic article of faith, widely held and almost universally taught: they were asked to 'abhorre, detest, and abiure, as impious and hereticall, this damnable doctrine and position, That Princes which bee excommunicated or depriued by the Pope, may be deposed or murthered by their subjects, or any other whatsoeuer'.[36] The King and his advisers heatedly denied that it was a matter of faith, arguing that it referred only to an illegitimate papal pretension to have the right to intervene in the temporal disposition of Christian realms. It was not denied that the Pope had the responsibility of caring for the spiritual welfare of Catholics

---

[32] William Barlow, *An Answer to a Catholike English-man (so by himself entituled) who, without a Name, passed his Censure upon the Apology, made by the Right High and mightie Prince Iames ... for the Oath of Allegeance* (London, 1609); for details of the works by Bellarmine and Andrewes, and the further ramifications of the controversy, see Milward, *Religious Controversies of the Jacobean Age,* pp. 89–94, 109–114.

[33] Robert Persons, *A Discussion of the Answere of M. William Barlow ... to the Booke intituled: The Judgment of a Catholike Englishman ... concerning the Apology of the new Oath of Allegiance* (St Omer, 1612), henceforth referred to as *A Discussion of the Answere of M. William Barlow.* On the composition, see Edward Coffin, 'Preface to the Reader', sig. b1v–b2r.

[34] See, for example, *An Apologie for the Oath of Allegiance,* pp. 117–18.

[35] Barlow, *An Answer to a Catholike English-man,* p. 42; *A Discussion of the Answere of M. William Barlow,* p. 108.

[36] 3 Jac. I, c. 5, in *A Collection of Sundry Statutes,* p. 1304.

everywhere, but he was not entitled, James believed, to recourse to any but spiritual means; neither directly nor indirectly could he employ military power. The full extent of what was demanded here is evident from the examination of Blackwell after he had taken the oath; it was not enough, his examiners asserted, simply to repudiate, in theory, the Pope's right to act against kings at will; they wanted a guarantee that Catholics would remain loyal if the Pope should in fact move against England:

> It was told this Examinate, that all these points so well by him enlarged, did come farre short of the meaning of the said oath: because it is very vncertaine, what the Roman Catholickes in England would doe, if the Pope should *de facto* proceede with his Maiestie, as some of his predecessours did with the late Queene of worthy memorie; which vncertaintie the State may not endure.

There could be no question of any residual political allegiance to the Pope in any form whatsoever.[37]

Persons's basic stance towards the Oath was that it was an assault on the Catholic conscience, that to deny the papal deposing power was to leave the Church unprotected from tyranny, and that it was of no practical benefit to the state. His initial response was to appeal to Robert Bellarmine in May 1606 to denounce the appellant loyalist doctrine that he believed was responsible for the Oath. In other words, he intuited that the Oath was designed to pressurize Catholics into joining the appellant camp; it was an extension of Bancroft's earlier policy of encouraging collaboration.[38] In the same year he composed 'A discourse against taking the oath in England', which dismisses the various devices or evasions, as he calls them, by which Catholics could square the Oath with their conscience in order to avoid temporal loss.[39] In so doing he anticipated Blackwell's plea to save the Catholic community from ruin of body and soul. It was no good turning to authorities such as Salmeron, Covarrunias and St Gregory of Nazianzus to claim that since the papal deposing power was necessarily destructive, it was *ipso facto* null and void and could be renounced; it all depended on how the power was applied in practice, and

> we should doe the Pope our Superior an injury to presume upon our own imagination that he would execute a thing *in destructionem Ecclesiae* before we see the end of it, and not rather think that it should fall-out *ad aedificationem* if he did it, considering he would both doe it with deepe deliberation and alsoe by direction and assistance of the Holy Ghost promised unto that Sea for the assured direction of the church.[40]

---

[37]   *A Large Examination taken at Lambeth … of M. George Blackwell*, p. 13.

[38]   Memorial to Cardinal Bellarmine, 18 May 1606, *ABSI*, Persons Letters 46/12/7 fols 1586–7. Persons notes that 11 or 12 books containing this doctrine (of denying the papal supremacy) have been delated to the Inquisition.

[39]   *ABSI*, Persons Letters 46/12/7, fols 1590–1617.

[40]   Ibid., fol. 1601; cf. Blackwell's reply to Bellarmine, *A Large Examination taken at Lambeth … of M. George Blackwell*, sigs c4v–e2r.

To take the oath would do the Pope an injury and the King no favour; no Catholic, even if he believed in the papal deposing power, was obliged to act on it;[41] neither could any Catholic who repudiated the deposing power be trusted not to betray his King as readily as he betrayed the Pope.

It was particularly futile, Persons argued, for the authorities to try to make assurance doubly sure by requiring the oath-taker to forswear equivocation. If they were afraid of equivocators, there was no way of securing them. Persons provides a satirical cameo of this figure of anti-Jesuit propaganda:

> By what wordes or meanes can a magistrate tye these men men to aunswere truly or directly ... this strongest Sampson no Philistin power can bridle.
>
> But what? is there no Dalila can powle or shave away the very haire wherein his principal strength resteth? behold himself can play that feate with his owne rasore by forswearing all equivocation ... do you not see how these slipslings wil stil remayne untyed? and in what sorte Sampsons haires by cutting are multiplyed, or which is more wonderfull that being cleer shaven to the skinne yet his strength remaineth without foundation. A man would thinke that he might safely give credit unto a deepe dissembler, if by oath he would testify to use noe dissimulation.[42]

The cutting sarcasm of the final sentence reflects Persons's scorn for the irrational fear aroused by the limited use of equivocation under persecution.

The discourse was presumably written to provide direction to Catholics, and its main thrust was to warn against playing into the authorities' hands. The following year, in 1607, Persons felt it necessary to reiterate the case against attending church, recognizing that with the confirmation and even augmentation of the recusancy laws, the appeal for sanctioned church papism was on the increase again. The Blackwell case for compassion in the face of hardship seemed strong. Persons confessed that he had received a Latin translation of an English work on hearing Protestant sermons; this, too, was too dangerous to allow. In response he wrote a Latin tract entitled *Quaestiones duae de sacris alienis non aduendis, ad vsum praximque Angliae breuiter explicatae*.[43] Here too his intention was to persuade Catholics to hold the line.

In his published works against the Oath of Allegiance Persons was concerned to discredit the official policy and to present a reasoned account of conscientious Catholic solidarity against the Oath. In dealing with his royal opponent, he had to resist compromise but also avoid unnecessary provocation. We have to assume that he did not take long to recognize the King's hand in the *Triplici nodo, triplex cuneus*. In *The Judgment of a Catholicke English-man* he affected to believe that the author was either Thomas Morton or another divine somewhat nearer his Majesty. He was thus able to write boldly about the author and then excuse himself by pleading mistaken identity. More than

---

[41] *ABSI*, Persons Letters 46/12/7, fols 1611–12.

[42] Ibid., fols 1615–16.

[43] Robert Persons, *Quaestiones duae de sacris alienis non aduendis, ad vsum praximque Angliae breuiter explicatae* (St Omer, 1607), esp. pp. 10–11, 41–2.

this, he could shame the King into acknowledging his authorship or distancing himself from the *Triplici nodo*.

Helping himself, then, to a licence for satire, Persons assumed mock surprise and disbelief. How did such ranting against Bellarmine consort with the moral gravity to which the new king pretended and which he paraded in his admonition to Catholics and Puritans?

> That other iniurious and stinging conclusion also, that, *There is no greater difference betweene* God *and* Belial, *light and darknes, heauen and hell, then there is betweene the doctrine of the Scriptures, and Card[in]all Bellarmines workes, concerning the dignity of temporall Princes,* I can not imagine that the equity, and grauity of his Ma.tie would euer allow of it, being apparently a passionate exaggeration, and refuted euery where by *Bellarmine* himselfe.[44]

The terms 'apparently' and 'passionate' signal the very same extremism James was so anxious to suppress in his subjects. And what of his reputation for learning? He had dissected an analogy of Bellarmine's: Persons rebuked him, as he might an ignorant pupil, for not realizing that all analogies can be made to look false by concentrating on irrelevant aspects of the similitude. The result of this 'trifling', as he put it, was that 'we should ouerthrow all similitudes whatsoeuer, and consequently we should eneruate many most heauenly speaches of our Sauiour in the Ghospell, that stand vpon similitudes'.[45]

Persons sought to embarrass James further by mistaking the king's own words for those of an intolerant Puritan. Here he sarcastically questions which side is being unreasonable in the debate over liberty of conscience:

> From such a King (I say) for vs to expect liberty of Conscience, and equality with other Subiects (in this poynt at least of freedome of soule) *what height of pryde* may it be called? May it not rather seeme *height of pryde* in this Minister, & his fellowes, that hauing byn old enemyes, and always borne a hard, & hatefull hand, and tongue against his Ma[ies]tie both in their Sermons, Bookes, Speaches, all the tyme of the late Queenes raigne; now vpon the suddayne *sine* ... will needs be so priuiledged, & assume vnto themselues such a confident presumption of his Ma[ies]ties speciall fauour, as to suffer no man to stand by them, but to hold it for *height of pryde* in vs, to hope for any freedome and liberty of our Conscience at all?[46]

The high moral tone of reproach to which James felt he was entitled sounded like arrogant spitefulness from a mere minister, glad that his party at least was not in the firing line. To expect 'such a King', a king, that is, who had so generously shown his due appreciation of Catholic loyalty, and who felt so injured by the unkind response of gunpowder and papal briefs, to sanction such Puritan intolerance, was unthinkable. Persons thus deployed the satirical shift of perspective presented by James's anonymity to shame the king into recognizing his overweening pretension.

---

[44]   *The Judgment of a Catholicke English-man*, p. 5.
[45]   Ibid., p. 106.
[46]   Ibid., p. 40.

Perhaps the most telling exposure of the inadequacy of James's argument was a bald summary that came so close to parody that Persons could put it in mock quotation marks, referring to 'iniurious inferences ... to witt':

> 'That Catholicks suffer nothing for their Conscience, That there is no persecution at all in *England*, That there is nothing exacted by this last oath, but *only* and *meerly* Cyuill Obedience, and that in this, the Pope exhorteth them to disobey the Temporall Prince in Temporall dutyes, and thereby giueth iust occasion to the Prince to vse his sword against them, and consequently that he is cause of the effusion of their bloud, and of the infamy of Catholicke Religion: as though no Catholicke by his Religion could be a true Subiect to his Temporall Prince.'[47]

All of this is intended to be read ironically. By shifting the blame to the Pope, and interpreting all conflict of allegiance as an interference in the temporal realm, James provides himself with a pretext to act against his Catholic subjects. Thus Persons insinuates that in defending the Oath of Allegiance James has revealed its real purpose: not (as was claimed) to give Catholics the chance of proving themselves loyal, but to identify true Catholics as traitors. The irony invites us to reverse the final clause to read: 'no subject to this temporal Prince can be a true Catholic (in the light of this Oath)'.

Having characterized the writer of the *Triplici nodo* as a logically inept, emotionally irresponsible and morally presumptuous embarrassment to the King's cause, Persons offered James the opportunity of a dignified retreat. He invited him, at the very end of *The Judgment of a Catholicke English-man*, to repudiate the *Triplici nodo*, act as a father to the nation and fulfil the Catholics' expectations of becoming reconciled – though unrepentant – to the rest of the family:

> Would God it might please his dyuine Ma.tie so to inlighten and illustrate that excellent vnderstanding of our Prince and Soueraigne, as he may see the many & great inconueniences, that do & must follow vpon so violent courses as these men for their own vtlitie do suggest, & prosecute. Nothing can be more pitifull, then to see a Noble House diuided in itselfe, & the one to beate, hunt, & pursue the other, & this to be their continuall exercise, especially of Children, vnder the sight of their owne Father, louing them all, and desyring to be beloued. Ah! what sollicitude must there needs be in that Fathers hart! And were it not a great synne to increase the same, by casting in oyle to augment the same?[48]

This was just the kind of self-image – the wise and loving patriarch of a noble household – that would appeal to James. It was reinforced by the *persona* that Persons adopted, of the 'Catholicke English-man, living in banishment for his Religion', writing 'to his private friend in England'. This was, like most of Persons's *noms-de-plume*, not a real disguise but the presentation of a point of view. An exile would not have to take the Oath himself and so would not be subject to the personal dilemma it enforced. He could see the bigger picture,

---

[47] Ibid., p. 63.
[48] Ibid., pp. 123–4.

the unity of the Catholic Church: English recusants, Englishmen in exile, the Pope and his cardinals. From his own superior vantage point he beckoned to James to rise above the pettiness of religious faction.

Apart from stripping bare the false assumptions of the *Triplici nodo*, Persons was concerned in *The Judgment of a Catholicke English-man* to defend the Catholic conscience that was being treated with such suspicion. This was not a simple task, because the Catholic conscience did not seem to be speaking with one voice. Some English Catholics had already taken the Oath. Did this mean that they had sundered themselves irrevocably from their brethren? Were they unforgivable apostates? Persons found himself in a dilemma here: when he tried to dissuade Catholics from taking the Oath (in 'A discourse against taking the oath in England'), he could admit no excuses; now, in *The Judgment of a Catholicke English-man*, he sought to repair the damage by conceding that oath-takers had not intended to exclude the Pope absolutely from any interest in the political dispensation in England:

> To deny simply and absolutely, *That the Pope as supreme Pastour of the Catholicke Church, hath any authoritie left him by Christ, eyther directly or indirectly, with cause or without cause, in neuer so great a necessity, or for neuer so great and publicke an vtility of the Christian Religion, to proceed against any Prince whatsoeuer temporally, for his restraint or amendment, or to permitt other Princes to doe the same:* this, I suppose, was neuer their meaning that tooke the *Oath*.[49]

He reaffirmed his total opposition to any equivocation in taking the oath;[50] but to maintain a putative unity of doctrine among all English Catholics, those who would take the Oath and those who would not, he had to accept that some of his co-religionists had lapsed into a form of equivocation.[51]

This looks like special pleading. But there was an important principle at stake. James's contention in tendering the Oath was that there was already an implicit division among Catholics between the loyal and the dissident, the moderate and the extremist, and the Oath would simply make the division manifest. Persons's interpretation of what the oath-takers had done repudiated this inherent division and offered another in its place: it was not the loyal and the moderate who took the oath, merely the weak. All Catholics were faced with a crisis of conscience. Some broke under the pressure, played hide and seek with their conscience, and equivocated. But conscience was uniformly against the oath. This is also what the documentary evidence suggests: it is impossible to predict, from earlier allegiances, whether a given Catholic would take the oath or not. The Oath polarized Catholics as never before: there was a sharp

---

[49]   Ibid., p. 19.

[50]   Ibid., p. 96.

[51]   For a sympathetic view of equivocating with the Oath, see Megan Matchinske, 'Gendering Catholic Conformity: The Politics of Equivocation in Elizabeth Grymeston's *Miscelanea*', *Journal of English and Germanic Philology* 101 (2002): 329–57, who argues that for women, especially, being part of a network of human relationships was more important than asserting difference: 'accommodating Catholics like Grymeston refuse to imagine their community as severed, as radically transformed into a separatist Catholic state by direct Romanist intervention' (p. 353).

increase in conformism in 1606, but at the same time the French ambassador, La Boderie, confessed that he was astonished by the fervour of the Catholic reaction. Many were prepared to go into exile, he claimed, even if they were so old that all they sought was a foreign grave. Others remained in England despite the threatening circumstances. This was not, perhaps, exactly what Henri IV, who was usually rendered uneasy by signs of Catholic extremism in England, wanted to hear.[52]

Such a view that Catholics took the oath not out of conscience but for expediency, lent weight to the charge of persecution implied by Persons's emphasis on the distress brought about by the pressure on conscience. He described graphically what it was like to give in:

> For that the griefe of their new wound of conscience remayning still within them, and stirring them to more auersion of hart, for the iniury receaued, must needes worke contrary effects to that which is pretended. And whosoeuer will not sticke to sweare against his conscience for feare, fauour, or some other like passion, may be presumed, that he will as easily breake his *Oath*, after he hath sworne, vpon like motiues, if occasion doe mooue him. And among all other passions, none is more strong, then that of reuenge for oppressions receaued.[53]

In this passage he applies the kind of psychological analysis familiar from *The Christian Directory*:[54] the struggle with temptation and the agony of the sinner – thus bringing the politics of the Oath of Allegiance into the context of the spiritual journey. One cannot dismiss this outcrop of pastoral concern as mere sentimentalism or manipulation. It is made clear that the Oath is a sham. It might satisfy the King's absolutist sentiments to have the Catholics abjure a doctrine so limited in its application that no hostile act against Elizabeth or James could be attributed to it.[55] It could not guarantee that anyone would not turn traitor; nor did it reliably distinguish the dangerous from the rest of the Catholic community. Persons thus calls the *bona fides* of the Oath into question and questions the justification of the suffering caused.

The language of moral theology evokes a universal agony of soul. In a familiar manoeuvre, Persons implicitly contrasts the reality of that experience – so vividly called to mind – with the vanity of the King's policy. The motif

---

[52]   Antoine Lefevre de la Boderie, Letter to Villeroy, 1 July 1606, *Ambassades de Monsieur de la Boderie, en Angleterre, Sous le regne d'Henri IV. & la minorite de Louis XIII. depuis les annees 1606. jusqu'en 1611* (5 vols; n.p., 1750), vol. 1, pp. 161–2; cf. Michael Questier, *Conversion, Politics and Religion in England, 1580–1625* (Cambridge, 1996), who writes: 'In fact, the number of conformists after the Plot started to increase sharply in 1606' (p. 137).

[53]   *The Judgment of a Catholicke English-man*, p. 21.

[54]   *The First Booke of the Christian Exercise, appertayning to Resolution* (Rouen, 1582, revd 1585, 1607), henceforth referred to as *The Christian Directory*. Quotations from the 1582 version are taken from *The Christian Directory (1582): The First Booke of the Christian Exercise, appertayning to Resolution*, ed. Victor Houliston (Leiden, 1998).

[55]   This is debatable; the excommunication of Queen Elizabeth, the Northern Rebellion and the Spanish Armada might be cited against the deposing power, although technically this was not the doctrine used to justify these acts.

recurs wherever he exposes the apologer's learning as mere showcasing, or his advisers as mere placemen.

> And yet doth he so insist on it, and so dilateth himselfe vpon this false surmised principle (*that Cyuill Obedience is denyed*) as though all his Discourse and Treatise dependeth only of this (as indeed it doth,) and therfore he entreth into the confutation therof with a great florish of Scriptures, Fathers, and Councells (wherin he and his do abound, when they say the same that we do, but otherwise are altogether barren) as though in earnest we did deny it: which thing neuer so much as passed through our cogitations, but do hold and teach that Subiects are bound to obey their Temporall Princes in all things lawfull, and those not only good Princes, but bad also: and not only out of feare or flattery, but out of Conscience, as the Apostle teacheth *propter Conscientiam,* for Conscience sake, but not *contra Conscientiam,* against Conscience.[56]

Against the plethora of misapplied 'florish of Scriptures, Fathers, and Councells', Persons counterposes his reasonable doctrine, in which every phrase counts. Beyond all the argumentation, refutation and (at its lowest) point-scoring, *The Judgment of a Catholicke English-man* engages in real negotiation: as if to say, we have a weighty concern, based on a solid foundation of learning and teaching, and we are willing to meet with you if you will take our doctrine seriously and not dismiss it as popish corruption.

What, then, is the settlement Persons wishes to propose in *The Judgment of a Catholicke English-man*, given his dismissal of the oath's expectations? First, he explains in what sense he is willing to grant supreme ecclesiastical authority to the king: namely, that the king has ultimate temporal authority over all his subjects, whether lay or clerical;[57] hardly a concession, one might protest, since James clearly had this authority *de facto*, but it should be remembered that St Thomas Becket had in effect denied what Persons is here allowing; and he was a powerful presence in post-Reformation English Catholic minds.[58] Where James was scandalized by Bellarmine's version of the basis of royal authority, Persons patiently explains that it still proclaims divine sanction:

> So as the former proposition, *That Kings haue not their Authority nor office from God nor his Law,* is very fraudulently sett downe. For if he vnderstand, that their forme of Principality and Office therin, is not immediatly from Gods institution, but by meanes of humane lawes, of succession, election, or the like; it is true. But if he meane, that their Authority is not from God, eyther mediate, or immediate, or induceth not obligation of Conscience in obeying them, as it seemeth he would haue his Reader to thinke; it is most false. And the Apologer ought not to haue walked in these obscurities, if he had not meant vprightly.[59]

---

[56] *The Judgment of a Catholicke English-man*, p. 50.

[57] Ibid., p. 73.

[58] See Victor Houliston, 'St Thomas Becket in the Propaganda of the English Counter-Reformation', *Renaissance Studies* 7 (1993): 44–70.

[59] *The Judgment of a Catholicke English-man*, p. 121.

Here he issues another invitation to James to accept obedience on reasonable terms. This is not the grand theory to which James subscribed, but it could assure loyalty none the less for that. The more modestly it was affirmed, the more convincing, in the long run, it was likely to be.

***

Would James have the nerve to acknowledge the *Apology* as his after this? Even though he had plenty of competent controversialists at his disposal, who could cover his shame and flatter his eloquence, he could not resist responding to these barbs in person. He took the effrontery of Persons's denunciation of Queen Elizabeth in high dudgeon and assigned to William Barlow the task of answering *The Judgment of a Catholicke English-man* point by point. There is no evidence that he was goaded by either Bellarmine or Persons into turning the screw on the recusants. Fortunately he did not allow personal pique or his appetite for intellectual debate to affect his judgment on policy issues.[60] But it seems the debate may have clarified a shift in thinking about the royal ecclesiastical supremacy. Put on his mettle, William Barlow proffered some arguments in *An Answer to a Catholike English-man* that could be interpreted to mean that the exaggeration of the king's claim to absolute political authority led paradoxically to the diminution of his ecclesiastical power.

For James, it was more pressing to eliminate the last vestiges of foreign political jurisdiction within his domain, the papal deposing power (whether it made any practical difference or not), than to assert his rights as Governor of the Church of England. In a sense he wanted the Church of England to include the Catholics, if they would submit to the reform of Romish corruptions. On these terms, he was prepared to concede a form of spiritual authority among Catholics to the Pope. Just what this implied in relation to the established Church of England it was hard to say, and he left Barlow to try to work out a definition of royal ecclesiastical authority in regard to things temporal and spiritual. With hindsight, this may have been a strategic blunder, because Barlow was not astute enough to pre-empt Persons's skill in recognizing an opening. To separate religion and politics has been a fatal attraction for many regimes; to separate temporal and spiritual authority in the immediate post-Reformation period was practically unthinkable.[61] All kinds of scholastic distinctions, chiefly concerning the distinction between the order of grace and the order of nature, could be invoked in order to draw the line of demarcation as clearly as possible, but ultimately there was nothing that could be defined as purely spiritual or purely temporal. Barlow got himself tied up in knots, and Persons was not the man to spare him.

---

[60]   See Milton, p. 55.

[61]   On this point, see Ferrell, p. 92: 'To concede the pope's spiritual authority within England, as the king protested he was willing to do in his *Apology*, was to unhitch secular loyalty from the shared religious premises that made it secure. To depend on the force of language alone to negotiate the gulf yawning between civil and religious loyalty was asking not only the improbable but also the hitherto unimaginable.'

The terms of the argument forced Barlow to be very wary of allowing the secular ruler judgment in religious matters other than the purely practical or 'executive'. Accordingly, he approved of St Ambrose's refusal to deliver some church vessels to the Emperor Valentinian. The emperor's demand was hardly an interference with the definition of church doctrine but nevertheless entered tentatively on the realm of the sacred. Persons wondered whether Barlow, as Bishop of Lincoln, would refuse to hand over the communion cup to the king's officers:

> If he would, what kind of Supremacy doth he allow his Maiesty in spirituall matters, if he may be denyed and disobeyed in these also that are in a certain sort mixt, and in some part conioyned with temporall resepcts?
> And truly when I do consider with my selfe, with what degrees M. Barlow doth descend and go downeward in defending of the Ecclesiasticall Supremacy of his Maiesty, bringing it as it were to nothing from that high pitch, wherin King Henry the eight both placed it, and left it, & his children King Edward and Queene Elizabeth continued the same; I cannot but wonder and admire the prouidence of Almighty God, that hath wrought the ouerthrow in effect of that new Protestant Idoll, of spirituall Authority in temporall Princes, euen by Protestants themselues.[62]

Barlow's sycophancy and his trivializing of royal authority are savagely attacked. To such a low pitch had the pretensions of caesaropapism been reduced. Persons also seized on Barlow's defensiveness towards the Puritans, such that the term 'ceremony' was used to cover anything that caused offence to them. 'Is all the dignity, and preheminence, which his sayd Lord hath aboue all the Ministers in England', he asked satirically, 'his superiority ouer the Cleargy, his being Archbishop & Primate, his spirituall Iurisdiction, his Courtes of the Arches, his power of dispensations, his making Ministers, and giuing them power to preach, teach, & administer Sacraments: Is all this but a ceremony?'[63] Once Barlow had defined this authority as 'executive' rather than 'definitive' it was open to Persons to argue that there could be no further claim that matters of doctrine required royal or imperial assent. The idea, enshrined in the Oath, that James could condemn as 'impious and heretical' a long-standing Catholic doctrine thus lost all foundation.[64] The difficulty of drawing the line – and the advantages this afforded the Catholic argument – was further reinforced by Persons's assertion that the Pope did not pose the same kind of threat as a foreign secular power: 'there is a great difference betweene this temporall power of the Pope deriued from his supreme spirituall authority, as vniuersall Pastour (which no temporall Prince is) and the pretension of any meere temporall Potentate'.[65] The clash of jurisdictions is not like that between two sovereigns, but between two powers quite different in nature and origin.

As a polemical work, then, A Discussion of the Answere of M. William Barlow shifts the debate away from the immediate politics of the Oath in

---

[62]   A Discussion of the Answere of M. William Barlow, pp. 296–8, 303.
[63]   Ibid., p. 258.
[64]   Ibid., p. 315.
[65]   Ibid., p. 82.

the direction of general principles. Although the book, incomplete as it is, is considerably longer than any of the others involved in the controversy, its method is not to deal exhaustively with every dispute in detail but to select the topics – in order as they have arisen in the controversy so far – and develop them fully.[66] The result is to lower the temperature from the pitch where Barlow had tried to excuse his own bitter style by his opponent's alleged abuse.[67] The very fact that Barlow felt it necessary to apologize in this way is testimony to the constraints of moderation that the dispute itself seemed to dictate.[68] In *A Discussion of the Answere of M. William Barlow* Persons was not above rebuking his opponent soundly for lapses of logic, documentation and relevance, and towards the end of the work, as he appears to lose patience with his opponent, we find increasing numbers of witty ripostes of a personally abusive nature. Thus he would use the faith/works dichotomy as a common source of witticism: 'This is his confidence, which I grant commeth not of merits, but of onely faith, or rather presumption, and therefore I meane not to impugne it',[69] but the rhetorical flourishes of contestation are generally well balanced with exposition.

It could be said that *The Judgment of a Catholicke English-man* had failed spectacularly to change James's attitude to Catholics, or, for that matter, to Robert Persons. In *A Discussion of the Answere of M. William Barlowe* Persons therefore maintains the satirical thrust against the king, and his predecessor, partly to reassure and entertain his Catholic readers. This is the king with whom they have to do; humour is a form of submission that is compatible with integrity of conscience. Even though – perhaps because – James has peremptorily withdrawn from the arena, Persons continues to target his vanity. Virtually admitting that he had known all along that it was James who had written the *Triplici nodo, triplex cuneus*, he excuses himself from his own finesse by mocking the King's doctrine of monarchical obscurity:

> Yea in all duty and good manners I had obligation to conceale his Maiesties name, for so much as himselfe concealed the same: and when any Prince will not be knowne to be a doer in action, as in this it seemeth he would not at that tyme, I know not with what dutifull respect any subiect might publish the same, though he did suspect that he had part therin. For that subiects must seeme to know no more in Princes affaires then themselues are willing to haue known. And consequently, when I saw that his Maiesty concealed his name, I thought it rather duty to seeke reasons to confirme

---

[66] Persons himself puts it like this: 'Yet shall I endeuour to recompence somewhat to the Reader this losse of time, by choosing out the principall matters only, & by drawing to light my said Aduersaries voluntary, and affected obscurity, vsing also the greatest breuity that I may, without ouermuch preiudice to perpecuity, which I greatly loue, as the lanterne or rather looking glasse wherby to find out the truth' (ibid., p. 2).

[67] Barlow, *An Answer to a Catholike English-man*, sigs. A1v-3r; and the 'Admonition to the Reader'.

[68] Milton, p. 261.

[69] *A Discussion of the Answere of M. William Barlow*, p. 437.

& couer the same, then by presumption to enter into Princes secrets, and to reueale them.[70]

With ironic courtesy he insinuates that such lack of transparency (as we should call it today) by breaking down the trust between governor and governed simply invites subjects to act deviously. More expansively, he glances at James's reputation for deipnosophistry, imagining what it would be like if some of the more prominent Church Fathers were to join the King at his table.[71] As a ploy to mollify James, who at one time looked as if he would be open to learned persuasion, this would only have been provocative, but by this stage in the debate Persons was more interested in cutting him down to size.

With Queen Elizabeth, Persons also became more openly satirical. His treatment of Elizabeth throughout his career had been somewhat ambivalent. Practically, he was convinced that she was a hindrance to the Catholic cause, and he worked consistently to have her replaced with someone more promising: Mary Queen of Scots, James VI or the Infanta Isabella. He presumed that her religious policy was chiefly determined by Burghley, and that this was not going to change, even after his death in 1598. But there was propaganda value in presenting her as a crypto-Catholic unable for various reasons to practise the religion of her heart's inclination. In the *Philopater* he exonerated her from the harsh measures against Jesuits and seminary priests.[72] After her death, and so beyond her contradiction, he recounted this story on the authority of Sir Francis Englefield:

> Not long before the death of Q. *Marie*, a commission being giuen to certaine of the priuie Counsell, to goe and examine the said Ladie *Elizabeth* ... shee taking occasion to talke with one of them a part in a window, said vnto him with great vehemencie of spirit, and affliction of mynd, as it seemed, laying her hands vpon his: *Oh Syr! and is it not possible, that the Queene my sister will once be persuaded that I am a good Catholicke?* Yes, Madame, quoth the Counsellor, if your Grace bee so indeed, God will moue her Maiestie to beleiue it. Wherevpon the said Ladie both sware and protested vnto him, that she did as sincerely beleiue the Roman Catholicke religion, as anie Princesse could doe in the world: & in proofe thereof, alleadged the order of her familie, which was to heare masse euery daie, and the most of them two, one for the dead, the other for the liuing.[73]

If he could at times show pastoral compassion towards the Queen (to the indignation of many), he was ultimately more concerned to lament her weakness. After all, it was his belief that most of the English people were similarly inclined to Catholicism but held in check by expediency. The Queen epitomized the half-heartedness that he was devoted to combating.

---

[70]   Ibid., p. 6.

[71]   Ibid., p. 235.

[72]   *Elizabethae Angliae Reginae haeresim Caluinianum propugnantis, saeuissimum in Catholicos sui regni edictum ... Cum responsione ad singula capita ... Per D. Andream Philopatrum* (Antwerp, 1592). See above, Chapter 3.

[73]   *An Answere to the Fifth Part of Reportes Lately set forth by Syr Edward Cooke Knight, the Kinges Attorney generall* (St Omer, 1606), p. 363.

A Discussion of the Answere of M. William Barlow takes the treatment of Queen Elizabeth further by including a somewhat sensational eye-witness account of her death by one of her waiting-women, Elizabeth Southwell. If Persons had originally intended to urge James not to make the same mistakes as his predecessor, he had done nothing but stir up indignation – although James deliberately departed from her religious policy, he was not going to do this in response to Jesuit pressure. Now Persons elaborated his depiction of Elizabeth as the very opposite of a saint. To publish in full what he had only hinted at in *The Judgment of a Catholicke English-man* was something of a polemical *coup*.[74] To counter the fulmination of James (against impertinence) and the extravagance of Barlow (in praise of the late Queen), he was able to produce hard evidence. Moreover, there was the threat of further revelations: from the original text Persons deliberately omitted references to Robert Cecil, and darkly hinted at the involvement of court personages. Perhaps the most damaging piece of information that he kept in reserve – and this must have taken some restraint – was the evidence that Cecil had taken an extremely dubious indication of the preferred successor as authorization for James's succession.[75]

Persons claimed that the reason for recounting Elizabeth's misery was to give comfort in adversity to the persecuted Catholics: 'I do heerin but imitate the first ancient Fathers ... who to comfort the afflicted, and to honour more their cause, did put them in mynd what manner of people their first persecutours were'; he felt 'it must needes be some comfort to Catholicke people, that God chose such an instrument to be their first scourge, out of all woman kynd'.[76] But there were several lively controversial points to be made. The heyday of glorifying good Queen Bess was still to come,[77] but already Barlow was describing her as 'the *Diamond among Princes, the glory of Royall Maiestie, and the ioy of the Christian world, for her Sex*'.[78] Persons dismisses this as narrow little-Englandism, invoking a wider perspective both geographically – what does the rest of the world think?[79] – and chronologically – what would former ages have thought?

---

[74] 'The story of which [pittifull end] I haue read written by a person of much credit that was present at her last sicknes, combats, and death, and relateth all that passed as an eye witnesse, which I passe ouer for breuity and modestyes sake' (*The Judgment of a Catholicke English-man*, pp. 31–2; the relation is given at length in *A Discussion of the Answere of M. William Barlow*, pp. 217–20). See Catherine Loomis, 'Elizabeth Southwell's Manuscript Account of the Death of Queen Elizabeth [with text]', *English Literary Renaissance* 26 (1996): 482–509. The text is also to be found in Hugh Tootel [Charles Dodd (pseud.)], *The Church History of England: From the Commencement of the Sixteenth Century to the Revolution in 1688*, ed. M.A. Tierney (5 vols; London, 1839–43), vol. 3, pp. 70–74.

[75] 'Diuers other particularities, for that they concern speciall Personages, I haue thought good for some causes to conceale' (*A Discussion of the Answere of M. William Barlow*, p. 220). For the succession, see Loomis's text, lines 72–9.

[76] *A Discussion of the Answere of M. William Barlow*, pp. 35–6.

[77] See John Watkins, ' "Old Bess in the Ruff": Remembering Elizabeth I, 1625–1660', *English Literary Renaissance* 30 (2000): 95–116.

[78] Barlow, *An Answer to a Catholike English-man*, p. 253.

[79] *A Discussion of the Answere of M. William Barlow*, p. 423.

Neither did I say any more [than that the best spiritual doctors would pronounce her spiritually dead] of the spirituall death of Queene *Elizabeth* most likely to accompany her corporall. I beseech the mercie of Almighty God that it be not so.

And here I might adde also another plaine & familiar proofe, out of the said ancient Fathers, and namely out of S. *Augustine,* to the end we may see how his Church did agree with ours, or rather the vniuersall knowne Catholicke Church in his dayes, with that Church that hath the same name & note in ours.[80]

This should give comfort to his Catholic readers, reassured that Elizabeth's persecution identified them as inheritors of the tradition. Another device Persons uses against Elizabeth is to satirize Barlow's suggestion – faced with the Queen's life of luxury and self-indulgence – that she was sanctified by the trials of greatness:

This [to be a King, and govern as a King] is the largest way (I suppose) of mortification that he can lay before vs: for of this kind he will find, no doubt many mortified people, both of men and women, that would be content to accept of this mortification, to be Kings & Queenes, and to gouerne well in their owne conceipts .... And if to be a *Bishop* also be a mortification, then hath M. *Barlow* in like manner proued himselfe a mortified man, & then those words of S. *Paul* to the *Colossians, Mortificate membra vestra quae sunt super terram:* Mortify your members which are vpon earth, may haue this sense also among other; do you mortify your self with some good Bishopricke.[81]

The idea that wealth and power constitute a form of mortification was too rich for Persons to let it pass, and inevitably his wit lights on the moral state of the flatterer.

Beyond all these polemical fireworks there lies a concern for the exposition of the good life, the life that comes from dying to self. Apart from the negative examples of Queen Elizabeth and the Emperor Frederick II (who is treated at length, pp. 461–95), there are 'praises' of Mary Queen of Scots (pp. 214–15) and Pope Paul V (pp. 56–7). The account of Mary's martyrdom, admittedly, is open to the charge of opportunism: Persons was prepared to make propaganda use of her whenever it suited him, exploiting her popularity among Catholics and her memory with the King, but he had been involved in invasion plans in 1582–85 in which her life would almost certainly have been sacrificed. How much she would have welcomed this martyrdom is open to question; and Persons was sensitive to accusations of cowardice imputed to his flight and safety in exile.

Readers will be divided in their response to Persons's treatment of Queen Elizabeth. Barlow rated him for passion, asserting that such bitterness towards Elizabeth proved that Persons's reputation for holiness, built on his authorship of *The Christian Directory*, was false:

---

[80]   Ibid., p. 226.
[81]   Ibid., p. 173.

If *Parsons* were euer famous for any good thing, he woon himselfe credit by the book of *Resolution,* though not inuented (as the Priests say) but borrowed *peece-meale* from others; *translated only,* and *methodized* by him: which when a man reades, hee will take the *Compiler,* or *translater* to be *that* very *Crucifix* of *Mortification* described by Saint *Paul, The world Crucified vnto him, and hee vnto the world:* now, that HEE should fal into such *passionate, prophane* and *Barbarously-distempered reuiling of a Christian Princesse,* the *mirror of the world* while she liued, some yeres dead, and laid vp in rest with her *Fathers;* as if the very mention of HER *Sacred Name,* were an *Eleborous purge* to make him disgorge the gall of his cankred heart, by his *Rabshakeis pen;* no man that professeth the name of Christ, can beleeue it to bee the labour of one that is ingrafted into Christ.[82]

Yet the formative aims of *The Christian Directory* come nearer to the surface in this work than in almost any other: there are discussions of the role of the papacy in resolving questions of conscience, how an erring conscience can be reformed, the degree to which one should put one's confidence in good works, and so forth. Although each of these disquisitions is strictly occasional, arising from a specific point of dispute, they would not be out of place in an extension of *The Christian Directory.* This should not surprise us, since the writing of *A Discussion of the Answere of M. William Barlow* interrupted Persons's work on the more important project. He laments that he is forced 'to leese so much good tyme, from other more profitable exercises';[83] and so he seizes on opportunities to write on topics that are suitable to a part following the making of a resolution: putting it into effect by self-discipline, forming the conscience, and becoming integrated into the liturgical, pastoral and institutional life of the Church.

At the deepest level, Persons believed that the principle informing resistance to the Oath was liberty of conscience. By this he meant the freedom for the Catholic conscience to be what it is. Barlow protested against the assumption that such liberty should be like 'breathing and vsing the Common-ayre',[84] because for Protestants the priest-ridden Catholic had a conscience that was contrived, distorted and unnatural. Persons, in turn, contrasts the Protestant conscience, which depends only on personal conviction, with the Catholic, which is grounded upon the Church's good counsel. Although it might be objected that the Catholic conscience is unstable because it depends on the Pope – and one Pope may differ from the next – Persons characterizes it as 'assured':

We depend vpon the Catholicke Church, as propounding vnto vs and expounding Gods word, and we depend of the Supreme Pastour as head of that Church, vnto whom we rest assured by Gods owne word and promise,

---

[82]   Barlow, *An Answer to a Catholike English-man,* p. 4.
[83]   *A Discussion of the Answere of M. William Barlow,* p. 2.
[84]   Barlow, *An Answer to a Catholike English-man,* p. 119.

that he will assist him with his spirit for all resolutions in matters of fayth, which shalbe necessary for his sayd Church.[85]

Where Barlow argues that the clergy have turned the Oath, quite gratuitously, into a rock of offence, creating, that is, a false scruple of conscience, Persons retorts that the Oath tempts Catholics to play hide-and-seek with their conscience, clouding the clear vision of obligation as taught by an unbroken tradition:

> He that layeth forth the truth of Catholike doctrine vnto Catholike men, may not iustly be sayd to threaten, or terrify, but to deale sincerely and charitably with them, laying truth before their eyes, what their obligation is to God, before man, and how they are bound as members of his true Catholike Church, to hould and defend the vnity and integrity of faith, and doctrine deliuered by the same, though it be with neuer so much temporall danger. And as for laying a scandall, wherby they may fall into the ruine of their soules, it is easy to iudge, whether wee do it rather, that teach them to deal sincerely with God and their Prince, wherby they shall preserue their peace, and alacrity of conscience; or you that indeauour to induce them to sweare, and doe against the same, whereby they shall be sure to leese both their peace in this life, and their euerlasting inheritance in the next.[86]

This view of a settled and educated conscience is one that chimes with much contemporary thinking, in other fields, about the compact between nature and art, and this is what gives Persons's instruction such moving power.[87]

The defence of the nature of the Catholic conscience – that it is not something that can be manipulated or abused, but is based on reason, Scripture and tradition – is crucial in the appeal for toleration. To allow freedom of conscience is not to concede licence to lawbreakers, the freedom to do evil without punishment. Barlow avers that just as the state has the right to constrain the criminal and vicious by making them face the consequences of their actions, so the Oath simply makes Catholics subject to the consequences of an act that is itself free. Persons exposes this argument as sophistry; it confuses freedom of conscience with freedom of will. The state, he agrees, is entitled to use coercion to interfere with the freedom of the will because

---

[85] *A Discussion of the Answere of M. William Barlow*, pp. 124–5, cf. Barlow, *An Answer to a Catholike English-man*, pp. 51–2.

[86] *A Discussion of the Answere of M. William Barlow*, pp. 139–40. Cf. Robert Tynley, *Two Learned Sermons. The one, of the mischievous subtiltie, and barbarous crueltie, the other of the false Doctrines, and refined Haeresies of the Romish Synagogue* (London, 1609), pp. 25–6: 'Is there not, iudge ye, great cause, that libertie of their conscience & Religion, which threatneth such dangers both to Prince and Countrie, should be as common *amongst vs in this Kingdome, as the vse of the aire & breathing is common to all?* or rather is there not great neede that the Statutes concerning obstinate Recusants, were put more duely in execution, and not lie sheathed so much as they doe in the scabbard?'

[87] Cf. Sir Philip Sidney's notion of poetry as creating 'another nature', in *An Apology for Poetry* [first published 1595], ed. Geoffrey Shepherd (London, 1965), pp. 51–5 (Shepherd's introduction) and pp. 99–101 (Sidney's text); and Polixenes' argument for the naturalness of an art that mends nature, in *The Winter's Tale*, IV, iv, 88–97, discussed by H.S. Wilson, 'Nature and Art in *Winter's Tale*', *Shakespeare Association Bulletin* 18 (1943): 114–20.

criminals are governed by their passions; the penalties of the law introduce a new passion – fear of punishment – into the emotional conflict to curb evil passion. But with conscience the case is altered: Catholics are governed not by passion but by the educated '*dictamen* of their consciences', with which no government has the right to interfere.[88]

By such recourse to moral categories, Persons attempts to defuse the controversy. The papal deposing power does not lay the nation open to some uncontrolled, sinister force, impelled by papal greed; it is a rational check on the power of kings, a protection against the abuse of that power. As he had written in his 'Discourse against taking the oath in England', the Pope in these matters is subject to reason and the guidance of the Holy Spirit. That is to say, liberty of conscience is a more assured guarantee of peace than the reduction of selected aspects of Catholicism to 'matters indifferent'.

---

[88] *A Discussion of the Answere of M. William Barlow*, pp. 41–2.

CHAPTER EIGHT

Mastering the Polemical Scene

The works I have discussed in this study represent a major contribution to the religious discourse of early modern England. In them, Persons elaborated an impressive version of a national Catholic community based on the faith commitment of the Spiritual Exercises of St Ignatius Loyola. What kind of political responsibility did recusants have? How and why should the training of priests challenge the Protestant establishment? How did the history of the national religion help to shape the present church and prepare for its future? What could be done about slander and backbiting as they sapped the clergy's spiritual energies? How could you keep the Catholic community whole, avoiding the fracturing of conscience and consensus that James's programme for reconciliation entailed? Through all of these questions and their ramifications Persons kept before him a clear and unalterable ideal of uncompromising reformed English Catholicism.

This singleness of purpose, this resolution of all conflict into a single vision, gave Persons a great advantage as a polemicist. In today's fashionable terms, one could say that he always had his eye on the 'big picture'. While his opponents were seizing on points of detail and engaging in abuse with little purpose other than discrediting or embarrassing him, he would subordinate debating niceties to the larger issues. This superiority showed itself most obviously in the disposition of material, the clear pointers in chapter headings and the deliberate definition of the debate and its implications, so that Persons's books often provide the best overall guide to a controversy. His final work, *A Discussion of the Answere of M. William Barlow*, is a particularly good example. Its expository character is evident in the bibliographical features of the book itself. James had established the basic pattern of the controversy with his *Triplici nodo, triplex cuneus*: a tripartite structure derived from but not altogether aligned with the three documents to which he was responding: a general first section, a section on the papal breves, and a section on Bellarmine's letter.[1] Persons, in *The Judgement of a Catholicke English-man*, had retained these three sections, confusingly called 'paragraphs',[2] and Barlow answered in sequence. So preoccupied was Barlow with simple refutation that his book, *An Answer to a Catholike English-man*, has no structural signals besides

---

[1]   King James I, *Triplici nodo, triplex cuneus: or, An Apologie for the Oath of Allegiance, Against the two Breves of Pope Paulus Quintus, and the late Letter of Cardinal Bellarmine to G. Blackwel the Arch-priest* (London, 1607 [*vere* 1608]).

[2]   Robert Persons, *The Judgment of a Catholicke English-man, living in banishment for his Religion ... Concerning A late Booke set forth, and entituled; Triplici nodo, triplex cuneus, Or, An Apologie for the Oath of Allegiance* (St Omer, 1608), henceforth referred to as *The Judgment of a Catholicke English-man*.

paragraph numbers (in the modern sense) and there was not even a page break or significant gap on the page between the three main sections.[3]

In stark contrast, Persons's reply, *A Discussion of the Answere of M. William Barlow*, is divided into chapters, within the three 'paragraphs': each chapter boldly positioned on a new page with a printer's rule and chapter heading, cast as a discursive topic, such as 'Whether the Pope in his breue did forbid temporall obedience to his Maiesty of *England?*'[4] Each chapter also has its own running title. In this way Persons sought to take control of the debate, clarify the issues and provide a definitive, lucid account of each.[5]

* * *

The distinguishing feature of Persons's polemical style is restraint. Although this is pertinent to many of his controversial exchanges, especially those with the appellants, King James and William Barlow (as we have seen), it is most instructive in this regard to examine the long-running dispute, first with Sir Francis Hastings and Matthew Sutcliffe and then with Thomas Morton, Protestant apologists who sought to expose the treachery and corruption of Rome. To put the matter briefly, Hastings, Sutcliffe and Morton practised a kind of 'maximizing' anti-Romanist rhetoric, presenting Catholic priests and lay people in exaggerated and frightening terms. Persons, in response, tried to reduce the debate to something more manageable and measured. Where they piled up the abuse and recoiled in horror, he set out the facts calmly, as he wanted them to be seen.

Of all Persons's Protestant opponents, Sir Francis Hastings was perhaps the most ineptly extremist in his anti-Romanist rhetoric. In 1599 Persons savaged his scare-mongering *Watch-word to all religious, and true hearted Englishmen* with *A Temperate Ward-word, to the turbulent and seditious Wach-word of Sir Francis Hastings knight.*[6] The title implied that Hastings's kind of heated

---

[3]   William Barlow, *An Answer to a Catholike English-man (so by himself entituled) who, without a Name, passed his Censure upon the Apology, made by the Right High and mightie Prince Iames ... for the Oath of Allegeance* (London, 1609).

[4]   Robert Persons, *A Discussion of the Answere of M. William Barlow, D. of Divinity, to the Booke intituled: The Iudgment of a Catholicke Englishman ... concerning The Apology of the new Oath of Allegiance. Written by the R. Father, F. Robert Persons of the Society of Jesus. Wherunto since the said Fathers death, is annexed a generall Preface, laying open the Insufficiency, Rayling, Lying and other Misdemeanour of M. Barlow in his writing* (St Omer, 1612), paragraph 2, ch. 7, henceforth referred to as *A Discussion of the Answere of M. William Barlow.*

[5]   Persons himself puts it like this: 'Yet shall I endeuour to recompence somewhat to the Reader this losse of time, by choosing out the principall matters only, & by drawing to light my said Aduersaries voluntary, and affected obscurity, vsing also the greatest breuity that I may, without ouermuch preiudice to perpecuity, which I greatly loue, as the lanterne or rather looking glasse wherby to find out the truth' (*A Discussion of the Answere of M. William Barlow*, p. 2).

[6]   Sir Francis Hastings, *A Watch-word to all religious, and true hearted English-men* (London, 1598); Robert Persons, *A Temperate Ward-word, to the turbulent and seditious Wach-word of Sir Francis Hastinges knight, who indevoreth to slaunder the whole Catholique cause, & all professors therof, both at home and abrode. Reduced into eight seuerall encounters, with a particuler speeche directed to the Lordes of her Maiesties most honorable Councel. To whom*

discourse was very damaging to the realm, by stirring up hatred amongst the Queen's subjects. This was a persistent theme: anti-Romanism was ostensibly concerned with religious unity yet it did nothing to defuse strife. At the end of *A Temperate Ward-word* Persons tries to set some limits to polemical abuse by putting Hastings beyond the pale. Claiming that 'the wiser sorte of our nation, haue learned euen by the lawes of moral ciuilitie, that a man must speake moderately also of his enemy', he proceeds to create a caricature of Hastings as the stereotypical boastful soldier, a Falstaffian figure without shame or honour: 'our *cockish knight*', 'malitious sycophant', 'counterfayt knight' (guilty of 'trecherous cogging and shameles forgerie'), 'our rash and falstongued English knight', 'our English *hastie-hote-spurre*, that sheweth malice in euery syllable', 'this fond knight', 'this unciuil knight', 'this good fellow', 'this slanderous *wach-word-giuer*'.[7] It is hard to believe, given this set of terms, and the reference to Hotspur, that Persons was unacquainted with Shakespeare's *1 Henry IV*, published in quarto in 1598.[8]

Although he opens himself to the charge of merely meeting abuse with abuse, insult with insult, Persons takes pains to ensure that his prose is immediately distinguishable from that of Hastings. In this chapter, for example, he gradually eases into the standard practice of quoting chunks from his opponent and refuting each in turn, thus interleaving the two styles, casting into relief Hastings's unmitigated hostility. What he quotes from Hastings is carefully chosen to represent bald assertion; his own replies exhibit patient demonstration laced with ironic references to 'the discouerie he promiseth of great hydden mysteries', 'the credyt of so new and weightie, and incredible a secret'.[9]

Such engagement contributes to an argument about the value of polemic. Wild or anarchic vilification, shooting at a venture, can only be destructive, whereas ordered and temperate response may bring the opposing parties to a better understanding. Accordingly, Persons concludes with an extended appeal to the Privy Council to adopt a more moderate policy to the recusants, elaborating a vision of peace, order and freedom in the realm:

> And further I appeale to your Lordships wise consideration what a comfort it might be to her Maiestie, now in her elder age, and later part of her gouernment, and to your Lordships also to see once all sortes of people merry, contented, louing, and confident within the realme, al to laugh and

---

the arbitrement of the whole is remitted (Antwerp, 1599), henceforth referred to as *A Temperate Ward-word*.

7   *A Temperate Ward-word*, pp. 103–118.

8   William Shakespeare, *The History of Henrie the Fourth; With the battell at Shrewsburie, betweene the King and Lord Henry Percy, surnamed Henrie Hotspur of the North. With the humorous conceits of Sir Iohn Falstaffe* (London, 1598). Persons deals extensively with Henry IV's right to the throne in R. Doleman (pseud.), *A Conference about the Next Succession to the Crowne of Ingland* (Antwerp, 1594 [vere 1595]), henceforth referred to as *A Conference about the Next Succession*. See above, Chapter 4.

9   *A Temperate Ward-word*, p. 118.

sing together, all to pray to God most hartely for her Maiesties health, wealth, and prosperous long continuance.[10]

This, he maintains, is the purpose towards which all the humble, learned, gentle martyrs from the seminaries tended. But peace, he implies, is not just the absence of war; it depends on conducting the war in such a manner that the two parties actually engage with each other.

Several metaphors point to Hastings's not merely missing the mark, but scarcely acknowledging that a mark needs to be aimed at. He is 'our harebrain and headlong knight',[11] 'a wilde beast without a bridle',[12] and a foolhardy mariner: 'he wilbe both maister and pilot, and boteswayne himself, to gouerne the barke at his pleasure, for he admitteth no iudge, no interpreter, no authoritie, no antiquitie, nor anie other manner of triall; which is the greatest madness and malediction that euer could happen amonge men of reason'.[13] Hastings's presumed exemption from the standards of debate derives from his unquestioned belief in an 'unholy trinity' of ignorance, slavery and carelessness, the marks of Roman Catholic lay piety. Each of these Persons turns effortlessly back on the author. It requires no heightening of emotional appeal or subtlety of logic to show that Catholic devotion, so far from being born of ignorance, begins with meditation on God's virtues, and ends with the fruit of good works.[14] It is only the Protestant fixation with a narrow theology of grace, he implies, that leads to the dismissal of a rich and learned tradition in these loaded terms.

The ease and confidence with which Persons deflects Hastings's allegations and warnings derive much of their strength from the Jesuit reinvigoration of that Catholic tradition. Protestants who assumed that Catholicism consisted primarily of a conservative attachment to a collection of outworn practices and a benighted dependence on works and merit (having failed, somehow, to see the 'light' of justification by faith alone and be free) were disarmed by the evidence that Jesuit spirituality and counsel rested firmly on properly established first principles:

> By their zeale and industrie many a separation is made between good and bad, many a heat enkindled in Christian hartes, where deadly cold occupied the place before, many a batterie geuen to fortes possessed by Satan, many an heathen and heretique made Christian, many a frostie catholique made a hoat recusant, many a vitious lyuer made obseruant, many a a [sic] careles and earthly mynd stirred vp to apprehend and think of eternitie, many a groueling soule plucked from the ground and quickened with the warmth of true Christian spirit.[15]

---

[10]   Ibid., p. 128.
[11]   Ibid., p. 96.
[12]   Ibid., p. 40.
[13]   Ibid., p. 6.
[14]   Ibid., pp. 18–19.
[15]   Ibid., pp. 65–6.

The kind of Christian faith commitment enjoined, for example, in *The Christian Directory* was immune to the slanders of someone as prejudiced and ignorant as Hastings.[16] Persons had only to adumbrate the Jesuit programme to make this clear.

Persons's *Temperate Ward-word* forced Hastings onto the defensive. His reply, *An Apologie or Defence of the Watch-word*, only made his position worse and he virtually disqualified himself from further participation in the contest. He made the strategic blunder of taking personally the attack on his argument and tone. In disputes of this kind both sides tended to accuse the other of 'railing', that is, leaving the real issues and descending to personal abuse. It took considerable skill to take advantage of one's opponent's weaknesses, the evidence of polemical ineptness, lack of learning, and so on, without exposing oneself damagingly to this charge. In rhetorical terms, it was a matter of managing the balance between *ethos* (the trustworthiness of the speaker) and *logos* (the validity of the argument). Persons was particularly adept at walking this line, but Hastings faltered by dwelling on the hits made against him personally. Peevish and pusillanimous, he appears preoccupied with his own performance. In the preliminaries he complains that Persons has fawned on the Lords of the Privy Council and treated him with contempt. Later, he makes himself even more vulnerable by being candid about his own shortcomings: 'Surely I willingly confesse my wants in learning to be verie great, and I doe bewaile my losse of time in that behalfe' – an admission that does not function as an artful modesty *topos* but simply identifies him as a novice.[17]

When Hastings leaves the personal *apologia* for matters of substance he back-pedals frantically and merely embarrasses himself. On the question of papist ignorance, he pleads that he is only concerned with lack of access to the Scriptures in the mother tongue – a dishonest redefinition of terms – and dismisses the Rheims–Douay translation project on the grounds that Catholics are not all permitted to read the Scriptures 'indifferently'.[18] That open and unguided Scripture-reading might breed a new and more dangerous ignorance does not seem to have occurred to him. There is a case to be made, but Hastings has too many prejudices to be able to conduct his part of the debate proficiently. A few Protestant shibboleths are inadequate when one's opponent stands in such a comprehensive intellectual tradition.

* * *

---

[16]   *The First Booke of the Christian Exercise, appertayning to Resolution* (Rouen, 1582, revd 1585, 1607), henceforth referred to as *The Christian Directory*. Quotations from the 1582 version are taken from *The Christian Directory (1582): The First Booke of the Christian Exercise, appertayning to Resolution*, ed. Victor Houliston (Leiden, 1998).

[17]   Sir Francis Hastings, *An Apologie or Defence of the Watch-word* (London, 1600), sig. A4v and p. 166. Orators were taught to affect inadequacy at the beginning of their speeches but this was normally managed in such a way as to imply authority to speak on the subject in hand.

[18]   Ibid., pp. 29–55.

Matthew Sutcliffe, Dean of Exeter, entered the fray with an exaggerated sense of his own scholarly credentials. He saw himself as the champion of the Protestant cause, a status in which he was confirmed by his appointment in 1610 as head of King James's Chelsea College, for the writing of Protestant propaganda. Entering the controversy in 1600 with his *Briefe Replie to ... N.D.* and his *New Challenge made to N.D.*,[19] he produced several more books between 1602 and 1606,[20] attacking Persons's *Temperate Ward-word* and subsequent *Warn-word*,[21] and then targeting *A Treatise of Three Conversions*.[22] To add weight to his argument, he used devices such as leaving Latin quotations untranslated, enumerating his points and invoking the language of formal logic, and he made much of Persons's pseudonymous initials N.D. to caricature his opponent as 'the Noddy'. His method was also superior to Hastings's in that he developed a strong theme, that of the true and false Catholic church: but like Hastings his argument depended too much on mere abuse and logic-chopping. Of Roman Catholics he wrote:

> So apes clad with purple iackets, beare themselues verie proudly among other beasts, and all for their gaie apparel. But as apes by their apish trickes bewray themselues to bee apes, so papists by their apish, popish and fonde deuises shewe themselues to be factious heretikes, and no true catholikes.[23]

Of their ignorance, the persistent indictment, he will not allow that unlearned knowledge of Scripture can be dangerous. If it is argued that 'the letter killeth' – applied by Catholics to a literalist or uninstructed scripturalism – he rejoins that this cannot possibly refer to the Bible, because all Scripture is profitable.[24] Such glossing over a real concern is an ideologically inspired refusal to acknowledge the difficulties or intractabilities over open access to Scripture.

---

[19]   Matthew Sutcliffe, *A Briefe Replie to a certaine odious and slanderous libel, lately published by a seditious Jesuite, calling himselfe N.D.* and *A New Challenge made to N.D.* (London, 1600; bound together).

[20]   Matthew Sutcliffe, *A Challenge concerning the Romish Church* (London, 1602); *A Full and Round Answer to N.D. alias Parsons the Noddie his foolish and rude Warne-word* (London, 1604); *The Subversion of Robert Parsons His confused and worthlesse worke, Entituled, A treatise of three Conversions* (London, 1606); *A Threefold Answer unto the third part of a certaine Triobular Treatise of three supposed Conversions of England* (London, 1606).

[21]   Robert Persons, *The Warn-word to Sir Francis Hastinges Wast-word: Conteyning the issue of three former Treatises, the Watch-word, the Ward-word and the Wast-word (intituled by Sir Francis, an Apologie or Defence of his Watch-word), togeather with certaine admonitions & warnings to the said knight and his followers. Wherunto is adioyned a breif reiection of an insolent, and vaunting minister masked by the letters O.E. who hath taken upon him to wryte of the same argument in supply of the knight. There go also foure several Tables, one of the chapters, another of the controversies, the third of the chief shiftes, and deceits, the fourth of the particular matters conteyned in the whole book. By N.D. author of the Ward-word* (2 vols; Antwerp, 1602), henceforth referred to as *The Warn-word*.

[22]   Robert Persons, *A Treatise of Three Conversions of England from Paganisme to Christian Religion* (3 vols; St Omer, 1603–1604), henceforth referred to as *A Treatise of Three Conversions*.

[23]   Sutcliffe, *A New Challenge made to N.D.*, pp. 1–2.

[24]   Ibid., p. 47, alluding to 2 Tim. 3.

Sutcliffe may be relying on a Calvinist consensus which regards these matters as settled and beyond dispute.[25] But Persons's strategy in response is to demonstrate that, so far from inculcating and encouraging ignorance, the Jesuit apostolate of writing is concerned not only to confute the enemy but instruct the faithful. His extensive *Warn-word to Sir Francis Hastinges Wast-word* is ostensibly directed at Hastings (the easier prey), but its real target is Sutcliffe's *Briefe Replie to a certaine odious and slanderous libel, lately published by a seditious Jesuite, calling himselfe N.D.*, which is dealt with parenthetically, as it were. The response to Sutcliffe is grafted on the reply to Hastings's *Apologie* rather as Bunny was dealt with in *A Christian Directorie* in 1585 – as a kind of afterthought or in brief inserts.[26] In so doing Persons denies him the status of the superior adversary that he had arrogated. Instead, Sutcliffe is described as one who prefers 'to follow the warders words [i.e., Persons's *Temperate Ward-word*], as a dog at his heeles, barking, and gnybling at euery step, but yet ... confusedly'.[27]

The *Warn-word* represents a masterly exposition of the reasonableness of the Roman position, expertly negotiating the balance between witty, light-hearted riposte and patient demonstration. We can observe the difference in the way the two authors, Persons and Sutcliffe, make personal attacks on their opponents. Sutcliffe's method is first to abuse and then to try to justify the abuse:

> But his conclusion is nothing, but a wicked calumniation of gods holy scriptures: and his proofes consiste of a packe of lies, & both declare him to be a sclanderous lying enymy of Gods truth. For it is not reading of scriptures ... but neglect of scriptures, that bringeth foorth error and heresie.[28]

In reply, Persons first deals playfully with the 'Noddy' appellation, and then turns to genuine satire:

> As though he were not only that Terentian Thraso, or Philistian Goliath, but euen Behemoth, or Leuiathan himselfe whose lips (as the Scripture saith) do cast foorth burning lampes, and his nostrels fyerie smoke, who esteemeth iron as straw, and contemneth brasse as rotten wood, which is spoken of a proud contemptuous spirit discouered euery where in this fellow, not only by his fuming, fretting and facing throughout this ydle Epistle, but by his contumelious words, and reprochful speaches also in all other partes of his writing, prouoking and chalenging as a gyant, and yet when he cometh to grypes he sheweth himselfe one of the poorest, and weakest wormes, that euer lightlie hath come to combat in these affayres

---

[25] See Nicholas Tyacke, *Aspects of English Protestantism, c. 1530–1700* (Manchester, 2001), p. 165.

[26] *The Warn-word*, vol. 1, fols 83v–84r, and vol. 2, ch. 6. For Persons's bibliographical treatment of Bunny, in *A Christian Directorie Guiding men to their Salvation* (Rouen, 1585), see above, Chapter 2.

[27] *The Warn-word*, vol. 1, fol. 25v.

[28] Sutcliffe, *A Briefe Replie to a certaine odious and slanderous libel*, p. 49.

as after yow wil fynd by experience, now let vs heare him a litle cracle if yow list.[29]

The portrait here is comical and entertaining as well as demeaning, and ends with an invitation to the reader to see for himself. This is Persons's method in dealing with more substantial points of difference, especially. He so disposes the evidence, with a minimum of commentary or authorial intervention, that it appears to speak for itself, to bring, as he puts it 'euery thing to methode & perspicuous order'.[30] What emerges most forcefully from such exchanges is Sutcliffe's repetitiveness and Persons's resourcefulness. Each felt utterly convinced of the justice of his cause and the validity of his church's position. But this confidence manifested itself in quite different ways. Like many Protestants, Sutcliffe assumed that the purity of the Reformation, its fidelity to Scripture and the early church, was as self-evident as the corruption of Rome. The basic points did not need debating; they simply needed to be made often enough and stridently enough. Each reiteration in each successive book expressed greater wonder or exasperation at the opponent's obtuseness; there was an increase in abuse and expostulation; but seldom the reinvention of an argument. Persons, who was always looking for new angles on a controversial crux, came to see Sutcliffe's mere prolixity as a sign that Protestantism is one-dimensional. Sutcliffe had become fixed in a single line of argument that ultimately depended on premises he regarded as unquestionable. For Persons, this simply reconfirmed his own sense of belonging to a much richer and more generative tradition.

* * *

During the contest with Sutcliffe, the Gunpowder Plot intervened and Thomas Morton, one of the King's chaplains, became the most prominent anti-Romanist by seizing on the question of equivocation. His *Full Satisfaction concerning a double Romish Iniquitie* was a vicious attack on Catholics, and especially the clergy, as untrustworthy and deceitful.[31] Persons's two responses to Morton, *A Treatise tending to Mitigation* and *A Quiet and Sober Reckoning with M. Thomas Morton* are among his most magisterial polemical works.[32]

---

29   *The Warn-word*, vol. 1, fol. 3r.

30   Ibid., vol. 1, fol. 26r.

31   Thomas Morton, *A Full Satisfaction concerning a double Romish Iniquitie; hainous Rebellion, and more then heathenish Aequivocation* (London, 1606); in response to Persons he later wrote *A Preamble Unto an Incounter with P.R. the Author of the deceitfull Treatise of Mitigation* (London, 1608); and *The Encounter against M. Parsons* (London, 1610).

32   Robert Persons, *A Treatise tending to Mitigation towardes Catholicke-Subiectes in England. Wherin is declared, That it is not impossible for Subiectes of different Religion, (especially Catholickes and Protestantes) to live together in dutifull obedience and subiection, under the government of his Maiesty of Great Britany. Against The seditious wrytings of Thomas Morton Minister, & some others to the contrary. Whose two false and slaunderous groundes, pretending to be drawne from Catholicke doctrine & practice, concerning Rebellion and Equivocation, are overthrowne, and cast upon himselfe. Dedicated to the learned Schoole-Devines, Cyvill and Canon Lawyers of the two Universities of England. By P.R.* (St Omer, 1608), henceforth referred to as

In essence, they constitute a contestation for the centre. Doctrines such as the papal deposing power and the legitimacy of equivocation frightened – or could be used to frighten – Englishmen in the immediate context of the Gunpowder Plot and the recent history of the Spanish threat and insecurity over the succession. That the Pope could license rebellion and that priests and laymen might withhold crucial strategic information from those in authority went against the grain of the state campaign to elevate civil obedience to a divinely sanctioned absolute. From an official point of view, therefore, these doctrines could be used to make Catholics look like dangerous extremists, and this was of course Morton's tactic. In *A Treatise tending to Mitigation*, Persons used several devices to make the official position look absolute and therefore extremist, in conflict with common sense and established, universal perspectives. Could one really claim that there were no circumstances in which an oppressed people might look to the Pope to sanction resistance?[33] How could distressed innocents survive if they could never under any circumstances conceal anything from hostile interrogators?[34] This was to deny God's Providence. Against the extravagant dismissal of these doctrines and practices Persons opposed the limited and carefully circumscribed applications of the papal deposing power and equivocation. These doctrines were of long-standing and wide acceptance; they were associated with stability.[35] Their denial was part of a general subversion of the provisions of Christendom for civil society.

There is much in common between this strategy and the argument about Catholic ignorance. Protestant outrage is in both instances represented as a fixation on narrow definitions: of the gospel, of obedience, of the practice of truth. Equivocation obviously offends against a literal sense of the truth, because what is understood by the hearer is contrary to what is in the mind of the speaker. To consider it properly, Persons argues, you need to broaden your conception of what a speech act entails. There is the right of the hearer to know, which is not absolute. There are the legitimate needs of the speaker and his or her dependants. There is the ambiguity of language, provided by God to negotiate these rights and needs, and there is the complexity of grammar

---

A Treatise tending to Mitigation; and *A Quiet and Sober Reckoning with M. Thomas Morton somewhat set in choler by his Adversary P.R. concerning Certaine imputations of wilfull falsities obiected to the said T.M. in a Treaties of P.R. intituled Of Mitigation, some part wherof he hath lately attempted to answere in a large Preamble to a more ample Reioynder promised by him. But heere in the mean space the said imputations are iustified, and confirmed, & with much increase of new untruthes on his part returned upon him againe: So as finally the Reckoning being made, the Verdict of the Angell, interpreted by Daniell, is verified of him. Daniel 5. Vers. 27. You have byn weighed in the ballance, & are found to want weight. There is also adioyned a peece of a Reckoning with Syr Edward Cooke, now L. Chief Justice of the Common Pleas, about a Nihil dicit, & some other points uttered by him in his two late preambles, to his sixt and seaventh Partes of Reports* (St Omer, 1609), henceforth referred to as *A Quiet and Sober Reckoning with M. Thomas Morton.*

[33]   *A Treatise tending to Mitigation*, pp. 174–7.
[34]   Ibid., pp. 406–438.
[35]   Ibid., pp. 32–3.

and syntax that allows for an incomplete sentence to convey only what the hearer has a right to know. One should see these things as a whole, and not restrict one's scrutiny to a part.[36] Persons is able to assemble many instances of equivocation where truth is served, so that Morton's total embargo on the practice seems mean-spirited.

Perhaps the most telling – and daring – defence of equivocation relates to the general problem of concealment in an age of persecution. Jesuits in particular had to become habituated to a life of disguise; their whole existence was perforce a kind of equivocation. To live such a double life was naturally a strain, which could only be endured with a stable defence of the legitimacy of a contradiction between the testimony of conscience (to God) and speech or signal (to man). There was thus a psychological imperative to rest in and affirm the traditional teaching on equivocation, and to ground it in the life of Christ. So much of what Christ said and taught had a hidden meaning – plain to the reader but obscure to the disciples – that it could be said that he led one life to God and another to men.[37] This view of equivocation has close affinities with dramatic irony, so it is no wonder that it resonates throughout Shakespeare's *Macbeth*, which offers both a superficial satire on equivocation and a highly complex treatment of multivalency in speech.[38]

Persons's skill in opening up the definition of equivocation makes his doctrine seem humane. Nevertheless, he is very careful not to sanction all kinds of deception or concealment based on ambiguity or reservation. Instead, he turns the argument on Morton and his fellows by charging them with equivocating with patristic and other venerable authorities. Nor is this mere ingenuity, for he insists that the condemnation of equivocation is itself a misreading of Christian tradition. They are in this equivocating against equivocation.[39] But the charge is more general: he claims that Protestant authors consistently misrepresent authorities, in ways that involve dishonest exploitation of ambiguity or disregard of context.

* * *

Equivocation ultimately is a form of avoidance, an immunity from responsibility. It provides a refuge for the innocent; even Christ himself needed a place of retreat. What Persons sees in Morton, and in his other Protestant opponents, is an abuse of this shelter: evasion rather than avoidance. It was Morton's response to *A Treatise tending to Mitigation, A Preamble Unto an Incounter with P.R.*, that brought to the surface Persons's frustration with his adversaries' refusal to engage. It was not just a matter of empty abuse, Protestant propaganda and stereotypical allegations, although this kind of retreat into assertion rather than argumentation also drew his wrath. It was

---

[36]   Ibid., pp. 330–31, 338–43.

[37]   Ibid., pp. 380–81, 398–9.

[38]   On Shakespeare's *Macbeth*, Garnet and equivocation, see Garry Wills, *Witches and Jesuits: Shakespeare's 'Macbeth'* (New York, 1995), ch. 5.

[39]   *A Treatise tending to Mitigation*, pp. 488–9.

rather that Morton laid claim to consistency with the patristic tradition, with a whole range of common authorities, but knowingly distorted their testimony. There was a show of learning that actually evinced a total exemption from authority. It was as if Morton and his fellows were living a disguised double life among the Fathers, outwardly conforming but actually betraying their teaching. Persons saw in Morton a kind of horrible mockery of the necessary and legitimate equivocation of Catholic priests, and that is one reason why he turned on him the full weight of his scorn, in his next work, *A Quiet and Sober Reckoning with M. Thomas Morton*. The distaste for Morton and all he represented came from very deep down. After all, what was recusancy itself but a refusal to equivocate?

A Quiet and Sober Reckoning with M. Thomas Morton is Persons's most sustained appeal for higher standards of controversy, involving honesty, charity and modesty. In *The Christian Directory* he had called for controversy to be put to one side;[40] having realized in the intervening years that the resolved life could not be isolated from controversy, he now sought to set some ground rules for controversy that would make it compatible with the accountability to God that underlies *The Christian Directory*. The put-down of Morton, the withering scorn, the pity, the wonder at his audacity, the piercing through his rhetorical flourishes of triumph and protestation before God, the exposure of his futile attempt to shelter within a larger body of Protestant divinity, the satirical treatment of the conspicuous gap between promise and delivery – all these are directed at Morton as an extreme and vicious example of the dishonest scholarship Persons attributes to Protestant polemicists generally.

Apart from Morton, Persons also levelled allegations at Sir Edward Coke. Coke had not deigned to reply to Persons's *Answere to the Fifth Parte of Reports Lately set forth by Syr Edward Cooke*,[41] but Morton had undertaken to defend him in *A Full Satisfaction concerning a double Romish Iniquitie*, only to neglect, in *A Preamble Unto an Incounter with P.R.*, the subsequent attacks on Coke contained in *A Treatise tending to Mitigation*. Persons accordingly gave Coke's evidence further extended treatment in *A Quiet and Sober Reckoning with M. Thomas Morton*. The fundamental point at issue in these works was whether Morton and Coke on the one hand, or Persons and other Catholic writers on the other, were guilty of 'such falsitie, as can not be excused either by ignorance, ouersight, negligence, error of print, translation, diuersitie of editions, or the like, but that it must needs be presumed, that he knew the vntruth, and yet would set it forth'.[42] Morton accepted this challenge,[43] and much of the exchange, in *A Quiet and Sober Reckoning with M. Thomas Morton* and Morton's *Encounter against M. Parsons*, was taken up with this question of wilful falsification.

---

40 See above, Chapter 2, pp. 37 ff.
41 Robert Persons, *An Answere to the Fifth Part of Reportes Lately set forth by Syr Edward Cooke Knight, the Kinges Attorney generall* (St Omer, 1606).
42 Persons, *A Treatise tending to Mitigation*, p. 489.
43 Morton, *A Preamble Unto an Incounter with P.R.*, p. 50.

It is difficult, at this distance, to settle the dispute: both sides could expose errors and make the case that the opponent must have known that he was misrepresenting the evidence. In general, however, we can say that the terms defined by Persons in this controversy helped to establish a sense that polemicists should be less concerned with scoring points than with addressing the main issue. One particular example may make this clear. Morton liked to point out disagreement among Catholic authorities, and particularly to accuse the prominent contemporary Catholic apologists, Robert Bellarmine, Cesar Baronius and Francesco Suarez, of misusing tradition:

> Heere, heere had been a large field of falsities, for Mr. *Parsons* his pen to galloppe in, and to play his Rhetoricall curuets, if that his *Holy itch,* (as he calleth such his desire to be meddling with Protestants) had not mooued him, rather to calumniate the manifest truthes of his Aduersaries, then to acknowledge the *Falsifications* committed by the Principall Authors of his owne side.[44]

Apart from the fact that internal debate within Catholicism – as, indeed, within Protestantism – was so lively and widespread that one could not expect the kind of consistency among Catholic authors that a monolithic ideology might produce, Morton's propensity for seizing on error, as he sees it, evinces an insensitivity to context of a kind that convinces Persons that he is not really taking the issue seriously. In *A Preamble Unto an Incounter with P.R.*, for instance, Morton accuses Bellarmine of misrepresenting Augustine's position on the sufficiency of Scripture. In a dispute over the re-baptism of heretics, Cyprian had given way to an outburst against the authority of tradition, because it seemed to be given more weight than Scripture. Augustine responded that the animosity was misplaced because Cyprian had misapplied Scripture on this particular matter. Bellarmine concluded that Augustine had thereby reproved Cyprian's 'manner of reasoning from the sufficiency of Scripture'. Morton's point, ultimately, is that since Augustine had used Scripture itself to refute Cyprian, what appeared to be a defence of tradition was actually an affirmation of Scripture as the only true authority. He goes on to quote further from Augustine, to the effect that if Scripture is not clear, man should keep silent.[45]

Persons did not live to comment on this, but the instance bears out his general criticism of Morton. The burden of Augustine's argument is that although tradition needs to be controlled by Scripture, one should be very cautious about applying Scripture to later disputes about Church practice – and this is Bellarmine's concern. Indeed, Bellarmine had already anticipated the further reference to Augustine that Morton so triumphantly produced.[46]

---

[44]   Morton, *The Encounter against M. Parsons*, p. 13.

[45]   Morton, *A Preamble Unto an Incounter with P.R.*, p. 66; Persons, *A Quiet and Sober Reckoning with M. Thomas Morton*, pp. 186–8; Morton, *The Encounter against M. Parsons*, pp. 108–109.

[46]   Robert Bellarmine, SJ, *De Verbo Dei* IV.11, in *Disputationes de controuersiis Christianae fidei aduersus huius temporis haereticos* (4 vols; Ingolstadt, 1601), vol. 1, pp. 250–52.

Tracking Morton through the folio tomes of Bellarmine and Augustine reveals the characteristic close fighting of Reformation controversy, and there is plausibility in his case. But what continually frustrates Persons is the violence done to the vast and subtle body of Catholic authorities when it is raided in this way to gain a momentary advantage over an adversary. How important this issue was to him is evident from the fact that he turned, in his controversy with Morton, from the immediate issue of rebellion and equivocation to focus on the use of authorities. It was becoming clear to him that controversy could not be conducted under these conditions, when (as he saw it) sycophancy and opportunism covered up intellectual dishonesty or shoddiness, as in Morton's case, or when opponents could shield behind denunciation and professional mystery, as in Coke's.

Perhaps it is fairest simply to note that the Gunpowder Plot had placed Persons at such a propaganda disadvantage that Sutcliffe, Coke, Morton and Barlow (his chief adversaries at this time) could operate with impunity. Persons sensed that his own arguments and the tradition he represented were not being treated with the kind of respect that true debate demands. There was also the question of his place in this tradition. William Barlow alluded to a common perception that Persons was in an inferior league to Bellarmine and tried to bring the cardinal down to Persons's level:

> For whereas the generall opinion, conceiued commonly of the *Cardinall*, hath beene *this*, by those that haue not pondered his works, (and Prefaces especially) that *Father Rob. Bellarmine* hath beene no *base pragmaticall Fa. Parsons*, but an honest, quiet ingenuous Student; now, by this his *Letter to Blackwell*, he is truly made knowen.[47]

Without actually referring to this jibe, Persons responded with a searing assault on Barlow's case in the matter of the Pope's disrespect to the body of the Emperor Henry IV. His concluding flourish is so extravagant as to seem quite disproportionate to the significance of the point at issue:

> Hath he a generall licence, to take away or adde what he listeth to his Authors words? And finally those last words, *that they would not indure it*, written in great letters, where doth he find them? And if he find them not, who gaue him leaue to add them, and crowne his owne inuention with Capitall letters? Is there no law of truth or sincerity? Is it lawfull for euery man to deuise, add, alter, cut of, or disguise what he wil without controlment? Is this the liberty of *Ghospellers*? There haue bene now alleadged by him about this point some eight seuerall authors, *Cuspinian, Helmodus, Vrspergensis, Nauclerus, Sigonius, Binnius, Baronius,* and *Petrus Diaconus,* and euery one hath receaued his cut. Will euer Catholicke writer be found that dealeth so with authors?[48]

Apart from this, the scholarly care, the deliberate style, of the work as a whole seem designed to rebut Barlow's disparagement. Persons wanted to be known

---

[47]   Barlow, *An Answer to a Catholike English-man,* p. 228.
[48]   *A Discussion of the Answere of M. William Barlow,* pp. 409–410.

as an 'honest, quiet, ingenuous Student'. This can be seen most clearly, perhaps, in the historical sections of *A Discussion of the Answere of M. William Barlow*. There is an inordinately long but meticulously researched piece on Frederick II, in which he takes Barlow apart point by painstaking point.[49] The intention may be to imply a parallel with the life of Queen Elizabeth: both denied the true Catholic faith and had dubious dealings with Moslem potentates. They were colourful but heterodox rulers. Here Persons returns to the manner of *A Conference about the Next Succession* and the early parts of *A Treatise of Three Conversions*: the inscription of Roman orthodoxy into the history of kings.

In establishing scholarly credentials, an even more telling passage of arms concerns Frederick Barbarossa, said by James in his *Apology* to have been betrayed on the crusade by Pope Alexander III. In this dispute with Barlow there are two points at issue: what do the authorities say, and do James and Barlow deliberately misrepresent them? James gives 'Paulus Jovius, lib. 2 hist.' as his reference, for confirmation of which Persons searches in vain, and says so, in *The Judgment of a Catholicke English-man*.[50] Barlow does a bit of homework and realizes that Paulus Jovius should actually be attached to James's next example, that of Innocent VI, and crows: Persons has come back, like Saul, without the asses, because he looked in the wrong place. Why get so indignant, he asks, about a mere printer's slip? After all, a similar slip occurs in *The Judgment of a Catholicke English-man*, only a page or two away, and he (Barlow) will treat this much more charitably; he will not rant at Persons for falsifying the evidence.[51] Once Persons points out, in his response to Barlow, that it was not only the position of the sidenote but its corresponding letter that sent him off on the fruitless search, the argument has reached the level of the school playground. But there is a much more important point here: never mind whether Paulus Jovius is a misattribution (and what scholar can escape blushing?): where *is* the evidence against Pope Alexander III? To Persons's credit, this is the question that preoccupies him: he spends several pages probing the historical records before playing his trump card of the sidenote letter. The fact that Alexander III died eight years before Frederick Barbarossa went on crusade clinches it.[52]

Ultimately Persons's view that he and his fellow-Catholic apologists were not being treated as worthy adversaries derived from his deeply held belief that the Protestantism of the English state was expedient. In Elizabeth's reign, the Queen and her counsellors were less interested in the truth of the Reformed religion than in its usefulness – a point made most forcibly in the *Philopater*.[53]

---

[49]   Ibid., pp. 461–95.

[50]   James I, *Triplici nodo, triplex cuneus*, p. 73; also in *An Apologie for the Oath of Allegiance* (London, 1609), p. 74; *The Judgment of a Catholicke English-man*, p. 103.

[51]   Barlow, *An Answer to a Catholike English-man*, pp. 298–9.

[52]   Persons, *A Discussion of the Answere of M. William Barlow*, pp. 524–33.

[53]   Robert Persons, *Elizabethae Angliae Reginae haeresim Caluinianum propugnantis, saeuissimum in Catholicos sui regni edictum ... Cum responsione ad singula capita ... Per D. Andream Philopatrum* (Antwerp, 1592). See above, Chapter 3.

Protestant apologists thus knew they were secure so long as they were serving the state's interests; none needed to be too scrupulous about fact or argument so long as a decent show of learning could be put up as a gloss on political realities. Catholic arguments could be met with bluster and commonplace and superficial approximations. With James on the throne, things were slightly different. He certainly seemed interested in getting to the truth of a debate. How sincerely he was prepared to entertain the possibility that the Catholics could be right, in some points at least, might be open to question. But his vaunted theological acumen had this advantage at least for Persons, that the exposure of wilful falsification was much more damning than under the previous dispensation. No apologist could pretend to be doing the King's cause any good if he were not being scrupulously honest with the evidence.

* * *

The moral dimension – the *ethos* – of controversy is most nearly touched in *A Quiet and Sober Reckoning with M. Thomas Morton*, the opponent who had tried, in *A Preamble Unto an Incounter with P.R.*, to defend his previous record, blasted by *A Treatise tending to Mitigation*. In withering tones Persons now demonstrated that Morton had ineptly and flagrantly compounded his errors, untruths and fallacies. The picture of his adversary is pitiable indeed: a cowardly verbal warrior and a reckless gambler with his immortal soul. In his own *Preamble Unto an Incounter with P.R.*, Morton wanted to appear like a general marshalling his arguments, and so began with some 'light skirmishes' over isolated inaccuracies and lapses in argument in Persons's *Treatise tending to Mitigation*, thus impugning the Jesuit's memory and wit. Such quibbles over inconsequential details represented, in Persons's view, a reluctance to enter upon the main argument. Admittedly, it was also a favourite tactic of his own to expose a particularly weak spot in his opponent's argument, before engaging with the more substantial matter of controversy, but this was made to appear, in contrast with Morton's pusillanimity, as a deliberate clearing of the ground for battle: 'By little and little we draw towards the substance of our chief point of controuersie'.[54]

Persons's art of caricature contributes to the *ethos* of debate: the creation of a polemical identity of a master controversialist engaging with a mere novice. Morton as portrayed in *A Quiet and Sober Reckoning* has no strength, only the bravado of a gambler. His boasting and abuse are shown to be generated mechanically and so to be entirely arbitrary. When he boldly asks: 'How now would my reader hear this noble equivocator confuted? By Fathers? Or by his own Doctors? or by sensible readers?' Persons compares him to a 'bragging bankrupt debtor' who asks his creditors,

> Come Syr, what sort of gold will you be paid in? will you haue it in Spanish Pistolets? Portugall Cruzadoes? French Crownes? Zechines of *Venice*? Dallers of *Germany*, or English Angels? and his creditor should answere

---

[54]   Persons, *A Quiet and Sober Reckoning with M. Thomas Morton*, p. 221.

him, Syr any kind of coyne would content me, although it were but halfe-
faced groates, or single-pence, so I might haue it. And that then the other
should reply as M. *Morton* doth here: Well, I hope, God willing, to pay
you in tyme; and so leaue him with lesse probability of payment then euer
before.[55]

The multiplication of currencies gives no more ground for confidence than
Morton's advertised variety of evidences, which are never realized. Such
oratorical indecorousness enables Persons to rebuke Morton for gambling
with his soul. In a dispute over the existence of purgatory Persons writes:

> And as for the last matter handled by you heere against *Purgatory* ... I
> cannot but lay before you a certaine frendly consideration, tending to your
> eternall good. You and I, that are now so contrary in this point one against
> the other: you in denying, and I in belieuing the truth of that dredfull purging
> fire, cannot but assure our selues, though our age perhaps be vnequall, yet
> that shortly we shall both come to try the matter by experience, and theorf
> will depend our euerlasting good or euill.[56]

This places the *agon* of controversy in the context of the final reckoning,
providing a fit restraint to the excesses of eloquence.

A further aid in the quest for *gravitas* was the contrast between the security
of English apologists like Morton and the hardships of the Jesuits. In a much
earlier engagement Persons had characterized his Protestant opponents thus:
'You feared the fire, and therefore you ascended not up the mountain',[57]
implying that they feared the state more than God. Consequently they were
free from crises of conscience over attending church, taking oaths, equivocation
and political resistance, all of which derived from the dictum of fearing God
rather than men. Thomas Morton epitomized this complacency. It was easy
for him to dismiss reports from India of the miracles of the Blessed Virgin
Mary. Accordingly, Persons demanded:

> How then doth this arrogant-sylly-gras-hopper insult here in fauour of
> Infidels, and disgrace of Christians, calling them, *lying miracles amongst
> the Indians*? Hath he perchance euer byn there? Hath he aduentured his
> life to gaine those soules vnto Christ, that dyed for them, as others haue
> donne? Hath he suffered hunger and thirst, could and heates, persecution
> and affliction with losse of his bloud for gayning of those poore *Indian*
> soules, as others haue suffered, and doe dayly? Noe. He hath done nothing
> of this, but contrary wise stood a farre of in *England*, hath attended to
> good cheare and ease, procured benefices and fauour of the State, and now
> vpon the suddaine is become an aduocate for the *Indian* Pagans, to scorne
> at the Christian miracles wrought by Gods power among them, though
> testified by neuer so great and graue Authority vnto vs. And is not this a
> pious man thinke yow.[58]

---

[55]   Ibid., p. 92.
[56]   Ibid., p. 217.
[57]   Robert Persons, Epigraph (Deut. 5:5) to *A Brief Censure uppon two bookes written in
answere to M. Edmund Campion's offer of disputation* (London, 1580), sig. B3v.
[58]   *A Treatise tending to Mitigation*, 'Epistle Dedicatory', para. 31.

Persons was adept at guaranteeing his views by reference to state suppression, exploiting to the full his unenviable advantage of persecution.

The polemical advantage of appealing to a broad universal, rather than a narrow national, perspective, could be exploited by condescension to the English language. Persons affected a kind of embarrassment about the conduct of controversy in English. He argued that the only effect of making the Bible available to the people in the vernacular was to encourage eccentric readings.[59] It was a mercy that most of the controversies in which he had been engaged were opaque to a European readership, or England's divines would be disgraced: luckily for William Barlow, the Inquisition's request for a reply to his tome was based on the fact that it was in English and thus unreadable.[60] Persons was scandalized that the appellants were not ashamed to publish their calumnies in Latin.[61] He thus offered himself as the representative of Latin Christendom, rebuking his English adversaries in the privacy of their own tongue. He claimed to be alarmed for the reputation of England's ancient universities. In *A Treatise tending to Mitigation* he wondered what foreigners would think about Thomas Morton's arguments, and suggested, in the 'Epistle Dedicatory. To the learned school-divines and lawyers of both faculties in the universities of England', that they would 'infer that either their sciences are not studied in our universities, or that the students profit little in them, or that the worst learned of all are suffered to write books'.[62] Conversely, in his Latin writings he posed as the ambassador of English Catholics, interpreting the religious conflict in his country to the outside world. Facing both ways, he could draw on the still lively idea of Christendom to confer authority on his works.

***

Persons could write with authority because of his experience of remarkable success in influencing opinion at a more personal level. His leadership of the English mission had arrested the decline of the demoralized English Catholics and given them direction and resolution. He had focused the energies of a new generation of priests by founding seminaries in Valladolid, Seville and St Omer, as well as establishing Jesuit control over the Venerable English College at Rome. His understanding of the revolution he had effected in 1580–81 is registered in his unfinished *Life of Campion*.[63] He had to be persuaded, by an appeal to his celebrated readiness to advance the cause at whatever personal cost, to overcome his reluctance to write the history that would have to record his own exploits. Richard Gibbons wrote to the General, Claudio

---

[59]   *The Warn-word*, ch. 8.

[60]   *A Discussion of the Answere of M. William Barlow*, preface, sig. b2.

[61]   Robert Persons, *A Briefe Apologie, or Defence of the Catholike Ecclesiastical Hierarchie, & subordination in England* (Antwerp, 1601), fol. 44.

[62]   *A Treatise tending to Mitigation*, 'Epistle Dedicatory', para. 4.

[63]   'Of the Life and Martyrdom of Father Edmond Campion', *Letters and Notices*, 11 (1877): 219–42, 308–339, and *Letters and Notices*, 12 (1878): 1–68.

Acquaviva, in 1593, urging him to ask Persons to write the *Life* despite the unwelcome publicity it would bring. If he left out his own part in the story, 'the whole force of the account would perish'.[64] The *Life of Campion* corroborates Gibbons's assessment of his leader's modesty, for the narrative shows little straining for effect. There is a quiet insistence on the operation of divine Providence, from the conversion of Persons himself through to the details of movements and decisions on the mission. For the most part the style is that of reportage, allowing events to declare their own significance. The contribution of Persons, especially to the shaping of policy, tends to be shaded by impersonal constructions such as 'it was resolved'.

It is clear from all Persons's correspondence and activity that his experiences in England during the mission left him with two unshakeable convictions: that the majority of the English population was Catholic at heart, ready to respond unreservedly to the old faith as it was made accessible, and that the restoration of Catholicism in England could be achieved only through a united effort. This would have to be led by the Jesuits and carry the authority of the Pope. Even in 1605 he was still convinced that God had singled out England, above all other Protestant nations, for 'a certain spiritual movement towards the preservation and revival of the Catholic religion in our time'.[65] Whether justified or not, the intensity of Persons's vision was extraordinarily persuasive. 'His address and suavity in conversation quickly dissipated aversion', recorded Hugh Tootel in the eighteenth century.[66] This was most manifest in his intervention in the English College at Rome in 1597. Dissatisfaction with the Jesuit control of the college had been brewing ever since the death of Cardinal Allen in 1594. The breach between those who sought tolerance through compromise with the English authorities and those who supported the unyielding position of the Jesuits was widening. Many of the college students, due to return to England before long, joined the anti-Jesuit faction and became ostentatious Hispanophobes. Protests against Jesuit authority came close to rebellion. On 3 April 1597, Persons, sent in by Pope Clement VIII as peacemaker, delivered an address to the students that temporarily won them all over. In the following year, when Persons himself became rector, unity was finally restored.

The speech to the college is the only surviving record of Persons's oratory.[67] His skill is shown in the economy with which he manages his personal

---

[64] 'Pereat ... totus neruus historiae', Richard Gibbons, Letter to Acquaviva, Valladolid, 6 Oct 1593, *ARSI*, Hisp. 136, fols 92–3.

[65] 'Motum quendam animorum ... ad religionem Catholicam tuendam, ac recuperandam nostra hac aetate', 'Epistola pro Anglia, Regnisque Septemtrionalibus', Robert Persons, Letter to Pope Paul V, Rome, 30 June 1605, State Archives, Turin, Raccolta Mongardino, 61, No. 4, fol 2b.

[66] Hugh Tootel [Charles Dodd (pseud.)], *The Church History of England, From the Year 1500, to the Year 1688. Chiefly with regard to Catholicks: together with The Lives of the most eminent Catholicks* (3 vols; London, 1737–42), vol. 2, pp. 402–408.

[67] *ABSI*, MS Collectanea N/II, fols 77–94 (formerly at Stonyhurst). Part of the speech is quoted in *The Copie of a Letter written to a very worshipful Catholike Gentleman in England, of greif conceaved about some scandalous dissention, and bookes set forth, tending to the disgracing one of another, by such as labour in the same cause. By S.N. that dearely loveth them all* (Antwerp, 1601), fols 10v–16v.

antagonism to the anti-Jesuit party. At first he poses as a grave but impartial observer, an Englishman above all, driven by love of his country to probe the causes of dissension. Only when he has patiently laid out the evidence does he become impassioned and appeal to the students to join him in devoting themselves again and entirely to the college's common cause:

> I desire nothing else at God's hands but that He will vouchsafe to remember me to do me good and pardon my sins. As I have always been desirous and endeavoured what hath been in me to do good to this kind of people, to men of your vocation and the like, I must and will do ever by His divine grace, let it be taken or construed how it will. In fine I am wholly yours: use me to your best commodity. God's holy grace and benediction be upon us all, and upon the cause of our country. And this is all I have now to say.[68]

This affecting peroration flows naturally from the incremental feeling of loss of that golden age when English Catholics were united under Cardinal Allen and guided by Providence; and Persons is conscious of his own role in building that former unity.

The governing conceit of the speech is an elaboration of the biblical parable of the second sowing, from Matthew 13:24–30. By judicious comparison of the fruits of the Allen days and those of more recent agitation, especially in the English College, Persons succeeds in identifying the anti-Jesuit party as enemy agents whose tares have sprung up, unwanted, among the expected wheat:

> When I do call to mind the first seed that was sowed by God in his garden, when it was planted (for I was present and had my part in the planting, as some here will bear me witness), when I do remember (I say) what sweet, pure, and holy seed God did put into that ground at the beginning … peace, patience, longanimity, humility, obedience, love, zeal, alacrity, and other such seed, which St Paul testifieth to be true seed of Gods spirit –, and what suitable fruits this seed brought forth presently in the first plants and trees of this garden, whereof many have been martyrs, other confessors, and the rest great labourers in the vineyard of the afflicted country, to the high glory of God, renown of our nation, and edification of the whole world abroad, when I think (I say) of this, and consider withall what loathsome and pernicious cockle hath appeared since, at divers times, of discontentments, griefs, unquietness, and open breaches, I have nothing else to say, but that which Christ Himself said in the like case, *Inimicens homo hoc fecit*. God's enemy hath done this; his hand goeth in this matter; it is of his planting, of his sowing; his malice, his craft, his diligence hath done it. *Non enim fuit sic ab initio:* it was not so from the beginning; it is of a later date, of a second sowing; it is *superseminatum*, that is, oversprinkled and oversown upon that which was well sown before, even as heresy is upon the Catholic religion, and therefore of the same hand and finger, and of the self same malice, though in different objects.[69]

Direct accusation is suspended, and Persons so diplomatically presses the analogy that it gradually takes sure hold on the imagination. Considering the

---

[68]   *ABSI*, MS Collectanea N/II, fol. 94.
[69]   Ibid., fols 81–2.

intensity of feeling against him at this time, the speech bears testimony to his gift for dislodging suspicion with the imaginative force of his convictions. The student leader Edward Bennett commented: 'He whom we most feared, and whom we accounted for our greatest enemy, hath been our greatest friend; yea, and the only man that hath satisfied us.'[70]

An important source of Persons's assurance was the confidence placed in him by the Catholic authorities in Rome. His close association with the Cardinal Nephew, Aldobrandino, ensured that his authority as rector of the English College was never questioned. This may have given him a false sense of security about the tractability of the English Catholic Church at large.[71] Yet his diplomatic status gave him a larger perspective that in some ways elevated him above the internal problems of English Catholicism. In 1588, for example, when he was sent by Acquaviva to intervene in a dispute between the Society of Jesus and the Inquisition in Spain, the General affirmed Persons's unique contribution to the preservation of the company's sense of vocation and identity.[72] Again, when Pope Paul V succeeded in 1605, he asked Persons to draw up a prospectus for the Catholic Reformation in northern Europe. In his reply, Persons argued that the conversion of England was God's chosen first step to the recovery of all the Protestant kingdoms.[73]

Persons's last days, in April 1610, were described in hagiographical fashion by his secretary Edward Coffin. A Latin translation survives in the Roman archives of the Society of Jesus.[74] Once allowances have been made for Coffin's partiality, this document remains good evidence for the regard in which Persons was held, and the ideal of life that he maintained to the end. Three themes emerge: the demands made on him as a spiritual director, the tributes paid to him by the Roman authorities, and his immersion in liturgical discipline. Despite the onset of illness, he kept the Lenten fast with all rigour, responded wholeheartedly to the devotions of Holy Week and welcomed the last rites. When it was objected that this represented a premature despair of life, he insisted on the sacrament, not so much submitting to death as fortifying himself for the final conflict. The image of a priest supernaturally attuned and passing on, in an entirely collected spirit, to the next world, is impressive. Again, Coffin effectively creates the aura of a great man dying, the news rippling through ecclesiastical Rome, the princes of the Church competing for a chance to pay their respects, and the Jesuit fathers attempting to protect him from over-excitement. Whenever there was an interval in the fever, more students, colleagues and friends poured in, seeking his final blessing.

---

[70]   Anthony Kenny, 'The Inglorious Revolution 1594–1597', *Venerabile* 16 (1956): 240–58, and *Venerabile* 17 (1957): 7–25, 77–94, 136–55 (vol. 17, p. 91).

[71]   Michael E. Williams, *The Venerable English College, Rome: A History 1579–1979* (London, 1979), p. 21.

[72]   Claudio Acquaviva, Letter to Persons, Rome, 30 Oct 1588, *ARSI*, Tolet. 4, fol. 41.

[73]   'Epistola pro Anglia, Regnisque Septemtrionalibus', State Archives, Turin, Raccolta Mongardino, 61 no. 4.

[74]   *ARSI*, MS. Anglia 38/2.

Pope Paul V recognized his stature by granting him a plenary indulgence *in amplissima forma*, a distinction normally reserved for cardinals. This placed him on the same level as Allen, and indeed he was to be buried alongside him. Acquaviva described him as a martyr, 'his old age broken by his labours'.[75] Not only was Persons at this time under almost ceaseless pressure for spiritual counsel or advice on mission strategy, until first his voice and finally consciousness failed, but he had recently completed, in a remarkably short time (even for him), the lengthy *Discussion of the Answere of M. William Barlow*, when he would much rather have been expanding *The Christian Directory*. His ability to hold firmly to his spiritual vocation is well represented by Coffin's final scene: he died with the words of the Psalms on his lips as if hedged in by pure devotion on the one hand and dedication to the service of the English mission on the other.

Such further glimpses of Persons's personal qualities as a leader as can be obtained from scattered sources confirm this sense of an equilibrium between spirituality and 'policy'. The epitaph inscribed on his tomb in the English College includes the tribute: 'always prepared, always alert, always magnanimously rushing into the midst of the flame of the most dangerous conflict'.[76] Expressions of gratitude and confidence were the staple of much of the correspondence of his colleagues and pupils.[77] His tirelessness derived from a sense of priorities: his laconic comment on plans to make him a cardinal was 'God is not so short of material that when He wants to make a new suit He has it made from a rough old overcoat'.[78] In his letters, whatever his own discouragement, he was full of consolation for others. In 1595 he reported the loss of six pupils to Acquaviva with the words: 'It is the Lord: let Him do what has seemed good in his eyes ... and if we have received good from His hands, why not evil as well?'[79] He encouraged Henry Garnet:

> You must have still (as hitherto) great patience on the one side and on the other great confidence and courage in Him, for He will not forsake you now the work He hath begun. If we be faithful, humble and perseverant, notwithstanding the difficulties He permitteth *a dextris et a sinistris*, which Himself will overcome, to His own great glory and our more singular comfort in the end.[80]

'Difficulties', indeed, is the lexical crux around which Persons's whole endeavour turns. It suggests both the spiritual category of affliction and the political

---

[75]   Ibid., fols 150, 156, 161.

[76]   'Semper paratus semper erectus semper in mediam flammam periculosissimae concertationis irrumpens animae magnae' (see above, Chapter 1 for the full epitaph).

[77]   E.g., *Registers of the English College at Valladolid 1589–1862*, ed. Edwin Henson; CRS, 30 (London, 1930), pp. 90–93; *Letters of Thomas Fitzherbert*, ed. L. Hicks, SJ; CRS, 41 (London, 1948), p. 80.

[78]   Henry More, SJ, *The Elizabethan Jesuits*, ed. and trans. Francis Edwards, SJ (London, 1981), part 6, p. 291.

[79]   Robert Persons, Letter to Acquaviva, Seville, 15 May 1595, *ARSI*, Hisp. 138, fol. 264.

[80]   Robert Persons, Letter to Garnet, Rome, 12/13 July 1598, in *The Archpriest Controversy*, ed. T.G. Law (2 vols; London, 1896–98), vol. 1, pp. 21–2.

category of obstacles to a desired end. The former meaning predominates in *The Christian Directory*, where the 'impediments which hinder [resolution]' are handled. Here the reader often encounters the term 'difficulties' in a spiritual sense. The political meaning is reflected in a letter of advice to George Blackwell, the archpriest: 'But of necessity we must sail here according to the winds and weather, not respecting only what reason equity and justice would require (for that is evident) but what the condition of times and men both there and here do bear'.[81] Blackwell, as it turned out, could not bear very much, but Persons kept writing to the end, fighting the enemy and feeding his flock.

---

[81]   Robert Persons, Letter to Blackwell, Rome, 30 Apr 1601, *ABSI*, Coll P, fol. 344.

A Chronology of Persons's Printed Works, 1580–1622

1580   *A Brief Discours contayning certayne reasons why Catholiques refuse to goe to Church*

        A Brief Censure uppon two bookes written in answere to M. Edmonde Campions offer of disputation

1581   *A Discoverie of I. Nicols Minister, misreported a Jesuite, lately recanted in the Tower of London*

        The Copie of a Double Letter ... containing the true advises of the cause, and maner of death, of one Richard Atkins, executed by Fire, in Rome, the second of August 1581

        De persecutione Anglicana, epistola. Qua explicantur afflictiones, aerumna, & calamitates grauissimae, cruciatus etiam & tormenta, & acerbissima martyria, quae Catholici nunc Angli, ob fidem patiuntur

1582   *A Defence of the Censure, gyven uppon two bookes of William Charke and Meredith Hanmer mynysters, whiche they wrote against M. Edmond Campian preest, of the Societie of Jesus, and against his offer of disputation*

        The First Booke of the Christian Exercise, appertayning to Resolution

1585   *A Christian Directorie Guiding Men to their Salvation ... with reprofe of the corrupt and falsified edition of the same booke lately published by M. Edm. Buny*

1590   *Relacion de Algunos martyrios, que de nueuo han hecho los hereges en Inglaterra, y de otras cosas tocantes a nuestra santa y Catolica religion*

1592   *A Relation of the King of Spaines Receiving in Valliodolid, and in the Inglish College of the same towne, in August last past of this yere, 1592*

        Elizabethae Angliae Reginae haeresim Caluinianum propugnantis, saeuissimum in Catholicos sui regni edictum ... Cum responsione ad singula capita

        Relacion de un Sacerdote Ingles ... de la venida de su Magestad ... al colegio de los Yngleses

1593   *Newes from Spayne and Holland conteyning. An information of Inglish affayres in Spayne with a conference made theruppon in Amsterdame of Holland*

1595   *A Conference about the Next Succession to the Crowne of England*

1598   *A Christian Directorie Guiding Men to their Salvation*

1599   *A Temperate Ward-word, to the turbulent and seditious Wach-word of Sir Francis Hastinges knight*

1601   *A Briefe Apologie, or Defence of the Catholike Ecclesiastical Hierarchie, & subordination in England*

       An Appendix to the Apologie, lately set forth, for the defence of the Hierarchie, & subordination of the English Catholike Church

1602   *A Manifestation of the Great Folly and bad spirit of certayne in England calling themselves secular priestes*

       The Warn-word to Sir Francis Hastinges Wast-word: Conteyning the issue of three former Treatises, the Watch-word, the Ward-word and the Wast-word (intituled by Sir Francis, an Apologie or Defence of his Watch-word)

1603   *A Treatise of Three Conversions of England from Paganisme to Christian Religion*

1604   *The Third Part of a Treatise, Intituled: of three Conversions of England: conteyning. An Examen of the Calendar or Catalogue of Protestant Saints, Martyrs and Confessors, divised by John Fox, and prefixed before his volume of Acts and Monuments …. The first six monethes*

       The Third Part of a Treatise Intituled Of Three Conversions of England. Conteyning an examen of the Calendar or Catalogue of Protestant Saintes, Martyrs and Confessors, devised by Fox, and prefixed before his huge Volume of Actes and Monumnets … The last six monethes

1606   *An Answere to the Fifth Part of Reportes Lately set forth by Syr Edward Cooke Knight, the Kings Attorney generall*

1607   *The Christian Directory Guiding men to eternall salvation*

       Quaestiones duae de sacris alienis non aduendis, ad vsum praximque Angliae breuiter explicatae

1608   *A Treatise tending to Mitigation towardes Catholicke-Subiectes in England*

       The Judgment of a Catholicke English-man. Concerninge A late Booke set forth, and entituled: Triplici nodo, triplex cuneus, Or, An Apologie for the Oath of Allegiance

1609   *A Quiet and Sober Reckoning with M. Thomas Morton somewhat set in choler by his Adversary P.R. concerning Certaine imputations of wilfull falsities obiected to the said T.M. in a Treaties of P.R. intituled Of Mitigation*

1612   *A Discussion of the Answere of M. William Barlow, D. of Divinity, to the Booke intituled: The Judgment of a Catholicke Englishman*

1622   *A Christian Directory, Guiding men to Eternall Salvation: commonly called the Resolution*

Bibliography

I. Manuscript Sources

Archives of the British Province of the Society of Jesus (ABSI)

Anglia III. Letters of English Jesuits.
Collectanea N/II. Containing Persons's speech to the English College, Rome, 1597.
Collectanea P. Christopher Grene's 17th century transcripts, section P.
46/12/1–7. Persons Letters: transcriptions and translations, chiefly by L. Hicks, SJ.

Archivum Romanum Societatis Iesu (ARSI)

Angl. 38/2. Latin translation of Edward Coffin's account of Persons's death.
Angl. 42. Scottish history.
Cast. 6. Castilian Letters.
Fl. Belg. 1/II. Belgian Letters.
Hisp. 136. Spanish Letters.
Hisp. 138. Spanish Letters.
Tolet. 4. Letters of the Generals.
Tolet. 5/I–II. Letters of the Generals.
Fondo Gesuitico 651. Selected Letters from England.

British Library

Harleian 35 # 36. Copy of Verstegan's *Advertisement.*

Corpus Christi College Library, Oxford

CC 200. 'Lord Burleigh's Commonwealth'.

Lambeth Palace Library

648. Bacon Papers.

State Archives, Turin

Raccolta Mongardino 61 no. 4. Persons's memorandum to Pope Paul V, 1605.

II. Primary Printed Sources

Allen, William, *A Briefe Historie of the Glorious Martyrdom of xij Reverend Priests, executed within these twelve monethes for confession and defence of the Catholike Faith* (Rheims: Jean Foigny, 1582).

—— *The Copie of a Letter written by M. Doctor Allen: concerning the yeelding up, of the citie of Daventrie* (Antwerp: Joachim Trognaesius, 1587).

—— *The Letters and Memorials of William Cardinal Allen (1532–1594)*, ed. Fathers of the Congregation of the London Oratory; introd. T.F. Knox (London: David Nutt, 1882).

—— *A Treatise of Treasons against Q. Elizabeth, and the Croune of England* (Louvain: John Fowler, 1572).

—— *A True, Sincere and Modest Defence of English Catholiques that suffer for their Faith both at home and abrode: against a false, seditious and slaunderous Libel intituled; The Execution of Justice in England* (Rouen: Fr Persons' Press, 1584).

'An Apologie and Defence of the King of Scotland', in *Documents Illustrating Catholic Policy in the Reign of James VI*, ed. T.G. Law; Publications of the Scottish History Society, 15 (Edinburgh: University Press, 1893).

Anon. [S.N. (pseud.)], *The Copie of a Letter written to a very worshipful Catholike Gentleman in England, of greif conceaved about some scandalous dissention, and bookes set forth, tending to the disgracing one of another, by such as labour in the same cause. By S.N. that dearely loveth them all* (Antwerp: Arnout Conincx, 1601).

The Archpriest Controversy: Documents Relating to the Dissensions of the Roman Catholic Clergy, 1597–1602: from the Petyt MSS of the Inner Temple, ed. T.G. Law; Camden Society, n.s. 56 (London: Camden Society, 1896) and 58 (London: Longmans, Green & Co., 1898).

Assheton, William, *The Royal Apology: or, An Answer to the Rebels Plea: wherein, the most noted anti-monarchical tenents, first, published by Doleman the Jesuite, to promote a bill of exclusion against King James. Secondly, practised by Bradshaw and the regicides in the actual murder of King Charles the 1st. Thirdly, republished by Sidney and the associators to depose and murder his present Majesty, are distinctly consider'd. With a parallel between Doleman, Bradshaw, Sidney and other of the true-Protestant party* (London: T.B. for Robert Clavel, 1684).

Bacon, Sir Francis, *The Works of Francis Bacon*, ed. James Spedding, R.L. Ellis and D.D. Heath (14 vols; London: Longman & Co., 1857–74).

Bagshaw, Christopher, *Relatio Compendiosa Turbarum quas Iesuitae Angli … Sacerdotibus Seminariorum populoque Catholico concivere* (London: Thomas Creede, 1601).

—— *A Sparing Discoverie of our English Jesuits, and of Fa. Parsons proceedings vnder pretence of promoting the Catholike faith in England* (London: Felix Kingston, 1601).

—— *A True relation of the faction begun at Wisbich, by Fa. Edmons, alias Weston, a Jesuite* (London: Felix Kingston, 1601).

Barlow, William, *An Answer to a Catholike English-man (so by himself entituled) who, without a Name, passed his Censure upon the Apology, made by the Right High and mightie Prince James ... for the Oath of Allegeance* (London: Thomas Haveland for Matthew Law, 1609).

Baxter, Richard, *Reliquiae Baxterianae* (London: T. Parkhurst, J. Robinson, J. Laurence and J. Dunton, 1696).

Bellarmine, Robert, SJ, *Responsio Matthaei Torti Presbyteri et Theologi Papiensis, ad Librum inscriptum, Triplici Nodo Triplex Cuneus* (St Omer: English College Press, 1608).

—— *De Verbo Dei*, in *Disputationes de controuersiis Christianae fidei aduersus huius temporis haereticos* (4 vols; Ingolstadt: A. Sartorius, 1601), vol. 1.

Belloy, Pierre de, *A Catholicke Apologie against the Libels, Declarations, Advices, and Consultations made, written and published by those of the League, perturbers of the quiet estate of the Realme of France* (London: n.p., 1590) [*Apologia catholica ad famosos et seditiosos libellos Coniuratorum* (Paris, 1584)].

Benet of Canfield, *The Miraculous Life, Conversion and Conversation of the Reverend Father Bennett of Canfield* (Douay: n.p., 1623).

Bennet, John, *The Hope of Peace. By laying open such doubts and manifest untruthes as are divulged by the Arch-priest in his Letter or Answere to the Bookes which were published by the Priestes* (London: Thomas Creede, 1601).

Bishop, William, *The Copies of certaine discourses, which were extorted from divers ... to purge themselves of the most greevous crimes of schisme, sedition, rebellion, faction, and such like, most unjustly laid against them for not subscribing to the late authoritie at the first sending thereof into England* (London: Thomas Creede, 1601).

Bluet, Thomas, *Important Considerations, which ought to move all true and sound Catholikes who are not wholly Jesuited ... to acknowledge ... that the proceedings of her Maiesty ... have bene both mild and mercifull* (London: Richard Field, 1601).

Breaking the Silence on the Succession: A Sourcebook of Manuscripts & Rare Elizabethan Texts (c. 1587–1603), ed. Jean-Christophe Mayer; Astraea Texts, 1 (Montpellier: Université Paul Valéry Montpellier 3, 2003).

Brutus, Junius. See Philippe de Mornay.

Buchanan, George, *De iure regni apud Scotos, dialogus* (Edinburgh: John Ross for Henry Charteris, 1579).

Calendar of the Manuscripts of the Most Honourable the Marquess of Salisbury, Historical Manuscripts Commission (24 vols; London: HMSO, 1883–1976).

Calvin, Jean, *Institutes of the Christian Religion*, ed. J.T. McNeill; trans. F.L. Battles; The Library of the Christian Classics, 20–21 (2 vols; London: SCM Press, 1961).

Camden, William, *Annales rerum Anglicanum, et Hibernicarum regnante Elizabetha, ad annum salutis MDLXXXIX* (Frankfurt: I. Bringerus, 1616).

Campion, Edmund, SJ, *Ambrosia*, ed. Jos. Simons (Assen: Van Gorcum, 1969).

—— *A Historie of Ireland* [1570], ed. Rudolf B. Gottfried (New York: Scholars' Facsimiles and Reprints, 1940).

—— *A Jesuit Challenge: Edmund Campion's Debates at the Tower of London in 1581*, ed. James V. Holleran (New York: Fordham University Press, 1999).

—— *Rationes decem quibus fretus, certamen aduersariis obtulit in causa fidei* (Stonor Park: Fr Persons' Press, 1581).

Cecil, Sir William, *The Execution of Justice in England for maintenance of publique and Christian peace, against certeine stirrers of sedition, and adherents to the traytours and enemies of the Realme, without any persecution of them for questions of Religion, as is falsely reported and published by the fautors and fosterers of their treasons* (London: Christopher Barker, 1583).

Certaine Sermons or Homilies appointed to be read in Churches, 2 parts (London: J. Bill, 1623) [*Certain Sermons, or Homilies, appoynted...to be declared and redde ... in ... Churches* and *The Second Tome of Homelyes* (London: C. Barker and H. Middleton, 1582; J. Charlewood & T. East, 1587; E. Allde, 1595)].

Charke, William, *An answere to a seditious pamphlet lately cast abroade by a Jesuite, with a discoverie of that blasphemous sect* (London: Christopher Barker, 1580).

Clarke, William, *A Replie unto a certaine Libell, latelie set foorth by Fa: Parsons, in the name of united Priests, intituled, A manifestation of the great folly and bad spirit, of certaine in England, calling themselves secular Priestes* (London: James Roberts, 1603).

Coke, Sir Edward, *The Fift Part of the Reports of Sr. Edward Coke Knight, the Kings Attorney Generall: Of divers Resolutions and Iudgments given upon great deliberation, in matters of great importance & consequence by the reverend Iudges and Sages of the Law: together with the reasons and causes of the Resolutions and Iudgements* (London: Stationers' Company, 1605).

A Collection of Sundry Statutes, ed. F. Pulton (London: Flesher and Young, 1940).

Colleton, John, *A Just Defence of the Slandered Priestes: Wherein the reasons of their bearing off to receive Maister Blackwell to their Superiour before the arrivall of his Holines Breve are layed down, and the imputation of disobedience, ambition, contention, scandall, &c., is by able arguments and authorities removed, the obiection of the adverse part suficiently answered, and the Popes sentence in the controversie truly related* (London: Adam Islip, 1602).

Constable, Henry, *A Discoverye of a Counterfecte Conference helde at a counterfecte place, by counterfecte travellers, for thadvancement of a counterfecte tytle, and invented, printed, and published by one (PERSON) that dare not avowe his name* (Cologne [*vere* Paris]: for Charles Paget, 1600).

The Copie of a Leter, wryten by a Master of Arte of Cambridge. See Leicester's Commonwealth.

Copley, Anthony, *An Answere to a Letter of a Jesuited Gentleman, by his Cosin, Maister A.C. Concerninge the Appeale; State, Jesuits* (London: Felix Kingston, 1601).

Creswell, Joseph, SJ [Ioannes Pernius (pseud.)], *Exemplar literarum, missarum, e Germania, ad Guilielmum Cecilium, Consilium Regium* (Rome: Vincento Accolti, 1592).

Didymus Veridicus Henfildanus. See Thomas Stapleton, *Apologia pro Rege Catholico Philippo II.*

Documents Illustrating Catholic Policy in the Reign of James VI, ed. T.G. Law; Publications of the Scottish History Society, 15 (Edinburgh: Edinburgh University Press, 1893).

Dodd, Charles. See Hugh Tootel.

Doleman, R. See Robert Persons, A *Conference about the Next Succession.*

Donne, John, *The Poems of John Donne,* ed. Herbert J.C. Grierson (2 vols; Oxford: Clarendon Press, 1912).

—— *Pseudo-Martyr. Wherein out of certaine Propositions and Gradations, This Conclusion is evicted. That those which are of the Romane Religion in this Kingdome, may and ought to take the Oath of Allegeance* (London: W. Stansby for W. Burre, 1610).

English Prose: Selections, ed. Henry Craik (5 vols; London: Macmillan, 1893–96), vol. 1, *Fourteenth to Sixteenth Century.*

Erasmus, Desiderius, *Moriae encomium, sive Stultitiae laus* (Paris: G. Gourmont, 1511).

Field, John, *A Caveat for Parsons Howlet, concerning his untimely flight and screeching in the clear daylight of the gospel, necessary for him and all the rest of that dark brood and unclean cage of papists, who with their untimely books seek the discredit of the truth, and the disquiet of this Church of England* (London: R. Waldegrave for T. Man and T. Smith, 1581).

Fitzherbert, Thomas, *Letters of Thomas Fitzherbert,* ed. L. Hicks, SJ; CRS, 41 (London: Catholic Record Society, 1948).

For Matters of Greater Moment: The First Thirty Jesuit General Congregations, ed. John W. Padberg, SJ et al. (St Louis: Institute of Jesuit Sources, 1994).

Foxe, John, *Actes and Monuments of matters most speciall and memorable, happening in the Church, with an universall history of the same* (London: Peter Short, 1596).

Gerard, John, SJ, *The Autobiography of an Elizabethan,* trans. Philip Caraman, SJ (London: Longmans, Green and Co., 1951).

Gibbons, John, *Concertatio Ecclesiæ Catholicæ in Anglia, adversus Calvinopapistas et Puritanos, a paucis annis singulari studio quorundam hominum doctrina et sanctitate illustrium renovata* (Trier: E. Hatot, 1583; rpt. Trier: H. Bock, 1588).

Greene, Robert, *The Life and Complete Works, in Prose and Verse, of Robert Greene,* ed. A.B. Grosart (15 vols; London and Aylesbury: The Huth Library, 1881–86).

Hanmer, Meredith, *The great bragge and challenge of M. Champion a Jesuite, commonlye called Edmunde Campion, latelye arrived in Englande, contayninge nyne articles here severallye laide downe, directed by him to the Lordes of the Counsail, confuted & aunswered by Meredith Hanmer, M. of Art, and Student in Divinitie* (London: T. Marsh, 1581).

Harington, Sir John, *Orlando Furioso* [1591], ed. R. McNulty (London: Oxford University Press, 1972).

Harpsfield, Nicholas, *Dialogi Sex contra Summi Pontificatus, monasticae vitae, sanctorum, sacrarum imaginum oppugnatores, et pseudomartyres* (Antwerp: Christopher Plantin, 1566).

Harvey, Gabriel, *Pierces Supererogation* [1593], extracted in *Elizabethan Critical Essays*, ed. G. Gregory Smith (2 vols; London: Oxford University Press, 1904), vol. 2.

Hastings, Sir Francis, *An Apologie or Defence of the Watch-word* (London: Felix Kingston, for Ralph Jackson, 1600).

—— *A Watchword to all religious, and true hearted English-men* (London: Felix Kingston for Ralph Jackson, 1598).

Hopkins, Gerard Manley, SJ, *Poems and Prose*, ed. W.H. Gardner (Harmondsworth: Penguin, 1953).

Hotman, Francois, *Francogallia* [1573], ed. R.E. Giesey; trans. J.H.M. Salmon (Cambridge: Cambridge University Press, 1972).

Ignatius of Loyola, St, *Personal Writings*, ed. Joseph A. Munitiz, SJ and Philip Endean, SJ (Harmondsworth: Penguin, 1996).

James I, King of England, *An Apologie for the Oath of Allegiance: first set forth without a name, now acknowledged by James, King. Together with a premonition to all most mightie monarches* (London: R. Barker, 1609).

—— *Basilikon doron, Or His Maiesties instructions to his dearest sonne, Henrie the prince* (London: Richard Field for John Norton, 1603).

—— *Triplici nodo, triplex cuneus: or, An Apologie for the Oath of Allegiance, Against the two Breves of Pope Paulus Quintus, and the late Letter of Cardinal Bellarmine to G. Blackwel the Arch-priest* (London: R. Barker, 1607 [*vere* 1608]).

James, Thomas, *The Jesuites Downefall … Together with the Life of Father Parsons an English Jesuite* (Oxford: Joseph Barnes, 1612).

Kingsley, Charles, *Westward Ho!* (Cambridge: Macmillan, 1855).

A Large Examination taken at Lambeth, according to his Maiesties direction, point by point, of M. George Blakwell (London: Robert Barker, 1607).

Leech, Humphrey, *Dutifull and Respective Considerations upon foure severall heads of Proofe and Triall in matters of Religion. Proposed by … Iames King … for clearing his Royall Person from the Imputation of Heresy* (St Omer: English College Press, 1609).

Lefévre de la Boderie, Antoine, *Ambassades de Monsieur de la Boderie, en Angleterre, Sous le regne d'Henri IV. & la minorite de Louis XIII. depuis les annees 1606. jusqu'en 1611* (5 vols; n.p.: n.p., 1750).

[Leicester's Commonwealth] *The Copie of a Leter, wryten by a Master of Arte of Cambridge, to his friend in London, concerning some talke past of late between two worshipful and grave men, about the present state, and some procedinges of the Erle of Leycester and his friendes in England. Conceyved, spoken and publyshed, wyth most earnest protestation of al duetyful good wyl and affection, towardes her most excellent Ma. and the Realm, for whose good onely it is made common to many* (?Paris (cf. Mush): n.p., 1584).

—— *Leicester's Commonwealth. Conceived, spoken and published with most earnest protestation of all dutiful good-will and affection towards this realm. By Robert Parsons* (London: n.p., 1641).

—— *Leicester's Commonwealth: 'The Copy of a Letter written by a Master of Art of Cambridge' (1584) and Related Documents*, ed. D.C. Peck (Athens: Ohio University Press, 1985).

Loarte, Gaspar de, [*Essercitio della vita christiana* (Venice, 1561)] *The Exercise of a Christian Life. Written in Italian by … Gaspar Loarte … and newly translated into Englishe. By I.S.*, trans. James Sancer [Stephen Brinkley (pseud.)] (London: William Carter, 1579).

—— *The Exercise of a Christian Life. Written in Italian by … Gaspar Loarte … and newly translated into Englishe. By I.S. Newly perused and corrected by the translator*, trans. Stephen Brinkley (Rouen: Fr Persons' Press, 1584).

Luis de Granada, [*Guia de Pecadores* (Salamanca, 1556–57, 1567)] *The Sinners Guide. A Worke Contayning the whole regiment of a Christian life*, trans. Francis Meres (London: James Roberts for Paul Linley, 1598).

—— [*Libro de la Oración y Meditación* (Salamanca, 1554, 1556)] *Of Prayer, and Meditation*, trans. Richard Hopkins (Paris: Thomas Brumeau, 1582; rpt. Rouen: George L'Oyselet, 1584).

—— [*Memorial de lo que debe hacer el cristiano* (Lisbon, 1561)] *A Memoriall of a Christian Life*, trans. Richard Hopkins (Rouen: George L'Oyselet, 1586).

Memoirs of the Reign of Queen Elizabeth, From the Year 1581 till her Death, ed. Thomas Birch (2 vols; London: A. Millar, 1754).

Middleton, Thomas, *A Mad World, My Masters* [1608], in *Selected Plays of Thomas Middleton*, ed. D.L. Frost (Cambridge: Cambridge University Press, 1978).

Miscellanea II, ed. J.H. Pollen; CRS, 2 (London: Catholic Record Society, 1906).

Moffet, Thomas, *Healths Improvement: or, Rules Comprizing and Discovering The Nature, Method, and Manner of Preparing all sorts of Food Used in this Nation* (London: Thomas Newcomb for Samuel Thomson, 1655).

More, Henry, SJ, [*Historia Missionis Anglicanae Societatis Iesu* (1660)] *The Elizabethan Jesuits*, ed. and trans. Francis Edwards, SJ (London: Phillimore, 1981).

More, Sir Thomas, *Libellus vere aureus nec minus salutaris quam festivus de optimo reipublicae statu deque noua insula Utopia* (Louvain: T. Martens, 1516).

Mornay, Philippe de [Junius Brutus (pseud.)], *Vindiciae contra Tyrannos: siue, De principis in populum, populique in principem, legitima potestate* (Basle: C. Waldkirch, 1579).

Morton, Thomas, *The Encounter against M. Parsons* (London: J. Bill, 1610).

—— *A Full Satisfaction concerning a double Romish Iniquitie; hainous Rebellion, and more then heathenish Aequivocation* (London: Richard Field for Edmund Weaver, 1606).

—— *A Preamble Unto an Incounter with P.R. the Author of the deceitfull Treatise of Mitigation* (London: M. Bradwood for John Bill and Edmund Weaver, 1608).

Mush, John, *Declaratio Motuum ac Turbationum quae ex controversiis inter Iesuitas ... & Sacerdotes Seminariorum in Anglia* (London: ?Thomas Creede, 1601).

—— *A Dialogue betwixt a Secular Priest, and a Lay Gentleman. Being an abstract of the most important matters that are in controversie betwixt the priests and the Spanish or Jesuiticall faction* (London: Adam Islip, 1601).

Newman, John Henry, *An Essay in Aid of a Grammar of Assent* [1870], ed. Nicholas Lash (Notre Dame: University of Notre Dame Press, 1979).

Pelling, Edward, *The Apostate Protestant. A Letter to a Friend, occasioned by the late Reprinting of a Jesuites Book. About Succession to the Crown of England* (London: W. Davis and J. Hindmarsh, 1682).

Pernius, Ioannes. See Joseph Creswell, SJ.

Persons, Robert, SJ, *An Answere to the Fifth Part of Reportes Lately set forth by Syr Edward Cooke Knight, the Kings Attorney generall* (St Omer: François Bellet, 1606) [= *An Answere to Coke*].

—— *An Appendix to the Apologie, lately set forth, for the defence of the Hierarchie, & subordination of the English Catholike Church* (Antwerp: Arnout Conincx, 1601).

—— *A Brief Censure uppon two bookes written in answere to M. Edmonde Campions offer of disputation* (London: 'Greenstreet House' Press, House of Francis Browne, Southwark, 1580).

—— [John Howlett (pseud.)], *A Brief Discours contayning certayne reasons why Catholiques refuse to goe to Church* (London: 'Greenstreet House' Press, East Ham, 1580) [= *Reasons of Refusal*].

—— *A Briefe Apologie, or Defence of the Catholike Ecclesiastical Hierarchie, & subordination in England, erected these later yeares by our holy Father Pope Clement the eyght; and impugned by certayne libels printed and published of late ... under the name of Priests of the Seminaries* (Antwerp: Arnout Conincx, 1601) [= *A Defence of the Catholike Ecclesiastical Hierarchie*].

—— [*Certamen Ecclesiae Anglicanae*: selections] *Certamen Ecclesiae Anglicanae: A Study of an Unpublished Manuscript*, ed. Jos. Simons (Assen: Van Gorcum, 1965).

—— [*The Christian Directory*] *The First Booke of the Christian Exercise, appertayning to Resolution. Wherein are layed downe the causes and reasons that should move a man to resolve hym selfe to the service of God: And all the impedimentes removed, which may lett the same* (Rouen: Fr Persons' Press, 1582).

—— [*The Christian Directory*: revised version] *A Christian Directorie Guiding Men to their Salvation. Deuided into three Bookes. The first wherof apperteining to Resolution, is only conteined in this volume, devided into two partes, and set forth now againe with many corrections, and additions by th'Authour himself, with reprofe of the corrupt and falsified edition of the same booke lately published by M. Edm. Buny* (Rouen: Fr Persons' Press, 1585; rpt. Louvain: Laurence Kellam, 1598).

—— [*The Christian Directory*: a further revision] *The Christian Directory Guiding men to eternall salvation, Devided into three Bookes. The First wherof teacheth how to make a good resolution. The Second, how to begin well. The Third, how to perservere and end happily. In this volume is onely contayned the first booke, consisting of two Partes, wherof the former layeth downe the motives to Resolution: and the other remoueth the impediments: both of them having byn lately reviewed, corrected, and not a little altered by the author himselfe for the greater commodity and utility of the Reader* (St Omer: François Bellet, 1607).

—— [*The Christian Directory*: a further revision, possibly authorial] *A Christian Directory, Guiding men to Eternall Salvation: commonly called the Resolution. The first wherof, teacheth how to make a good Resolution. The second, how to begin well. The third, how to perservere, and end happily. Written By the R. Father Robert Persons, Priest of the Society of Jesus. The Sixt. and last Edition* (St Omer: English College Press, 1622).

—— [*The Christian Directory*: modern edn] *The Christian Directory (1582): The First Booke of the Christian Exercise, appertayning to Resolution*, ed. Victor Houliston (Leiden: E.J. Brill, 1998).

—— [*The Christian Directory*: a Protestant adaptation] *A Booke of Christian exercise, appertaining to Resolution, that is shewing how that we should resolv our selvs to becom Christians indeed: by R.P. Perused, and accompanied now with a Treatise tending to Pacification: by Edmund Bunny*, ed. Edmund Bunny (London: N. Newton and A. Hatfield for John Wight, 1584).

—— [R. Doleman (pseud.)], *A Conference about the Next Succession to the Crowne of Ingland, divided into two partes. Whereof the first conteyneth the discourse of a civill Lawyer, how and in what manner propinquity of blood is to be preferred. And the second the speech of a Temporall Lawyer, about the particuler titles of all such as do or may pretende within Ingland or without, to the next succession* (Antwerp: Arnout Conincx, 1594 [*vere* 1595]).

—— [R. Doleman (pseud.)], *A Conference About the Next Succession to the Crown of England* (London: n.p., 1681).

—— [A Conference about the Next Succession: an adaptation] Severall Speeches Delivered at a Conference concerning the Power of Parliament, to proceed against their King for Misgovernment, ed. Henry Walker (London: Robert Ibbitson, 1648).

—— [A Conference about the Next Succession: an abridgement] A Treatise Concerning the Broken Succession of the Crown of England. Inculcated, about the later end of the Reign of Queen Elizabeth. Not impertinent for the better Compleating of the General Information intended (London: n.p., 1655).

—— The Copie of a Double Letter sent by an Englishe Gentilman from beyond the seas, to his frende in London, containing the true advises of the cause, and maner of death, of one Richard Atkins, executed by Fire, in Rome, the second of August 1581 (Rheims: Jean Foigny, 1581).

—— A Defence of the Catholike Ecclesiastical Hierarchie. See A Briefe Apologie, or Defence of the Catholike Ecclesiastical Hierarchie.

—— A Defence of the Censure, gyven uppon two bookes of William Charke and Meredith Hanmer mynysters, whiche they wrote against M. Edmond Campian preest, of the Societie of Jesus, and against his offer of disputation (Rouen: Fr Persons' Press, 1582).

—— A Discoverie of I. Nicols Minister, misreported a Jesuite, lately recanted in the Tower of London (Stonor Park: Fr Persons' Press, 1581).

—— A Discussion of the Answere of M. William Barlow, D. of Divinity, to the Booke intituled: The Judgment of a Catholicke Englishman living in banishment for his Religion & c. concerning The Apology of the new Oath of Allegiance (St Omer: English College Press, 1612).

—— Elizabethae Angliae Reginae haeresim Caluinianum propugnantis, saeuissimum in Catholicos sui regni edictum .... Cum responsione ad singula capita (Antwerp: Richard Verstegan, 1592) [= Philopater].

—— 'Father Persons' Autobiography, 1546–1584', ed. J.H. Pollen, SJ, in Miscellanea II, CRS, 2 (London: Catholic Record Society, 1906), pp. 12–47.

—— The First Booke of the Christian Exercise, appertayning to Resolution. See The Christian Directory.

—— The Jesuit's Memorial, for the Intended Reformation of England Under their First Popish Prince, ed. Edward Gee (London: Richard Chiswel, 1690) [= A Memorial for the Intended Reformation of England].

—— The Judgment of a Catholicke English-man, living in banishment for his Religion: Written to his private friend in England. Concerninge A late Booke set forth, and entituled: Triplici nodo, triplex cuneus, Or, An Apologie for the Oath of Allegiance (St Omer: English College Press, 1608).

—— Letters and Memorials of Father Robert Persons, S.J.: Vol. I (to 1588), ed. L. Hicks, SJ; CRS, 39 (London: Catholic Record Society, 1942).

—— A Manifestation of the Great Folly and bad spirit of certayne in England calling themselves secular priestes (Antwerp: Arnout Conincx, 1602).

—— A Memorial for the Reformation of England. See The Jesuit's Memorial, for the Intended Reformation of England Under their First Popish Prince.

—— *Newes from Spayne and Holland conteyning. An information of Inglish affayres in Spayne with a conference made theruppon in Amsterdame of Holland* (Antwerp: Arnout Conincx, 1593).

—— *De persecutione Anglicana, epistola. Qua explicantur afflictiones, aerumna, & calamitates grauissimae, cruciatus etiam & tormenta, & acerbissima martyria, quae Catholici nunc Angli, ob fidem patiuntur* (Rouen: Fr Persons' Press, 1581; rpt. Paris: Thomas Brumen, 1582; Rome: English College and Francesco Zanetti, 1582; Ingolstadt: Wolfgang Eder, 1582) [French translation by Matthieu de Launoy; Paris: Thomas Brumen, 1582. Italian translation, translator unidentified; Bologna: Alessandro Benacci, 1582. German translation by Johann Christoff Hueber; Ingolstadt: David Sartorius, 1583].

—— [*De persecutione Anglicana, epistola*] *An Epistle of the Persecution of Catholickes in Englande* .... *To whiche there is added an epistle by the translator to the right honorable Lordes of her meiesties preevie councell towchynge the same matter*, trans. G.T. (Rouen: Fr Persons' Press, 1582).

—— *Philopater*. See *Elizabethae Angliae Reginae haeresim Caluinianum propugnantis*.

—— 'A Preface, written by Father Robert Parsons, S.J., to the History of the Wanderings of Syon', in Dom Adam Hamilton, OSB, *The Angel of Syon: The Life and Martyrdom of Blessed Richard Reynolds, Bridgettine Monk of Syon, Martyred at Tyburn, May 4, 1535* (Edinburgh, 1905).

—— 'Punti per la Missione d'Inghilterra', ed. and trans. J.H. Pollen, SJ, in *Miscellanea IV*, CRS, 4 (London: Catholic Record Society, 1907).

—— *Quaestiones duae de sacris alienis non aduendis, ad vsum praximque Angliae breuiter explicatae* (St Omer: François Bellet, 1607).

—— *A Quiet and Sober Reckoning with M. Thomas Morton somewhat set in choler by his Adversary P.R. concerning Certaine imputations of wilfull falsities obiected to the said T.M. in a Treaties of P.R. intituled Of Mitigation* (St Omer: English College Press, 1609).

—— *Reasons of Refusal*. See *A Brief Discours contayning certayne reasons why Catholiques refuse to goe to church*.

—— *Relacion de Algunos martyrios, que de nueuo han hecho los hereges en Inglaterra, y de otras cosas tocantes a nuestra santa y Catolica religion. Traduzida de Ingles en Castellano, por el padre Roberto Personio, etc.* (Madrid: Pedro Madrigal, 1590).

—— *A Relation of the King of Spaines Receiving in Valliodolid, and in the Inglish College of the same towne, in August last past of this yere, 1592* (Antwerp: Arnout Conincx, 1592).

—— [*A Relation of the King of Spaines Receiving in Valliodolid*] *Relacion de un Sacerdote Ingles ... de la venida de su Magestad ... al colegio de los Yngleses* (Madrid: Pedro Madigal, 1592).

—— 'Robert Parsons and Claudio Acquaviva: Correspondence', ed. Thomas M. McCoog, SJ, *Archivum Historicum S.I.* 68 (1999): 79–182.

——— 'A Storie of Domesticall Difficulties in the Englishe Catholike cause', ed. J.H. Pollen, SJ, in *Miscellanea II*, CRS, 2 (London: Catholic Record Society, 1906).

——— *A Temperate Ward-word, to the turbulent and seditious Wach-word of Sir Francis Hastinges knight* (Antwerp: Arnout Conincx, 1599).

——— *A Treatise of Three Conversions of England from Paganisme to Christian Religion. The First under the Apostles, in the first age after Christ: The Second under Pope Eleutherius and K. Lucius, in the second age. The Third, under Pope Gregory the Great, and K. Ethelbert in the sixth age* (St Omer: François Bellet, 1603).

——— [*A Treatise of Three Conversions*: vol. 2] *The Third Part of a Treatise, Intituled: of three Conversions of England: conteyning. An Examen of the Calendar or Catalogue of Protestant Saints, Martyrs and Confessors, divised by John Fox ... The first six monethes. Wherunto in the end is annexed a defence of a certaine Triall, made before the King of France upon the yeare 1600. betweene Monsieur Peron Bishop of Evreux, and Monsieur Plessis Mornay Governour of Saumur, about sundry points of Religion* (St Omer: François Bellet, 1604).

——— [*A Treatise of Three Conversions*: vol. 3] *The Third Part of a Treatise Intituled Of Three Conversions of England. Conteyning an examen of the Calendar or Catalogue of Protestant Saintes, Martyrs and Confessors .... The last six monethes. Wherunto is annexed in the end, another seuerall Treatise, called: A re-view of ten publike Disputations, or Conferences, held in England about matters of Religion* (St Omer: François Bellet, 1604).

——— *A Treatise tending to Mitigation towardes Catholicke-Subiectes in England* (St Omer: François Bellet, 1608).

——— *The Warn-word to Sir Francis Hastinges Wast-word: Conteyning the issue of three former Treatises, the Watch-word, the Ward-word and the Wast-word (intituled by Sir Francis, an Apologie or Defence of his Watch-word)* (2 vols; Antwerp: Arnout Conincx, 1602).

——— (ed.), *Acta in comitiis parlamentaribus Londini die X. Aprilis huius anni praesentis 1593. tam contra Catholicos quam Puritanos seu Caluinistas rigidos ... Collecta & in sermonem latinum traducta per Ioannem Dodritium Londini commorantem* (Antwerp: Jan van Keerberghen, 1593).

Philopater, Andreas. See Robert Persons, SJ, *Elizabethae Angliae Reginae haeresim Caluinianum propugnantis*.

Preston, Thomas, *Apologia Cardinalis Bellarmini pro iure principum* (London: Richard Field, 1611).

Proceedings in the Parliaments of Elizabeth I, ed. T.E. Hartley (3 vols; Leicester: Leicester University Press, 1981–95).

Rainolds, John, *John Rainolds's Oxford Lectures on Aristotle's 'Rhetoric'*, ed. Lawrence D. Green (Newark: University of Delaware Press, 1986).

Records of the English Province of the Society of Jesus: Historic Facts Illustrative of the Labours and Sufferings of its Members in the Sixteenth and Seventeenth Centuries, ed. Henry Foley, SJ (7 vols in 8; London: Burns & Oates, 1875–83).

Registers of the English College at Valladolid, 1589–1862, ed. Edwin Henson; CRS, 30 (London: Catholic Record Society, 1930).

Report on the Manuscripts of Lord de L'Isle and Dudley Preserved at Penshurst Place, Historical Manuscripts Commission (6 vols; London: HMSO, 1925–66).

The Responsa Scholarum of the English College, Rome, ed. Anthony Kenny; CRS, 54–5 (2 vols; London: Catholic Record Society, 1962–63).

Ribadeneira, Pedro de, SJ, *Bibliotheca Scriptorum Societatis Jesu* (Rome: Jacobus Antonius de Lazzaris Varesii, 1676).

—— *Historia ecclesiastica del scisma del reyno de Inglaterra* (Emberes: M. Nucio, 1594).

Sander, Nicholas, *De origine ac progressu Schismatis Anglicani liber ... Editus & auctus per Edouardum Rishtonum* (Cologne: n.p., 1585).

—— *De origine ac progressu Schismatis Anglicani, Libri Tres ... Aucti per Edouardum Rishtonum ... nunc iterum locupletius & castigatius editi* (Rome: Bartholomaeus Bonfadinus, 1586).

—— *De origine ac progressu Schismatis Anglicani, Libri Tres ... Aucti per Edouardum Rishtonum ... nunc iterum locupletius & castigatius editi* (Ingolstadt: Wolfgang Ederus, 1588).

Select Statutes and Other Constitutional Documents Illustrative of the Reigns of Elizabeth and James I, ed. G.W. Prothero; 4th edn (Oxford: Oxford University Press, 1946).

Shakespeare, William, *The Cronicle History of Henry the fift, With his battell fought at Agin Court in France. Togither with Auntient Pistoll* (London: Thomas Creede for Thomas Millington and Iohn Busby, 1600).

—— *The History of Henrie the Fourth; With the battell at Shrewsburie, betweene the King and Lord Henry Percy, surnamed Henrie Hotspur of the North. With the humorous conceits of Sir Iohn Falstaffe* (London: P.S. for Andrew Wise, 1598).

—— *King Henry V*, ed. Andrew Gurr; rev. edn (Cambridge: Cambridge University Press, 2005).

—— *King Richard II*, ed. Andrew Gurr (Cambridge: Cambridge University Press, 1984).

—— *Shake-speares sonnets Neuer before imprinted* (London: G. Eld for Thomas Thorpe, 1609).

—— *The Tragedie of King Richard the second* (London: Valentine Simmes for Andrew Wise, 1597).

—— *The Winter's Tale*, ed. J.H.P. Pafford (London: Methuen, 1963).

Sidney, Sir Philip, *An Apology for Poetry*, ed. Geoffrey Shepherd (London: Nelson, 1965).

—— *The Defence of Poesie* (London: William Ponsonby, 1595).

Southwell, Robert, SJ, *An Humble Supplication to her Maiestie* [1595], ed. R.C. Bald (Cambridge: Cambridge University Press, 1953).

—— *A Short Rule of Good Life. To direct the devout Christian in a regular and orderly course* (St Omer: John Heigham, 1622).

Spenser, Edmund, *The Faerie Queene* [books I–III] (London: William Ponsonby, 1590).

—— *The Faerie Queene* [books I–VI] (London: William Ponsonby, 1596).

—— *Prosopopoia. Or Mother Hubberds Tale* (London: William Ponsonby, 1591).

Stapleton, Thomas [Didymus Veridicus Henfildanus (pseud.)], *Apologia pro Rege Catholico Philippo II … Contra varias & falsas accusationes Elisabethae Angliae Reginae* (Antwerp: n.p., 1592).

—— *A Counterblast to M. Hornes Vayne Blast against M. Fekenham … touching, the Othe of Supremacy* (Louvain: John Fowler, 1567).

—— *A Fortresse of the Faith, First planted amonge vs englishmen, and continued hitherto in the universall Church of Christ* (Antwerp: Jan Laet, 1565).

Stow, John. *The Annales of England, faithfully collected out of the most autenticall Authors, Records, and other Monuments of Antiquitie* (London: R. Newberry, 1592).

Strype, John, *Memorials of the Most Reverend Father in God, Thomas Cranmer* (London: n.p., 1694).

Stuart Royal Proclamations, Vol. 1: Royal Proclamations of King James I, 1603–1625, ed. James F. Larkin and Paul L. Hughes (Oxford: Oxford University Press, 1973).

Suarez, Francisco, SJ, *Selections from Three Works of Francisco Suarez, S.J.*, trans. G.L. Williams et al. (2 vols; Oxford: Oxford University Press, 1944).

—— *Tractatus de legibus ac deo legislatore* (Coimbra: D. Gomez de Loureyro, 1612).

Sutcliffe, Matthew, *A Briefe Refutation of a certain calumnious relation of the conference passed betwixt the Lord of Plessis Marli and I. Peron, calling himselfe bishop of Evreux* (London: Arnold Hatfield, 1600).

—— *A Briefe Replie to a certaine odious and slanderous libel lately published by a seditious Jesuite, calling himselfe N.D. … entitled A temperate ward-word* (London: Arnold Hatfield, 1600).

—— *A Challenge concerning the Romish Church* (London: A. Hatfield, 1602).

—— *A Full and Round Answer to N.D. alias Robert Parsons the Noddie his foolish and rude Warne-word* (London: G. Bishop, 1604).

—— *A New Challenge made to N.D.* (London: Arnold Hatfield, 1600).

—— *The Subversion of Robert Parsons His confused and worthlesse worke, Entituled, A treatise of three Conversions of England from Paganisme to Christian Religion* (London: J. Norton, 1606).

—— *A Threefold Answer unto the third part of a certaine Triobolar Treatise of Three supposed Conversions of England to the moderne Romish Religion published by Rob. Parsons under the continued Maske of N.D.* (London: for J. Norton, 1606).

Swift, Jonathan, *Prose Works*, ed. Herbert Davis et al. (14 vols; Oxford: Oxford University Press, 1939–68).

Tootel, Hugh [Charles Dodd (pseud.)], *The Church History of England: From the Commencement of the Sixteenth Century to the Revolution in 1688*, ed. M.A. Tierney (5 vols; London: Charles Dolman, 1839–43).

—— *The Church History of England, From the Year 1500, to the Year 1688. Chiefly with regard to Catholicks: together with The Lives of the most eminent Catholicks* (3 vols; London, 1737–42).

Tudor Royal Proclamations, ed. Paul L. Hughes and James F. Larkin (3 vols; New Haven: Yale University Press, 1964–69).

Tynley, Robert, *Two Learned Sermons. The one, of the mischievous subtiltie, and barbarous crueltie, the other of the false Doctrines, and refined Haeresies of the Romish Synagogue. Preached, the One at Paules Crosse the 5. of November, 1608. The Other at the Spittle the 17. of Aprill. 1609* (London: W. Hall for T. Adams, 1609).

Unpublished Documents Relating to the English Martyrs: Vol. I: 1584–1603, ed. J.H. Pollen, SJ; CRS, 5 (London: Catholic Record Society, 1908).

Verstegan, Richard, *An Advertisement written to a Secretarie of my L. Treasurers of Ingland, by an Inglishe Intelligencer as he passed through Germanie towards Italie* (Antwerp: Joachim Trognaesius, 1592).

—— *A Declaration of the True Causes of the great troubles, presupposed to be intended against the realm of England* (Antwerp: Joachim Trognaesius, 1592).

—— *Letters and Despatches of Richard Verstegan (c. 1550–1640)*, ed. Anthony G. Petti; CRS, 52 (London: Catholic Record Society, 1959).

Watson, William, *A Decacordon of Ten Quodlibeticall Questions concerning Religion and State: Wherein the Author framing himself a Quilibet to every Quodlibet, decides an hundred crosse Interrogatorie doubts, about the generall contentions betwixt the Seminarie Priests and Jesuits at this present* (London: Richard Field, 1602).

Weston, William, SJ, *The Autobiography of an Elizabethan*, trans. Philip Caraman, SJ (London: Longmans, Green and Co., 1955).

Winwood, Ralph, *Memorials of Affairs of State in the Reigns of Q. Elizabeth and K. James I, Collected (chiefly) from the Original Papers of … Sir Ralph Winwood*, ed. Edmund Sawyer (3 vols; London: W.B. for T. Ward, 1725).

The Wisbech Stirs (1595–98), ed. P. Renold; CRS, 51 (London: Catholic Record Society, 1958).

Yepes, Diego de, *Historia Particular de la Persecucion de Inglaterra* [1599], ed. D. M. Rogers (London: Gregg International, 1971).

III. Secondary Sources

Allison, A.F. and D.M. Rogers, *The Contemporary Printed Literature of the English Counter-Reformation between 1558 and1640* (2 vols; Aldershot: The Scolar Press, 1989–94).

Anstruther, Godfrey, *The Seminary Priests: Vol. I: Elizabethan 1558–1603* (Durham: Ushaw College, 1968).

Arblaster, Paul, *Antwerp & the World: Richard Verstegan and the International Culture of Catholic Reformation* (Leuven: Leuven University Press, 2004).

Aveling, Hugh, *Northern Catholics: The Catholic Recusants of the North Riding of Yorkshire 1558–1790* (London: Geoffrey Chapman, 1966).

Basset, Bernard, SJ, *The English Jesuits: From Campion to Martindale* (London: Burns & Oates, 1967).

Beales, A.C.F., *Education Under Penalty: English Catholic Education from the Reformation to the Fall of James II* (London: Athlone, 1963).

Black, Joseph, 'The Rhetoric of Reaction: The Martin Marprelate Tracts (1588–89), Anti-Martinism, and the Uses of Print in Early Modern England', *Sixteenth Century Journal* 28 (1997): 707–725.

Borja Medina, Francisco de, SJ, 'Intrigues of a Scottish Jesuit at the Spanish Court: Unpublished Letters of William Crichton to Claudio Acquaviva, 1590–1592', in McCoog (ed.), *The Reckoned Expense*, pp. 215–45.

Borot, Luc, 'Is Father Robert Parsons's *Memorial* a Utopia? A Few Thoughts about the Question of Succession', in Mayer (ed.), *The Struggle for the Succession*, pp. 179–97.

Bossy, John, *The English Catholic Community 1570–1850* (London: Darton Longman and Todd, 1975).

—— 'The Heart of Robert Persons', in McCoog (ed.), *The Reckoned Expense*, pp. 141–58.

—— 'Henry IV, the Appellants and the Jesuits', *Recusant History* 8 (1965): 80–122.

Breight, Curtis C., *Surveillance, Militarism and Drama in the Elizabethan Era* (London: Macmillan, 1996).

Broderick, Edwin B., 'Robert Persons *The Christian Directory*: Prolegomena to an Edition' (diss., Fordham University, 1951).

Brodrick, James, SJ, *The Life and Work of Blessed Robert Francis Cardinal Bellarmine, S.J. 1542–1621* (2 vols; London: Burns, Oates and Washbourne, 1928).

Brooke, Christopher, *The Medieval Idea of Marriage* (Oxford: Oxford University Press, 1989).

Brown, Peter Robert Lamont, *Augustine of Hippo: A Biography* (London: Faber, 1967).

Caraman, Philip, SJ, *Henry Garnet 1555–1606 and the Gunpowder Plot* (London: Longmans, 1964).

Carrafiello, Michael L., *Robert Parsons and English Catholicism, 1580–1610* (Selinsgrove: Susquehanna University Press, 1998).

Clancy, Thomas H., SJ, 'Notes on Persons's "Memorial for the Reformation of England" (1596)', *Recusant History* 5 (1959): 17–34.

—— *Papist Pamphleteers: The Allen-Persons Party and the Political Thought of the Counter-Reformation in England, 1572–1615* (Chicago: Loyola University Press, 1964).

Code, J.B., *Queen Elizabeth and the English Catholic Historians* (Louvain: Louvain University, 1935).

Coffey, John, *Persecution and Toleration in Protestant England 1558–1689* (Harlow: Longman, 2000).

Collinson, Patrick, 'Truth and Legend: The Veracity of John Foxe's Book of Martyrs' [1985], rpt. in *Elizabethan Essays* (London: The Hambledon Press, 1994), pp. 151–78.

Corthell, Ronald, 'Robert Persons and the Writer's Mission', in Arthur F. Marotti (ed.), *Catholicism and Anti-Catholicism in Early-Modern English Texts* (London: Macmillan, 1999), pp. 35–62.

Crehan, Joseph, SJ, 'Father Persons, SJ', in Charles Davis (ed.), *English Spiritual Writers* (London: Burns & Oates, 1961), pp. 84–96.

Crosignani, Ginevra, *'De adeundis ecclesiis Protestantium': Thomas Wright, Robert Parsons, S.J., e il debattito sul conformismo occasionale nell'Inghilterra dell'età moderna*, Bibliotheca Instituti Historici S.I., 56 (Rome: Institutum Historicum S.I., 2004).

Dillon, Anne, *The Construction of Martyrdom in the English Catholic Community, 1535–1603* (Aldershot: Ashgate, 2002).

Duffy, Eamon, *The Stripping of the Altars: Traditional Religion in England, c. 1400–c. 1580* (New Haven: Yale University Press, 1992).

Edwards, Francis, SJ, *The Jesuits in England: From 1580 to the Present Day* (Tunbridge Wells: Burns & Oates, 1985).

—— *Robert Persons: The Biography of an Elizabethan Jesuit, 1546–1610* (St Louis: Institute of Jesuit Sources, 1995).

Eguiluz, Federico, *Robert Persons 'El Architraidor'* (Madrid: Fundacion Universitaria Española, 1990).

Evans, John X., 'The Art of Rhetoric and the Art of Dying in Tudor Recusant Prose', *Recusant History* 10 (1970): 247–72.

Ferrell, Lori Anne, *Government by Polemics: James I, the King's Preachers, and the Rhetorics of Conformity 1603–1625* (Stanford: Stanford University Press, 1998).

Fincham, Kenneth and Peter Lake, 'The Ecclesiastical Policy of King James I', *Journal of British Studies* 24 (1985): 169–207.

Flynn, Dennis, ' "Out of Step": Six Supplementary Notes on Jasper Heywood', in McCoog (ed.), *The Reckoned Expense*, pp. 179–92.

Freeman, Thomas S., ' "Great searching out of bookes and autors": John Foxe as an Ecclesiastical Historian' (diss., Rutgers University, 1995).

—— 'John Bale's Book of Martyrs?: The Account of King John in *Acts and Monuments*', *Reformation* 3 (1998): 175–223.

Gregory, Brad S., 'The "True and Zealouse Seruice of God": Robert Parsons, Edmund Bunny, and *The First Book of the Christian Exercise*', *Journal of Ecclesiastical History* 45 (1994): 238–68.

Haller, William, *Foxe's Book of Martyrs and the Elect Nation* (London: Jonathan Cape, 1963).

Hamilton, Donna B., 'Catholic Use of Anglo-Saxon Precedents, 1565–1625', *Recusant History* 26 (2003): 537–55.

Heal, Felicity, 'What can King Lucius do for you? The Reformation and the Early British Church', *English Historical Review* 120 (2005): 593–614.

Helgerson, Richard, *Forms of Nationhood: The Elizabethan Writing of England* (Chicago: University of Chicago Press, 1992).

Hicks, L., SJ, 'Father Persons, S.J., and the Seminaries in Spain', *The Month* 157 (1931): 193–204, 410–17, 497–506, and *The Month* 158 (1931): 26–35, 143–52, 234–44.

—— 'Father Robert Persons S.J. and *The Book of the Succession*', *Recusant History* 4 (1957): 104–137.

—— 'The Growth of a Myth: Father Robert Persons, S.J. and Leicester's Commonwealth', *Studies: An Irish Quarterly Review* 46 (1957): 91–105.

—— 'Sir Robert Cecil, Father Persons, and the Succession, 1600–1601', *Archivum Historicum S.I.* 24 (1955): 95–139.

Hill, Christopher, *Intellectual Origins of the English Revolution* (Oxford: Oxford University Press, 1965).

Holmes, P.J., '*An Epistle of Pious Grief*: An Anti-Appellant Tract by Robert Persons', *Recusant History* 15 (1981): 328–35.

Holmes, Peter, 'The Authorship of "Leicester's Commonwealth" ', *Journal of Ecclesiastical History* 33 (1982): 424–30.

—— *Resistance and Compromise: The Political Thought of the Elizabethan Catholics* (Cambridge: Cambridge University Press, 1982).

Houliston, Victor, 'The Martyr Tallies: Robert Persons and his Anonymous Respondent', in David Loades (ed.), *John Foxe at Home and Abroad* (Aldershot: Ashgate, 2004), pp. 47–50.

—— 'Robert Persons's Comfortable History of England', in Thomas S. Freeman and Thomas F. Mayer (eds), *Martyrs and Martyrdom in England, c. 1400–1700* (Woodbridge, Suffolk, 2007), pp. 180–202.

—— 'St Thomas Becket in the Propaganda of the English Counter-Reformation', *Renaissance Studies* 7 (1993): 44–70.

—— 'Why Robert Persons would not be Pacified: Edmund Bunny's Theft of *The Book of Resolution*', in McCoog (ed.), *The Reckoned Expense*, pp. 159–78.

Hudson, Elizabeth K., 'The Catholic Challenge to Puritan Piety, 1580–1620', *Catholic Historical Review* 77 (1991): 1–20.

Hughes, Philip, *Rome and the Counter-Reformation in England* (London: Burns Oates, 1942).

Hutchison, Ann M., 'The Life and Good End of Sister Marie', *Bridgettiana* 13 (2002): 33–89.

—— 'Mary Champney a Bridgettine Nun under the Rule of Queen Elizabeth I', *Bridgettiana* 13 (2002): 3–32.

Jenkins, Gladys, 'The Archpriest Controversy and the Printers, 1601–1603', *The Library*, 5th series, 2 (1948): 180–86.

Johnson, Paul, *The Offshore Islanders: A History of the English People*, rev. edn (London: Weidenfeld and Nicholson, 1985).

Jusdado, Sandra, 'The Appellant Priests and the Succession Issue', in Mayer (ed.), *The Struggle for the Succession*, pp. 199–216.

Kennedy, D.E., 'King James I's College of Controversial Divinity at Chelsea', in D.E. Kennedy, Diana Robertson and Alexandra Walsham (eds), *Grounds of Controversy: Three Studies in Late 16th and Early 17th Century English Polemics* (Melbourne: History Department, University of Melbourne, 1989), pp. 97–126.

Kennedy, T. Frank, SJ, 'Jesuits and Music: Reconsidering the Early Years', *Studi Musicali* 17 (1988): 71–100.

Kenny, Anthony, 'The Inglorious Revolution, 1594–1597', *Venerabile* 16 (1956): 240–58, and *Venerabile* 17 (1957): 7–25, 77–94, 136–55.

—— 'Reform and Reaction in Elizabethan Balliol, 1559–1588', in John Prest (ed.), *Balliol Studies* (London: Leopard's Head Press, 1982), pp. 17–51.

Keynes, Geoffrey, *The Library of Edward Gibbon* (London: St Paul's Bibliographies, 1980).

Kilroy, Gerald, *Edmund Campion: Memory and Transcription* (Aldershot: Ashgate, 2005).

—— 'Eternal Glory: Edmund Campion's Virgilian Epic', *Times Literary Supplement* (8 March 2002): 13–15.

King, John N., 'Fiction and Fact in Foxe's *Book of Martyrs*', in David Loades (ed.), *John Foxe and the English Reformation* (Aldershot: Scolar Press, 1997), pp. 12–35.

Laursen, J.C. and C.J. Nederman (eds), *Beyond the Persecuting Society: Religious Toleration Before the Enlightenment* (Philadelphia: University of Pennsylvania Press, 1998).

Law, T.G., 'Robert Parsons', in Leslie Stephen and Sidney Lee (eds), *Dictionary of National Biography* (63 vols; London: Oxord University Press, 1885–1904), vol. 43, pp. 411–18.

Levy, F.J., *Tudor Historical Thought* (San Marino, Calif.: Huntington Library, 1967).

Lewis, C.S., *English Literature of the Sixteenth Century: Excluding Drama* (London: Oxford University Press, 1954).

Lock, Julian, ' "Strange Usurped Potentates": Elizabeth I, The Papacy and the Indian Summer of the Medieval Deposing Power' (diss., Oxford University, 1992).

Loomie, Albert J., SJ, 'The Armadas and the Catholics of England', *Catholic Historical Review* 59 (1973): 385–403.

—— 'The Authorship of *An Advertisement written to a Secretarie of M.L. Treasurer of England* ....', *Renaissance News* 15 (1962): 201–207.

—— 'Philip II and the Printing of "Andreas Philopater" ', *The Library*, 5th series, 24 (1969): 143–5.

—— 'Philip III and the Stuart Succession in England', *Revue belge de Philologie et d'Histoire* 43 (1965): 492–514.

—— *Spain and the Early Stuarts, 1585–1655* (Aldershot: Variorum, 1996).

—— 'Spain and the English Catholic Exiles, 1580–1604' (diss., London University, 1957).

—— *The Spanish Elizabethans* (New York: Fordham University Press, 1962).

Loomis, Catherine, 'Elizabeth Southwell's Manuscript Account of the Death of Queen Elizabeth [with text]', *English Literary Renaissance* 26 (1996): 482–509.

Martin, Patrick and John Finnis, 'The Identity of "Anthony Rivers" ', *Recusant History* 26 (2002): 39–74.

Matchinske, Megan, 'Gendering Catholic Conformity: The Politics of Equivocation in Elizabeth Grymeston's *Miscelanea*', *Journal of English and Germanic Philology* 101 (2002): 329–57.

Mattingly, Garrett, *The Defeat of the Spanish Armada* (London: Jonathan Cape, 1959).

Mayer, Jean-Christophe (ed.), *The Struggle for the Succession in Late Elizabethan England: Politics, Polemics and Cultural Representations*, Astraea Collections, no. 11 (Montpellier: Université Paul Valéry Montpellier 3, 2004).

Mayer, Thomas F., 'A Sticking-Plaster Saint? Autobiography and Hagiography in the Making of Reginald Pole', in Thomas Mayer and D.R. Woolf (eds), *The Rhetorics of Life-Writing in Early Modern Europe: Forms of Biography from Cassandra Fedele to Louis XIV* (Ann Arbor: University of Michigan Press, 1995), pp. 205–222.

McCoog, Thomas M., SJ, 'Construing Martyrdom in the English Catholic Community, 1582–1602', in Ethan H. Shagan (ed.), *Catholics and the 'Protestant Nation': Religious Politics and Identity in Early Modern England* (Manchester: Manchester University Press, 2005), pp. 95–127.

—— *English and Welsh Jesuits, 1555–1650*, CRS, 74–5 (2 vols; London: Catholic Record Society, 1994–95).

—— 'The English Jesuit Mission and the French Match, 1579–1581', *Catholic Historical Review* 87 (2001): 185–213.

—— 'The Establishment of the English Province of the Society of Jesus', *Recusant History* 17 (1984): 121–39.

—— 'Harmony Disrupted: Robert Parsons, S.J., William Crichton, S.J. and the Question of Queen Elizabeth's Successor, 1581–1603', *Archivum Historicum S.I.* 73 (2004): 149–220.

—— '"Playing the Champion": The Role of Disputation in the Jesuit Mission', in McCoog (ed.), *The Reckoned Expense* (1996), pp. 119–39.

—— *The Society of Jesus in Ireland, Scotland, and England 1541–1588: 'Our Way of Proceeding?'* (Leiden: E.J. Brill, 1996).

—— (ed.), *The Reckoned Expense: Edmund Campion and the Early English Jesuits* (Woodbridge, Suffolk: The Boydell Press, 1996).

McGrath, Patrick, 'The Bloody Questions Reconsidered', *Recusant History* 20 (1991): 305–319.

—— *Papists and Puritans Under Elizabeth I* (London: Blandford Press, 1967).

McNulty, Robert, 'The Protestant Version of Robert Parsons' *The First Booke of the Christian Exercise*', *Huntington Library Quarterly* 22 (1959): 271–300.

—— 'Robert Parsons's *The First Booke of the Christian Exercise* (1582): An Edition and a Study' (diss., Columbia University, 1955).

Meyer, A.O., *England and the Catholic Church under Queen Elizabeth*, trans. J.R. McKee; 2nd edn; introd. John Bossy (London: Routledge and Kegan Paul, 1967; New York: Barnes and Noble, 1969).

Milton, Anthony, *Catholic and Reformed: The Roman and Protestant Churches in English Protestant Thought, 1600–1640* (Cambridge: Cambridge University Press, 1995).

Milward, Peter, SJ, *Religious Controversies of the Elizabethan Age: A Survey of Printed Sources* (London: Scolar Press, 1978).

—— *Religious Controversies of the Jacobean Age: A Survey of Printed Sources* (London: Scolar Press, 1978).

Mozley, J.F., *John Foxe and his Book* (London: SPCK, 1940).

Muddiman, J.G., 'Puritan Piracies of Father Persons' "Conference"', *The Month* 117 (1911): 270–78.

North, Marcy L., 'Anonymity's Subject: James I and the Debate over the Oath of Allegiance', *New Literary History* 33 (2002): 215–32.

Nussbaum, Damian, 'Reviling the Saints or Reforming the Calendar? John Foxe and his "Kalender" of Martyrs', in Susan Wabuda and Caroline Litzenberger (eds), *Belief and Practice in Reformation England: A Tribute to Patrick Collinson from his Students* (Aldershot: Ashgate, 1998), pp. 113–36.

O'Connell, Marvin R., *Thomas Stapleton and the Counter Reformation* (New Haven: Yale University Press, 1964).

O'Malley, John W., SJ, *The First Jesuits* (Cambridge, Mass.: Harvard University Press, 1993).

Parish, John E., *Robert Parsons and the English Counter-Reformation*, Rice University Studies, 52 (Houston: Rice University, 1966).

Parmelee, Lisa Ferraro, *Good newes from Fraunce: French Anti-League Propaganda in Late Elizabethan England* (Rochester: University of Rochester Press, 1996).

Parry, Glyn, 'John Foxe, "Father of Lyes", and the Papists', in David Loades (ed.), *John Foxe and the English Reformation* (Aldershot: Scolar Press, 1997), pp. 295–305.

Patterson, Annabel, *Reading Holinshed's Chronicles* (Chicago: Chicago University Press, 1994).

Patterson, W.B., *King James VI and I and the Reunion of Christendom* (Cambridge: Cambridge University Press, 1997).

Pilar, Scott, SJ, *Robert Southwell, S.J. and the Mission of Literature* (Aldershot: Ashgate, 2003).

Pollen, J.H., SJ, 'The Accession of King James I', *The Month* 101 (1903): 572–85.

—— *The Institution of the Archpriest Blackwell: A Study of the Transition from Institutional to Paternal and Local Church Government among the English Catholics, 1595 to 1602* (London: Longmans and Co., 1916).

—— 'The Politics of English Catholics during the Reign of Queen Elizabeth. No. III. – Revival of Spiritual Life and of Political Aspirations, 1580–1582', *The Month* 99 (January–June 1902): 290–305.

Pritchard, Arnold, *Catholic Loyalism in Elizabethan England* (London: Scolar Press, 1979).

Questier, M.C., 'Conformity, Catholicism and the Law', in Peter Lake and Michael Questier (eds), *Conformity and Orthodoxy in the English Church, c. 1560–1660* (Woodbridge, Suffolk: The Boydell Press, 2000), pp. 237–61.

—— *Conversion, Politics and Religion in England, 1580–1625* (Cambridge: Cambridge University Press, 1996).

—— 'Loyalty, Religion and State Power in Early Modern England: English Romanism and the Jacobean Oath of Allegiance', *Historical Journal* 40 (1997): 311–29.

—— (introd.), *Newsletters from the Archpresbyterate of George Birkhead*, Royal Historical Society Camden, 5th series, 12 (London: Cambridge University Press, 1998).

Reynolds, E.E., *Campion and Parsons: The Jesuit Mission of 1580–1* (London: Sheed and Ward, 1980).

Robertson, Diana, 'Bishop Lancelot Andrewes and his Gunpowder Treason Sermons, 1606–1618', in D.E. Kennedy, Diana Robertson and Alexandra Walsham (eds), *Grounds of Controversy: Three Studies in Late 16th and Early 17th Century English Polemics* (Melbourne: History Department, University of Melbourne, 1989), pp. 49–96.

Rowse, A.L., *Eminent Elizabethans* (London: Macmillan, 1983).

—— *The England of Elizabeth* (London: Macmillan, 1950).

Salmon, J.H.M., 'Catholic Resistance Theory, Ultramontanism, and the Royalist Response, 1580–1620', in J.H. Burns and Mark Goldie (eds), *The Cambridge History of Political Thought, 1450–1700* (Cambridge: Cambridge University Press, 1991), pp. 219–53.

Sanders, Wilbur, *The Dramatist and the Received Idea: Studies in the Plays of Marlowe and Shakespeare* (London: Cambridge University Press, 1968).

Scarisbrick, John J., 'Robert Persons' Plans for the "True" Reformation of England', in Neil McKendrick (ed.), *Historical Perspectives: Studies in English Thought and Society in Honour of J.H. Plumb* (London: Europa, 1974), pp. 19–42.

Shell, Alison, *Catholicism, Controversy and the English Literary Imagination, 1558–1660* (Cambridge: Cambridge University Press, 1999).

—— '"We are Made a Spectacle": Campion's Dramas', in McCoog, *The Reckoned Expense*, pp. 103–118.

Simpson, Richard, *Edmund Campion: A Biography*, 2nd edn (London: John Hodges, 1896).

Sinfield, Alan, *Literature in Protestant England, 1560–1660* (London: Croom Helm, 1983).

Solomon, David A., 'Examinations of Conscience: Robert Parsons' *Christian Directory* and Catholic Spirituality in Post-Reformation England' (diss., University of Connecticut, 1999).

Steuart, Dom Hilary, 'The Place of Allen, Campion and Parsons in the Development of English Prose', *Review of English Studies* 20 (1943): 272–85.

Strathmann, Ernest A., 'Ralegh and the Catholic Polemicists', *Huntington Library Quarterly* 4 (1945): 337–58.

Sullivan, Ceri, 'Cannibalizing Persons's *Christian Directorie*, 1582', *Notes and Queries* 239 (1994): 445–6.

—— *Dismembered Rhetoric: English Recusant Writing, 1580–1603* (Madison/ Teaneck: Farleigh Dickinson University Press, 1995).

—— '"Oppressed by the Force of Truth": Robert Persons Edits John Foxe', in David Loades (ed.), *John Foxe: An Historical Perspective* (Aldershot: Ashgate, 1999), pp. 154–66.

Sweeney, Anne, *Robert Southwell: Snow in Arcadia: Redrawing the English Lyric Landscape, 1586–1595* (Manchester: Manchester University Press, 2007).

Taunton, Ethelred L., *The History of the Jesuits in England 1580–1773* (London: Methuen & Co., 1901).

Turchetti, Mario, 'Religious Concord and Political Tolerance in Sixteenth- and Seventeenth-Century France', *Sixteenth Century Journal* 22 (1991): 15–25.

Tyacke, Nicholas, *Aspects of English Protestantism, c. 1530–1700* (Manchester: Manchester University Press, 2001).

Vickers, Brian, *In Defence of Rhetoric* (Oxford: Clarendon Press, 1988).

Walsham, Alexandra, *Church Papists: Catholicism, Conformity and Confessional Polemic in Early Modern England* (Woodbridge, Suffolk: Boydell & Brewer, 1993).

—— '"Yielding to the extremity of the Time": Conformity, Orthodoxy and the Post-Reformation Catholic Community', in Peter Lake and Michael Questier (eds), *Conformity and Orthodoxy in the English Church, c. 1560–1660* (Woodbridge, Suffolk: The Boydell Press, 2000), pp. 211–36.

Watkins, John, '"Old Bess in the Ruff": Remembering Elizabeth I, 1625–1660', *English Literary Renaissance* 30 (2000): 95–116.

Waugh, Evelyn, *Edmund Campion, Jesuit and Martyr* [1935], in *Two Lives: Edmund Campion – Ronald Knox* (London: Continuum, 2001).

Williams, Michael, *St Alban's College Valladolid: Four Centuries of English Catholic Presence in Spain* (London: C. Hurst, 1986).

—— *The Venerable English College, Rome: A History 1579–1979* (London: Associated Catholic Publications, 1979).

Williams, J.B. See J.G. Muddiman.

Williams, Penry, 'Elizabethan Oxford: State, Church and University', in T.H. Aston et al. (eds), *The History of the University of Oxford* (8 vols; Oxford: Oxford University Press, 1985–2000), vol. 3 (ed. James McConica), pp. 397–440.

Wills, Garry, *Witches and Jesuits: Shakespeare's 'Macbeth'* (New York: Oxford University Press, 1995).

Wilson, A.N., *C.S. Lewis: A Biography* (London: Collins, 1990).

Wilson, H.S., 'Nature and Art in *Winter's Tale*', *Shakespeare Association Bulletin* 18 (1943): 114–20.

Woolf, D.R., 'Erudition and the Idea of History in Renaissance England', *Renaissance Quarterly* 40 (1987): 11–48.

—— 'The Rhetoric of Martyrdom: Generic Contradiction and Narrative Strategy in John Foxe's *Acts and Monuments*', in Thomas Mayer and D.R. Woolf (eds), *The Rhetorics of Life-Writing in Early Modern Europe* (Ann Arbor: University of Michigan Press, 1995), pp. 243–82.

Index